Financial Markets in Transition

Global financial markets are on the threshold of a new age. After two decades of dramatic transformation in the structure and functions of national financial markets and financial service industries, a more or less perfectly integrated and globalized system has emerged. Global financial markets have become noticeably more efficient, while the financial service industry has been reduced to little more than an information industry. However, the transformation has not been without implications. For many stakeholder groups in many countries it has meant crises and difficult adjustments. This study focuses on the way in which different sequences of events in this globalization process affect the ability of financial markets to attract and channel savings in order to improve real national growth.

The empirical analysis is regional in scope and involves the four major Nordic countries – Denmark, Finland, Norway and Sweden. Being public-sector dominated economies, they provide examples of all the problems faced by other countries looking for an opening of their financial markets. In addition to intra-Nordic comparisons, the development of the region is compared to the US, UK, German and Japanese markets.

Two avenues of investigation are followed – one describing structural changes in national bond markets, the other measuring the levels of international integration of these markets and the potential effects that the process of globalization may have had on national economic growth. Both these aspects are central to a full understanding of the transition from national financial markets to well-integrated parts of the global market.

Lars Oxelheim is Professor at the Institute of Economic Research, Lund University and Senior Researcher at the Industrial Institute for Economic and Social Research (IUI) in Stockholm.

Financial Markets in Transition

Globalization, Investment and Economic Growth

Lars Oxelheim

INTERNATIONAL THOMSON BUSINESS PRESS
I ⓣ P An International Thomson Publishing Company

London • Bonn • Boston • Johannesburg • Madrid • Melbourne • Mexico City • New York • Paris
Singapore • Tokyo • Toronto • Albany, NY • Belmont, CA • Cincinnati, OH • Detroit, MI

Financial Markets in Transition

Copyright ©1996 Lars Oxelheim

 A division of International Thomson Publishing Inc.
The ITP logo is a trademark under licence

British Library Cataloguing-in-Publication Data
A catalogue record for this book is available from the British Library

First published by Routledge 1996
Paperback edition published by International Thomson Business Press 1996

Typeset in Garamond by Solidus (Bristol) Limited
Printed in the UK by Biddles ltd, Guildford and King's Lynn

ISBN 1-86152-099-9

International Thomson Business Press
Berkshire House
168–173 High Holborn
London WC1V 7AA
UK

International Thomson Business Press
20 Park Plaza
13th Floor
Boston MA 02116
USA

http://www.thomson.com/itbp.html

To Tina, Josephine, Karolina and Gustaf

Contents

Figures

Tables

Preface

The last twenty years have been a time of upheaval and transformation in the national financial markets, which have become more closely linked to one another to form a global market. This transformation can be very largely explained by the evolution in information technology which has done so much to undermine the efficiency of the various barriers previously in force. But the development was also made inevitable by the growing internationalization of banks and businesses. In some countries the politicians recognized the high price that would have to be paid for another couple of years of sheltered national markets, and hastened to deregulate their internal markets before that protection had vanished completely. In other countries the politicians long resisted the forces impelling the globalization, and insisted on keeping inefficient capital controls in place. Thus the globalization process has evolved in quite a different way in different countries. In the mid-1990s we can look back and see many alternative models for achieving the perfect integration of a national market into the global financial market. The different approaches to the necessary transition have had implications for the savings–investment relationship, i.e. for the way savings are channelled into growth-enhancing investments. The aim of this book is to offer some insights on this crucial situation.

The empirical part of the book relates the globalization of a region composed of small open economies to the development of the markets within the financial 'triad' – Japan, the USA and the EU. The task of providing empirical support for the links between the different markets in a rapidly changing financial landscape has been Herculean. As a researcher it was interesting if daunting to discover how much more difficult the data-gathering process has become in a deregulated world, now that the former control authorities no longer require detailed reports about cross-border operations. Nevertheless I think I have ultimately managed to get a consistent set of data which I hope will provide the diverse categories of my readers with some useful ideas. The readers I am addressing here include, first, researchers and students in the field of international economics and finance; second, policy-makers who are interested in finding the 'optimal' sequence for their deregulative measures, who need to consider the 'cost' involved and particularly the cost of deviating from the optimal sequence; and third, business executives and bankers concerned about various issues in which they are both interest parties: the development of corporate indebtedness, the development of various types of market efficiency, securitization, financial innovation and fund-raising during the process of transition.

The book was born of a regional research venture undertaken by the Nordic Perspective Group. At the many seminars I have held at different stages in this project I have benefited from comments by researchers from the five industrial research institutes which comprised the group. I would thus like to thank Pentti Vartia, Olavi Rantalla, John Rogers and Pekka Ylä-Anttila from ETLA, Finland; Uffe Palludan from IFF, Denmark; Per Heum and Einar Hope from SNF, Norway; Gudmundur Magnusson, University of Iceland: and, finally, Pontus Braunerhjelm, Gunnar Eliasson, Stefan Fölster, Jonas Häckner, Erik Mellander, Karl Markus Moden, Sten Nyberg and Roger Svensson from IUI, Sweden. For many valuable comments I would also like to thank Art Stonehill, Oregon State University, Clas G. Wihlborg, University of Gothenburg and Finn Östrup, Copenhagen School of Economics.

I am also grateful to Gunnar Eliasson, former director of the Industrial Institute for Economic and Social Research (IUI) in Stockholm, and Ulf Jacobsson, its present director, for giving me access to the various facilities of the Institute while I have been writing this book. At different stages of the research process many people have helped me with a variety of tasks such as data gathering, calculations, typing and layout. I thus owe many thanks to Torsten Dahlqvist, Pontus Engström, Harri Kanerva, Jan Michelson, Jörgen Nilsson and John Rogers for their work and their patience. I have also benefited from Nancy Adler's help in making my language more comprehensible, and am grateful to her for the discussions we have had together.

Finally, the generous financial support of the Nordic Economic Research Council is gratefully acknowledged, as is the sponsoring I received from NorFA for organizing a network on the topic of this book, from which the book has also benefited.

All these people, while extremely important to the book, are free of blame for any errors that may remain, which are mine and mine alone.

Lars Oxelheim
Stockholm

Chapter 1

Towards perfect international financial integration

Global financial markets are on the threshold of a new age. After two decades of dramatic transformation in the structure and functions of the national financial markets and the financial service industries, a more or less perfectly integrated and globalized system has emerged: the global financial markets have become noticeably more efficient, while the financial service industry has been reduced to little more than an information industry. However, the transformation has not been without complications. For many stakeholder groups in many countries it has meant crisis and difficult adjustments. And in some national markets – predominantly in small and/or developing countries – the new order has not yet been fully established. In this book I shall be looking at certain elements in the transformation process, and will do so by examining the globalization of the financial markets in a region of small open economies. In particular I shall examine the impact of various events on the ability of markets in general, and bond markets in particular, to attract and channel savings in order to improve real national growth.

Globally, the transformation was propelled by a variety of forces, of which improvements in information technology and a general wave of deregulation were the strongest. Major shifts in stocks and flows of global financial resources and increased economic integration were other forces at work.[1,2] The deregulation was to some extent an acknowledgement (*de jure*) by the authorities that existing regulations had eroded and had (*de facto*) become inefficient. But deregulation was also an expression of a change in the philosophy underlying national economic policies in the 1980s, reflecting a growing recognition that excessive controls are not compatible with efficient resource allocation and solid and balanced economic growth. In the 1980s it became increasingly evident that controls discourage financial savings, distort investment decisions and render the intermediation between savers and investors ineffective.

The transformation of financial markets has involved a dramatic change in the regulatory environment that affects national financial markets, although the regulatory changes differed significantly between countries as regards:

- timing;
- the nature of external deregulative measures (e.g. abolition of exchange controls);
- the opening of domestic markets to foreign financial institutions;
- the nature of internal deregulative measures (e.g. phasing-out the interest rate ceiling on the deposit and lending activities of the financial intermediaries);
- tax reductions and the elimination of tax wedges;
- the relaxation of limits on the financial activities of institutions;
- the activities of the supervisory authorities.

With hindsight, it may be argued that the transformation was not effected in an 'optimal' way. Although it is too early to sum up the costs and benefits of the transformation of the global financial markets, the fact that the deregulation of financial markets has often been associated with undesirable macroeconomic outcomes suggests that the deregulation may not have been optimal. For instance, the growing reliance on credit markets for buying homes, consumption goods, financial assets and whole companies (take-overs) not only led to a substantial and unstable build-up of household and/ or corporate debt, but also contributed to a decline in household savings, and damaged the prospects for the balance of payments and inflation. Empirical studies indicate that, at the beginning of the 1990s, countries with high inflation and current account deficits tended to be those which moved most quickly towards financial liberalization.[3,4]

The global financial crisis of the early 1990s generated concern about the financial transformation and, more specifically, about the interaction between markets and policy-makers. In the case of the *internal deregulation* one might argue that, in liberalizing interest rates, the authorities should have anticipated the vulnerability of the banking system to such a change and have taken precautionary action before the liberalization was implemented. This could have been effected, for instance, by making a thorough review of the soundness of the domestic banking system and the adequacy of the mechanisms for bank supervision. It could also be argued that the authorities in several countries have aggravated the effects of the global financial crisis manifested in their national markets by forcing BIS capital-adequacy requirements on the domestic banking industry.[5] In the long run, such harmonization does bring benefits. However, in the short run, and to get some degree of freedom in the transitional stage, different minimum standards would probably have been preferable to identical regulation. The crisis in the US saving and loan industry is another case in which different elements in the transformation process have interacted in an unfortunate way. The existence of deposit insurance schemes as a safety net generated problems of moral hazard, once the industry had been deregulated.

In the case of *external deregulation*, one might question the adequacy of the macroeconomic and financial policies adopted, with a view to sustaining capital account convertibility once the external liberalization had taken place. Thus, did the politicians try to minimize the differences between domestic and external financial market conditions? Were measures undertaken to strengthen the safety and soundness of the domestic financial system? And finally, were restrictions which inhibited the flexibility of wages and prices removed or reduced, to help the domestic economy to adjust more smoothly to real and financial shocks?

The transformation has resulted in a global financial system relying on the interaction between national financial systems. Although the global system has the same tasks as the national systems, it differs when it comes to the existence of institutions. In the mid-1990s there are as yet no global financial institutions or regulating mechanisms.[6] All institutions acting on the global market – central banks, supervisory institutions or others – are based on a national financial system and are under the regulation of the jurisdiction where they operate. This applies also to other market participants. The development of the global financial system and its vulnerability to different shocks is thus determined by the 'strength' of the linkages between national markets.

Dramatic technological changes in telecommunications, electronic trading and data processing have increasingly strengthened the linkages between national markets by helping to make their potential incompatibility more transparent. Since international compatibility is a crucial test for the survival of a market, governments have become increasingly aware of the pressure to adjust regulations and macroeconomic policies to external forces.[7] This pressure has provided a further incentive for individual governments to look for a 'refuge' within an appropriate regional entity. The regional entity provides a rationale for unpopular economic policy measures, as well as an insurance against a prolonged crisis in the international financial system, since individual governments can rely on the 'survival' of the larger entity.[8] Regionalism influences the transformation process by providing a shift in the adjustment mechanism, making for easier adjustment within the bloc and more difficult adjustment between blocs.[9]

Regionalism may have seemed particularly attractive to small countries.[10] Before the deregulation wave began, most of these countries had opted for national policy autonomy and the power to regulate internally by imposing capital controls combined with a fixed exchange rate regime.[11] At the time when the pressure for external deregulation started to make itself felt, the opportunity costs of pursuing internal regulations were rising dramatically. Governments had no choice. If they did not initiate internal deregulation before the external deregulation was upon them they would be more or less forced into it. In the government perspective, the transformation process involved switching from internal regulations based on economic political motives to regulations based on concern about the soundness of the markets.

For market actors the external deregulation provided additional financial alternatives. Savers were allowed to invest globally and to reap the benefits of holding an internationally diversified portfolio, while investors were able to finance their real investment with capital from abroad. However, a general weakness at the time when the transformation started was that these actors had been fostered in an isolated financial market environment, or in the embryo of such a market. They were inexperienced in dealing with the new risks and opportunities. Existing financial institutions, for instance, were unfamiliar with ways of dealing with foreign competition or with the pricing of international risks.

Moreover, since banks and finance companies domiciled in small economies are relatively small compared to their competitors in the global market, they were acting upon the general view that only large banks and finance companies would survive the increased competition from abroad following the external deregulation. Many banks thus started to grow by taking larger risks. The alternative to this strategy for survival, as they perceived it, was to disappear by being acquired or liquidated. Their inexperience in pricing risks undoubtedly contributed to the development of national financial crises. Since this development can be ascribed to some extent to the national authorities, it emphasizes the critical role of the interaction between politicians and markets in the transformation of small national financial markets.

The interaction between politicians and markets is also evident in the global market perspective. Political concern about systemic risk[12] may have affected the transformation process.[13] National financial markets gradually became so closely interlinked, that a disruption in one market could hardly be prevented from spreading to others. Naturally, this fuelled concern about a breakdown in the whole global financial system, i.e. a return to barter trade. The improved access to information resulting from progress in information technology justified, and still justifies, such fears.[14]

From past experience it is possible to identify the conditions most conducive to financial fragility.[15] They appear in combinations of factors such as:

- a real economic shock, such as the 1973 oil price rise;
- a major change of regime, such as the shift from fixed to flexible exchange rates;
- a sharp tightening of monetary policy following earlier relaxation;
- heavy debt accumulation by major classes of borrowers, or
- intense competition between financial intermediaries in new instruments leading to the underpricing of risk premiums and concentration in high-risk assets.

It is easy to visualize the crucial role of politicians behind most of these factors.

Since increased international financial integration – either *de facto* or *de jure* – seems to be of crucial importance to the process of transformation, there is every reason to emphasize the role of external deregulation and related policy issues. Two major questions can then be identified. First, what kind of difficulties are encountered when capital controls are relaxed or removed? Second, what type of policies would have helped to avoid these difficulties and to facilitate the transition to an open capital account and sustained capital account convertibility? History shows that the opening up of the capital account is often accompanied by difficulties in the shape of a sharp expansion of gross capital inflows and outflows, a large net capital inflow and an appreciation in the real exchange rate.[16]

In the mid-1990s many structural crises of a regional as well as a global character have emerged, indicating that in a global welfare perspective the transformation has been 'suboptimal'. What, then, has been the effect on the national economies of deviations from the optimal path?[17] This overall question can be split into subquestions as follows:

- To what extent has a smooth and adequate flow of financial resources been channelled in a direction where they were truly needed?
- To what extent has this flow been distorted during the transformation of national financial markets, and by what factors?
- To what extent has international regulatory arbitrage occurred?[18]
- To what extent have the changing national financial scenarios affected the international competitiveness of domestic non-financial and financial companies?
- What factors have provided incentives for actors in the national market, including the financial service industry, to carry out their tasks in a socially 'optimal' way, or what factors hindered them from doing so?

A study of the transformation process which provides answers to these and similar questions, will increase our understanding of the delicate process of interaction between policy and markets, and should help to promote appropriate policy-making in the new financial environment. Such a study will also increase our knowledge of the determinants of systemic risk and should lead to a more insightful approach in ensuring the safety and soundness of the markets.

THE AIM OF THE STUDY

The aim of this book is to promote a better understanding of the process of transformation by providing answers to some of the questions mentioned above. As indicated previously, the study will focus on the way in which different sequences of events affect the ability of financial markets to attract and channel savings in order to improve real national growth. This is a vast task, since the process of transformation has been extremely complex, involving many interacting dimensions and factors. The whole situation offers an infinite number of combinations which could be investigated.

In order to narrow the task somewhat I shall focus on the transformation of bond markets and will pay particular attention to the availability of funds for real investment. I am assuming that the liberalization process has influenced the national interest rate and the cost of capital. The impact may have been temporary or permanent, and may have expressed itself in effects on the size of potential inefficiencies and risk premiums. The influence runs from interest rate, via cost of capital and investment, to economic growth in the particular country.[19] This makes the concept of financial integration, focusing on the implications of various market imperfections, a relevant object of study. The present study also includes an analysis of the extent to which policy-makers have contributed to rising interest rates by influencing various kinds of risk premiums.

The empirical analysis will be regional in scope and involves the four major Nordic countries.[20] In addition to intra-Nordic comparisons, the development of the region will also be compared to the development of the US, UK, German and Japanese markets. The presentation will proceed along two avenues, one describing structural changes in national bond markets and another measuring the levels of international integration of these markets and the potential effects that disintegration may have had on national economic growth. Both these aspects – the *formal* (to the extent that the structural changes have consisted of deregulative measures) and *informal* degree of integration – are to be seen as important to an understanding of the transition from national financial markets to well-integrated parts of the global market, and of the implications of this process for the national economy.

DEVELOPMENT OF THE BOND MARKET IN FOCUS

The focus on the transformation of bond markets is justified by the importance of these markets to economic activity.[21] The government bond rate also has an important function as a benchmark rate: the risk-free rate in the investment decision. A bond is a contract whereby an issuer undertakes to make payments to an owner or beneficiary when certain events or dates specified in the contract occur. Public bonds appeared in their modern form for the first time with the establishment of the Monte in Florence in 1345.

Bond markets perform two important functions. First, they facilitate the transfer of investable funds from economic agents with a financial surplus to others with a financial deficit. This is achieved by selling (issuing) bonds to those with surplus funds. New cash is raised in exchange for financial claims on the *primary market*. In this manner companies, governments, local authorities, supranational organizations and others gain access to a larger pool of capital than would be the case if they had to rely on internally generated funds only. Primary market activity is designated as domestic, foreign or Euro depending on where the issue takes place, the nationality of the issuer and the currency of the issue.[22]

What distinguishes bonds from most other types of loan is that they are transferable and negotiable. Hence, the second important function of bond markets is to provide an adequate *secondary market* for bonds issued in the past. To the extent that the secondary market exists and performs its functions well, it makes the primary market operate more effectively. It also lets the bonds offer the issuer the advantage of borrowing 'long', while maintaining an acceptable degree of liquidity for any given investor. The secondary market determines the price at which the bond is sold in the primary market; investors pay the issuing corporation no more than the price they expect the secondary market will set for its bonds. Hence, the state of the secondary market is of utmost importance to the corporation which is issuing the bonds. A well-functioning secondary market is characterized by:

- a high degree of transparency;
- a multiplicity of maturities and issuers;
- low spreads;
- high and stable liquidity (easy to sell even in times of economic turbulence).

In addition to these qualities of static efficiency, a well-functioning secondary market is also *innovative* and responds quickly to its customers' demand for new products, i.e. it is efficient in a dynamic sense. The US treasury bond market is the most attractive market in both these respects, and is often used as a benchmark.[23]

Participants in the secondary markets are investors, market-makers and other securities companies, and brokers who mediate between market-makers. Trading between these participants takes place mainly in central public market-places such as stock exchanges[24] or in over-the-counter (OTC) markets.[25] Many transactions in the OTC markets are never reported since they are made in-house, with the securities company itself arranging both sides of the transaction. Any analysis of market efficiency in terms of liquidity requires an effort to capture the transactions in both trading alternatives. Until the beginning of the 1980s, stock exchanges around the world had a monopoly on dealing in the bonds quoted there. However, progress in information technology has weakened the case for a central market-place. The decline in activity on the floor of the London Stock Exchange following the introduction of the SEAQ[26] system in London at the time of Big Bang, provides a good example of this. The convention in the US offers another example, with all US treasury bonds listed on the New York Stock Exchange but with trading taking place overwhelmingly in the OTC market.[27] Generally speaking, a listing of an issue on an exchange is no longer a guarantee that it is only traded there.

In retrospect, the international development of global bond markets shows that governments in the 1960s and 1970s intervened actively, which hindered the emergence of well-functioning national bond markets. The governments' objectives were often to control the supply side, predominantly through issuing controls, but also the demand side, through investment obligations for pension funds and insurance companies and by imposing reserve requirements on banks. In addition to these measures the use of interest rate regulations was also common. The absence of adequate price-setting in secondary markets made the voluntary purchase of bonds virtually non-existent. The reasons for this extensive government regulation were twofold: (1) an attempt to create a degree of freedom in domestic policy-making, and (2) to finance the housing sector or a fiscal deficit cheaply.

In this book the process of globalization is exemplified by the development of the Nordic national bond markets between the 1970s to the early 1990s.[28] Two aspects in particular will be considered: (1) the role played by Nordic national bond markets in the funding of domestic non-financial companies, and (2) the way the efficiency of Nordic secondary national markets has developed.

MOTIVATION FOR THE REGIONAL APPROACH

A study of the Nordic region makes sense for two reasons. First, it allows a comparison of similar countries with different regulatory approaches. Previous parts of this chapter have focused entirely on the link between integration and regulation (including taxation). However, disintegration or segmentation has many other possible causes, such as *information barriers, transaction costs, home-country bias, take-over defences, small-country bias,* and *the dominance of privately owned companies.*[29,30] Taking the Nordic countries as the examples means that one can disregard many of these causes as they are more or less similar in the four countries, which in turn allows us to concentrate on a few of them.

Second, the regional approach makes it possible to discuss the importance of the region as a political 'refuge'. It will be seen how the Nordic economies have coordinated the general transformation through cooperation and simultaneous policy changes.

The institutional setting for long-term credit varies in the Nordic countries. Whereas banks have played a leading role in Finland, Norway and Sweden, mortgage credit institutions have been the major supplier of long-term credit in Denmark. When it comes to the structure of the entire national credit market, Table 1.1 shows big differences between the Nordic markets as well as between them and the markets in major OECD countries. In 1990

Table 1.1 Structure of national credit markets (percentage of total credit stock)

End of year	Denmark 1990	Denmark 1980	Finland 1990	Finland 1980	Norway 1990	Norway 1980	Sweden 1990	Sweden 1980	Germany 1990	Japan[a] 1990	UK[b] 1990	USA[c] 1990
Bond market	47	48	13	9	17	18	23	31	26	24	13	41
Money market	3	2	10	0	4	4	8	4	2	6	9	9
Loans	50	50	77	91	79	78	69	65	72	70	78	50
Total	100	100	100	100	100	100	100	100	100	100	100	100

Sources: Based on data from Denmark's Nationalbank, Annual Report, various issues; Copenhagen Stock Exchange, Annual Report, various issues; Central Statistical Bureau of Denmark, Statistisk Årbog, various issues; Finanstilsynet, 1991, Beretning fra Finanstilsynet; Central Statistical Bureau of Finland, Financial Market Statistics, various issues; Central Statistical Bureau of Norway, Bank-og Kredittstatistikk, various issues; Bank of Norway, Database; Central Statistical Bureau of Sweden, Financial Accounts: Database, SDB KR805; OECD, Financial Accounts, Germany 1976/1991; Deutsche Bundesbank, 1993, Monthly Report, August; Deutsche Bundesbank, 1993, Kapitalmarktstatistik, August; OECD, Financial Accounts, Japan 1976/1991; M. Takeda and P. Turner, 1992, The liberalization of Japan's financial markets: Some major themes, No. 34, Bank for International Settlements; Central Statistical Bureau of United Kingdom, 1992, National Accounts; R. Benzie, 1992, The development of the international bond market, No. 32, Bank for International Settlements; J.S. Alworth and C.E.V. Borio, 1993, Commercial paper markets: A survey, No. 37, Bank for International Settlements; OECD, Financial Accounts, United States 1975/1990; Federal Reserve, 1991, Federal Reserve Bulletin, June; own calculations and estimates.

Notes: [a]Excluding foreign issues in Japan and including loans issued abroad.
[b]The size of money market is an estimated value.
[c]Excluding long-term loans, issued abroad and by foreigners in the USA

bonds issued in Denmark represented about 47 per cent (as compared to 48 per cent in 1980) of the total Danish domestic credit stock, which was well above the US standard of 41 per cent for that year.[31] The corresponding figures in Finland and Norway were 13 (9) and 17 (19), which were at par with the UK standard for that year, whereas the relative size of the Swedish bond market was 23 (31) per cent and equal to the German market. The figures also indicate that, with the exception of Finland, the significance of Nordic domestic bond markets, as reflected by their share of the domestic credit stock, has declined slightly between 1980 and 1990.

CAPITAL CONTROLS, MONETARY POLICY AND THE COST OF CAPITAL

The abolition of capital controls has been the major ingredient in the process of globalization. Capital control embraces a very large set of measures. All these measures or types of restriction, albeit highly diversified, have a common goal: to restrain non-governmental cross-border investment decisions. According to the OECD classifications of capital flows, the aim is to control:

- foreign direct investment (FDI);
- financial assets, stocks, bonds, and derivatives;
- credit and loans;
- purely financial operations, FOREX;
- personal capital operations.

The relative importance of the different groups has varied over time. The IMF *Balance of Payment Statistics* shows that a large part of these cross-border investments consists of foreign direct investment. Between 1975 and 1979 the size of FDI flows from fourteen major industrialized countries was twice that of the flow of portfolio investment, i.e. bonds and equities.[32] A temporary change occurred between 1985 and 1989, when the flow of securities was twice that of FDI due to a heavy increase in bond investments. From 1990 onwards the opposite applied again.

In general the imposition of capital controls has been justified on four grounds:

- They help to manage balance-of-payment crises or unstable exchange rates generated by excessively volatile short-run capital flows.
- They help to ensure that domestic savings are used to finance domestic investments rather than to acquire foreign assets, and to limit foreign ownership of domestic assets.
- They enable governments to tax financial activities, income and wealth, and thus to maintain the domestic tax base.
- They prevent capital flows from disrupting reform programmes.

By imposing external regulations, governments have also paved the way for internal regulations such as interest rate ceilings and reserve requirements, which have created opportunities for low-priced domestic financing to boost domestic economic growth.

Efficient capital controls provide governments with some degree of freedom in national policy-making: governments can exert a certain influence on inflation, interest and exchange rates. By 'managing' these variables they may also influence the relative attractiveness of their country in the eyes of international investors. Depending on which variables policy-makers emphasize, they can choose an appropriate policy regime. The role of capital controls in this context is demonstrated by the triangle in Figure 1.1 which describes three optional monetary regimes (the corners) based on three policy elements that can only be combined in pairs. The 'impossible' triangle produces three policy regimes as paradigms. One combines fixed exchange rates, capital controls and national monetary autonomy (1). The second combines a fixed exchange rate, perfect capital mobility and no autonomy (2), while the third regime is based on a floating rate, perfect capital mobility and national monetary autonomy (3).

A characteristic feature of many small economies with a high degree of openness to international trade has been the striving for a fixed exchange arrangement. Generally, these small economies have also opted for monetary autonomy.[33] In order to create this combination they have had to reduce capital mobility by imposing capital and exchange regulations. Hence, small economies have opted for corner (1) in the figure. The erosion or abolition of capital controls then moved them to corner (2). A characteristic feature of the monetary turbulence in Europe following the problems of launching the

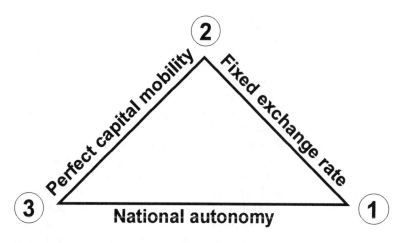

Figure 1.1 The monetary policy option triangle

European Monetary Union (EMU) in 1992 and 1993, was that a row of straddle-vaults from corner (2) to corner (3) appeared.[34]

A central hypothesis underlying the present study is that the isolation of a small economy through the adoption of capital controls can lead to high societal costs in the long run. One major determinant of this cost is the interest gap between the global and domestic interest rates. In its broadest version – from the saver to the ultimate user – the gap includes:

- margins and transaction costs;
- political and exchange risk premiums;
- market- and policy-generated inefficiencies.

These elements will be discussed in detail below. The basic view underlying the above hypothesis is that the transition affects competitiveness between companies within a particular country as well as between countries. This influence will express itself in the extent to which different kinds of company have to bear the above-mentioned cost elements. A large part of a bigger interest rate gap, experienced in the transition phase by companies located in a country with a small and segmented market, is a *learning cost* incorporated in margins and transactions costs. Furthermore, the transition will involve some policy-making of a 'trial and error' character, producing temporary policy-generated inefficiencies.[35]

By pursuing a particular policy politicians may increase relative risk premiums, thus further adding to the interest gap, thereby imposing a net cost on society during the transition process. 'Net cost' means here the difference between the real benefits from adopting a particular policy and the costs generated by potentially increased risk premiums. A relatively high national interest rate will affect economic activity in three ways: via income, substitution and exchange rates.

The logic behind the non-neutrality of the process of transition is that 'fine-tuning' measures, or rather the investors' perceived threat of such measures, will increase the relative political risk premium charged for investing in a particular country. In an international context this means relatively higher national interest rates in that particular country, with implications for domestic investments and the international competitiveness of the country's companies. The national policy option will be reflected in an increasing national *relative cost of capital*, in a way that may have detrimental long-run implications for the domestic economy. By discussing relative costs we circumvent the problem of assessing the overall global impact of the increased international financial integration, for instance in terms of a global interest rate lower than the rate that would otherwise have prevailed. Moreover, the isolation of a country reduces the availability of risk capital, with serious implications in terms of lost opportunities for small and medium-sized companies in particular. The isolation may also leave small and medium-sized companies especially vulnerable when it comes to meeting competition in their home markets, as well as being less able to exploit the opportunities – financial as well as real – arising from an external deregulation.

The size and direction of capital flows are important sources of information in the assessment of international competitiveness. The imposition of capital controls distorts this source and reduces its value as a signal. Thus, there are reasons to believe that industries enjoying protection from border controls will find themselves less competitive and will experience a deterioration in their profit prospects as integration proceeds. This reinforces the negative effects of the relatively high cost of capital. The Nordic banking industry serves as a good example here, since this industry has been sheltered during the post-war period and will be hit in many ways by greater financial integration. It is easy to imagine that banks in general will lose many of their cash cows once the world market reaches a state of perfect integration, and that the 'loss' will be relatively bigger for banks that work predominantly in countries with a sheltered banking industry.

THE IMPORTANCE OF THE ORDER IN WHICH DEREGULATIVE MEASURES OCCUR

In this study we will investigate whether the particular order in which deregulative measures appear in a country has influenced the benefits of the liberalization, or affected the emergence of a financial crisis in the country concerned. For instance, does the order matter in which internal deregulation, tax reforms and external deregulation occur? Further, how serious is the gap between the formal (*de jure*) and actual (*de facto*) degree of integration in terms of the prospects for national growth?

Denmark was the first Nordic country to complete a formal deregulation. Did the Danes reap relatively higher benefits from their way of deregulating the financial markets? If so, did Danish politicians, as opposed to their Nordic colleagues, perceive at an early stage that the *actual* level of the international financial integration of their market was high? And did this in turn lead them to speed up the *formal* integration as well? Why were the Danes first in the field? Did politicians in the other Nordic countries fail to understand what was happening, or did they simply ignore signals of a very high degree of *de facto* financial integration, and persist in pursuing what they believed to be autonomous monetary policies? The extent to which this led to more serious financial crises, and what other consequences there were, such as international bargain prices for domestic companies, relatively lower rates of investment, etc., will be discussed in the course of this book.

CHARACTER OF THE DESCRIPTION AND ANALYSIS

The description will cover relevant aspects of the transformation process, as presented in Chapter 2. In the analysis the international integration of capital markets is measured in terms of bond market integration. To some extent this makes the empirical part of the study vulnerable to the criticism of being partial in character, or of ignoring indirect effects that would be captured in a general equilibrium approach.

The multiplicity of market segments in a national market – if the segments are disintegrated – would also require a simultaneous study of all the segments before anything could be said about the international integration of the national market as a whole.[36] In a country with more or less well-functioning exchange controls, for example, the financial integration of the money market may differ greatly from the integration of the markets for long-term investments, loans or stocks. Consequently the empirical analysis that follows below does not provide any grounds for generalization from the bond market segment to the national market as a whole, unless we can assume that the different segments making up the domestic market are perfectly integrated.

The liberalization and the decline in political influence and control on the Nordic markets in the form of administratively determined interest rates, have probably also affected the delay before influence from abroad takes effect. In order to say something about changes in the level of integration over time, an analysis of subperiods will also be carried out.

There are four main ways of performing an analysis of the actual degree of financial integration:

- by studying the *relationship between the savings rate of an economy and its investment rate*;
- by measuring the *interest sensitivity of capital flows*;
- by measuring the *reflow of capital* and the offset coefficients;
- by analysing the relationship between interest rates in different countries, i.e. by studying the *law of one price for financial instruments*, and measuring the difference in level and covariation for different interest rate combinations.

In our analysis we will briefly examine the relationship between saving and investment rates in Chapter 4, after which the fourth of the above alternatives is adopted, using the gap between bond rates in individual Nordic countries and foreign bond rates as the dependent variable. The choice of approach has been largely influenced by the statistical uncertainty that makes it difficult to determine the size of the capital flows over national borders. Moreover, by using the interest gap rather than the capital flow as the dependent variable, it is possible to avoid the dubious assumption that the interest rate is consistently used as a policy variable.

The monthly data on which the study is based encompasses (for most variables) the period January 1974 to December 1993, with the collapse of the Bretton Woods and the Smithsonian agreements motivating the choice of the starting date. The absence of any formal Eurorate for the Nordic currencies for the period as a whole excludes any short cuts, such as comparing domestic rates with Eurorates in the same currency, in order to avoid problems in estimating the expected change in exchange rates.

Which interest rate or aggregated interest rates influence the Nordic bond markets? For a long time the US rates exerted a powerful influence on most national interest rates, but their impact has been successively diminishing. Recent studies suggest that since the middle of the 1970s there have been two-way causal relationships between the US rates and their counterparts on the national markets in Europe.[37] This mutual influence is mediated in part by the Eurodollar rate.

In recent years it has been found that bond rates are increasingly subject to the influence of a common factor which can be called the 'global' bond rate.[38] This can be described as a weighted average of the rates in the largest OECD countries. The US bond rates are thus still exerting considerable influence through their weight in this proxy for the global rate.

In any empirical study of the effect of changes in the global bond rate on bond rates in a small open economy, the weighing procedure raises an interesting theoretical problem. Should we use trade weights – bilateral or multilateral – or capital market weights? The second of these alternatives would give more weight to the US rate. Trade weights appear more appropriate, since it seems reasonable that capital market weights covariate with the bond rate. In the present analysis we look at the influence of both the US rate and a trade-weighted OECD rate.

PLAN OF THE BOOK

In Chapter 2 some of the main elements of globalization are presented, and the post-war history of external financial market deregulation is reviewed. In Chapter 3 reasons for choosing the regional approach and the Nordic region as an object of study are given.

In Chapter 4 we will look at links between financial liberalization and deregulation on the one hand, and investment and growth on the other. Private saving behaviour, corporate funding decisions and financial market distortions are key words here. In this chapter the extent to which domestic savings are still important to domestic investment will also be examined.

Chapter 5 contains a brief survey of the conceptual apparatus and methodological problems connected with the analysis of financial integration. Here, the model for analysing the international integration of financial markets is introduced.

Various special institutional characteristics of the Nordic markets are described in Chapters 6, 7, 8 and 9. The importance of exchange controls as an instrument of segmentation is discussed in Chapter 6. The external deregulation of financial markets in general and of bond markets in particular is described. Whereas in Chapter 6 we examine the way governments can insert a wedge between domestic and foreign prices, in Chapters 7, 8 and 9 we turn to certain specific aspects of this wedge. Chapter 7 is concerned with internal deregulation and includes an analysis of relative tax burdens. The choice of monetary regimes and recent historical patterns in exchange rate movements and related issues are discussed in Chapter 8. In Chapter 8 the magnitude of exchange rate risks is also examined, while in Chapter 9 we look at different expressions of the magnitude of political risks.

Chapter 10 highlights the development of primary bond markets, and growth in these markets is analysed. The importance of functioning bond markets to companies is then described and analysed in Chapter 11. Here, fund raising, cash management and securitization are the key words.

Chapter 12 is devoted to an analysis of the static and dynamic efficiency of the Nordic bond markets, while the historical patterns in Nordic bond rates and the correlation between them are analysed in Chapter 13. National bond rates and foreign bond rates are then juxtaposed in Chapter 14. Here we look for indications of increasing integration in the adjustment of domestic interest rates to major shifts in foreign rates. The gap between domestic rates and the corresponding global rates and US rates is illustrated, as well as the correlation between these international rates and successive Nordic interest rate quotations. Growth effects generated by the gaps are discussed. Finally, in Chapter 15, the results are summarized.

NOTES

1   Deregulation and liberalization are used more or less synonymously in the literature to emphasize the relaxation and removal of constraints and barriers that have limited competition or insulated markets from general economic forces. The two concepts, which embrace efforts made by the market as well as by regulators, will be used interchangeably in this book.

2   Conceptually, the two forms of integration – economic and financial integration – overlap, as both include foreign direct investment. In causal terms it can be claimed that the financial integration was triggered and made inevitable by the increasing internationalization of companies.

3   See e.g. Blundell-Wignal et al. (1990). At the beginning of the 1990s inflation above 3 per cent and current account deficits worse than 1 per cent of GDP were regarded as high.

4   It is difficult to decide whether the new regulatory situation is sustainable or is just an overreaction of the kind that often accompanies radical social changes. Perhaps the pendulum will swing back and forth several times before reaching a stable equilibrium which may properly be regarded as the end of the transformation process.

5   The BIS (Bank for International Settlements) capital-adequacy requirement, which is also in accordance with an EU directive, states that a bank's equity must

exceed 8 per cent of its assets from 1 January 1993. During the years immediately preceding that date, rules implying a gradual approach to these figures have been applied in most industrial countries.

6   In a long-term perspective the G-10 Supervisory Committee, the World Bank, the International Monetary Fund and the Bank for International Settlement are potential candidates to become true global financial institutions acting with supernational jurisdiction.

7   The development of the Euromarket in the 1960s as a response to the introduction of capital controls in New York should have been a lesson to national authorities.

8   See Dufey (1993).

9   This will mean a tendency to less volatile asset prices and exchange rates within each bloc and increased variability between blocs.

10   The arguments put forward in this book apply to a good many countries, since 'small' refers to the inability to influence global markets rather than to the size of a country's population or area. Generally speaking these countries can be described as price-takers in a financial perspective.

11   The financial markets remained in general rudimentary, and were simply a means for governments to channel cheap financing into public investments.

12   A plausible sequence of events in the emergence of a crisis in the whole financial system is as follows. It starts with a shock in a single national securities market. Impelled by its establishment in one market, the shock is then transmitted to other national and international securities markets, and subsequently to the whole global financial system of which they are part. The ultimate consequence may be the demise of the global financial system with tremendous effects on the real-world economy.

13   Concern about systemic risks and the safety and soundness of markets was frequently expressed by politicians, business people and researchers as the global financial crisis intensified at the beginning of the 1990s.

14   One more reason for concern is that information technology has reduced the 'filtering' of information in a way that, at least until the market participants learn how to deal with the new situation, may cause destabilizing effects on financial markets. For instance, it may mean that false but sensational news makes a greater impact on the market compared to accurate but unspectacular news.

15   See, for instance, Kanda (1992).

16   In some cases, and predominantly in developing countries, there have also been high ex post real interest rates and a large gap between domestic and foreign interest rates. See, for example, Mathieson and Rojas-Suarez (1992).

17   The 'optimal' way for individual countries may differ, depending on differences in characteristic features of the particular economies.

18   International regulatory arbitrage may express itself in a race between national regulatory authorities in introducing reforms aimed at strengthening the competitive position of the financial markets in the countries over which they preside. The competition may concern the easing of the interest-free reserve requirements imposed by the national monetary authorities on the banks' deposit liabilities, as well as fiscal regulations such as withholding taxes or stamp duties.

19   Hence, it is assumed here that financial markets determine the development of the real side of an economy, and do not only reflect it. See, for instance, Galbraith (1955), Temin (1976), Minsky (1982,1986), Blanchard and Watson (1982), Shiller (1984) and Gertler et al. (1991).

20   The region is made up by five countries: Denmark, Finland, Iceland, Norway and Sweden. Because of its relatively small size, Iceland has been excluded from

the present study but its case will be examined in a separate one.

21   The distinction between money markets and bond markets is expressed here in terms of maturities, letting the bond market consist of maturities exceeding one year. Referring to traditional terminology, the bond market thus encompasses long-term as well as medium-term loans. Some authors make a further split between bond market issues, labelling issues with maturities not exceeding 7–10 years 'notes', and issues with maturities exceeding that time-span 'bonds'. Other authors use other distinctions, such as a promise to pay (note) and an order to pay (bond). No such further distinction will be made here, but 'bond' will be used as a comprehensive designation for medium- and long-term issues.

22   As a rule of thumb a bond can be said to belong to the Eurosector if it is issued through an international (with respect to ownership) syndicate of securities houses. Transactions in the Euromarket are all denominated in Eurocurrencies, i.e. funds held in an account outside the country of the currency's origin. Non-Euro issues belong to the domestic sector if the issuer's country of residence corresponds to the bond's currency of denomination, and otherwise to the foreign sector.

23   The US treasury notes are seen as risk-free from a credit risk point of view. Hence, the general demand for a multiplicity of issuers to diversify credit risks in a market does not contradict the given assessment.

24   As a general rule, stock exchanges provide a trading environment, negotiated spreads, rules, transparency and a clearing house.

25   OTC markets are characterized by having no central market-place. Transactions take place either by telephone or through computers between geographically dispersed participants.

26   SEAQ stands for Stock Exchange Automatic Quotations, a system for continuously updating quotations and trade reports for UK and Irish securities.

27   The listing obligation is for the benefit of those overseas institutional investors whose charters only permit the purchase of listed securities.

28   The assessments were made in the first part of 1995. Due to the availability – or non-availability – of data, some descriptions and comparisons come to an end during 1990.

29   See Stonehill and Dullum (1981) for a further description.

30   The existence of home-country bias implies that international portfolio investment activities are influenced by foreign exchange risk, political risk and the 'old boys' network', while small-country bias means lack of liquidity for foreign investors (flowback of shares) and lack of economies of scale and scope.

31   As measured in common currency, the total credit stock in Sweden in 1990 was more than double the Danish and almost three times as big as the Finnish and Norwegian domestic credit stocks.

32   The Group-10 countries (Switzerland being the eleventh) plus Austria, Australia and Spain.

33   This autonomy does not necessarily mean that the country has achieved independence in terms of monetary policy; rather it has succeeded in differentiating prices. The distinction is a matter of aggregated versus selective monetary policy.

34   Since the beginning of the 1980s there has been a trend towards flexible exchange rates. According to the IFS-classification in IMF (1995), 64 per cent of the member countries in IMF pegged the value of their currency at the end of 1984, while at the end of 1994 the proportion had fallen to 40 per cent. During this period the proportion of member countries with independent floating exchange rates rose from 8 to 33 per cent of the member countries.

35   Stemming from lags in information, regulatory arbitrage, and a need to

harmonize deregulation in an uncertain global economic environment.

36 It has to be emphasized that it is very difficult to integrate (internationally) one market completely, say the financial market, without integrating completely all other markets, i.e. goods markets and labour markets. For instance, within the EU a complete integration of the labour market may be impossible, which means that in the final stage of EMU the social costs of adjusting to asymmetric shocks in different EU countries may be considerable. Despite this 'cost', the integration may nevertheless be beneficial for other reasons.

37 See, for example, Hartman (1984) for nominal rates and Cumby and Mishkin (1984) for real rates.

38 See, for example, Oxelheim (1990).

REFERENCES

Alworth, J.S. and C.E.V. Borio, 1993, *Commercial Paper Markets: A Survey*, No. 37, Bank for International Settlements, Basle.

Benzie, R., 1992, *The Development of the International Bond Market*, No. 32, Bank for International Settlements, Basle.

Blanchard, O.J. and M.W. Watson, 1982, 'Bubbles, Rational Expectations, and Financial Markets', in Wachtel P. (ed.) *Crises in the Economic and Financial Structure*, Heath & Company, Lexington, Mass.

Blundell-Wignal, A. *et al.*, 1990, 'Monetary Policy in Liberalized Financial Markets', *OECD Economic Studies*, No. 15, Autumn.

Cumby, R.E. and F. Mishkin, 1984, 'The International Linkages of Real Interest Rates: the European–US Connection', *NBER Working Paper No. 1423*, New York.

Dufey, G., 1993, 'The Instability of the International Financial System and its Implications for Trade and Investment', in Oxelheim, L. (ed.) *The Global Race for Foreign Direct Investment – Prospects for the Future*, Springer Verlag, Heidelberg.

Galbraith, J.C., 1955, *The Great Crash*, Houghton Mifflin, New York.

Gertler, M., R.G. Hubbard and A.K. Kashyap, 1991, 'Interest Rate Spreads, Credit Constraints and Investment Fluctuations: An Empirical Investigation', in Hubbard R. (ed.) *Financial Markets and Financial Crises*, University of Chicago, Chicago, pp. 11–31.

Hartman, D., 1984, 'The International Financial Market and US Interest Rates', *Journal of International Money and Finance*, Vol. 3, pp. 91–103.

IMF, 1995, *Annual Report on Exchange Arrangements and Exchange Restrictions*, Washington, DC.

Kanda, H., 1992, 'Systemic Risk and International Financial Markets', in Edwards, F.R. and Patrick, H.T. (ed.) *Regulating International Financial Markets; Issues and Policies*, Kluwer Academic Publishers, Dordrecht.

Mathieson, D.J. and L. Rojaz-Suarez, 1992, 'Liberalization of the Capital Account: Experiences and Issues', *IMF Working Paper*, No. 46, IMF, Washington, DC.

Minsky, H.P., 1982, *Can 'it' Happen Again?: Essay on Instability and Finance*, M.E. Sharpe, Armonk.

Minsky, H.P., 1986, *Stabilizing an Unstable Economy*, Yale University Press, New Haven.

Oxelheim, L., 1990, *International Financial Integration*, Springer Verlag, Heidelberg.

Shiller, R.J., 1984, 'Stock Prices and Social Dynamics', *Brookings Papers on Economic Activity*, Brookings Institution, Washington, DC, pp. 457–98.

Stonehill, A. and K. Dullum, 1981, *Internationalizing the Cost of Capital*, Wiley, Chichester.

Takeda, M. and P. Turner, 1992, *The Liberalization of Japan's Financial Markets: Some Major Themes*, No. 34, Bank for International Settlements, Basle.

Temin P., 1976, *Did Monetary Forces Cause the Great Depression?*, MIT Press, Cambridge, Mass.

Chapter 2

The transformation of national financial markets

The transformation of national segmented financial markets into integrated parts of the global financial market – the globalization process – involves complex cross-border and cross-sectoral integration in which capital movements and financial services are key determinants. The corporate sector plays a major role in this process, since it is in practice the large corporations that have the widest range of funding options. They can engage in arbitrage between less efficient and more efficient markets on a global scale. In this chapter we will look first at the way the national financial system, in terms of tasks and institutional data, compares with the final outcome – namely, the global financial system. In the first section, the bond market will thus be viewed in terms of its place in the financial system. In the second section a framework for analysing the process of financial market transformation will be developed, and certain key factors and elements will be highlighted. In the third part of the chapter financial market activities will be considered in a saving-to-economic-growth perspective. Particular attention will be paid to the link between investment and economic growth. The aim here is to pave the way for a clear focus in the rest of the book on the role of bond markets in the narrower saving-to-investment context. The chapter concludes with an examination of historical patterns in external deregulation.

THE NATIONAL VERSUS THE GLOBAL FINANCIAL SYSTEM

The key elements involved in the globalization process are the national segmented financial markets and the integrated global market. National markets compete both with each other and with international markets. The national market is part of the *national financial system*, which has two essential functions – namely, the payment and credit functions.[1] In general, the government plays an important role in the first of these functions by having the power to create money, a power which it exercises through a central bank or some similar monetary institution. Money is expected to be created at a non-inflationary rate and to be compatible with macroeconomic stability. Commercial banks and other institutions meeting the public demand for deposit facilities complement the central bank by fulfilling the payment function. The payment system makes a wider range of transactions feasible, permitting a greater degree of specialization in economic activity. In addition to the markets, the national financial system consists of financial intermediaries and an infrastructure embracing a regulatory body, information and payment channels.[2]

The major financial markets, or aggregates of submarkets, are the credit market, the stock market and the foreign exchange market. The credit and stock markets contribute to economic efficiency by performing the credit function, i.e. the channelling of funds from actors who do not have a productive use for them to those who do. These markets are used by lenders (savers), i.e. households, business firms and government in channelling their funds to borrowers (users), i.e. households, firms and government. The flow of funds involved here can be called direct finance, as opposed to indirect finance whereby lenders channel their funds to ultimate borrowers via financial intermediaries. In this second case, savers may make deposits in savings or commercial banks, or they may buy 'secondary' financial claims or liabilities issued by financial institutions. Savers thus expect to benefit in terms of liquidity, convenience and safety from the financial institutions' ability to diversify risk and improve credit quality. The financial intermediaries can then choose to channel funds direct to the borrowers in the shape of loans, or via financial markets by buying securities.[3]

In the case of direct finance, borrowers raise funds directly from lenders in financial markets by selling publicly issued securities (financial instruments), which are liquid financial claims on the borrower's future income and assets. Alternatively, they can raise funds by offering privately issued securities in direct contact with lenders. A broker and/or an informal or organized security market can then be used as a facilitating agency. These two alternatives open up a broader range of options for investors than assets direct from the publicly and privately issued debt and equity instruments available. The direct finance model characterizes the market-based financial system, while indirect finance predominates in the bank-based system.

The issuing and reselling of securities gives rise to a further distinction between different markets, which is important to note in assessing a financial system. Primary markets are markets in which new issues of securities such as bonds or stocks are sold to initial buyers, while secondary markets are markets where these securities are resold. As was emphasized in Chapter 1, the existence of secondary markets is instrumental in increasing liquidity and represents an important step towards the development of an efficient financial system.[4] These markets can be organized as exchanges where buyers and sellers meet in a common location to conduct trade, or as over-the-counter (OTC) markets in which dealers at different locations, who have an inventory of securities, stand ready to buy and sell to anyone willing to accept their prices. However, the difference in competitiveness between exchanges and OTC markets is not significant, since dealers in the OTC market are in computer contact with each other and know the prices the others are offering.

Markets can also be classified on the basis of the maturity of the securities traded or on the kind of funds channelled there. When maturity is the criterion, then 'money market' means a financial market in which only short-term debt instruments (maturity less than one year) are traded, and 'capital market' refers to a market in which longer-term debt and equity instruments are traded.[5] When the kind of funds provides the classification instruments, then 'capital market' becomes a comprehensive designation for the credit and stock markets, and 'credit market' a comprehensive designation for the money and bond markets. In the present book I shall adopt this last solution, distinguishing markets from one another according to the kind of funds involved.

The government and monetary authorities in a country are largely responsible for market regulations, supervision and insurance. At the same time they are important actors in connection with the credit function in most national financial markets, and they undertake:

- the issuing of government securities (primary market for government securities);
- the buying and selling of government securities (secondary markets for government securities);
- lending to financial institutions.

Financial markets are characterized by actors endlessly looking for new profit opportunities resulting from unevenly distributed information, tax wedges, market inefficiencies or inefficiencies created by the regulating authorities. In a competitive environment this drive for profits generates financial and organizational innovations, of which the successful ones are then emulated by other actors, with the resulting erosion of the profits to be made from them. The emergence of the 'information age' paved the way for the development of highly sophisticated financial engineering systems, such as the swap market in the 1970s and the subsequent development of markets for options and futures. Once financial engineering was established, the likelihood increased of new solutions appearing to bypass every new regulation imposed. This is the process of combined innovation and 'creative destruction' which Schumpeter (1943) identified as the driving force of a capitalist economy. Since the 1970s this process seems to have become increasingly typical of financial markets.

The *global financial system* consists of the interaction of national financial systems. In the absence of a global central bank and global institutions, the creation of a truly global market has to be assessed in terms of the closeness of this interaction, i.e. how high is the level of international financial integration. This integration is often measured in terms of capital flows, which take place through the foreign exchange market and the markets for various financial assets. Among these markets we can distinguish between the market for intermediated credit and the market for securities. In the first of these, claims are transferred via financial intermediaries, while in the second market liquid claims such as equity, various fixed income securities and derivatives[6] are traded across borders. The homogeneity of the global financial system can also be assessed on the basis of the degree of coordination in policies which affect the financial interaction.[7] In this context, the choice of exchange rate regime is of crucial importance.

Now, in the mid-1990s, the global financial system is in fact less than global in scope, since many countries – mostly developing countries – have only rudimentary systems and are more or less cut off from the global financial system. Rather, the global system of the mid-1990s is constituted of a hard core of financially sophisticated countries. At the centre of this core we find the financial 'triad': the three major financial centres London, New York and Tokyo. Around the core we then see a number of countries which are dependent on but only loosely linked to the global market. History has seen many periods of increasing partial integration, followed by a return to segmentation. The absence of global institutions certainly leaves the global system very vulnerable, but this time the development of information technology does suggest a possibility that integration will continue towards a global financial system, eventually embracing all national markets.

ON THE ANALYSIS OF FINANCIAL MARKET TRANSFORMATION: FACTORS AND CONCEPTS

When the aim, as here, is to analyse and understand a process of transition, some fundamental factors and sources of change have to be identified. Some of these factors are related to the initial state, while others refer to the process itself. The *initial state*, or point of departure for the exposition, is characterized here in terms of institutional attributes of the national economy, the objectives underlying existing regulations, the starting time for the process and the infrastructure of the financial market at that point. The *process* will be discussed and analysed in terms of (1) driving forces, catalysts and influences from the global macroeconomic environment; (2) factors in domestic policy-making and market behaviour with tangible action parameters in the form of regulations and institutional change; (3) time-related factors, which measure changes in the lapse of time between informal and formal deregulation, the length of the transition period and the order in which liberalization occurs; and (4) factors reflecting implications for the market. The last category includes such things as market efficiency, flexibility and credibility, viewed not only on a basis of financial theory but also in a real macro- and microperspective.

Factors relating to the initial state

Information about the *objectives* underlying the regulations existing when the liberalization started will help in the analysis of the liberalization process. Regulations can be of a political kind, perhaps introduced to prevent 'international capitalism' from taking root in the domestic economy. By their very nature such regulations have fostered an institutional setting quite different from regulations introduced to bridge a period of temporary balance-of-payments problems.

Consideration of regulatory devices[8] is necessary to any understanding of the transformation process. The devices also deserve attention here because the very fact of their existence is an important attribute of the initial state. They can be divided into two kinds, namely internal and external regulations. By *internal deregulation* or liberalization is meant here the relaxation of four kinds of internal regulation or national controls:

- Rate or quantity controls on bank deposits and loans, including ceilings on bank deposits, lending rates and quantitative measures with similar effects (credit ceilings, liquidity ratios, etc.).
- Rules governing the activities of individual financial institutions authorized to carry out various borrowing and lending functions and whose actors are allowed to participate in the payment system or in securities underwriting, equity, insurance, etc. Also included are regulations governing the nature of the financial 'products' offered, and participation in domestic markets.
- Rules governing the activities of individual households, non-financial companies and local governments. These rules determine what activities the actors are allowed to participate in and the limits imposed on different kinds of activity.
- Rules governing tax obligations, such as rules about possible deductions of interest expenses, withholding of taxes, etc.

External deregulation refers to measures such as the abolition of capital controls and exchange rate regulations, and involves the relaxation of national controls on cross-border activities belonging to the second- and third-mentioned categories above. Other restrictions commonly included in external deregulation are the elimination of dual or multiple exchange arrangements and taxes on external financial transactions.

Another factor is the *starting time*. When did the process take off? The time perspective has no explanatory value of its own, but it can help in our interpretation of the development of the process and our understanding of the way it is monitored. It can also help us to identify the general macroeconomic setting that characterizes the start in any particular country. For instance, did the process start during a recession or in a boom? Was the starting-point characterized by a monetary overhang stemming from an imbalance between the price level and the stock of money?[9] As a global phenomenon the start of the current wave of deregulations can be dated to the mid-1960s.

The initial state can also be described in terms of the *infrastructure of the financial market*. For instance, what was the basic set-up regarding financial and supervisory institutions? What weaknesses were there in access to information? How was the particular national system classified in terms of market behaviour and infrastructure?

A common way of answering this last question is to refer to the two major cases previously touched upon: a market-based system with little government influence, and a bank-based system with heavy government influence.[10] As a general rule deregulation appears to have pushed national financial systems in the direction of market-based financial systems. At the beginning of the 1990s the UK system provides an excellent example of a European market-based system, while Germany exemplifies the opposite, i.e. a bank-based system with heavy government influence on the allocation of capital.

In any analysis of the financial market infrastructure, the close involvement of industry in the development and transformation of national financial systems has to be emphasized. The financial systems differ across countries in this respect. For instance, there is no direct equivalent in the US of the German system whereby the lead bank acts as equity holder and management supervisor, or of the Japanese *keiretsu* system. These different market structures have to be considered whenever comparisons are made. We may wonder, for example, whether identical leverage ratios imply different levels of risk in the different countries. If they do, what light does this shed on cost-of-capital-induced differences in competitiveness between countries?[11] Many specific characteristics of a market will have emerged as a result of the long interaction between industry, financial institutions and government policies.

Greater flexibility in the financial infrastructure is a desirable outcome of the transformation. In any particular country flexibility determines the extent to which the national financial market can resist price volatility without transmitting the shocks and forcing them on to the real side of the economy. Hence, in assessing any improvement, the flexibility at the starting point has to be taken into account. And in analysing the path of the change in flexibility, attention must be paid to the microelements of financial institutions and markets, and to the extent to which policy-makers have cooperated over sectors and national borders. Consideration of all these many dimensions makes for an extremely complex analysis, something which must be borne in mind when we embark on the analysis of a fast-changing financial landscape.

Triggering and impelling mechanisms in the process of globalization

Let us now turn to the process itself. It has to be remembered that the process is dynamic and is generated by the interaction of all the dimensions and factors mentioned above. One central question concerns how the process started. Is it possible to single out a major triggering mechanism for the global wave of deregulation that we have witnessed in the 1980s? The answer is no. We have rather to list a number of *driving forces* interacting with each other. If any of these should be mentioned before the others, it must be the improvements in information technology which have eroded regulations generally and made international differences between regulations unsustainable. However, the increase in economic integration and the regional redistribution of financial resources are also important. In the second case, public borrowing was often a significant force. Economic integration and regional redistribution generated competitive pressure, which made a *de jure* deregulation more or less unavoidable in most countries. The formal relaxation of barriers or the abolition of controls have often simply confirmed that the authorities have surrendered and accepted the fact that informal deregulation is a *fait accompli.*

Very similar to these basic driving forces are other forces designated as *catalysts.* These speed up the liberalization process and make the transition phase shorter. The most important catalyst consists of financial innovations, which have continuously developed in response to regulations and fuelled the competitive pressure by eroding them. The massive supply of financial innovations made possible by the developments in information technology has been triggered by the markets' demand for the following:[12]

- new instruments and securities for handling risk; here it is a matter of sharing, pooling or hedging new risks or 'slices' of old risks;[13]
- improved opportunities in the intertemporal and geographical allocation of resources;
- lower transaction costs and increased liquidity;
- bridging over information asymmetries;
- influence on corporate asset allocation;
- ways of circumventing taxes, regulations and accounting rules.[14]

All these types of innovation are more or less directly related to the process of transformation. According to Jensen (1989), financial innovations have in general had a positive impact on the economy, as they have improved corporate access to capital and communication between management and corporate stakeholders. However, they have also reduced the usefulness of current international statistics in the monitoring of international capital flows.

Something else that can be described as a catalyst is that the process of deregulation is contagious: spill-over effects will appear. If one sector is deregulated, an imperfection in another sector will appear relatively more painful and its elimination will be called for, perhaps through further deregulation.

The spill-over effects appear across national borders, since the removal of regulations in some countries and the development of global markets soon undermine controls in other less liberalized countries. Maintaining a high level of regulation in this group of countries would lead to a decline in their domestic financial institutions due to their inability to compete effectively with foreign rivals.

However, spill-over effects in the pace of development across financial products are also important. Of the major industrial countries, Germany's system has in the past been based on universal banking, whereas financial institutions in the United States (the Glass–Steagal Act) and in Japan (Article 65 of the Securities Act) were prevented from engaging in either commercial or investment banking.[15] To date, in the mid-1990s, spill-over effects can be seen to have contributed to the erosion of the Glass–Steagal Act and Article 65, symbolizing the fall of the last major barriers separating different financial services in national financial markets.

The *global macroeconomic environment* and, more specifically, different kinds of global shocks and disturbances have also influenced the way the financial market transformation has proceeded, as well its final outcome in terms of the implications for the national economy. We can separate policy from non-policy, domestic from foreign and monetary from real shocks here, since the market participants make these distinctions themselves in assessing their profit prospects.[16]

In the recent past there have been many examples of shocks which have affected the whole macroeconomic setting, as well as the route and the speed of the transformation. One example of a policy-generated shock of monetary character and of such magnitude was the increase in US interest rates at the beginning of the 1980s. This was triggered to a certain extent by the change in US monetary policy in 1979, when the Federal Reserve Board started to set – and to comply with – money supply targets intended to curb the inflation that was expected to follow the second oil crisis. Abandoning the previous interest targeting and embarking on a 'new' fiscal policy meant higher US interest rates; a wave of interest rate increases around the world, as well as a realignment of exchange rates, followed. The extent to which the increase in the US rate was a shock to participants in different national markets depended on the efficiency of individual countries in preventing the US increases from affecting their own domestic rates. In many countries dramatic increases in real rates left the transformation process very vulnerable. The market actors were also faced with high real rates at the end of the 1980s in a low inflationary environment, creating a similar vulnerability in the transformation process.

Examples of policy-generated shocks of an aggregated real character are provided by the three oil price increases in 1973, 1979 and 1990. For industrialized countries these shocks can be compared to substantial drops in the productivity of the labor force and the capital stock. Big fiscal and monetary policy adjustments and gigantic flows in international markets have sometimes accompanied these shocks, as oil producers' revenues have been recycled. The combination of reduced productivity and policy responses have had drastic effects on the level of aggregate demand, inflation rates, interest rates, exchange rates and the relative prices of various commodities and services. The oil crises of the 1970s created a need for a recycling of OPEC revenues. A surplus of financial capital in the OPEC area induced actors in this area to search for the highest rate of return in a global perspective.[17] This new 'global interest-sensitivity' propelled the international financial integration.

'Rules' for policy responses in the form of exchange rate regimes, money supply growth targets, etc., determine how a particular disturbance affects exchange rates, inflation rates, interest rates and relative prices. Uncertainty about such rules or regimes is an important aspect of the political risk which has to be assessed and priced by the actors in the financial markets. In order to diversify this risk, market participants have circumvented national barriers and contributed to globalization.

Policy-making, action parameters and market behaviour

The filtering of foreign shocks and the existence of domestic shocks are largely matters of the general *policy-making* in a country. This dimension can also be classified as a catalyst, depending on the extent to which the policy-making has been conducive to changes in the financial market. Our understanding of the process of transition can be enhanced by an analysis of the way the different dimensions of it have interacted with changes in monetary and fiscal policies. One aspect of this interaction is credibility, i.e. that a government undertakes measures that are consistent with a continuously ongoing process of transition, and which signal that the government will implement and sustain the policies necessary to complete this transition. Undertaking a fiscal reform, which noticeably reduces any fiscal deficit and which finances any remaining deficit in a non-inflationary manner prior to the opening of a capital account, is a measure that will significantly enhance the credibility of the process of transition.[18]

In order to increase credibility, any supportive policies implemented prior to the external deregulation should be geared towards ensuring the following:

- an exchange rate consistent with equilibrium in the balance of payments;
- sufficient liquidity in a country to eliminate or reduce its vulnerability to unforeseen external shocks;

- the presence of incentives for domestic households and producers to adjust supply and demand in response to price changes, and their ability to do so.

These policy issues constitute a prerequisite for a country being able to reap the intended benefits of external deregulation. When these supportive policies are implemented, the external deregulation can be seen as sustainable and credible.

In decisions about *timing* a government has to consider how quickly it can implement supportive economic reforms with a view to restructuring the corporate and banking sectors, and to creating the infrastructure needed to generate private direct investment and financial intermediation. Some countries may be tempted to remain in a transitional stage and to benefit from certain transitional measures, but there will then be a risk of these transitional arrangements becoming permanent. The aim of policy-making can be stated in terms of efficiency as well as increased stability in the financial market. Hence, a trade-off between these aims has to be recognized in the assessment of national policy-making in a globally competitive financial environment.

The *devices* available to policy-makers and markets consist of rules and institutional changes. The rules have already been addressed above in our discussion of the initial state. Thus we need only comment here on institutional changes. At a general level these involve changes in financial infrastructure, as mentioned above. At the level of detail they appear in the form of new market segments, new supervisory authorities, etc.

The regulatory and supervisory institutions differ both between countries and over time. In Japan, for instance, regulation is centralized in the Ministry of Finance, whereas in the United States there are several regulators – governmental as well as self-regulating exchanges. This multiplicity has led to jurisdictional disputes among the regulators, most notably the Securities and Exchange Commission (SEC) and the Commodity Futures Trading Commission (CFTC). In the United Kingdom the regulatory system is similar to the US system, albeit with greater reliance on self-regulation, fewer formal mechanisms of compliance, and less definite areas of jurisdiction and lines of responsibility. Furthermore, the British Security and Investments Board (SIB)[19] operates as a statutory public body, but it delegates many of its regulatory powers to self-regulatory organizations.[20] However, their powers are conferred by statute and their rules must be approved by SIB. Government and self-regulators are seen as complementary actors in the regulatory framework.

In the absence of global supervisory institutions, international cooperation has to be informal – a system that is tested in times of crisis. Judging from the way the Drexel Burnham bankruptcy was handled, the cooperation between the regulatory agencies of the United States and the United Kingdom seems to have worked effectively, while the way the BCCI crisis was dealt with provides an example of successful cooperative action in which even more countries were involved.

Changes in *market behaviour* may result from changes in policy. Market behaviour can be said to involve

- risk attitude;
- market discipline;
- vendor–customer relationships;
- degree of competition.

Market participants have the option of moving from one behaviour paradigm to another. For instance, the relaxation of liquidity constraints as part of the transformation process could result in savings behaviour of quite a new kind. The transformation may also affect the market's appetite for risk. For instance, in the small economies of northern Europe, the transformation pushed the financial institutions towards a state of risk neutrality, whereby they treated the 'old style' risk premium as a mark-up open to negotiation in doing business.[21]

Another important element is market discipline, and the way it has changed. Market discipline means that financial markets can send appropriate signals to prevent market actors from following an unsustainable path in their financial operations. Lane (1992) emphasizes four general conditions connected with borrowing which must be fulfilled if market discipline is to be effective:

- capital markets must be open;
- lenders must have good information about the borrower's existing liabilities;
- there should be no prospect of a bailout;
- the borrower must respond to the signals provided by the market.

Lane sees the bailout condition as the Achilles' heel of market discipline, because of the difficulty of making a 'no-bailout' commitment seem credible. Although one cannot rely solely on market forces to prevent unsustainable behaviour, they do have the potential to play an important disciplinary role in financial markets. If, then, institutions are designed to complement rather than to suppress these forces, the efficiency and stability of the whole financial system will be enhanced.

It is often claimed that a relatively free market for corporate control, as in the US for instance, has a disciplinary effect, making the system very efficient.[22] However, some researchers point to the Japanese system as a key explanation of the competitive advantage enjoyed by Japanese companies. Some members of this school also stress the role of governmental regulatory power in the old Japanese system in the creation of comparative advantage.[23]

The *vendor–customer relationship* is another behavioural mechanism that is important to the process of transformation. Since the 1970s this relationship has changed and the customers have become more demanding and more selective.[24] This demand, together with the pressure of competition, led sellers to favour deregulation. In a deregulated system, they expected to be able to provide a wider range of products and services to attract more customers, even while considering giving up some of their present turf.

Liberalization – the sequence of events

An important dimension of the transformation process is the *order* in which different liberalizing measures occur. The effects of a process in which internal liberalization is undertaken before external deregulation may differ from the effects when this order is reversed. Or again, the timing of a tax harmonization, for instance, is crucial to the outcome of external deregulation and the achievement of financial integration. Tax reforms which involve greater harmonization should be implemented before the external deregulation to avoid excessive social adjustment costs – otherwise, certain categories of financial market transactions will be outlocated to foreign markets with the resulting erosion of the corresponding segment in the domestic financial market.

When it comes to the sequence of events in a liberalization process, three main patterns can be distinguished: one in which the external deregulation precedes the internal, another in which internal and external liberalization occur simultaneously, and lastly one in which the internal deregulation precedes the external. The completion of the external deregulation is a key event, as it signals the credibility of sustained internal liberalization. However, in regulated economies a typical sequence is that the authorities start to recognize that capital controls are no longer as effective as they were (*de facto* external liberalization), and find themselves more or less forced to adapt the domestic financial market to the new situation by deregulating (*de jure* internal liberalization), after which they deregulate externally (*de jure* external liberalization). At the level of detail, the order in which individual measures of internal and external liberalization are undertaken also has to be considered. The UK is an example of a country that embarked on external deregulation before its internal deregulation had matured.

Liberalization can also occur at different times in different segments of a national market. Many countries liberalize segments of their financial system in a stepwise process, and the sequence of events – the order in which liberalization embraces non-bank institutions, private banks, state-owned banks and government securities – varies from one country to another; the appropriate sequence is determined among other things by the initial regulatory and institutional features.[25] For instance, in some Eastern European countries (e.g. Poland and the Czech Republic), interest rates in the deposit and loan markets for enterprises were liberalized first, and the household and enterprise markets were integrated in a second stage.

Another measure which can be used, and which is still related to the sequence of deregulating events, is the *lapse of time* between the informal (*de facto*) and the formal (*de jure*) liberalization of a national financial market. Structural adjustments, for example in the regulatory body of the financial markets and in the whole institutional setting, represent formal changes, while measures of financial integration reflect actual changes. As we have noted, competitive forces have frequently contributed to the completion of an informal liberalization, which is afterwards confirmed by a formal deregulation. Politicians basing their decisions on the formal structure may endanger the whole domestic economy, if that formal structure does not reflect actual integration. Pursuing an autonomous policy in an integrated market can thus generate a high social cost. The most powerful force in this game is capital mobility. It is reasonable to assume that the greater the lapse of time between the formal degree of financial integration and the degree of integration that actually applies, the more serious the policy-induced consequences for the domestic economy.[26]

Market implications of the process of transformation

The last step in the analysis of the transformation is to analyse the *implications* for the country's economy. It has to be asked how far the transformation has affected the ability of financial markets to enhance production of goods and services, and how it has contributed to the real side of the economy. Consequences implying improvements in allocational efficiency are classified as intermediate, while the ultimate effects can be real, financial or organizational.[27]

When it comes to measuring the ultimate consequences of external deregulation in a broader context, measures in terms of a reduction in direct and indirect costs for the country can be used. The direct costs for a particular country are related to lost international competitiveness and increased vulnerability to domestic financial shocks, while indirect costs are generated by the enforcement of capital controls. Further, external deregulation means new constraints on the formulation of macroeconomic and structural policies, as the government will find it increasingly difficult, for instance, to tax financial incomes, transactions and wealth. It seems likely that these constraints contribute to a reduction in both direct and indirect costs.

Financial theory claims that as a general rule the elimination of barriers to cross-border capital movements will increase efficiency and make way for an optimal allocation of financial resources. However, it is also emphasized that this generally occurs at the cost of undermining the efficiency of the national stabilization policy.

More specifically, the major benefits of external deregulation in a financial context are the following:

- efficiency gains in the international economy due to specialization in the production of financial services;
- increased efficiency in individual national financial sectors as a result of stiffer competition from abroad;
- improved global intermediation of resources between savers and investors by ensuring that savings are allocated to the most productive investment (assuming that financial markets appropriately price the risks and returns inherent in financial claims);
- an increase in internationally diversified asset portfolios among those resident in a country, making their incomes less vulnerable to domestic shocks;
- easier access to international financial markets;
- reduced transactions costs for financial operations.

In the case of real economic consequences, changes in the degree of efficiency can be seen as intermediate effects which obviously influence the national and global allocation of resources. Financial services can be viewed as inputs into a country's overall production process and to its efficiency, and thus also as helping to determine the rate of national economic growth. The way the transition affects the volume of business investment and, ultimately, economic growth, represents a permanent[28] real effect, while a short-lived rise in interest rates due to an increase in the risk premium is a transitory financial effect. Quite often a financial effect can be seen as intermediate to a real effect. The creation of new supervisory institutions in connection with the transition is an example of an organizational effect.

An inefficient financial service industry is a major obstacle to a country's overall economic performance. It is an impediment to the final consumer of financial services and it reduces the level of private and social welfare. Producers are also affected as their costs increase, which in turn undermines their competitiveness.

In a macroperspective, positive permanent effects arising from the process of national financial liberalization and external deregulation will materialize, in that the influence of liquidity constraints in the economy will be reduced. This then allows greater scope for private agents to achieve their portfolio investment and spending objectives, and for market expectations to be reflected in financial prices. Meanwhile, all this leads to more market integration internationally, i.e. globalization, and gives individual agents a better chance of diversifying their risks. Savings in one country can increase investment in another. The deregulation will also tend to push borrowing away from 'grey' markets and towards registered markets. Closer integration reduces the likelihood of one market being drained of liquidity, and limits the extent to which liquidity problems can spread. Reduced transaction costs will improve the operational efficiency of the financial markets.

On the negative side, it can also be argued that deregulation and innovation make the financial system more fragile. The vulnerability of the financial system to liquidity crises has also been heightened by the inter-action of deregulation and macroeconomic policy. Interest rates and the 'thrift institutions' in the US are just one example. Problems arising in one set of institutions are propagated, and their effects felt, far from the point of origin. The possibility of chain reactions spreading through increasingly integrated domestic and international markets is something that should be borne in mind.[29,30]

Various factors – interdependence among market participants,[31] required-time constraints for settlement[32] and unsettled large-amount transactions – are making exposure to systemic risk a problem of growing magnitude in the financial markets of the mid-1990s. Another transitory problem is that the machinery for managing crises may be inappropriate to the types of problem that can arise.[33] History has made us aware of many important factors that make financial markets vulnerable to crises. These have to be considered at every moment in the liberalization process. A feature of the transitory period can be that the situation regarding these factors may deteriorate, thus further fuelling the crisis. *Uncertainty* about the future among market actors is one such factor. A second is *confidence*, which is connected with the degree of uncertainty and is a central ingredient in virtually all financial transactions, while a third factor is *vulnerability* to runs on depository institutions, i.e. their susceptibility to loss of liquidity. However, as *market segmentation* is often stressed as a fourth important element of risk in systemic crises, the greater integration should reduce that risk.

To understand the transitional phase it is also necessary to consider one more element in the pattern of macro implications, namely the *distributional* effect of the transition. Some sectors or actors will gain from the transition, while others will face losses or at least a reduced surplus.[34] Winners and losers can be identified, for instance, by comparing financial and non-financial companies and, within the second category, small companies and large ones.[35]

Major distributional effects will arise if the deregulation process is not neutral, competitively speaking. Small and medium-sized companies, for instance, will face higher risk-adjusted capital costs, at least as a transitory phenomenon, than internationally recognized companies based in the same country. This is because it takes the smaller companies longer to learn how to cope with the international financial markets and to improve their international status by sending out various appropriate signals. The transi-tion should thus go more smoothly in a market-based system of the US type than in a bank-orientated financial system, since in the first case companies are already used to marketing themselves financially, and they know how to deal with sending out or acquiring the necessary information.

Small and medium-sized companies in a regulated society are expected to be the winners in the process of globalization, and they are only worse off if the deregulation process temporarily contributes, in one way or another, to an increase in the national cost of capital due to higher transaction costs, exchange risk premiums and political risk premiums or to various inefficiencies in the market.[36] In many small economies this has been the case because of the link between the deregulation process and conditions in the banking industry. A drop in the creditworthiness of the banking industry has meant higher funding costs which, together with attempts to recoup credit losses, has also meant a higher cost of capital for companies which are restricted to borrowing from these particular banks.

In the microperspective, globalization means that companies are no longer 'locked in'. Before integration, someone wanting a deposit denominated in yen had no alternative but to accept the regulatory body of the Japanese authorities and the procedures and costs of the Japanese financial institutions. In the integrated world, however, that person can acquire whatever combination of market/jurisdiction, currency, interest structure and institutions that seems interesting. For instance, a depositor can keep a yen deposit in a Swedish bank in London as his or her preferred combination of political, currency, interest rate and credit risks.

Further, in a globally integrated financial market the modern international corporation has a broad range of options when it comes to meeting its financial needs. It can find optimal solutions to its three major financial tasks – namely, liquidity management, risk management and fund raising. A more mature financial market also provides companies with opportunities for tax arbitrage. When different financial systems come to resemble each other more closely, the implications for competitiveness between companies in different countries are likely to be less marked.

Finally, in an analysis of the implications of the process of transition, *structural* and *secular* effects are of particular interest. They have to be separated from *purely cyclical* effects, which are reversible. At the same time, however, information about the cyclical, the secular and the structural effects together can be important to an understanding of the overall process. For instance, cyclical effects may have aggravated the economic situation in a country and impelled a change in the regulatory set-up, which then causes structural effects. Although the ultimate state of integration is more or less positive in its effects on all participants, the transition itself may have drawbacks for certain groups in a particular country. Most of these disadvantages are transitory, but some can turn out to be permanent.

Globalization and efficiencies

To be able to evaluate and calibrate the functioning of a national financial system, we need a set of criteria for describing optimum performance-orientated financial systems which are at one and the same time efficient, creative in generating innovative financial products and processes, globally competitive and stable. In an assessment of the measures undertaken at different stages in the transition, such a set of criteria can help us to identify the contribution that the various measures have made to the long-run efficiency of the national financial system.

In measuring efficiency we can separate *static* from *dynamic* efficiency. According to Walter (1992), static efficiency can be modelled as the all-in weighted average spread (differential) between the rates of return for the ultimate savers on the one hand, and the cost of funds for users on the other. This gap, or spread, depicts the overall cost of financial intermediation. In particular it describes the direct costs of producing financial services.[37] The spread also reflects losses incurred in the financial process, monopoly profits and liquidity premiums. A statically inefficient system is characterized by large spreads due to high overhead costs, high losses, barriers to entry, etc.[38] Furthermore, a financial system characterized by dynamic efficiency exhibits high levels of financial innovation over time.[39] Successful product and process innovations help to broaden the range of financial services available to ultimate borrowers and/or ultimate savers. A financial system that is both statically and dynamically efficient is characterized by a minimum intermediation spread and a continuous stream of innovations to meet the ever-changing needs of the financial marketplace. Walter argues that the most advanced financial systems approach a theoretically 'complete' optimum with sufficient financial instruments and markets to span – individually or in combination – the entire state-space of risk and return outcomes.[40]

LIBERALIZATION AND THE LINK BETWEEN SAVINGS AND ECONOMIC GROWTH

With the 1990s an important question of public policy came to the fore: how much can an increase in the domestic savings rate be expected to do to improve long-term domestic economic growth? The question can be split into two parts. First, how important are domestic savings to national investment? Second, to what extent does increased investment contribute to improved domestic economic growth? Although it is easy to have an intuitive belief in a strong relationship between savings and economic growth, such a relationship is not indisputable in terms of causality, strength or models.

In connection with the first subquestion, we noted in the previous chapter that greater financial integration diminishes the role of domestic saving. Savings from one country can be used for real investment in others. However, as we also saw before, even in an integrated society some market participants come up against barriers that need to be eliminated or circumvented. Moreover, in empirical studies of the relationship between savings and growth, the question of 'what causes what' always comes up. Correlation studies provide no answer to the question; they just give an indication of the strength of the relationship. In Chapter 4 we will return to a discussion of the importance of savings to investment. For the time being we can simply consider the impact of financial liberalization on economic growth, and assume that it can be direct or indirect. By focusing on the second case at this early stage in the book, implying that the effect is expressed via investment, I will provide better grounds for narrowing down the savings-to-economic-growth chain to the saving–investment relationship in the later chapters.

The link between investment and growth

On the relationship between investment and economic growth, two main views can be identified. One is based on the traditional neoclassical growth model, and the other on more recent models of endogenous growth.

The *neoclassical growth model* states that an increase in the investment rate, while raising the medium-term growth rate (and the succeeding level of output) has no long-term effect on the growth rate in an economy.[41] To the extent that contribution of capital to growth is reasonably well approximated by its income share, this improvement in economic performance would be expected to be small relative to the underlying growth rate of the economy. In the basic neoclassical model, improvements in technology are assumed to be disembodied, i.e. they do not require an increase in factor inputs to be implemented.[42]

In recent years new models have emphasized that the income share of capital may significantly underestimate the contribution of capital to growth. Moreover, under certain conditions, shifts in the investment rate can permanently change the growth rate. The most important arguments here include: increasing returns to scale, learning-by-doing, human capital accumulation and spill-over effects.[43] Romer (1986, 1987a, 1987b and 1990) has contributed to this family of *endogenous growth models*.[44] He stresses the possibility that the returns from (physical) capital accumulation can be larger than in the neoclassical growth model, and that they do not decrease in response to faster rates of capital accumulation. He claims further that the economy as a whole can avoid diminishing returns if there are positive externalities associated with corporate investment decisions. For instance, if the acquisition of knowledge by one company expands the knowledge frontier of others, or if there are learning-by-doing effects associated with the investment, the social rate of return on the investment will exceed the (perceived) private rate of return and need not necessarily imply a decline as capital output increases.

In the endogenous growth model associated with Romer, in contrast to the traditional neoclassical model, the exponent on capital in the (Cobb–Douglas) production function for the whole economy is equal to α (income share of capital as in the neoclassical model) plus β, an externality.[45] Hence, in this model the implications for the relationship between investment and growth depend on the size of the exponent on the aggregated capital stock ($\alpha + \beta$). Given a positive externality, three cases exist: the exponent is below unity, it exceeds unity and, finally, it is equal to unity.

When the exponent is below unity, there are diminishing returns on capital (each successive increase in capital has a smaller and smaller effect on output) and the growth rate of the economy cannot be permanently raised by an increase in the investment rate, even though the social returns on investment in this case will exceed the (perceived) private rate. If, on the other hand, the exponent is above unity, there are non-diminishing returns on capital, and an increase in the investment rate will permanently raise the growth rate. In the final case the exponent describes a situation in which private companies perceive diminishing returns on their investments, while the social returns on investment are constant.

A difficulty associated with the endogenous growth model is its implication that the capital–output ratio will be constantly changing, if labour input is not fixed. Consequently, under general conditions, a steady state will not be approached.

The explanation as to why changes in the investment rate do not alter long-run growth in the neoclassical model lies in the existence of diminishing returns on capital. Consequently, and referring to the production function on which the model is based, only continuing increases in labour input and (exogenous) improvements in technology can sustain a positive growth rate. Although the neoclassical model implies that (exogenous) changes in the investment rate have no implications for long-term growth, such changes will influence the growth rate in the transition from one steady state to another. Moreover the transition can take a long time to be completed.[46] Also, the neoclassical model implies that a change in investment will influence the level of output (and other variables as well) across steady-state growth paths.[47] Thus, efforts to increase investment rates will lead to an improvement in economic performance. The effort will pay off in terms of a faster growth rate in the transition to a new long-run equilibrium and a permanently higher level of output and labour productivity. However, the efforts will probably not lead to big and sustained changes in the growth rate of the economy. Rather, a decline in the rate of return on capital will follow.

The relationship between investment and growth – some empirical findings

In the case of the United States Adams and Chadha (1992) find support for the neoclassical model, while in the case of many other countries De Long and Summers (1991) report a strong causal relationship supporting endogenous growth models of the type derived from Romer (1990a, 1990b). De Long and Summers also noted the existence of large gaps between private profitability and the social utility of investment. Their study is concerned with machinery investments, and the authors claim that this kind of investment can be seen as the single most indispensable prerequisite of industrialization. They argue that whatever sets of growth-causing factors are considered, the rate of machinery investment remains the most important factor determining rates of economic growth. In their view there is macroeconomic support for the belief that investment in machinery yields large social benefits, both directly through the more advanced technologies embodied in machinery, and indirectly by increasing the skills of workers and the experience of companies in organizing modern technologies. In a cross-countries comparison they find these social benefits to be equal to approximately three times the extra profits accruing to the investing companies. De Long and Summers proclaim their results as very robust.[48]

The link between savings and investment must be emphasized

Most empirical studies focus on the possibility that the neoclassical model may understate the growth contribution of capital. Summers (1990), however, suggests that we should also ask ourselves whether the neoclassical model does not in fact overstate this contribution. One important reason for this which he cites is that part of what is measured as profit in the national accounts may include returns on monopoly power, on research and development expenditures or extraordinary managerial talent. These returns should not be included in measuring the (social) rate of return on physical capital.[49] Another important reason, according to Summers, is that investments are risky and profits include risk premiums. He advocates exclusion of these risk premiums, and instead stresses the need to adopt a certainty-equivalent rate of return. Adams and Chadha (1992) claim that capital-generated income probably still provides a measure of the average but risky rate of return on investment, but point out that the value society places on this income, in risk-adjusted terms, may be much lower than the rate of return on capital. The way the financial transformation proceeds, influences the risk premiums. We will explore this issue in Chapter 6 and succeeding chapters.

Regardless of which model we subscribe to, it seems that investment promotes growth.[50] Hence, for our present purpose we need not involve ourselves any further in a discussion of the relationship between investment and growth; it is enough to bear in mind the dispute about the size and path of growth. The only relevant question remaining to be answered concerning the causal chain of growth-promoting activities, is why do some economies, but not all, manage to channel savings efficiently for investment by leading-edge companies? What role do politicians and markets play in creating distortions? What, for instance, distinguishes companies which are able to borrow from those which are not?

What biases in real economic activity are then triggered by the credit restrictions that markets impose (for whatever reasons)?[51] Theories of credit restrictions due to asymmetric information were well established in the theoretical literature by the mid-1970s. Historical studies have demonstrated the importance of taking behavioural aspects into consideration, since neither a high national savings rate, nor a balanced government budget, nor a commitment to free trade can guarantee a high rate of machinery investment. Lewis (1978) provides many interesting examples of the growth of high technology industries around the turn of the century, and of the deteriorating position of England in these industries. British companies were reluctant to issue bonds or raise new equity on the stock market, and their expansion slowed down. Investors preferred lending to foreign and colonial governments. England failed to turn its high savings rate and leading industrial position into a strong high-technology-based production capacity.[52] De Long (1990) argues that investment banks (in the US and Japan, and corresponding departments in other types of financial systems) have played, and will continue to play, an important role in this process. Moreover, close links between financial institutions and non-financial companies – like those found in contemporary Japan and Germany, and in the United States at the turn of the century – are an integrated part of well-functioning financial systems capable of channelling savings into companies investing in growing high-technology industries.

The role of financial liberalization in promoting growth

Economic growth can be affected in many ways by financial liberalization and external deregulation. And the impact may not necessarily take the route via investment. As we have noted, one highly influential factor consists of the *easing of liquidity constraints* due to the relaxing of rate and quantity regulations and the rising tide of financial innovations. A reduction in liquidity constraints affects private consumption and expenditure behaviour, as well as savings behaviour. Financial liberalization makes permanent income more important as an influence on private consumption, compared with current or transitory income. Spending behaviour is likely to be based far more on relative financial prices and expectations about longer-run permanent income and wealth, because capital and credit markets can now be used much more flexibly than in the past. As a result, current income and the availability of money (or current liquid wealth) will represent a less binding constraint on expenditure and portfolio behaviour. Financial liberalization will therefore tend to bring about a fall in private savings. None the less, as private agents are better placed to act on their expectations, policy is forced to operate largely through the incentives engendered by changes in relative financial prices. These prices are also affected by market perceptions about the implications of current policies for future demand and inflation, with expectations and financial portfolios being adjusted rapidly in response to new information.

Another major source of influence, intuitively positive to economic growth, consists of the *improvements in internal and external efficiency* that often follow financial liberalization and innovation. Competition imposes a downward pressure on prices, which forces financial intermediaries to operate more efficiently. Hence, the cost of their services falls as well. A reduction in non-price credit rationing will lead to improved internal efficiency in the allocation of resources.

In the perspective of the global financial market, liberalization and deregulation make saving a matter of purely relative financial prices. Consequently, countries in which distortions still obtain, will end up in a much worse position. They will either get no capital or, if they do, it will be at a relatively much higher price due to the difference in risk premiums. Distortions in a national tax system, for instance, will have implications for savings behaviour and, ultimately, for investment and growth in that particular country. In the internal perspective, as we have seen, the tax system can create a tax wedge with the result – of which the Nordic countries are an example – that real productive investments are crowded-out by investment in housing.[53] In an external perspective, frequent changes in tax rates, in rules of taxation, in withholding tax rates, etc. will generate demands for political risk premiums and increase the cost of capital, resulting in a decline in international competitiveness for real investment on the part of the residents of the countries concerned.[54]

What is to be achieved by monetary autonomy?

A country's main justification for protecting itself and conducting what it perceives as an autonomous national policy comes from the threat of *speculative international crises*, and the *high cost to society of financial instability*. The traditional assumption is that greater financial integration promotes greater efficiency in the international allocation of resources, but at the cost of the efficiency of the national stabilization policy. If we step outside this general framework, several other questions arise regarding the efficiency of the stabilization policy. To what extent can the government keep the domestic real return on a security beneath that on the equivalent paper in another currency? How much can it influence the cost of capital within the country and the level of real domestic investment? What can the government do to influence the relative cost of capital, and thus also the allocation of capital to various classes of domestic investment? The answer is that under increasing integration the opportunities in these respects remain unchanged, or are reduced. A more exact answer would call for a specification of the kind of integration we are talking about. Furthermore, the prevailing conditions as regards exchange rate systems, capital mobility, the efficiency of information and so on need to be clarified.

How can governments exercise autonomy in monetary policy and determine the gap between the expected domestic and foreign real interest rates, with a view to influencing investment and unemployment? By definition, perfect total financial integration does not allow governments any such opportunity. If integration is less than perfect, governments do have a chance of influencing the size of expected deviations from purchasing power parity and the size of the risk premiums. A gap is thus created between expected domestic and foreign real interest rates, because the market has been made to feel uncertain about exchange rates or about imminent political intervention. However, it is not at all certain that investment or employment goals can be achieved by exercising this sort of control.

Even if the government is doubtful about the value of 'managing' development by increasing the uncertainty in the market, there is still the possibility of exercising control by influencing the market's exchange expectations and/or by imposing regulations. However, market participants will probably not allow themselves to be systematically manipulated in the first of these ways. Instead, they will recognize the manoeuvre for what it is – an attempt to control things. In so far as the market fails to see through the mechanism, governments can exercise control without incurring too high a 'cost'. But if the market does see through it, high costs will fall on society as a whole. The greater uncertainty in the market can lead to undesirable outcomes for the country, perhaps in the shape of postponed investments.

There remains the alternative of using regulations to insert a wedge between domestic and foreign nominal interest levels. But even if a government succeeds in achieving this, the question remains as to what they have achieved in real terms. Attempts at disintegration, perhaps by imposing exchange controls, have a rarely mentioned price: by blocking off the effects of international shocks and disturbances, governments increase the vulnerability of the home economy to domestic non-policy-related disturbances. A globally growing network of flows between countries – in labour, capital, goods, services and information – reinforces the contention that individual countries are now less able to maintain an independent stabilization policy by imposing exchange controls and other regulations.

National monetary autonomy in the international investor's perspective

Under perfect (total) financial integration[55] the expected real interest rate on comparable investments in different countries and different currencies will be identical. Thus, if a (small) country's financial market is becoming more highly integrated, corporate capital costs in the country concerned – and consequently return requirements in real terms – will increasingly adjust to movements in the global interest level. Greater total financial integration also reduces the corporate incentive to establish operations in a large number of different countries.

On a perfectly direct integrated capital market the investor cannot increase his expected risk-adjusted nominal return by reinvesting his capital in other countries. A higher expected return converted into the domestic currency is accompanied by a higher risk in his portfolio. The ex ante differentials in nominal interest rates can be expected to compensate for expected exchange rate movements, risk premiums, and transaction and information costs. Thus, the profit from diversification consists simply of a reduction – globally speaking – in the possible non-systematic risk, i.e. the risk for which the investor obtains no compensation. But if investors are aware of the segmentation of the capital markets, they will have an incentive to seek *excess return*, i.e. a return over and above compensation for the above-mentioned risks and costs, by choosing the 'right' national market or combination of markets.

Opportunities for risk-free profits, as a result of covered interest arbitrage, are an indication that financial markets are not characterized by perfect (direct) financial integration. The profits are captured at the corporate level by cross-border transfers of forward-covered capital. Corporate profit opportunities lie in the existence of market inefficiency and/or politically generated inefficiency.

If there is a higher level of direct financial integration, there will also be better opportunities for the market actors to allocate and diversify risks, and this trade-off between risk and expected return can in turn improve the chances of greater welfare. Thus the (possible) loss in welfare due to reduced autonomy in the national stabilization policy has its counterpole in a more efficient allocation of capital in terms of risk and return.

Referring again to Figure 1.1, each leg of the triangle involves its own distortions. First, most of the countries opting for corner (1) are hoping for greater freedom in managing their domestic stabilization policy. Changes in financial market regulations (including tax rules) have been frequent in these countries. The price for this can be found in a *political risk premium*. Since it takes time for a market to regain credibility in terms of having stable rules, we can expect the political risk premium to remain at a high level for quite a while after a deregulation. Second, as a result of opting for corner (1) and isolating their market from international competition, a knowledge gap will appear in these countries at the time of the external deregulation. The price for this can be quite substantial, and domestic actors have to pay dear for their experience for some time after the external deregulation has been completed.

Third, the pursuit of a fixed exchange rate policy within the framework of corner (1) in the triangle, often leads to deviations in real exchange rates. The risk attached to these deviations can be substantial, and can result in claims for high-risk premiums which increase the level of domestic interest rates. These premiums will continue to be charged, so long as national politicians possess little credibility. What has to be emphasized is the trade-off between the exchange rate risk target and the political risk premiums. In pursuing a fixed exchange rate policy, a country will have to make extreme efforts to coordinate its policy with international standards in order to escape volatility in real exchange rates. Such policies, however, may require a lot of changes in market rules, e.g. tax changes, and will increase political risk premiums. All these premiums, together with higher funding costs for banks involved in financial crises, will primarily hit those who are locked into their home country on account of residual non-regulatory barriers, i.e. mainly small and medium-sized companies.

THE INTERNATIONAL DEREGULATION OF FINANCIAL MARKETS – A HISTORICAL REVIEW

The Second World War was followed by a period when policy-makers believed that the best way to heal the economic wounds of the war was to impose various forms of internal and external regulation on the financial markets. In this way the authorities did their best to create cheap domestic financing in order to boost domestic economic recovery.[56] By imposing external regulations they paved the way for the use of internal controls such as interest rate ceilings and reserve requirements.

A shift of opinion in favour of greater freedom for cross-border capital transactions appeared in the 1950s, manifesting itself for example in OECD's adoption of a Code of Liberalization of Capital Movements in 1961. None the less, international deregulation remained fairly modest, and even suffered a setback in the 1960s due to balance-of-payment problems. Liberalization started to accelerate in the 1970s, gained momentum in the 1980s, and by the mid-1990s, was nearing completion. In a global perspective, however, there is an alarming inconsistency in the policy path, as most countries implement further liberalization on the tariff side, while at the same time increasing the use of non-tariff barriers and measures that are incompatible with 'fair' competition. Regulators are also beginning to realize that the economic problems which appeared in the late 1980s were almost as much of a regulatory debacle as a financial one. This may mean that the 1990s will come to be described as a decade of regulatory rigour. Regulatory rules applying to financial institutions, for instance, have been hotly debated issues since the beginning of the 1990s. There is also growing concern about the solvency of insurance companies. Limits have been suggested to the kinds of investment that insurers should be allowed to make. Thus, in a long-term perspective, periods of regulation and deregulation have been recurrent phenomena.

As a general rule capital controls have been directed predominantly at capital outflows, usually with a view to preserving scarce domestic savings for domestic use and reducing the risk of capital flight during periods of exchange-rate pressure or balance-of-payments weakness. Restrictions on the inflow of capital from abroad have been imposed mainly for reasons of monetary control, or for non-economic reasons, as in the case of foreign acquisitions of domestic businesses or investments in real estate. Some OECD countries have operated comprehensive exchange control regimes involving restrictions on capital outflows and inflows, thereby attempting to isolate their domestic financial markets from external influences. According to OECD (1990) the most restrictive measures throughout the period have concerned the admission of foreign securities into domestic capital markets. Whereas some form of control has been considered necessary by most countries because of the size of potential foreign placements relative to the absorption capacity of the domestic market, restrictions on domestic companies and institutions in issuing securities abroad have been much less pronounced. Restrictions are also widely imposed on credits and loans unrelated to the international trade of the country concerned. Such capital movements have usually been regarded as less important to the 'real' side of the economy, as potentially destabilizing and as an easy conduit for circumventing other controls.

Restrictions on direct investments have also been common, especially with regard to inward flows. However, the tendency has been to widen the scope progressively for direct investments from abroad, among other things to allow entry for foreign technology. Operations in real estate represent another traditionally restricted area, with more than half the OECD countries still retaining reservations to the OECD capital movement code in the early 1990s. Capital movements relating to individuals (personal capital movements, life assurance and securities and guarantees, the physical movement of capital assets and the disposal of non-resident-owned blocked funds) have been among the most restricted areas, and the last to be liberalized. Commercial credits and loans have enjoyed a fairly high degree of freedom throughout the period, since most authorities believe restrictions in this area would be unduly harmful to normal business relations.

Will total deregulation be the end-station?

The role of regulations can always be disputed and this is reflected in the many schools of thought on the subject. History shows that periods of war and general distress are followed by periods of extensive regulations. The 'creative destruction' already mentioned forces authorities to acknowledge the inefficiency of regulations by formal abolition, or by imposing new regulations. Hence, the pendulum swings around a set of regulations that can be seen as the minimum regulation set required to guarantee the infrastructure of the financial market. This is a set of regulations that promotes the soundness of a financial market and guarantees competition. By aiming for this set of regulations, national authorities should improve the general confidence in the domestic market.

However, once national financial markets are approaching perfect global integration, there is a risk of policy-makers starting to compete in attracting investments in the financial industry, by adopting a 'looser' interpretation of the content of this minimum set of regulations in the national regulatory body.[57] Thus, they are potentially triggering a wave of re-regulation.

Financial liberalization and tax incentives interact

Financial liberalization and competition interact in many ways with tax incentives, and this has implications for the real side of an economy. Financial liberalization has eliminated or reduced credit rationing and has meant increased liquidity for the private sector, for instance by making it easier for households to use their homes and equity as collateral for other loans. Stiffer competition in the banking industry has also reduced margins on consumer or housing loans.

The major tax wedge consists of the preferential tax treatment of investment in owner-occupied housing. Moreover, in most countries the deductibility of mortgage interest is the single most costly expense-related tax relief. Tax wedges are large in countries which allow generous or complete deductibility of interest payments, and they grow even bigger with rising inflation. The United States, the United Kingdom, Australia, Finland, Norway and Sweden are all countries where tax relief has significantly distorted the housing market.[58] In the early 1990s Canada, Turkey and New Zealand were the only OECD countries which did not allow tax deductions or credits for mortgage interest payments.

It was often claimed in the early 1990s that financial liberalization was one of the main factors behind the contemporary financial crisis. One of the key arguments was that liberalization allowed households to take greater advantage of tax incentives relating to the purchase of housing or consumer goods, by borrowing at an earlier stage in their lives or by making bigger purchases.[59] Home loans represent the greatest liability of most households, but down payments were reduced as a result of the liberalization and competition. In the United Kingdom, for instance, over half of all first-time house buyers in 1987 were given mortgages of 95 per cent or more of the price.[60] At the end of the 1980s similar developments accompanied financial liberalization in the Nordic countries. Booming house prices in the second half of the 1980s increased personal net wealth. In combination with generous arrangements for deducting interest costs, this led to a rapid build-up of gross personal debt, particularly in the United States, France and the United Kingdom but also in Finland, Norway and Sweden. In general the credit could be used for other purposes, as mortgages credits were not tied to actual construction activities. Hence, the liberalization seems to have discouraged savings. Existing tax distortions meant that additional expenditures were directed towards areas where the tax relief was greatest.

As a general rule interaction between financial liberalization and existing tax wedges[61] has contributed to an 'overinvestment' in housing at the expense of productive business investment. Thus, in this case, financial liberalization appears to have aggravated the effects of any remaining distortions, and to have led to imbalances elsewhere in the economic system.[62]

External deregulation in a historical perspective

Later in this book we will be measuring financial integration on a basis of financial market prices. However, a brief historical overview of the deregulation process in major developed countries can help us to assess the persistence to date of the current liberalization. An overview can be obtained by looking at the development of reservations to the OECD Capital Movement Code as reported in OECD (1990). Members of the OECD have sought to liberalize capital movements by applying the principles of the Code, which has been changed only slightly since 1964. Member countries which imposed controls on capital movement operations have maintained reservations or derogations from items of the Code where restrictions have been in force.[63]

Changes in the number of liberalized items, full reservations, limited reservations, general derogations and specific derogations under the Code are shown in Figure 2.1.[64] This represents a useful and unique indicator of the progress of the liberalization of capital movement operations. The trend away from reliance on exchange controls is reflected in the number of reservations retained under the Code. During the period 1964–90 nearly all OECD member countries retained some exchange controls for a brief period at least. While some countries applied fairly heavy capital movement restrictions throughout the period, other countries – the traditionally more liberal – tended to restrict capital movements mainly during periods of balance-of-payments difficulties, exchange rate crises or undesired monetary developments.

In the 1960s some progress was achieved in relaxing capital controls, primarily as regards long-term capital movements. Several countries – notably the United States,[65] Germany, Switzerland and Canada – were already applying fairly liberal policies with respect to capital movements, but most other countries still maintained a substantial number of direct control measures, as well as other more market-orientated mechanisms such as two-tier exchange rate systems, which interfered with capital movement operations.

Periods of re-regulation occurred in 1964–90

Liberalization did not proceed smoothly throughout the period 1964–90. Rather, reservations on the capital outflow side tended to multiply up to the mid-1970s. This may have been partly due to the relatively restrictive stance

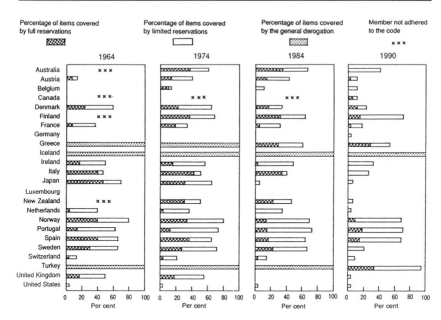

Figure 2.1 Evolving degree of liberalization of capital movements, 1964–90

Source: OECD (1990).

Note: The degree of liberalization – at any point in time – is measured by the number of 'reservations' or 'derogations' maintained under the terms of the OECD Code of Liberalization or Capital Movements. The presence of a reservation or derogation indicates that the members concerned can restrict the operations covered by specific 'item(s)' of the Code. Certain countries have in the past maintained a 'general derogation' allowing them to restrict the operations covered by all the items of the Code; only Iceland still does so. The diagram illustrates the degree of liberalization of capital movements by reference to the 'percentage of items covered' by limited reservations, full reservations or general derogations. Items covered by 'full reservations' may be totally restricted, although they are often less than totally restricted in practice. Where 'limited reservations' apply, the items concerned can be restricted only to the extent specified in the 'remarks' attached to the reservation concerned. The interpretation of the diagram has to be cautious, as until the 1989 amendment the Code did not cover all capital movement operations. Most short-term operations, except for commercial credits and loans, were excluded. Furthermore, certain measures – like taxes on transactions and payments, two-tier exchange rate systems and currency deposit requirements – which may impede capital movements were not considered to be restrictions in the meaning of the Code.

of countries that became members of the OECD in the late 1960s and early 1970s, but controls also became more common in several other countries during the 1960s and early 1970s.

Indirect methods of restraining capital movements, which do not immediately appear to conflict with the obligations under the Code, were also common, and even increased in importance during the period. Control devices were used extensively to minimize the balance-of-payments consequences of capital flows. Restrictions on the overall foreign position of financial institutions formed one such measure, which was adopted along with reserve requirements, restrictions on interest payments and other measures designed to discourage or penalize capital flows. These techniques were even adopted by traditionally liberal OECD members. For example they were used by the United States in 1963–64 to moderate capital outflows, when they also included a 'voluntary restraint' on direct investment abroad, an interest equalization tax, and in 1968–70 a reserve requirement on Eurodollar borrowing by banks. They were also used by Germany during 1971–74 in the shape of reserve requirements on bank and non-bank external liabilities and disincentives for German businesses to borrow abroad.

By the mid-1970s the liberalization of exchange controls was clearly moving forward. The process was dominated by the almost complete dismantling of capital movement restrictions in the United Kingdom and later in Japan. A number of other countries gradually began to reduce the scope of their exchange controls. In some countries, however, re-regulation was on the agenda. In 1978, for example, Switzerland imposed a negative interest charge on the deposits of non-residents, who were also prohibited from purchasing Swiss stocks and bonds.[66]

The liberalization process gained momentum in the 1980s, during which time many developed countries abolished most or all of their capital controls. Australia and New Zealand dismantled most controls early in the period (in 1983 and 1984 respectively), the Netherlands removed its last few restrictions in 1986, Denmark completed its external deregulation in 1988, France and Sweden achieved virtually full liberalization in 1989, and Italy and Ireland removed a substantial number of restrictions between 1988 and 1 July 1990, the deadline for achieving free capital movements for most EU countries.[67] During the 1980s only Denmark, France, Norway and Finland felt it necessary to suspend temporarily the freedom of operations not covered by reservations.

In the developed world, the liberalization process moved towards completion in the early 1990s. More and more countries have opened up their economies to FDI flows, as evidenced by the fact that of eighty-two changes made in foreign direct investment policies in thirty-five countries during 1991, eighty were in the direction of increased liberalization.[68] However, in 1992 capital restrictions in some form were still being applied in almost half the countries in the developed world.[69] Moreover, as a preview of what might come, Spain imposed limited foreign exchange controls in September 1992.[70]

Countries in the developed world have not been the only ones to liberalize during the past two decades: in a relative sense they have liberalized the least. Newly industrializing countries exhibit the greatest relative liberalization, followed by the developing countries.[71] In spite of the high speed of liberalization in developing countries completion still seems far off, since at the outset these countries were making extensive use of controls. In 1992, 114 of 136 developing countries still maintained some capital restrictions.[72]

Liberalization has varied across operations

On the capital import side, the most substantial progress has occurred on items which used to be restricted mainly for economic reasons, such as securities transactions, financial credits and loans, and the admission of domestic securities on foreign capital markets, although liberalization has been less pronounced in this last instance. In areas where special factors have motivated restrictions, (e.g. on inward direct investment and the building and purchase of domestic real estate by non-residents), liberalization has been less spectacular. Nevertheless, it has been of considerable importance, especially with regard to the establishment of new businesses by non-residents and investment in the financial sector. It is also interesting to observe that the process of liberalizing the trade in securities began much earlier than the liberalizations of borrowing abroad by residents or admission of the domestic securities to foreign financial markets.

In the case of capital exports liberalization seems to have been distributed slightly more evenly across items, including virtually complete removal of the last few restrictions on the granting of commercial credits to non-residents and substantial progress on operations in real estate. This is probably due to the dominance of economic considerations in the formulation of policies on outward capital movements. On the outflow side, progress was quite limited until the mid-1970s, when a more rapid liberalization as regards commercial credits and securities transactions began. Later in the 1970s, the dismantling of the 'hard core' of restrictions on capital outflows started to gain momentum, directed first towards the liberalization of financial credits and loans, and then towards the admission of foreign securities in domestic financial markets. In the 1980s, liberalization measures tended to be much more radical, but where only partial liberalization was undertaken it was outward direct investment that was given priority, along with other international operations on the part of companies and financial institutions. Investment abroad by individuals was generally given low priority.

Different national approaches to external deregulation

As for national approaches to deregulation, two diametrically opposite types can be identified: a gradual approach, or total abolition at one stroke. Deregulations since the 1960s suggest that most countries prefer the first approach rather than trying to dismantle foreign exchange controls all at one go, while the timing and scope of the liberalization measures have generally been determined by economic fundamentals and diverse market pressures. In the countries concerned it was often regarded as politically necessary to proceed step by step, analysing the effects of each phase before taking the process further. However, liberalization is contagious, and as it proceeds the pressures favouring progress gain momentum. Governments may find it successively more difficult to justify and administer the remaining controls, and are forced to speed up the process. The experience of the late 1980s and the early 1990s also shows that several OECD countries did abolish all exchange controls at one go. The need to win political support for liberalization led some governments to act decisively before special interests could organize resistance to measures that were being taken for the general good.

The Japanese authorities adopted a gradual approach

Japan provides an interesting example of the gradual approach. The country had an extensive array of restrictions in 1964 when it joined OECD, and it embarked on a liberalization programme the same year. Nearly all restrictions on capital movements were removed in a gradual process that continued until 1980.[73] In the initial phase of the programme the main focus was on gradually opening up more sectors to foreign direct investment, and facilitating inward and outward securities transactions. Removing the last few restrictions on personal capital movements, which were completely free by the end of 1970, was the final step in that process. A number of other liberalizing measures eventually resulted in the removal of all remaining restrictions on securities transactions and commercial credits and loans during 1975–76.

The Foreign Exchange and Foreign Trade Control Law of December 1980 marked the completion of the process of liberalizing Japanese exchange controls. Not only were restrictions on financial credits and loans and the issue of domestic securities abroad and foreign securities in Japan both liberalized, but the new law committed the Japanese authorities for the first time to the principle of freedom for capital movements by excluding the possibility of reintroducing restrictions except in certain specified circumstances. The process of liberalization appears rather gradual and smooth, but in fact it was closely linked to developments in Japan's economic circumstances. France, and later Denmark, provide two further examples of the gradual approach.

In some countries the authorities have preferred deregulation overnight

The United Kingdom (October 1979), Australia (December 1983), and New Zealand (December 1984) exemplify the 'single-stroke' approach. Shortly after new governments had been elected all three countries liberalized capital movements more or less 'overnight', making a fundamental break with past restrictiveness and the use of exchange control measures as an active tool of policy. Exchange controls had long been used to protect the balance-of-payments position and to support the management of the exchange rate, while providing autonomy for domestic monetary policy. Although all these countries chose the single-stroke approach, the decision to liberalize was taken under somewhat different economic circumstances in each one. As the decision to remove barriers to capital movements was less closely related to the immediate economic situation, it was more a question of a philosophical nature, reflecting a change in attitude and a shift in emphasis away from government intervention and towards almost complete reliance on market forces. To a large extent the dismantling of exchange controls was part of a wide-ranging structural reform programme and a fundamental change in the *modus operandi* of economic policy.

CONCLUDING REMARKS ON THE GENERAL PROCESS OF FINANCIAL MARKET TRANSFORMATION

The aim of this chapter has been to highlight some general issues connected with an analysis of financial market transformation. National bond markets have been viewed in the framework of the global financial system as a whole. This comprehensive presentation has shown us that by focusing entirely on that one sector of the financial market we may be led to draw the wrong conclusions about the importance of globalization to economic growth: inefficiencies in other sectors may be exerting a counterbalancing influence. For instance, it is easy to imagine that large corporations based in countries where the national banking sector came under pressure during the recent financial crises, with a consequent loss of creditworthiness, acquired an incentive to use their own superior creditworthiness to raise funds in the bond markets. However, Table 1.1 showed no major structural changes during the transition phase as regards the market shares of different sectors of the Nordic credit markets. Nevertheless, here and there throughout the book we will have to discuss developments in competing sectors in the financial market as a whole.

I have also addressed conceptual issues regarding the analysis of the process of financial market transformation. If we were only interested in the bottom line – the increase in economic growth resulting from the globalization – we could have followed a design similar to the approach in *The Cost of Non-Europe in Financial Services* (Vol. 9 in the report on *The Cost of Non-Europe* presented by the Commission of the European Communities in 1988), or have developed a model within a general equilibrium framework. But one problem in assessing the effects of the abolition of capital controls, for instance, is to measure the benchmark case: what would have happened if the abolition had not occurred? In view of the criticism which the EC report aroused, and of the lack of any generally accepted frameworks for estimating the bottom line, I shall adhere to my original objectives and concentrate mainly on how the process has developed. For this purpose I have therefore proposed a set of important dimensions. The choice of dimensions in this set is admittedly subjective. Although my aim is to describe developments as fully as possible, the set will have to be reduced somewhat when it comes to analysing the globalization of national bond markets.

The general purpose of the book is to study, in terms of economic growth, the impact of globalization on the channelling of savings. After analysing the link between investment and economic growth, I felt justified in stopping at investments, while still retaining the possibility of extrapolating the findings to economic growth. The remainder of the book will thus focus on the impact of the globalization of national bond markets on the relationship between savings and investment.

NOTES

1   In addition it can be argued that the financial system serves as a *store of value* which makes possible the intertemporal allocation of consumption, as a source for information processing and transmission, and as a provider of the means of risk management.

2   According to Walter (1992) the value-chain of securities market services comprises the global financial market infrastructure and encompasses:

- information gathering and dissemination;
- trading mechanisms, both on exchanges and over-the-counter markets;
- clearance and settlement, both for payments and for financial instruments and derivatives;
- post-trade custody, safekeeping and reporting on investment performance.

3   The first alternative is by far the most important. In some countries financial institutions are not even allowed to hold shares.

4   In the absence or limited availability of a liquid secondary market, investors have to be rewarded with a higher yield.

5   As was discussed in Chapter 1, longer term includes both intermediate term (with maturities of one to five years) and long term (maturities exceeding five years). The limit between intermediate term and long term is by no means definite, and is sometimes set at ten years.

6   Such as futures, options and swaps.

7   Intergovernmental coordination of regulatory structures and macroeconomic policies has been common since the mid-1980s.

8   Some of these elements may be imposed to alleviate market failure, while others are policy-induced. The elements in the former group constitute the regulatory body concerned with the set of issues that have been described here as systemic problems. They are designed to preserve the confidentiality of commercially sensitive information and to enhance the efficiency (liquidity) of the payments and settlements system. The other group of elements constitutes the body of business, monetary and fiscal regulations.

9   It is feared that the monetary overhang will lead to increased inflation along with the liberalization process. This argument has perhaps its greatest importance in the analysis of Eastern European countries.

10   See, for example, Zysman (1983).

11   See, for example, French and Poterba (1990, 1991).

12 See, for example, Altman (1987) and Merton (1989).
13 There is a tendency towards a decomposition of risks into increasingly refined 'slices'.
14 By the use of off-balance-sheet instruments.
15 Universal banking embraces engagement in commercial banking (making loans to clients) and investment banking (underwriting and trade in securities) as well.
16 See, for instance, Oxelheim and Wihlborg (1987).
17 It can be argued as to whether this sensitivity was to nominal unadjusted interest rates or to risk-adjusted rates, since many people blame the emergence of the global debt crisis on recycling behaviour and a related inability on the part of the banking sector to price country risks appropriately.
18 See, for example, Mathieson and Rojas-Suarez (1992), who emphasize that a large fiscal deficit financed by money creation would induce domestic residents to move money abroad to escape the inflation tax.
19 A statutory body, created under the provisions of the 1986 Financial Services Act, and with overall responsibility for regulation.
20 To retain the benefits of direct practitioner input, the principal day-to-day regulators are five self-regulatory organizations. From April 1988 it has been illegal to operate in the securities and investment business in the UK without authorization from either one of these organizations or from SIB.
21 The alternative argument was to claim that they were still risk-averse, but had mispriced the risk.
22 See, for instance, Jensen (1991).
23 See, for instance, Zysman (1983) and Hutchison (1984).
24 Securitization is a good example of a service prompted by such demands from customers.
25 As, for instance, Leite and Sundararajan (1992) have pointed out.
26 The adaptation of an adequate market structure is delayed, and confidence in market institutions is undermined.
27 The link between the development of the financial sector and the real sector is a well-established fact. The links usually emphasized are the role of financial markets in channelling savings towards investment and, more recently, the fact that financial intermediaries are able to solve informational problems that would otherwise lead to inefficient outcomes. See, for instance, McKinnon (1973) for a classical contribution, and Bencivenga and Smith (1991) for a recent contribution.
28 'Permanent' refers to implications after the process has terminated, while 'transitory' refers to effects appearing while the process is still going on.
29 Further advances in information technology and data processing, with implications for cross-border financial transactions, may mean that value-creating transactions migrate to jurisdictions that are more conducive to economic enterprise. Restrictions thus come to affect a smaller and smaller part of total activity, and in the end become self-defeating.
30 See also Chapter 1.
31 Kanda (1992) claims that the traditional understanding of systemic risk as a combination of credit risk and liquidity risk is analytically insufficient, and therefore suggests the breaking down of systemic risk into four sub-risks. These are pure credit or default risk, interdependence risk, time risk and large-amount risk. Time is important because payments and other transactions are subject to a relatively short time constraint, and some mechanical breakdown or a single bank's failure will give rise to a liquidity problem for other banks. A large transaction amount causes a liquidity problem to the extent that it remains unsettled.
32 Settlement and clearance are frequently taken for granted; yet it is precisely here

that default and systemic risks manifest themselves in a crisis.

33   According to the Minsky hypothesis, it is not just a matter of transitory problems but recurrent *self-enforcing* crises (see Minsky 1982 and 1986).

34   In a global perspective distributional effects may mean that regulatory developments in the US in due course jeopardize the position of the Eurodollar bond and deposit markets.

35   Small companies call for particular attention because they are more likely to come up against imperfections in the credit market. Moreover, Gertler and Gilchrist (1991) provide evidence that they are also particularly sensitive to macroeconomic disturbances, including shifts in monetary policy.

36   An exception may be if government has used the isolation of the domestic market as a means of providing cheap financing to these categories of companies.

37   Such as operating and administrative costs, cost of capital, etc.

38   In describing sectors of the financial markets in Chapters 12–14 I shall measure efficiency directly by focusing on the interest spread, for instance, and indirectly by focusing on the determinants of efficiency and fair pricing. Such determinants are liquidity, information and transaction costs and competition. *Liquidity* may be measured in terms of the ratio of turnover to capitalization, availability of intermediaries, degree of concentration (number of security holders) and spread of orders. *Information* may be measured in terms of quality (requirements as regards annual reports, for instance), quantity (number of suppliers) and handling (technical possibilities), while *competition* may be measured by numbers and size of market actors. Finally, *transaction costs* may be captured by the size of bid-ask spreads, discounts, commission fees, taxes and search costs.

39   According to Walter (1992), product innovations usually involve the creation of new financial instruments (e.g. caps, futures, options and swaps) besides the ability to replicate certain instruments by bundling existing ones (synthetic securities) or to highlight a new financial attribute by rebundling existing instruments. Process innovations include contract design, methods of settlement and trading, techniques for efficient margin calculation, new approaches to contract pricing, passive or index-based portfolio investment techniques, etc.

40   When determining the 'optimum', it has to be remembered that innovations can also be too rapid.

41   See, for example, Solow (1956).

42   For details, see Burmeister and Dobell (1970).

43   See, for instance, Romer (1986, 1987a, 1987b, 1990), Rebelo (1990) and Sala-i-Martin (1990a, 1990b).

44   For a review of endogenous growth models, see Sala-i-Martin (1990a, 1990b).

45   The assumption that factor markets are competitive is retained. Consequently, α and $(1 - \alpha)$ continue to represent the income shares of capital and labour respectively. For the possible size of the externality, β, there is very little direct evidence. See Summers (1990) for indications of size.

46   For a recent discussion, see Adams and Chadha (1992).

47   For a discussion about the steady-state of the neoclassical model, see Burmeister and Dobell (1970) and Sala-i-Martin (1990a, 1990b).

48   However, it has to be stressed that the close association is between growth and machinery and not between growth and investment in general.

49   See, for instance, Summers (1990) and Adams and Chadha (1992).

50   To measure this, Adams and Chadha (1992) suggest three major avenues: (1) to focus on the growth contribution of capital, (2) to study the time-series relationship between investment and growth, and (3) to study the behaviour of the rate of return on capital.

51   See, for example, Gertler and Gilchrist (1991), Gertler *et al.* (1990), Greenwald

and Stiglitz (1990) and Shleifer and Vishny (1991).

52 As Lewis points out: 'Organic chemicals became a German industry; the motor car was pioneered in France and mass-produced in the United States; Britain lagged behind in the use of electricity [and] depended on foreign firms ...'

53 Fukao and Hanzaki (1987) show that the tax wedge for housing investment in Sweden is considerable in an 'asset draw down' case of a size more than 10 percentage points given the 1985 tax parameter and assuming a real interest rate of 5 per cent and inflation at 15 per cent. At 10 per cent inflation the wedge is 8 percentage points and at 5 per cent inflation the wedge is slightly more than 5 percentage points. The wedge is almost double the wedge in the country which comes next after Sweden in terms of the size of this wedge. In a 'borrowing' case, the wedges are almost halved and the gap in relation to other OECD countries is substantially smaller.

54 Another reason is the inadequate pricing of credit risks in the second part of the 1980s. The risks started to make themselves felt at the end of the 1980s and, since the banks had not covered them, bank profitability was seriously depleted, thus aggravating the recession.

55 More on this in Chapter 5.

56 For instance, Laroque (1981) and Saint-Paul (1991) stress a milking of the capital market by the state as a cause of the underdevelopment of financial markets during French post-war reconstruction. This development corresponds to what McKinnon (1973) has called 'repressed financial markets'. Further, the state used bank nationalization and portfolio requirements to pre-empt for the state the funds that would otherwise have gone to entrepreneurs. Along with pre-emptive institutional arrangements, the French government repeatedly used discretionary policy in order to solve budgetary crises: 'exceptional taxes', abolition of anonymity for treasury bill-holders, suspension of exchange liberalization measures, etc.

57 See, for example, Oxelheim (1993).

58 See Dean *et al.* (1989).

59 In some small economies such as the Nordic, liberalization meant a substantial increase in borrowing from real estate and finance companies.

60 See Shields (1988).

61 Including subsidies to the construction sector.

62 Tax deductibility for interest payments would be justified with respect to investment in housing if the accrued income on housing investment (including capital gains and implicit rental income) were also fully taxed.

63 Reservations are either 'full' or 'limited', where 'remarks' to the reservation specify that a country allows certain capital movement operations to take place under the particular item, or permits transactions up to certain limits. The derogations may be classified as 'general' – namely, a special arrangement whereby an economically less strong member derogates from the obligations of the Code – and 'specific', permitting members to reintroduce restrictions temporarily on already liberalized items because of serious economic and financial disturbances or balance-of-payments problems.

64 IMF presents a similar view in its yearly assessments. At the end of 1989, 123 of the 153 member countries and territories were reported by IMF (1990) as using capital controls and/or separate exchange rates for capital account transactions. The corresponding figures for 1975 were 103 of 126 member countries. From 1975 to 1989 the number of industrial countries with capital account convertibility rose from three to nine. For developing countries, the number rose from twenty to twenty-one.

65 Major parts of the internal deregulation were completed in the early 1980s, while

some parts such as the Glass–Steagal Act still formally remain even though they are eroding gradually.

66 The restrictions were lifted in 1979.
67 The EU commission's 1992 target, however, can be seen as the date for completion of its internal deregulation as well.
68 See UNCTC (1992).
69 From IMF (1992) it can be seen that eleven of twenty-one developed countries still try to maintain control through capital restrictions.
70 Lifted in November 1992.
71 Based on a study of forty-six countries: twenty developed countries, five newly industrializing and twenty-one other developing countries, 1977–87 as reported in UNCTC (1991).
72 As calculated on data from IMF (1992).
73 However, the internal deregulation proceeded much more slowly and continued throughout the 1980s. At the beginning of the 1990s deregulation in Japan had not yet proceeded to the elimination of interest ceilings on small time-deposits at banks, and the postal savings system and about half of the banks' time-deposits (and all postal savings) remained regulated.

REFERENCES

Adams, C. and B. Chadha, 1992, 'Growth, Productivity, and the Rate of Return on Capital', *Working Paper*, 92:35, IMF, Washington, DC.

Altman, E.I., 1987, 'The Anatomy of the High-yield Bond Market', *Financial Analysts Journal*, New York, July–August, pp. 12–25.

Bencivenga, V. and B.D. Smith, 1991, 'Financial Intermediation and Endogenous Growth', *Review of Economic Studies* 58, No. 2, pp. 195–209.

Burmeister E.M. and P. Dobell, 1970, *Mathematical Theories of Economic Growth*, Macmillan, London.

Dean, A., M. Durand, J. Fallon and P. Hoeller, 1989, 'Saving Trends and Behaviour in OECD Countries', *OECD Econometrics and Statistics Department Working Papers*, No. 67 (June).

De Long, J.B., 1990, 'Did J.P. Morgan's Men Add Value? A Historical Perspective of Financial Capitalism', *NBER Working Paper No. 3426*, Cambridge, Mass.

De Long, J.B. and L.H. Summers, 1991, 'Equipment Investment and Economic Growth', *NBER Working Paper No. 3515*, Cambridge, Mass.

French, K.R. and J.M. Poterba, 1990, 'Japanese and U.S. Cross-Border Common Stock Investments', *Journal of the Japanese and International Economies*, December, No. 4.

French, K.R. and J.M. Poterba, 1991, 'Were Japanese Stock Prices Too High?', *Journal of Financial Economics*, Vol. 29, No. 2, October, pp. 337–63.

Fukao, M. and M. Hanzaki, 1987, 'Internationalization of Financial Markets and the Allocation of Capital', *OECD Econometric Studies*, No. 8 (Spring), pp. 35–92.

Gertler, M. and S. Gilchrist, 1991, 'Monetary Policy, Business Cycles and the Behavior of Small Manufacturing Firms', *NBER Working Paper*, No. 3892, Cambridge, Mass.

Gertler, M., R.G. Hubbard and A.K. Kashyap, 1990, 'Interest Rate Spreads, Credit Constraints, and Investment Fluctuations: An Empirical Investigation', *NBER Working Paper No. 3495*, Cambridge, Mass.

Greenwald, B. and J. Stiglitz, 1990, 'Macroeconomic Models with Equity and Credit Rationing,' in Hubbard, R. (ed.), *Asymmetric Information, Corporate Finance, and Investment*, University of Chicago Press, Chicago.

Hutchison, M.M., 1984, 'Official Japanese Intervention in Foreign Exchange Markets. Leaning Against the Wind?', *Economic Letters*, Vol. 15, pp 115–20, North-Holland, Amsterdam.

IMF, 1990, *Annual Report on Exchange Arrangements and Exchange Restrictions*, Washington, DC.

IMF, 1992, *International Capital Markets: Developments, Prospects, and Policy Issues*, Washington, DC.

Jensen, M.C., 1989, 'Eclipse of the Public Corporation', *Harvard Business Review* (September–October), pp. 61–74.

Jensen, M.C., 1991, 'Corporate Control and the Politics of Finance', *Journal of Applied Corporate Finance*, No. 4, pp. 13–33.

Kanda, H., 1992, 'Systemic Risk and International Financial Markets', in Edwards, F.R. and H.T. Patrick (eds), *Regulating International Financial Markets; Issues and Policies*, Kluwer Academic Publishers, Dordrecht.

Lane, T.D., 1992, 'International Monetary Fund', *IMF Working Paper No. 42*, Washington, DC.

Laroque, G., 1981, 'Conjoncture économique de l'immédiat après-guerre', *Economie et Statistique*, 129, pp. 5–16.

Leite, S. and V. Sundararajan, 1992, 'Issues in Interest Rate Management and Liberalization', *Staff Paper*, Vol. 37, No. 4, IMF, Washington, DC.

Lewis, W.A., 1978, *Growth and Fluctuations*, Allen & Unwin, London.

McKinnon, R., 1973, *Money and Capital in Economic Development*, The Brookings Institution, Washington, DC.

Mathieson, D.J. and L. Rojas-Suarez, 1992, 'Liberalization of the Capital Account: Experiences and Issues', *IMF Working Paper*, No. 46.

Merton, R.C., 1989, 'On the Application of the Continuous-Time Theory of Finance to Financial Intermediation and Insurance', *The Geneva Papers on Risk and Insurance*, Vol. 14, No. 52, July, pp. 256–61.

Minsky, H.P., 1982, *Can 'it' Happen Again?: Essay on Instability and Finance*, M.E. Sharpe, Armonk.

Minsky, H.P., 1986, *Stabilizing an Unstable Economy*, Yale University Press, New Haven.

OECD, 1990, *Liberalization of Capital Movements and Financial Services in the OECD Area*, Paris.

Oxelheim, L. (ed.), 1993, *The Global Race for Foreign Direct Investment – Prospects for the Future*, Springer Verlag, Heidelberg.

Oxelheim, L. and C. Wihlborg, 1987, *Macroeconomic Uncertainty – International Risks and Opportunities for the Corporations*, John Wiley & Sons, Chichester.

Rebelo, S., 1990, 'Long Run Policy Analysis and Long Run Growth', *NBER Working Paper No. 3325*, April, Cambridge, Mass.

Romer, P.M., 1986, 'Increasing Returns and Long-Run Growth', *Journal of Political Economy*, pp. 1002–37.

Romer, P.M., 1987a, 'Growth Based on Increasing Returns Due to Specialization', *American Economic Review* (papers and proceedings) 77, pp. 56–72.

Romer, P.M., 1987b, 'Crazy Explanations for the Productivity Slowdown', *NBER Macroeconomics Annual* 2, pp. 163–202.

Romer, P.M., 1990, 'Capital, Labor, and Productivity', *Brookings Papers on Economic Activity*, Brookings Institution, Washington, DC, pp. 337–67.

Saint-Paul, G., 1991, 'French Economic Reconstruction: 1945–1958', Presented at the Center for Economic Performance Conference on Reconstruction, Hamburg, Sept., pp. 6–7.

Sala-i-Martin, X., 1990a, Lecture Notes on Economic Growth (I): 'Introduction to the Literature and Neoclassical Models', *NBER Working Paper No. 3563*, Cambridge, Mass.

Sala-i-Martin, X., 1990b, Lecture Notes on Economic Growth (II): 'Five Prototype Models of Endogenous Growth', *NBER Working Paper No. 3564*, Cambridge, Mass.

Schumpeter, J., 1943, *Capitalism, Socialism and Democracy* (republished in Unwin Paperbacks, London, 1987).

Shields, J., 1988, 'Controlling Household Credit', *National Institute Economic Review*, August, pp. 46–55.

Shleifer, A. and R. Vishny, 1991, 'Asset Sales and Debt Capacity', *NBER Working Paper No. 3618*, Cambridge, Mass.

Solow, R.M., 1956, 'A Contribution to the Theory of Economic Growth', *Quarterly Journal of Economics* 20, February, pp. 65–94.

Summers, L.H., 1990, 'What is the Social Return to Capital Investment?', Diamond, P. (ed.), *Growth/Productivity/Unemployment*, MIT Press, Cambridge.

UNCTC, 1991, *Government Policies and Foreign Direct Investment*, Series A, No. 17, United Nations Center on Transnational Corporations, New York.

UNCTC, 1992, *World Investment Report*, United Nationals Center on Transnational Corporations, New York.

Walter, I., 1992, 'Understanding the Structure and Dynamics of Global Financial Flows', Conference Paper, The Perspectives on International Business Conference, Columbia.

Zysman, J., 1983, *Governments, Markets and Growth – Financial Systems and the Politics of Industrial Change*, Cornell University Press, New York.

Chapter 3

A regional study of deregulation

The consequences of financial liberalization vary most among small countries, which suggests that a closer examination of some of these countries could be rewarding. Among the small economies which have moved most rapidly towards financial liberalization since the mid-1980s, the Nordic countries have been prominent. Because these countries closely resemble each other in many important aspects, they have been chosen as the object of the following study.

The subject of this chapter will be regionalism in the Nordic countries and the general macroeconomic setting there. Potential inoptimalities in the deregulatory process, as expressed in measures related to economic growth, will also be focused upon.

As the Nordic region consists of a group of countries singularly free from intra-regional barriers, this high degree of transparency thus allows us to concentrate on differences in the transformation of their national financial markets without having to control for differences in language, accounting principles or disclosure norms.[1]

Economic relations between the Nordic economies are close-knit, and the countries enjoy a similar level of welfare and a common cultural and social background. A passport union and a common market were established at the beginning of the 1950s, and more than one-fifth of the exports of any of the countries goes to the other three. All in all, the official Nordic cooperation covers every area except foreign policy and defence.

In an international investor's perspective, the individual Nordic countries look so similar that they are often lumped together. This attitude means that a shock in one Nordic country may easily become contagious, i.e. it will have spill-over effects in the others.

REGIONALISM IN THE TRANSFORMATION OF NATIONAL FINANCIAL MARKETS

The problems of Nordic intra-integration and the need for improving intra-Nordic capital mobility have been the subject of considerable attention over the last twenty years or so. The Nordic Council explicitly included the achievement of such integration in its recommendation No. 23/1980. In November 1982 the Nordic prime ministers jointly declared that steps should be taken to increase the freedom of capital flows and investment between the Nordic countries. In January 1984 the Nordic Perspective Group suggested the creation of a Nordic capital market (Etla *et al.* 1984). Following an investigation of the whole issue, the Nordic Council recommended the Nordic Council of Ministers in February 1984 to take steps to increase the freedom of capital flows, to stimulate cooperation on exchange rate policy and to provide more freedom for the creation of a Nordic stock market. However, the OECD Capital Liberalization Act was seen at the time as an obstacle to regional freedom for capital flows and to the use of the Nordic region as a 'refuge'. The abolition of exchange controls, according to OECD, should be effected on a global rather than a regional scale.

The Nordic Council persisted in its vision of a regional Nordic financial market and initiated two further investigations. These were to examine the influence on industrial development of various obstacles to intra-Nordic capital movements and diverse investment regulations.[2]

Another body working for Nordic integration is the Nordic Monetary Committee (NMC or NFU, Nordiska Finansiella Utskottet), which is a forum for Nordic monetary cooperation composed of representatives from the central bank or ministry of finance and economic affairs in the five Nordic countries. Typical topics discussed by the committee include various exchange regulations relevant to these countries.

In 1983 the Nordic finance ministries decided that foreign exchange regulations in the Nordic countries should be monitored with a view to further liberalization, provided the balance of payments and monetary policy warranted such a move.[3] Feldt (1991) provides many examples of Nordic exchange rate cooperation up to the time of the major devaluation of the Swedish krona in 1982. He claims, however, that 1982 saw the last occasion of such cooperation during the 1980s.

A working group on capital movements and a single Nordic market was established in May 1988. Another working group on financial services and the single market was set up in September the same year. These two units were also part of a new economic plan. Reports produced[4] by both of them pointed out the danger of discriminating against third countries, not only in light of the international role of the Nordic countries but also for purely economic reasons. As OECD members the Nordic countries also had to respect the OECD's capital movement code and refrain from preferential treatment of each other to the detriment of other OECD members. Consequently, the liberalization was to cover the largest possible geographical area. The statement issued by NMC on these reports emphasized the importance of coordinating the liberalization of capital movements and financial services, with the overall objective of improving adaptability while also taking into consideration developments in the EC.[5] The view at the time was that the liberalization process should continue at about the same rate in the five Nordic countries, and that there should be more exchange of information. Hence, the emphasis on intra-Nordic integration was replaced by coordinated efforts in moving towards international financial integration.

INTRA-REGIONAL HOMOGENEITY

The Nordic countries are small economies and are relatively open to international trade. Exchange controls have been imposed to reduce the outflow of interest-sensitive capital, and to achieve autonomy for the national monetary policy. For most of the post-war period all four countries have opted for corner (1) in the monetary policy triangle (Figure 1.1). The policy regime corresponding to that corner, implying financial isolation and monetary autonomy, has expressed itself in numerous changes in Nordic market rules. But they have not appeared with equal intensity at the same time in the four countries. This situation, which suggests that the policies pursued or the perceived need for new market rules have differed from country to country, will be considered further in Chapters 6–9. In general, Nordic regulations during the 1960s and 1970s were geared to maintaining low interest rates with a view to securing cheap public sector financing at the expense of private savers.

As can be seen in Table 3.1, the Nordic countries have been very open to trade throughout the post-war period, although only in Sweden has the openness substantially increased. For the Nordic region as a whole, the degree of openness to trade is high compared, for instance, with the United States and Japan. In the mid-1990s, the results appear unchanged.

In contrast, the degree of financial openness has increased dramatically in all four countries (see Table 3.1). The measure used is the sum of all gross components of non-government capital flows related to GDP.[6] The base year is 1970. An index value is shown for 1950 in the case of Sweden, but due to lack of data this was not possible for the other countries. However, the Swedish data for 1950 may be inaccurate since foreign direct investments – inward and outward – were set at zero that year, implying a potential underestimation. Accordingly, the development for Sweden between 1950 and 1960 – 350 per cent – may be exaggerated, and recent figures may provide a more reliable view. A comparison between the 1980 and 1990 figures reveals an impressive increase of 817 per cent. But the increase in financial openness between 1980 and 1990 may be underestimated as well, as the deregulation has made it extremely difficult to capture all non-government capital flows in the statistics.

As will be emphasized many times below, capital-flow-based measures are generally unreliable. Bearing this in mind, we can none the less conclude that the developments for the different countries probably differ. Denmark,

Table 3.1 Measures of national openness

	Openness to international trade %					Financial external openness (index 1970 = 100)				
	1950	*1960*	*1970*	*1980*	*1990*	*1950*	*1960*	*1970*	*1980*	*1990*
Denmark	29	34	29	33	32	–	23	100	312	1350
Finland	19	23	26	33	23	–	39	100	94	209
Norway	41	38	42	44	40	–	90[a]	100	177	867
Sweden	22	23	24	31	30	8	36	100	276	2532
USA	4	5	6	10	11					
Japan	11[b]	11	10	14	10					

[a] Openness in 1965.
[b] Openness in 1955.

Source: Based on data from IMF, *IFS-Database*; OECD, *National Accounts*, various issues; Nordic central banks, unpublished data.
Note: Openness to international trade is calculated as the average of exports plus imports of goods and services as a percentage of gross domestic product. Financial openness is calculated as an index of the sum of non-government gross capital account (residential and non-residential) transactions as a percentage of gross domestic product. Resident capital includes foreign direct investments, investments in foreign securities and various forms of loans from abroad. Non-resident capital includes direct investment in a particular Nordic country, investment in securities from that country, and various forms of loans to abroad.

where *de facto* external liberalization began as far back as the beginning of the 1970s rather than in the 1980s as in the other Nordic countries, shows the highest index for 1980. The figures for 1990 show the biggest increase in openness to be in the Swedish market, followed by the Danish. Finland, which did not complete the abolition of exchange controls until late 1991, exhibits a low figure.[7]

All the Nordic countries have large public sectors, which in turn implies a heavy tax burden. Total government outlays as a percentage of GDP for Sweden, Denmark and Norway have historically been far above all aggregated OECD measures (see Table 3.2). Finland has stayed relatively close to these aggregates. Moreover, according to OECD (1994), Denmark had the highest tax burden in the world in 1993 (50 per cent). Sweden with 49.5, Holland with 48.2, Finland with 46.8 and Norway with 45.8 came next. Thus the Nordic countries are all among the top five high-tax countries in the world. This fact, together with potential tax wedges, may go a long way towards explaining the process of transition, as changes in taxes exert considerable influence on the development of national financial markets. In Denmark, for instance, differences in the taxation arrangements for stocks and bonds led the Danish bond market quite early on to become one of the largest in the world in relative terms.

As regards indebtedness, the four countries are fairly similar, as all are heavy net debtors, albeit Norway to a lesser extent (see Figure 3.1). Since the

Table 3.2 Total government outlays[a] (percentage of GDP)

Country	1960	1968	1974	1980	1981	1982	1983	1984	1985	1986	1987	1988	1989	1990
United States	27.0	30.7	32.2	33.7	34.1	36.5	36.9	35.8	36.7	37.1	36.8	36.1	36.1	—
Japan	17.5	19.4	24.5	32.6	33.4	33.6	33.9	32.9	32.3	32.6	32.8	32.2	31.5	32.3
Germany	32.4	39.1	44.6	48.5	49.4	49.6	48.5	48.1	47.6	47.0	47.3	46.9	45.5	46.0
Denmark	24.8	36.3	45.9	56.2	59.8	61.2	61.6	60.3	59.3	55.7	57.3	59.4	59.4	58.4
Finland	26.6	31.0	32.0	36.6	37.5	39.1	40.3	39.8	41.6	42.2	42.2	40.0	38.2	41.2
Norway	29.9	37.9	44.6	48.3	47.9	48.3	48.4	46.3	45.6	49.9	51.5	53.7	54.6	55.6
Sweden	31.0	42.8	48.1	61.6	64.2	66.3	66.0	63.5	64.7	63.0	59.2	59.5	59.9	61.4
Total smaller countries	26.8	30.3	34.6	43.0	45.7	47.3	48.0	47.6	48.2	47.5	47.0	46.2	47.0	51.0
Total OECD	28.1	36.9	34.7	38.7	40.1	41.7	42.0	41.3	41.7	41.6	41.1	40.4	40.0	43.8
OECD Europe	31.3	36.3	39.8	45.2	47.8	48.8	49.1	49.2	49.4	48.8	48.2	47.5	47.6	48.4
EU	31.8	36.9	40.0	45.2	48.0	49.2	49.2	49.4	49.6	48.9	48.3	47.6	47.7	48.7

[a] Total outlays consist of current disbursements plus gross capital formation and purchases of land and intangible assets.

Source: Based on data from OECD, 1992, Economic Outlook, Historical Statistics 1960–1990.

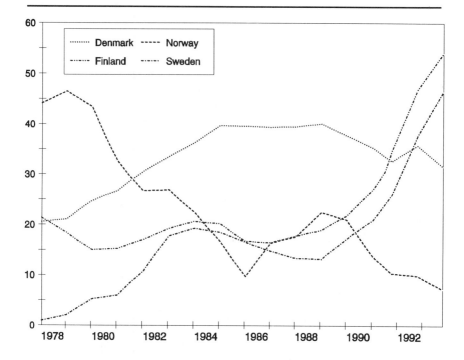

Figure 3.1 Net foreign debt in the Nordic countries (percentage of GDP, end of period)

Sources: Based on data from OECD, *National Accounts*, Vol. 1, 1992, 1994; Danmarks Nationalbank, *Annual Yearbook*, various issues, and *Monetary Review*, May 1994; Bank of Finland, *Database* and *Bank of Finland Bulletin*, Vol. 68, November 1994; Bank of Norway, *Database*; and the Swedish Central Bank, *Statistical Yearbook*, 1985 and *Sveriges tillgångar och skulder mot utlandet*, 1992:1, 1994:3.
Note: A new method for calculating the foreign debt was adopted in Denmark in 1991. Data prior to 1991 include a negative error term, and the trend for Denmark thus has to be taken as an approximation. For individual years these errors and omissions were modest, and they do not greatly affect the general trend.

1970s companies have also increased their net borrowing. These loans gave companies a way of circumventing external regulations by, for example, leads and lags in the debt service. They thus began the erosion of the efficiency of Nordic currency regulations, and helped to speed up the deregulation.

To sum up: the main similarities between the Nordic countries are that they are all small, open, political economies and all have opted for similar monetary policy regimes in the post-war period.

INTRA-REGIONAL DISSIMILARITIES

Denmark has been a member of the EU for a long time. Finland, Norway and Sweden, on the other hand, have belonged to EFTA. Sweden applied for membership of the EU in 1991, while Finland and Norway applied in 1992. In 1994 an agreement between the EU and EFTA to form a European Economic Area (EEA), came into force (enacted in 1993). For the EFTA countries this was seen as a transitional stage towards full EU membership. Referendums on membership were held in the three Nordic countries in 1994, with the result that Finland and Sweden became members of the EU of 1 January 1995, whereas Norway elected to stay outside. However, Norway will still have access to the single market through the EEA agreement, but a modification of this agreement will probably ensue as a result of the diminishing number of countries concerned.

In 1991 the Danish krone belonged to the European Monetary System (EMS), while the other Nordic currencies were unilaterally pegged to the European Currency Unit (ECU). At the end of 1991, however, the Finnish markka was devalued and floated for a few hours.[8] In September 1992 it had to float again, while turbulence in the European exchange rates caused the Swedish krona to float in November and the Norwegian krone in December the same year.

Another important difference, which is crucial to the path of the transformation and the credibility of the deregulative action, concerns the independence of the Nordic central banks. Starck (1992) assessed this independence, and although his study involves some discretionary elements it does provide an indication of the state of affairs. Starck compares twenty-three countries and finds that the central banks of Germany, Switzerland and Chile are the most independent. Finland is ranked sixth and is characterized as having considerable independence: Sweden follows in seventh place and Denmark in tenth, both characterized as having some independence; Norway, ranked twentieth, is described as having extremely little independence.

Previously, we have noted that differences in the degree of internationalization of industry affect the international integration of national financial markets. In terms of foreign direct investments, Sweden was ahead of her neighbours at the beginning of the 1980s. In the country's top ten companies, the number of employees working abroad was almost as high as the number working in Sweden, whereas the corresponding relative figures for the other three Nordic countries were in the range of 20–25 per cent.[9] In the early 1990s the proportion of employees abroad was about 60 per cent in the Swedish top ten group and slightly more than 40 per cent for companies from each of the other three countries. Thus, measured in this way, the economic integration of the Nordic region increased considerably during the 1980s and early 1990s.

The pattern of foreign direct investments from the Nordic countries as a whole shows a substantial increase, much of which was triggered by the development of the EU's single market. However, the pattern of FDI activities differs as between the Nordic countries, particularly if the gap between outflow and inflow is taken into account. In terms of net flows of

FDI as a percentage of GDP, Sweden exhibits the highest gap (1986–90) between outward and inward investment (3.44 per cent outward and 0.56 per cent inward) of any OECD country. Finland also exhibits a big gap (1.96 per cent outward and 0.46 inward) whereas Denmark (1.04 per cent and 0.54 per cent) and Norway (1.44 per cent and 0.90 per cent) show a tiny average net outflow of half a percentage point.[10]

The Nordic countries also differ as regards the share of non-factor services in total exports and imports. Exports from Norway reveal a high share of non-factor services. In the first half of the 1960s the share was over 50 per cent, after which it declined and by the early 1990s was about 30 per cent. The other Nordic countries have always had a considerably lower share; in the 1960s they were all in the range of 20–25 per cent and in the early 1990s of 15–25 per cent.

Yet another difference appears in the structure of manufacturing industry. The role of large multinationals has traditionally been important in Sweden, while small and medium-sized companies have been prominent in the other Nordic countries. Among the top 1,000 global publicly traded companies, according to market values as at May 1992, we find twenty-one Nordic companies: four Danish, no Finnish, two Norwegian and fifteen Swedish.[11] In per capita terms, Sweden occupies a top position in a European ranking.

Lastly, Denmark and Norway are self-sufficient as regards energy, whereas Finland and Sweden are not. Norway is a net oil exporter, whereas Finland and Sweden import substantial quantities.

CAUSALITY ISSUES IN THE ANALYSIS OF FINANCIAL MARKET RELATIONSHIPS

Criticism of empirical approaches to the measurement of international financial integration has often been levelled at the measurement and interpretation of *causality*. The main thrust of this criticism concerns the problem of distinguishing signs of *actual* economic dependence between countries from *spurious* dependence generated by some common underlying disturbance or factor, such as fluctuations in the business cycle. Thus, if we specify integration from some measure of covariation, we face the difficulty of eliminating from this measure any covariation, which could be due to such common underlying factors.

Many researchers recognize that the interpretation of causality is a serious analytical problem in the case of large countries such as the United States, Germany and Japan, whose relationship with their environments can be regarded as one of mutual dependence. But most researchers tend to regard the interpretive problem as less serious and more manageable when it comes to small open economies such as those in the Nordic region. In a financial context, they can all more or less be seen as price-takers.

INDICATORS OF SUBOPTIMALITY IN THE TRANSFORMATION PROCESS

Are there, then, any indications of structural or secular growth problems in the individual Nordic countries which might have been caused by the process of financial market transformation? Can we see in the Nordic countries any of the frequent problems that arise in global cases of external deregulation?[12]

Table 3.3 shows the long-term development of GDP per capita in the Nordic countries as compared with some of the OECD countries. GDP per capita in all the Nordic countries except Finland, corrected for deviations from purchasing power parity, has been above that of the EU since the beginning of the 1960s. The distance from the US figures has gradually diminished. Since the 1960s Finland and Norway have improved, while GDP per capita in Denmark and Sweden has been gradually falling towards the EU average. In general economies have not 'converged' in productivity levels or standards of living over the past century,[13] but the Nordic countries, with Norway as a borderline case, do roughly appear to have done so.

In terms of annual real growth,[14] Table 3.4 shows a depressing development for Sweden, which has remained constantly under every OECD average since 1985. The Finnish development is almost as gloomy. Even though in some years the Finnish growth rate did exceed the OECD

Table 3.3 GDP per capita in selected OECD countries[a] (index EU = 100)

Country	1960	1970	1980	1990
USA	190	165	151	150
Great Britain	129	109	101	105
Holland	119	116	111	103
Germany	118	113	114	113
France	106	110	112	109
Belgium	95	99	103	103
Italy	87	95	103	103
Spain	60	75	75	78
Japan	56	92	101	119
Portugal	39	49	55	56
Greece	39	53	58	53
Denmark	118	115	108	108
Finland	93	94	101	110
Norway	111	104	121	124
Sweden	130	128	116	113

[a] Corrected for deviations in purchasing power parity. Switzerland, Luxembourg, Canada and Iceland are not included in the table, but if they had been, they would all have been above Denmark in 1990.

Source: Based on data from Eurostat, *Database*; Nordic Statistical Secretariat, *Nordic Statistic Yearbook*; and Danish Ministry of Finance, *Database*.

Table 3.4 Growth of real GDP in selected OECD countries (percentage changes from previous period)

Country	Average 1967–76	1977	1978	1979	1980	1981	1982	1983	1984	1985	1986	1987	1988	1989	1990	1991	1992	1993
United States	2.6	4.5	4.8	2.5	−0.5	1.8	−2.2	3.9	6.2	3.2	2.9	3.1	3.9	2.5	1.2	−0.7	2.6	3.0
Japan	6.8	4.7	4.9	5.5	3.6	3.6	3.2	2.7	4.3	5.0	2.6	4.1	6.2	4.7	4.8	4.3	1.1	0.1
Germany	3.8	2.8	3.0	4.2	1.0	0.1	−0.9	1.8	2.8	2.0	2.3	1.5	3.7	3.6	5.7	4.5	2.1	−1.3
Denmark	3.2	1.6	1.5	3.5	−0.4	−0.9	3.0	2.5	4.4	4.3	3.6	0.3	1.2	0.6	1.4	1.0	1.2	1.2
Finland	4.5	0.1	2.2	7.3	5.3	1.6	3.6	3.0	3.1	3.3	2.4	4.1	4.9	5.7	0.0	−7.1	−3.8	−2.6
Norway	4.3	3.6	4.7	5.1	4.2	0.9	0.3	4.6	5.7	5.3	4.2	2.1	−0.5	0.6	1.7	1.6	3.4	2.2
Sweden	3.2	−1.6	1.8	3.8	1.7	0.0	1.0	1.8	4.0	1.9	2.3	3.1	2.3	2.4	1.4	−1.1	−1.9	−2.1
Total smaller countries	4.7	2.3	2.3	2.5	2.1	0.9	1.2	1.7	3.4	3.1	3.0	3.6	3.8	3.8	3.3	0.9	1.3	0.8
Total OECD	4.0	3.7	4.0	3.5	1.1	1.5	0.0	2.7	4.4	3.3	4.4	3.3	4.4	3.3	2.5	0.8	1.7	1.2
OECD Europe	4.1	2.8	3.0	3.5	1.5	0.3	1.0	1.8	2.4	2.7	3.0	3.0	4.1	3.5	3.2	1.3	1.1	−0.2
EU	4.0	2.9	3.1	3.5	1.3	0.1	0.8	1.7	2.3	2.5	2.9	2.9	4.2	3.5	3.0	1.5	1.0	−0.4

Source: Based on data from OECD, Economic Outlook, Vol. 55, 1994.

Table 3.5 Growth of gross private non-residential fixed capital formation in selected OECD countries (percentage changes from previous period, volume)

Country	Average 1970–76	1977	1978	1979	1980	1981	1982	1983	1984	1985	1986	1987	1988	1989	1990	1991	1992	1993
United States	2.3	10.8	13.3	8.7	-2.4	3.9	-4.6	-3.0	16.5	6.4	-4.1	-0.5	6.6	1.7	1.2	-5.9	2.9	11.8
Japan	0.6	-0.4	4.5	12.9	7.9	3.8	1.3	1.7	11.7	12.1	4.4	6.7	14.8	16.6	11.4	6.6	-4.0	-8.4
Germany[a]	-1.0	6.3	5.5	7.5	2.8	-3.9	-4.7	4.5	-0.4	5.0	4.3	3.8	5.6	7.4	10.1	7.5	-1.8	-12.2
Denmark	3.9	0.8	1.3	-2.0	-9.6	-16.5	19.9	2.7	12.1	18.9	18.8	-5.4	-7.3	5.8	2.6	-4.1	-12.1	-3.6
Finland	3.6	-9.1	-13.9	6.6	15.5	5.0	2.5	6.8	-1.7	6.3	3.6	5.2	8.5	19.1	-6.4	-24.2	-21.0	-22.3
Norway	10.6	3.5	-26.8	-6.3	-1.9	27.5	-15.5	7.3	15.5	-19.4	29.5	-5.4	1.9	-1.6	-32.7	5.7	7.2	25.8
Sweden	5.5	-5.8	-17.2	7.3	8.7	-6.8	1.6	3.9	7.7	12.2	2.7	8.8	5.0	14.4	-0.9	-13.9	-15.6	-16.5
Total smaller countries	3.2	1.7	0.8	2.5	3.2	-0.8	-0.6	-0.9	1.8	6.4	8.0	8.3	7.9	11.2	1.1	-3.9	-4.2	-7.0
Total OECD	1.9	5.6	7.2	7.7	2.2	1.1	-2.6	-1.6	9.5	7.1	1.5	4.7	9.4	7.0	3.5	-1.9	-1.4	-0.6
OECD Europe	1.8	3.4	2.7	4.3	3.1	-4.7	-1.7	-0.7	2.6	5.4	5.7	8.6	9.6	8.0	3.6	-1.1	-4.1	-9.8
EU	1.5	3.6	3.9	4.3	2.5	-5.5	-1.4	-1.2	2.3	5.3	5.3	8.8	10.0	7.9	4.2	-0.5	-3.7	-10.1

[a] Western Germany.

Source: Based on data from OECD, Economic Outlook, Vol. 55, 1994.

aggregate, the 1990s brought Finland the lowest rates of all the OECD countries. Denmark and Norway scored somewhat better and stayed close to the OECD average. For Finland and Sweden the decline in growth is considerable even in comparison with figures from the recession at the beginning of the 1980s. Thus the process of financial market transformation may have affected Nordic national growth development.

As can be seen in Table 3.5, the beginning of the 1990s has also meant low growth in Nordic gross fixed capital formation (except for Norway at the very beginning of the decade). If we look at the change over a longer period, from 1985 to 1993, we find that the growth of gross private non-residential fixed capital formation in the Nordic countries decreased significantly at the end of the 1980s and the beginning of the 1990s (with the exception of Norway from 1991–93). Even though the general trend for small countries and OECD Europe was a downward one, the decline was significantly stronger in the Nordic countries, and particularly in Sweden and Finland. If the investment development is compared with the figures at the end of the 1970s and beginning of the 1980s, i.e. from the previous recession, the impression is that this decline is not just a cyclical phenomenon.

Figure 3.2 shows the development of Nordic industrial investment as

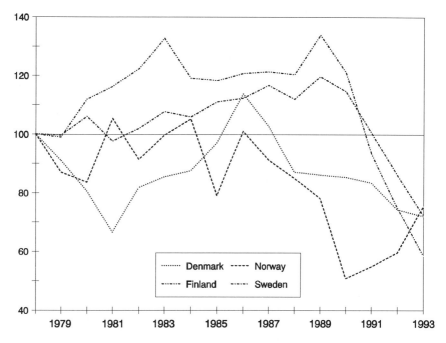

Figure 3.2 Index for industrial investment in individual Nordic countries as compared to the OECD average (index 1978 = 100)

Source: Based on data from OECD, *Economic Outlook*, Vol. 55, 1994.
Note: Industrial investment equals real gross private non-residential capital formation.

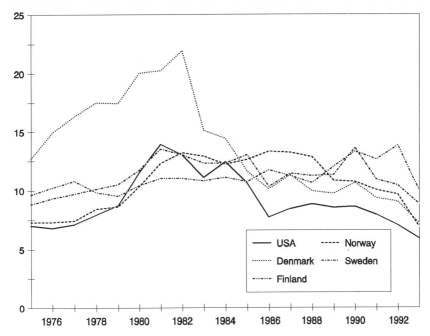

Figure 3.3 Nominal Nordic long-term interest rates (per cent per annum, government bond rates, yearly average)

Sources: Based on data from OECD, *Economic Outlook*, Vol. 55, 1994; OECD, *Historical Statistics*, 1993.

compared to OECD Europe since 1978. From the figure it is evident that the development of industrial investment was halted in Denmark and Norway in 1986, and in Finland and Sweden in 1989. For each of the Nordic countries the table indicates that the decline in growth may have followed the deregulation. A relevant question is thus: to what extent can the development be explained by the transformation of the Nordic national financial markets? Part of the decline may be explained by the growth of foreign direct investment as a means of replacing old capacity and finding new production facilities. Another part, however, may be seen as the result of falling prospects of profit, due to inoptimalities in the transformation process, i.e. by a cost of capital exceeding that of major competitors.

Finally, interest rates and exchange rates seem to have reacted in accordance with the usual outcome of post-deregulation. Nordic nominal interest rates exceeded the US rates, as shown in Figure 3.3, as from the mid-1980s. The end of the 1980s saw restrictive monetary and credit policies, with a view to slowing down rates of monetary and credit expansion. High real rates appeared at the beginning of the 1990s (see Figure 3.4) to balance a growing demand for money and slower monetary expansion.[15] Nordic real bond rates were all above the US bond rate from 1986–93. The powerful

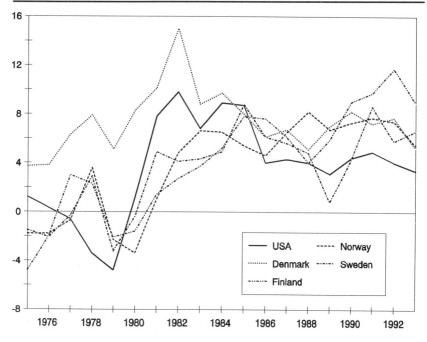

Figure 3.4 Real Nordic *ex-post* bond rates (per cent per annum, government bond rates, yearly average)

Sources: Based on data from OECD, *Economic Outlook*, Vol. 55, June 1994; OECD, *Historical Statistics*, 1983.
Note: The real bond rates are calculated as the nominal bond rate minus next year's inflation (period t + 1).

global trend, with low inflation, became apparent in the Nordic countries as well. However, the downturn in Swedish inflation had a late start – in 1990 – as can be seen in Figure 3.5.

The Nordic area at the end of the 1980s and the beginning of the 1990s was characterized by falling asset values, companies that could not raise prices, and stagnant wages. The exchange rate came under pressure in Finland and Sweden, reflecting the fact that market actors found the current macro-economic and exchange rate policies unsustainable. The real exchange rates had reached levels that were considered to be overvalued in terms of international purchasing power parity, giving rise to pressure for substantial intervention. For a short period the market's anticipation of large exchange rate depreciations in Finland and Sweden were reflected in domestic interest rates that reached a dramatic all-time high. Private and public borrowers had difficulty in complying with debt-service programmes, which meant that interest rates were embodying an implicit high default risk premium. All kinds of imperfections led to higher operating costs for domestic banks resulting in a big gap between lending and deposit rates. This sequence of

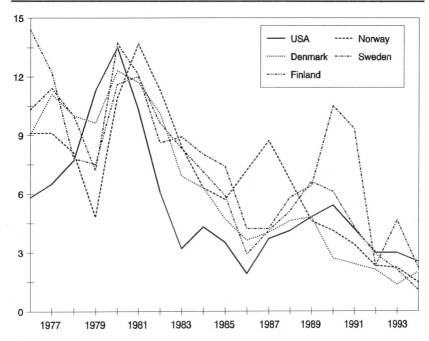

Figure 3.5 Rates of inflation (per cent change in consumer prices, yearly rates)

Source: Based on data from OECD, *Economic Outlook*, Vol. 55, 1994.

events meant that real interest rates were high compared with the 'global' real interest rate level. The global financial crisis was making itself felt even in the Nordic region, which meant that the radical change in savings behaviour following the deregulation went into reverse in recognition of a dawning national financial crisis. I will turn to a discussion about savings in the next chapter.

The development in Nordic national interest rates and the cost of capital may explain the poor growth development. On the national level the experiences of the 1980s reveal the powerful implications of changes in national nominal rates of interest for real economic development. In Denmark the impact of a 1 per cent increase in interest rates is a 0.8 to 1 per cent lower growth in GDP than would otherwise have obtained over a period of three to four years.[16] National models for Norway and Sweden show substantially less sensitivity to interest rates on the part of GDP in these countries, while the model for Finland reveals the highest sensitivity to interest rates among the Nordic countries.[17] However, some of the differences may be explained by differences in the models.

THE ROLE OF CREDIT MARKETS AS A SOURCE OF FUNDS FOR REAL INVESTMENT

In the early 1990s the need to strengthen Nordic competitiveness by developing new products and new companies was a hot topic in the public debate. One crucial question was: how far has the transformation of the small isolated Nordic national financial markets into well-integrated members of the global financial market been conducive to investment, and how far has it enhanced competitiveness and promoted growth? A major issue here concerned access to capital for research and development purposes in general, and for R&D in small and medium-sized companies in particular.

Large companies are generally also internationally recognized and have access to the international capital market, while small and medium-sized companies have to raise funds on their domestic markets. These last also have to pay a premium for distortions associated with their market, e.g. a political risk premium. They are particularly vulnerable in the transition phase of a transformation, since they have to bear costs that large companies can escape,[18] which temporarily gives the large company a competitive advantage over the small ones within the particular country.

The perceived problem of the availability of capital for R&D for small and medium-sized Nordic companies is illustrated in Table 3.6. For instance, at the end of the 1980s, just prior to the abolition of the Swedish capital controls, two-thirds of the small Swedish companies felt that they had difficulty in raising funds for R&D. Was this, then, a serious problem and a matter of national crowding out, or was the difference between small and large companies in this respect just a general indicator that risk capital in the Nordic countries was in short supply? Larger companies can escape the problem by raising funds abroad. Since Denmark, Finland and Norway – unlike Sweden – are dominated by small and medium-sized companies, R&D activities in these countries will be harder hit than they will be in Sweden. Table 3.7 shows that in 1989 funds from the domestic private sector were essential to national R&D activities in all the Nordic countries.[19]

Table 3.6 Lack of risk capital as a barrier to innovation, 1987 (percentage of respondents who see lack of risk capital as a barrier to innovation)

Size of company	Denmark	Finland	Norway	Sweden
Small	47.7	31.7 (65.4[a])	48.7	66.7
Medium	18.2	32.5	36.2	14.0
Large	16.1	32.8	12.2	5.6
Total	35.9	35.1	38.1	22.4

[a] Small and research-intensive companies.

Source: Nordic Industrial Fund, *Innovation Activities in the Nordic Countries*, Oslo, 1991.

Table 3.7 Research and development expenditures in Nordic manufacturing companies in 1989 (financing of R&D as a percentage of total R&D expenditures)

Financed by:	Denmark	Finland	Iceland	Norway	Sweden	Total
Private domestic sources	84	93	85	77	86	85
Public domestic sources	11	6	6	20	12	12
Foreign and other sources	5	1	9	3	3	3
Total Mill. SEK	5,770	8,268	66	6,092	22,362	42,558

Source: Nordic Industrial Fund, *Nordisk FoU-statistik for 1989 og Statsbudsjettanalyse 1991*, 1991.

The value of data such as that presented in the tables can always be disputed. What, in fact, is lack of capital? When credit-rationing obtains, it is easy to imagine that some risky projects, or projects that are hard to assess, will have difficulty in getting funds. Small and medium-sized companies, with no collateral and little recognition, will find it extra hard. But when there is no credit rationing, access to capital boils down to the price of capital and the size of the lending rates. Thus, companies like those in the tables may invoke a lack of risk capital when in fact it is the cost of risk capital that is higher than the price the companies are willing to pay. The problem is a matter of *information asymmetry*, *adverse selection*, and the *pricing of risk* rather than of the *availability of capital*. If the figures are to be interpreted as a lack of capital, i.e. capital provided at the same risk-adjusted rate as the rate their competitors have to pay for capital for similar projects, then the tables indicate a serious problem. But the question remains as to whether – or how far – the transformation of financial markets has aggravated or resolved this problem.

EARLIER STUDIES WITH A SIMILAR REGIONAL FOCUS

Since the Nordic countries belong individually to different supranational blocs, studies of these countries as a group are infrequent. However, a few reports have described the development of the Nordic financial markets in such a framework. Etla *et al.* (1987) is a publication from the Nordic Perspective Group which serves a descriptive purpose, covering developments up to 1986. However, the considerable structural changes that have recently occurred mean that more up-to-date data is urgently required, especially for those who are trying to understand the current deregulation process and its outcomes in terms of markets failure and successes.

Some studies touching on market integration do cover the Nordic countries as a whole, but most of them are concerned mainly with the interest-sensitivity of capital flows, as was pointed out in Oxelheim (1990). In this group we find studies such as Åkerholm and Tarkka (1987) and Virén (1989). Taken together, these studies of changes in capital flows and their relation to interest rate movements or other financial variables, suggest that Nordic financial markets in the mid-1980s were neither perfectly integrated nor perfectly segmented. At the time of writing, in the mid-1990s, no studies have so far been published which cover the period of transition as a whole for the Nordic financial markets in general, or for the bond markets in particular.

At the global level the available empirical studies have not come to any agreement about the appropriate form for an analytical model of integration. Empirical studies which take capital flow as the dependent variable can assume a variety of forms, due to the equally great variety of conditions on which the analyses are based. The main problem, and one which goes a long way towards explaining the sometimes contradictory conclusions, is to find a reliable measure of the size of the capital flow. With this problem in mind I have previously discussed ways of measuring financial integration (Oxelheim 1990). Taking up the Swedish case I then suggested that direct financial integration can be measured by comparing the risk-adjusted interest rate on securities in different currencies and/or on different markets. This approach, involving the modelling of different risk premiums, can be seen as a proxy for the capital flow approach, since the method focuses on the size of a single arbitrage or speculative argument. We will return to this approach in Chapter 5.

CONCLUDING REMARKS ON THE REGIONAL APPROACH

In this chapter we have seen how the Nordic countries constitute a very homogeneous region in many respects, with close-knit economic relations, similar high levels of welfare (and high taxes), and a common cultural and social background. Despite these similarities there are also some major differences between the countries, which suggests that the deregulative process may have proceeded differently in terms of both speed and outcome. The extent to which domestic industry is internationalized varies between the countries, a state of affairs which may also have affected the transformation of financial markets in the individual countries in different ways.

The fact that Denmark's membership of the EU dates back several years, while Sweden and Finland joined as late as 1995 and Norway has remained outside, means that intra-Nordic differences in the globalization process can be expected. Denmark is likely to have been tied more closely to the general European trend than Sweden and Finland. Norway, as a petro-economy, may have deviated from this trend, but in recent periods has remained close to the Nordic developments through the agreement on the European Economic Area (EEA).

The independence of the central banks, which is crucial to the transformation process, is another factor that differs between the Nordic countries. In Finland and Sweden the central banks enjoy considerable independence, while the Danish central bank has a little less. In Norway the central bank has little independence. As regards foreign direct investment, Sweden and Finland differ from Denmark and Norway in having traditionally had a bigger gap between inflow and outflow.

We have also noted deviations between the four countries in terms of real economic performance. During the 1980s and up to the mid-1990s a comparison shows that Denmark, and to some extent even Norway, has performed quite well relative to international standards, whereas Finland and Sweden have remained well below the standard for real economic growth and real growth in investment. Finally, the problem of a high real interest rate and an 'overvalued' currency, which has been found to follow deregulation on a global scale, has also characterized the aftermath of the Nordic deregulations.

NOTES

1　The Scandinavian languages – Danish, Norwegian and Swedish – are very similar, while Finnish belongs to another language family (Ural-altai) and is entirely different. However, a large proportion of the business and finance community in Finland has Swedish as their mother-tongue, or at any rate speak Swedish fluently.
2　NU 1987:2 and NU 1987:5.
3　The Nordic central banks agreed as far back as 1962 to support each other in case of short-term exchange rate problems. In 1976, 1984 and 1992 the agreement was revised.
4　Three main reports were produced concerning restrictions on the establishment of financial institutions, cross-border trade and currency exchange. Additional supplements were made in later years.
5　The terms EU and EC are often used interchangeably in the economic debate and will be so used even in this book.
6　A discussion of the problems in measuring capital flows can be found in Oxelheim (1990).
7　The Finnish figures are too low, as the central bank refers to statistical problems in providing gross figures for all components in the sum.
8　FIM floated for a few hours on 14 November, 1991.
9　'Top ten' refers to a ranking according to value added. See Oxelheim and Gärtner (1994).
10　See OECD (1992).
11　According to *Business Week*, 13 July 1992, these companies were as follows. Denmark: Dampskibsselskapet af 1912 (548), Novo-Nordic (610), Carlsberg (618), and Den Danske Bank (758); Norway: Norsk Hydro (337), and Hagslund Nycomed (753); Sweden: Astra (115), ABB (131), Procordia (217), Volvo (354), Ericsson (367), Sandvik (549), Investor (567), Electrolux (584), SCA (585), Stora (637), Skanska (776), Aga (808), SKF (839), Incentive (914) and Atlas Copco (964). The global rank is given in parentheses.
12　For instance, as has been mentioned above, a high real rate of interest and an 'overvalued' currency.
13　See, for example, De Long (1988).
14　In this case not corrected for deviations from purchasing power parity.
15　The growing demand for money reflected a lower anticipated rate of inflation.
16　See Danish Ministry of Finance (1992).
17　The different Nordic models ADAM (Denmark), BOF4 (Finland), MODAG (Norway) and KOSMOS (Sweden) and the resulting sensitivity of the national

economies to interest rates are compared in Whitley (1990) and in Danish Ministry of Finance (1992).

18   A representative sample of studies in the area of small business access to financial markets is made up of Leland and Pyle (1977); Jensen and Meckling (1976); Day *et al*. (1985); Pettit and Singer (1985); Fazzari *et al*. (1988); and Bates (1990).

19   Lindquist (1991), for instance, claims that funding is not as great a problem as is the lack of good innovative ideas. Gandemo (1989) reports from an interview study that no 'profitable' investment in small Swedish firms (in the sample) has been stopped due to lack of capital.

REFERENCES

Åkerholm, J. and J. Tarkka, 1987, 'Kan de nordiska länderna föra en självständig penningpolitik?', in *Nordiska Ekonomiska Forskningsrådets Årsbok 1986*, Nordic Economic Research Council, Lund, pp. 79–115.

Bates, T., 1990, 'Entrepreneur Human Capital Inputs and Small Business Longevity', *The Review of Economics and Statistics*, Vol. LXXII, No. 4, pp. 551–9.

Danish Ministry of Finance, 1992, *Finansredogørelse*, Copenhagen.

Day, T.E., H.R. Stoll, and R.E. Whaley, 1985, *Taxes, Financial Policy and Small Business*, Lexington Books, Lexington, Mass.

De Long, J.B., 1988, 'Productivity Growth, Convergence, and Welfare: Comment', *American Economic Review 78*, pp. 1138–54.

Etla *et al.*, 1984, *Economic Growth in a Nordic Perspective*, Helsinki.

Etla *et al.*, 1987, *Growth Policies in a Nordic Perspective*, Helsinki.

Fazzari, S., R. Hubbard and B. Petersen, 1988, 'Investment and Finance Reconsidered', *Brookings Papers on Economic Activity 1:1988*, Brookings Institution, Washington, DC, pp. 141–95.

Feldt, K.-O., 1991, *Alla dessa dagar*, Norstedts, Stockholm.

Gandemo, B., 1989, *Näringslivets behov av externt kapital;* in SOU 1989:25 Rapporter till Finansieringsutredningen, Department of Industry.

Jensen, M.C. and W.H. Meckling, 1976, 'Theory of the Firm: Managerial Behaviour, Agency Costs and Ownership Structure', *Journal of Financial Economics* 3, pp. 305–60.

Leland, H.E. and D.H. Pyle, 1977, 'Information Asymmetries, Financial Structure and Financial Intermediation', *Journal of Finance*, pp. 371–87.

Lindquist, M., 1991, *Infant Multinationals*, IIB, Stockholm.

NU, 1987:2, *Industrisamarbete och direkta investeringar*, Nordic Council.

NU, 1987:5, *Industrisamarbete och portföljinvesteringar*, Nordic Council.

OECD, 1992, *National Accounts*, Vol. 1.

OECD, 1994, *Revenue Statistics of OECD Member Countries 1965–1993*, Paris.

Oxelheim, L., 1990, *International Financial Integration*, Springer Verlag, Heidelberg.

Oxelheim, L. and R. Gärtner, 1994, 'Small Country Manufacturing Industries in Transition – the Case of the Nordic Region', *Management International Review*, Vol. 34, No. 4, pp. 331–56.

Pettit, A.R. and R.F. Singer, 1985, 'Small Business Finance: A Research Agenda', *Financial Management* Vol. 14, No. 3 (Autumn), pp. 47–60.

Starck, C., 1992, 'Centralbankens självständighet – argument och internationella erfarenheter', Mimeo, Bank of Finland, June.

Virén, M., 1989, 'Interest Rates, Capital Movements and Monetary Autonomy in the EFTA Countries', *Occasional Paper 26*, EFTA, Geneva.

Whitley, J.D., 1990, 'Comparative Properties of the Nordic Models', ESRC Macroeconomic Modelling Bureau, Mimeo, University of Warwick.

Chapter 4

Saving, investment and deregulation

In the previous chapter we made the point that there is a positive relationship between investment and growth. In the present chapter we will thus limit our study of the savings–growth chain to the link between savings and investment. How much does domestic saving mean to domestic investment? In addressing this question I shall start by discussing the supply and demand for savings, and will then measure the link between gross investment and gross savings in the Nordic countries.[1] This analysis is followed by a closer look at another question: who are the savers? This will be answered first in general terms and then with particular reference to the Nordic countries. The idea is to try to identify possible effects of the financial deregulation on savings patterns. The analysis starts with the relation between gross private and gross government savings. Public borrowing requirements have already been mentioned as one of the driving-forces in the transformation of national financial markets. The role of private domestic savings in meeting these requirements will be emphasized here, and the analysis will pave the way for a discussion of the importance of government bonds later in the book. I shall then discuss the link between household and business savings, with particular reference to the way corporate borrowing requirements are met, thus also highlighting the importance of corporate bonds.

After looking at the role of domestic savings as against savings from abroad in funding domestic investment, we can embark on an analysis of international financial integration. In the mid-1990s the adequacy of global saving flows is a hotly debated issue for the following reasons:

- concern about a potential increase in investment demand in central and Eastern Europe;
- a global wave of privatization;
- rising investments in infrastructure in the Asian NICs;
- the reappearance of certain developing countries as capital importers, and in a slightly longer perspective;
- the ageing population in the OECD countries.

Politicians may distort the channelling of savings in many ways

In many major OECD countries the 1980s meant a slowdown in investments as well as in economic growth. Some would argue that such a drop simply reflects a desired shift towards soft investments and a service-based society. Most economists, however, seem to agree about the importance of a sustained high level of real investment, and about the need to look for an explanation of the decline. The Nordic countries all experienced a sharp decline in the rate of industrial investment in the late 1980s and at the beginning of the 1990s as compared to the OECD average (see Figure 3.2). One may wonder whether this decline was caused by low expected returns or high costs of capital in any relative sense. Was it a policy-induced decline? Did politicians contribute negatively to profit prospects or distort the way savings were channelled into investments?

There are many obvious channels for government influence on corporate profit expectations. In a financial context this influence is exerted primarily by way of market regulations, market operations and taxation. Each of these devices has two dimensions: one *direct*, consisting of the actual size of a change in a tax rate, for instance, and the other *indirect*, consisting of a risk premium charged in compensation for the uncertainty about possible future changes.

Governments may reduce or eliminate some risk premiums by creating confidence in an absolute sense. However, at the same time the government may also increase risk premiums in other areas. By changing the rules of the markets they create a specific risk – a *political risk*. Whenever market rules are altered, companies perceive a change in the basis for their calculations of expected profit as well. Hence, if they are averse to risk they will claim a political risk premium.

To what extent has the slowdown in investment been aggravated, or possibly eased, by financial liberalization and deregulation? On the one hand, external deregulation means a reduction in the barriers to corporate access to international savings. On the other hand, the disappearance of liquidity constraints may change domestic saving behaviour and reduce savings. Weaker liquidity constraints could also, in combination with distorted expected profitability, channel savings away from productive business investment. Moreover, in practice, external deregulation is not neutral: it will mean immediate access to foreign savings for large and well-recognized companies only. Small and medium-sized companies face considerable information barriers which take time to cross. These companies have to take costly action, both internal and external, in order to gain recognition in the international financial markets. For some time at least, this gives the larger companies a competitive advantage in the domestic market. Gradual rather than instant deregulation can provide small and medium-sized companies with time for learning, thus reducing the competitive disadvantage they would otherwise have suffered.

One last question, depending on the outcome of the interaction between the deregulation process and the behaviour of politicians, concerns the extent to which this interaction has meant a higher *relative cost of capital*, in international terms, for companies based in a particular Nordic country. How, and how far, have politicians affected the demand for, and the supply of, savings and the realization of corporate investment plans in this context? In this chapter I shall focus on the savings issue. However, in order to pave the way for a later discussion of the role of political intervention, I will start by examining different definitions of 'cost of capital'.

SOURCES OF FINANCE AND THE COST OF CAPITAL

In principle there are three main ways of financing corporate investments:

- by retained earnings;
- by loans;
- by issues of new equity capital.

Among researchers there is general agreement that regardless of the size and nationality of the company concerned, retained earnings represent by far the most important source. Loans come next, denominated in domestic or foreign currency. As another option, loans can be raised in the banking sector or directly on the market, in which case the bond market is the chief alternative. In this last case there is a choice between borrowing on markets in other countries or in the Euromarket. A characteristic of small companies is that they rarely have direct access to foreign markets. Even if no regulations prevent them, these companies cannot meet the information requirement needed to attract interest in an issue on the bond market. A rating procedure is also generally required, and this costs a lot relative to the 'small' amount borrowed.

The third alternative is to raise capital through an equity issue. New equity can be issued at home or abroad and can be aimed at *insiders*[2] and/or *outsiders*. As in the case of bond issues, issuing equity abroad is generally a very expensive and time-consuming business for companies which are relatively small in global terms (see also Chapter 11). Before the first issue the company has to prepare the way thoroughly, in order to get the issue successfully placed on the market. One way of doing this is to start with a listing on a particular relevant stock market. An alternative is to start with an issue on a less demanding and less prestigious market, but one to which the company may have easier access. The company can then gradually upgrade itself. Some Nordic companies, for instance, have started with a listing on the London Stock Exchange, with the ultimate goal of a direct issue on the US market. If the institutional setting in a national financial market is conducive to bond issues rather than equity issues, a third way to gain international financial recognition for an equity issue may be to start with a bond issue.

The Nordic governments have often interfered in the process of raising funds abroad by imposing a variety of regulations affecting corporate timetables. When the deregulation in this particular context started in the mid-1970s, it took a long time for Nordic companies to catch up in developing an international financial reputation that would bring them access to the markets they were aiming for. By the mid-1990s some seventy Nordic companies, half of which were Swedish, had achieved international recognition such that they could successfully issue equity or bonds in some of the major global financial centres. In addition to these companies another seventy Nordic companies had probably acquired sufficient international recognition to provide themselves with opportunities to place international equity or bond issues successfully.

Cost of capital issues

The cost of capital encompasses debt and equity costs. The expected cost of capital is determined by the rate of return required by investors to purchase and hold equity and debt instruments. Further, the marginal cost of capital is the amount a company must pay to its creditors and stockholders to raise the next increment in the financing. This cost is assumed to increase as a company attempts to raise more and more funds from a given capital market. The corporate cost of capital will be equalized across countries on an ex ante, after-tax and risk-adjusted basis, provided efficiency obtains and there are no major distortional costs. Hence, the complete equalization of the cost of capital means perfect international financial integration.

In assessing the efficiency[3] of markets, and seeing whether or not companies can easily raise capital for investments, economic theory adopts a number of assumptions:

- that the market is composed of numerous individual and institutional participants;
- that the participants have access to sufficient funds to affect security prices;
- that transaction costs are low;[4]
- that consensus obtains when it comes to judging the implications for individual security prices of the available information.

In the real world these assumptions do not often apply. Many markets, for instance, are illiquid regardless of which measure we use, be it the trading volume or the degree to which a market can absorb the sale of a new issue of bonds at the current market price. The test of market liquidity should include the longer-run effect of a new issue on the bond price.

The illiquidity[5] of a market affects the cost of capital, as Figure 4.1 demonstrates. The figure exemplifies the theoretical relationship between the marginal cost of capital and the marginal return on capital (investment opportunity schedule). All projects available to a hypothetical company, ranked by the internal rate of return on investment, are represented by the DD line. The line SS_d is the supply curve of capital on the domestic market and reflects the marginal cost of capital when the company has access to the illiquid domestic capital market only. Further, the line SS_f is the supply curve of capital when the company has access to liquid foreign capital markets. This curve can be seen as representative of the situation of large companies before external deregulation. When the company has access to an illiquid domestic capital market only, its optimal capital budget is LC (local currency) 400 million and its marginal cost of capital, the point K_d, is 20 per cent. When the same company gains access to liquid foreign capital markets, its optimal capital budget is LC 500 million and its marginal cost of capital, the point K_f, drops to 15 per cent.

A company's cost of capital is also affected by market segmentation, as can be seen in Figure 4.1. The line SS_u is the supply curve of capital for a company in an integrated capital market. It shows a reduced marginal cost of capital for all projects in the budget. This curve can be seen as representative of the situation of large companies after external deregulation. Note that at all levels of the capital budget the marginal cost of capital is lower as compared to the situation when the same company was restricted to a liquid but segmented market (the line SS_f). As a result of gaining access to an integrated capital market, the firm's optimal capital budget increases in the example from LC 500 million to LC 600 million. Its marginal cost of capital drops from 15 to 11 per cent.

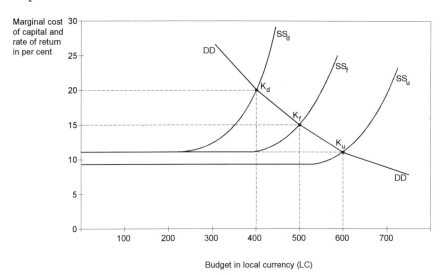

Figure 4.1 Market segmentation, availability of funds, and the marginal cost of capital

Source: Based on Stonehill and Dullum (1981).

The cost of capital concept is utilized in finance theory in two contexts: to measure the expected cost of funds used to finance a company, and as a potential discount rate to apply in discounting the future cash flows of a project. This book focuses on the first of these interpretations, which can be expressed theoretically by several different measures. However, the most common measure is an *expected weighted average cost of capital*. This is calculated by combining the company's expected cost of equity with its expected cost of debt (where the interest cost is assumed to be deductible):

$$K_a = K_e \frac{E}{V} + K_i(1 - t)\frac{D}{V}$$

(4.1)

where

K_a = the company's expected weighted average cost of capital after taxes;
K_e = the expected cost of equity capital;
K_i = the expected cost of debt before taxes;
t   = the company's marginal tax rate;
E   = the market value of the company's equity capital;
D   = the market value of the company's debt capital;
V   = the total market value of the company's equity and debt (E + D).

In estimating the expected costs of equity and debt we encounter a number of problems. We will concentrate in the rest of this book on the expected cost of debt in general, and on the cost of bond loans in particular. But first let us look briefly at the alternative of measuring the expected cost of equity only. Many analysts do this by assuming a 'normal' degree of leverage and cost of debt, and by focusing on the inverted traditional price-earning ratio as an indicator of the relative cost of equity capital. They further claim that this ratio should be seen as a good indicator of the relative overall weighted average cost of capital. However, this is disputable. If we want at least to improve the usefulness of the indicator, it should be corrected along the following lines,[6] allowing also for preferential tax treatment:[7]

$$\frac{s}{1 - z} = \left(\frac{1 - m}{1 - t}\right)\left(\frac{DI + R}{S}\right) + p$$

(4.2)

where

s   = nominal rate of return required by the typical shareholder, net of personal taxes;
z   = effective accruals tax rate on capital gains;
m   = tax rate on dividends;
DI = cash dividend per share;
S   = price per share;

R   = amount of retained earnings;
p   = inflation;
t   = the company's marginal tax rate.

It is clear from formula (4.2) that the after-tax required rate of return (s) can be inferred from ordinary earning-price data (DI + R)/S, provided corrections are undertaken to take preferential tax treatment of capital gains into account.

In empirical studies the cost of capital is often measured under a variety of alternative assumptions; generally, the measurements are based on observed corporate returns. A fundamental premise underlying such an approach is that, in the long run, companies will earn a before-tax rate of return just sufficient to cover their cost of capital, taking account of risks, taxes and the required returns to holders of debt and equity.[8] The measurement will then be based on observed market returns or on accounting returns. Using accounting returns in international comparisons then normally calls for numerous adjustments.[9]

As we have seen, there are many approaches to the concept of the cost of capital. However, regardless of which we choose, it can be stated that the economy of a country benefits from a lower cost of capital due to increased international financial integration. For the individual company the capital cost is conditioned by various company-specific factors such as the company's reputation and its transparency as perceived by creditors. The interest rate is just one source of information about the cost of capital for a company. None the less, in the rest of this book I shall be asserting that it is one of the most important. In Chapter 5 I will look at the cost of debt, and discuss the 'costs' of market segmentation in terms of different relative risk premiums and inefficiencies. The risk premiums are often policy-induced, an issue that will be addressed in Chapters 6–9. Changes in financial infrastructure will also be highlighted.

Problems in international comparisons of the cost of capital

It is generally assumed that in the case of Japan the country's historically high(er) saving rates led to low(er) interest rates. Japan is also regarded as having enjoyed greater advantages from financial leverage,[10] and from financial market structure. These are often referred to as explanations of the relatively low cost of capital in Japan. Many recent studies have focused on the difference between the cost of capital in the USA and Japan. French and Poterba (1991) find the difference to be 1–1.5 percentage points for the period since 1981, whereas McCauley and Zimmer (1989) report a slightly larger difference.[11]

Most of the variations observed in cross-country comparisons can be traced in general to differences in definitions, assumptions, methodology or the particular time period studied. The aim of all the comparisons is to study the cost of capital in terms of investors' pre-tax required (ex ante) returns. But, in practice, observed returns are frequently used as proxies for (ex ante) required returns. Many researchers reduce the analysis to the comparison of real, risk-adjusted interest rates. Some incorporate risk premiums on equity, others prefer a weighted average applying to industry as a whole. Yet another group uses the rental cost of capital needed for ultimately meeting the supply cost of capital. For this purpose, they use the corporate pre-tax required return on real investments, either in aggregate or for particular projects. Yet other researchers take account of differences in risk, referring perhaps to various forms of distress in Japan *vis-à-vis* the USA which might affect the rental cost and the supply cost of capital.[12]

CORPORATE FUNDING DECISIONS AND THEIR MACROECONOMIC IMPLICATIONS

In order to understand the macroeconomic implications of a deregulation it can be instructive to discuss what happens, from a financial point of view, to companies in a recession. The most probable effect will be a downturn in internal funds. Thereafter, the equity share will fall and, consequently, the debt ratio will increase. Any opportunity to raise external equity capital will be limited, and will be a function of direct costs, incentive and selection effects. A negative shock will increase the uncertainty about corporate profit prospects and the cost of capital accordingly. Insiders will find it too costly to sustain a high level of activity based on their own infusion of additional capital. In this situation the company needs new loans to offset the consequences of a negative shock. However, as the debt ratio may have increased, the creditors will be working the other way, trying to reduce the loans granted to the company. This means that the company may have to reduce its level of activity, lay off workers and postpone investments. Due to imperfect capital markets, a negative shock to an economy will cause a drop in the supply of capital to companies. The reduction in the level of corporate activity that follows will further increase the debt/equity ratio as earnings decrease. There will thus be long-term demand and supply effects. As the decline in economic activity influences corporate output negatively, capital market imperfections may explain stagflation. Even with high rates of unemployment, price increases will not be moderated to any great extent.[13]

Capital market imperfections may explain why neoclassical investment models have a very limited explanatory power and why the investment level can oscillate, even if the real rate of interest remains constant.[14] If the level of production reflects expectations about future profitability, the capital cost will be correlated with the company's production and internal funds will become important to it.[15] Theories about capital market imperfections may also explain why investments show much greater volatility than the gross national product.[16] This can be explained by the fact that companies see the postponing of investments as an effective way of reducing their need for capital in a recession. The alternative is to reduce the capacity or the utilization of already employed capital. However, this appears to be more expensive since the real capital has a low second-hand value.

What policy conclusion can be drawn regarding incentives for private sector saving? Bernanke and Gertler (1989, 1990), for instance, stress that it is not only the level of profits that determines the level of activity in an economy; rather, a time effect in allocating savings also has to be considered. It takes some time for savings to be channelled through the financial system to the investors. Direct improvements in access to internal funds and in the cost of these funds may have more immediate and stronger effects on the supply side of an economy. Easing corporate taxes or reducing payroll taxes are ways of increasing corporate access to internal funds and at the same time of reducing the debt/equity ratio. This aspect is important to policy-makers. Imperfections in capital markets imply that measures directed at households will only slowly and with allocative losses be channelled to companies through the financial system.

THE ADEQUACY OF DOMESTIC SAVING

It is a commonly held view in the economic debate of the mid-1990s that savings are allocated inefficiently. The authorities in many countries blame low investment and growth figures on 'inadequate' domestic saving. In this section, we will look for signs indicating that financial liberalization has contributed to distortions in the way capital markets allocate savings. Previously, we mentioned examples of such dysfunctions due to the interaction between financial liberalization and tax wedges.

Savings and investment decisions

Saving and investment decisions are based on intertemporal choices about consumption and production. Low saving rates are thus a case of a preference for current consumption. This preference would be of concern only if it is at the expense of savings required for financing the desired national investment. However, if other countries seem willing to cover any gap, low saving rates need not necessarily cause concern.

Low saving rates might reflect rates of private-sector time preferences due to policy-induced imperfections. In so far as they are seen as nonoptimal from a national viewpoint, policy-makers have to examine whether they are unduly distorting the private sector's saving and investment decisions. Such an examination should include:

- consideration of the level of government saving;

- the impact of social security policy;
- the effect of tax structures on the savings decisions of companies and households;
- the interaction of taxation changes with financial liberalization.

Government saving may be an important factor in mitigating a decline in national saving and investment rates. In a historic perspective changes in private-sector saving have generally been offset by changes in government saving. This substitution can take place in many ways, but is seldom complete. Policy-makers have to consider all possible problems in trying to achieve optimal saving one way or another. In their efforts to achieve an optimal level of national savings by changes in government saving, e.g. tax changes, policy-makers may seriously distort the incentive structure of the market. Thus, this seems to be a dangerous way of accumulating funds associated with high social costs.

A distorted incentive structure may lead to asset inflation of the kind that appeared at the end of the 1980s, contributing to lower savings. The rise in the value of housing and equities then allows household and corporate saving rates to fall without any deterioration in wealth positions. The asset inflation of the 1980s and 1990s, fuelled by the liberalization of the financial market, is generally regarded as having encouraged borrowing to an extent that led to the misallocation of resources, and the aggravation of the ongoing global financial crisis.

If saving is inadequate for the desired corporate domestic investments, funds can in many cases be raised abroad. However, as we have noted in earlier discussions in this book, this is a solution for large and well-known companies only. The small and medium-sized companies have to compete for scarce and more expensive funds in the domestic market.[17] Consequently, this group is exposed to all the policy-induced imperfections in the domestic financial markets, which in turn implies a competitive disadvantage with implications for the regeneration of the national industry. If it could be assumed that all information and other barriers were relaxed, then it would be possible to sustain the desired investment levels with the help of foreign capital inflows for quite long periods of time, i.e. as long as the marginal productivity of domestic capital equals or exceeds the marginal cost of foreign borrowing. Hence, if there were no major cross-border market barriers, a long mismatch between national savings and investment would hardly be a problem.

The international matching of savings and investment

As can be seen in Figure 4.2, a trendwise decline in national savings rates has been a global phenomenon. Generally speaking, the rates were higher in the 1960s and 1970s than in the 1980s and the early 1990s. In the OECD

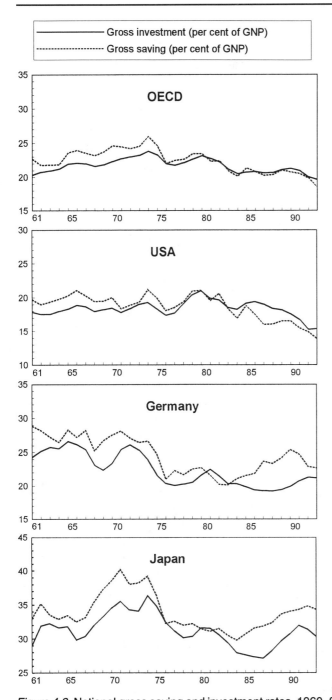

Figure 4.2 National gross saving and investment rates, 1960–92

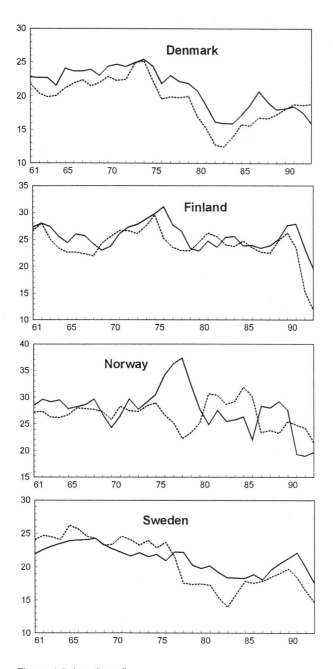

Figure 4.2 (continued)

Source: Based on data from OECD, *National Accounts*, Vol. II, various issues.

countries a substantial downturn in national saving occurred at the time of the first oil crisis. However, in terms of averages, savings and investments have matched each other quite well in an OECD perspective. In some countries such as the USA, Denmark, Finland and Sweden, domestic savings have been insufficient, whereas countries like Germany and Japan have enjoyed a savings surplus. Due to a period of huge investment in the oil-industry Norway shows no clear trend in the investment/saving gap. In terms of net saving ratios, Table 4.1 shows that Sweden and Denmark were below the OECD average in the 1970s and 1980s, whereas Finland and Norway were above it. A fall in net savings over time is obvious in all the OECD countries (except Norway), but it was considerably greater in Denmark and Sweden. One general explanation is provided by OECD (1990): the fall in net saving and investment in relation to net national product reflects a rise in the depreciation of fixed capital. Furthermore, the change in depreciation is due to changes in the composition of the capital stock which now contains more short-lived equipment and less long-lived structures; it is not due to changes in the service lives of assets of a given type.

Table 4.1 Net and gross national saving ratios (as percentage of net and gross national product)

		Averages					
		1960–70	*1971–80*	*1981–90*	*1990*	*1991*	*1992*
United States	Net	10.6	8.9	4.8	3.5	3.2	2.2
	Gross	19.6	19.5	17.3	15.5	15.4	14.5
Japan	Net	25.6	24.6	21.1	22.9	23.3	21.5
	Gross	35.0	34.4	32.2	35.8	34.9	33.6
Germany	Net	19.9	14.3	11.5	14.1	11.9	11.3
	Gross	27.3	23.7	22.5	24.8	22.9	22.7
Denmark	Net	17.4	13.3	7.1	10.2	9.6	10.2
	Gross	23.2	20.3	15.8	18.6	18.2	18.9
Finland	Net	15.7	14.2	10.3	9.2	–2.1	–6.5
	Gross	25.6	26.7	23.9	23.6	15.6	12.6
Norway	Net	16.1	14.0	14.1	11.1	10.5	7.2
	Gross	27.5	27.0	27.1	24.8	24.2	21.5
Sweden	Net	16.6	11.7	5.5	5.6	3.2	0.8
	Gross	25.0	21.0	17.7	18.4	16.4	14.6
Average of major	Net	14.6	13.5	9.4	9.2	8.5	7.4
OECD countries	Gross	23.3	23.5	21.2	21.0	20.3	19.3

Source: Calculations are based on data from OECD, *National Accounts*, Vol. II, various issues.
Note: Net national saving equals net saving/NNP (national income). Gross national saving equals (net saving + consumption of fixed capital)/GNP.

The adequacy of national savings for funding investment and promoting growth was a major concern for policy-makers in many countries at the beginning of the 1990s. But, as has been emphasized above, we are justified in asking how far domestic savings really matter. Concern may have been highly motivated in the 1960s and 1970s.[18] But since then access to global saving has increased and the relationship between domestic savings and investment can be expected to have grown gradually weaker. Many studies do in fact show that even if an increase in domestic saving still makes a substantial impact on a country's capital stock and the productivity of its workforce, the impact is less than it was in the 1960s and 1970s.[19] Among major industrialized countries, the international financial liberalization and integration in the 1980s facilitated the large capital flows necessary to sustain saving/investment gaps for quite long periods.

A declining covariation between national saving and investment rates is, as has been previously mentioned, one of four indicators of an increasing level of international financial integration. A study of the covariation for the Nordic countries reveals that the relationship has shifted over time (see Table 4.2). Denmark shows a gently falling 'saving retention' coefficient(b), indicating the declining but not negligible importance of domestic saving in the funding of domestic investment. In Norway, at the other extreme, gross saving and gross investment ratios were unrelated in the 1980s. In Finland the retention coefficient in the 1980s was still relatively high, whereas it was low and insignificant in Sweden. Moreover, it shows no clear trend in these two countries. Although the empirical result is not as convincing as the result based on pooled data on the period average for twenty-three countries published by OECD (1990),[20] we can conclude that

Table 4.2 Relation between gross national saving and gross investment ratios, 1960–90 (annual data)[a]

Period	Denmark			Finland			Norway			Sweden		
	a	b	R^2	a	b	R^2	a	b	R^2	a	b	R^2
1960 –90	0.05 (0.01)	0.83 (0.05)	0.89	0.10 (0.04)	0.63 (0.04)	0.30	0.45 (0.07)	−0.62 (0.26)	0.13	0.12 (0.01)	0.46 (0.05)	0.74
1960 –70	0.09 (0.04)	0.68 (0.21)	0.50	0.15 (0.05)	0.41 (0.22)	0.20	0.17 (0.17)	0.39 (0.66)	0.00	0.15 (0.01)	0.35 (0.28)	0.05
1970 –80	0.09 (0.01)	0.66 (0.06)	0.92	0.11 (0.09)	0.60 (0.36)	0.14	0.63 (0.10)	−1.20 (0.37)	0.49	0.18 (0.02)	0.18 (0.08)	0.30
1980 –90	0.10 (0.03)	0.51 (0.19)	0.39	0.10 (0.06)	0.59 (0.27)	0.29	0.32 (0.08)	−0.23 (0.30)	0.00	0.15 (0.03)	0.27 (0.19)	0.10

[a] The regression for each country is $I_t/Y_t = \alpha + \beta(S_t/Y_t)$ where I_t, S_t and Y_t are domestic gross investment, gross saving, and gross domestic product. Standard errors are shown below the coefficients.

Source: Calculations are based on data from OECD, *National Accounts*, Vol. II, various issues.

domestic saving still matters in Denmark and Finland and to some extent in Sweden as well.

Nordic countries help each other in financing investment

An analysis of the correlation between Nordic saving and Nordic investment provides a Nordic[21] retention coefficient for the whole period 1960–90, which is higher than the national retention coefficients of Finland, Norway and Sweden but lower than the surprisingly high Danish coefficient.[22] This can be interpreted as meaning that savings flow between the Nordic countries and support investment in the area. However, the coefficients of the subperiods indicate that the investment-promoting value of intra-Nordic saving is diminishing. Another observation that supports the intra-Nordic saving–investment relationship, at least for the 1980s, is the high figures for intra-Nordic foreign direct investment. Finland, for instance, was the most important individual country with respect to foreign direct investment in Sweden in 1988 and 1989; its share was above 30 per cent. Norway was the most important investor in Sweden in 1985 and 1986 (with Finland as the second most important).

Government versus private gross savings

According to the debt-neutrality hypothesis, the private sector anticipates the future tax burden associated with the government debt service, and adjusts its saving accordingly. It is claimed that the way public outlays are financed leaves the flow of funds available for investment and interest rates unaffected, and makes the choice between tax and debt finance irrelevant to macroeconomic outcomes.[23]

As Figure 4.2 shows, falling gross saving/GNP ratios in the Nordic countries reflect to a large extent falling government saving/GNP ratios. In the 1960s and the beginning of the 1970s, government saving contributed significantly to total saving; in all the Nordic countries the contribution was in the range of 20–25 per cent of gross national savings. The years following the first oil crisis brought a downturn in government saving in Denmark, Finland and Sweden. Norway experienced a downturn first following the inverted oil crisis in the mid-1980s. Figure 4.3 suggests that there is some validity in the debt-neutrality hypothesis in the case of the Nordic countries. The impression of a strong negative correlation between public and private sector saving[24] in individual Nordic countries is verified in Table 4.3. For Denmark, Finland and Sweden the correlation has increased considerably in the 1980s as compared to the 1970s. Hence, policy-makers have in some way increased their influence on private-sector saving.[25]

Table 4.4 shows that the average ratio of private saving to GNP in the Nordic countries has been well below that in the major OECD countries, in

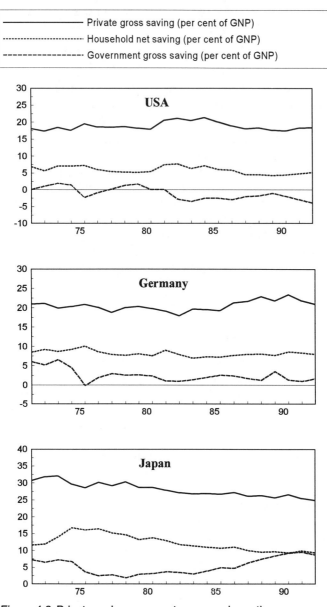

Figure 4.3 Private and government gross saving ratios

particular Japan. Another point to be noted in the table is that in the period 1971–90 the standard deviation in the Swedish savings ratio was considerably above that in the major OECD countries, but it was also above the ratios of the other Nordic countries. As a rule the standard deviations in the Nordic

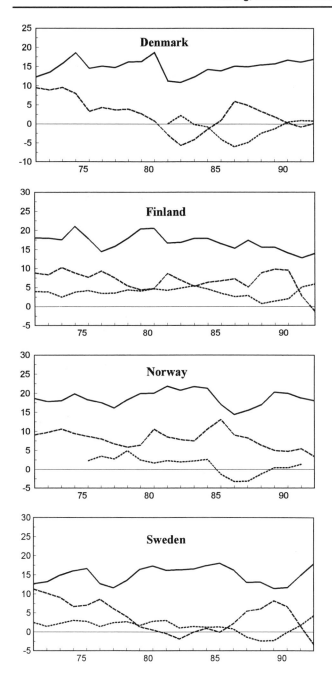

Figure 4.3 (continued)

Source: Based on data from OECD, *National Accounts*, Vol. II, various issues.

Table 4.3 Correlation between government and private saving, 1971–90 (annual data)

Country	1971–90	1971–80	1981–90
USA	−0.53*	−0.61	−0.24
Japan	−0.12	0.64	−0.72*
Germany	0.00	0.13	0.16
Denmark	−0.64*	−0.28	−0.86*
Finland	−0.50	−0.48	−0.80*
Norway	−0.11	0.26	−0.21
Sweden	−0.72*	−0.59	−0.92*

Source: Calculations are based on data from OECD, *National Accounts*, Vol. II, various issues.
Note: * indicates a significant negative correlation at the 1 per cent level. The test results have to be interpreted with caution, however, due to the small number of observations.

countries were above the standard deviations of the major OECD countries, indicating that the conditions for Nordic private saving were more uncertain than in these countries for the 1971–90 period as a whole, which in turn reflects frequent regulative changes in the rules for saving. The higher standard deviation is also consistent with the pattern in Table 4.3, i.e. a higher response on the part of private savings to changes in (expected) government saving. Negative government saving indicates a borrowing need that is sometimes met by domestic government bond issues, placed in the private sector.

As in the rest of the world, a comparison of the 1960s, 1970s and 1980s shows that the level of the average gross private-sector savings ratios in the Nordic countries remained more or less unchanged. The same holds for the Nordic net private savings ratios during the 1970s and 1980s (see Table

Table 4.4 Nordic private saving in an international perspective, 1971–90 (annual data, private gross saving as a percentage of GNP)

	Average			Standard deviation		
	1971–90	1971–80	1981–90	1971–90	1971–80	1981–90
USA	18.8	18.3	19.4	1.2	0.6	1.4
Japan	28.4	30.0	26.7	1.9	1.2	0.6
Germany	20.5	20.2	20.7	1.3	0.6	1.7
Denmark	15.1	14.8	15.4	1.9	0.8	2.5
Finland	17.3	18.2	16.4	1.9	2.0	1.2
Norway	18.7	18.5	19.0	2.0	1.2	2.6
Sweden	14.8	14.5	15.0	2.1	1.9	2.3

Source: Calculations are based on OECD, *National accounts*, Vol. II, various issues.

Table 4.5 Net and gross private sector saving ratios (percentage of net and gross national product)

		Averages			1990	1991	1992
		1960–70	1971–80	1981–90	1990	1991	1992
United States	Net	9.9	9.1	8.7	7.1	7.9	8.0
	Gross	17.7	18.3	19.4	17.5	18.3	18.4
Japan	Net	18.9	19.8	15.5	12.9	12.8	11.9
	Gross	28.7	30.0	26.7	26.6	25.4	24.9
Germany	Net	13.5	11.1	10.2	13.4	11.5	10.2
	Gross	21.1	20.2	20.7	23.5	21.9	21.0
Denmark	Net	–	8.1	7.7	10.9	11.6	11.2
	Gross	–	14.8	15.4	18.3	19.0	18.8
Finland	Net	8.1	6.8	3.0	–0.4	–3.5	–2.9
	Gross	18.2	18.2	16.4	14.1	12.9	13.9
Norway	Net	7.4	4.9	5.6	6.6	5.1	4.4
	Gross	19.4	18.5	19.0	20.0	18.7	–
Sweden	Net	–	5.9	4.0	0.1	3.6	6.8
	Gross	–	14.5	15.0	11.7	14.9	18.0
Average of major	Net	–	12.0	10.7	9.4	9.6	9.6
OECD countries	Gross	–	21.0	21.3	20.2	20.2	20.3

Source: Calculations are based on data from OECD, *National Accounts*, Vol. II, various issues.
Note: Net private sector saving equals (net saving – government saving)/NNP (national income). Gross private sector saving equals (net saving + consumption of fixed capital – government saving – government consumption of fixed capital)/GNP.

4.5). Further, the Nordic rates are consistently lower, and show a dramatic fall in the period following the liberalization. Part of the differences in level may be explained by differences in the definition of saving, but the main reasons are to be found in demographic factors like extremely high participation rates for women (see Table 4.6), insurance programmes, etc. Negative Nordic tax incentives which discourage saving may also explain some of the differences, in the case of both business and household saving. Table 4.7 shows that business saving in the Nordic business sector – as exemplified by Finland and Sweden – is quite low compared to that in Japan and the USA.

As a rule private-sector saving is by far the largest source of financing for national investment. Some of this saving has been intermediated, originating in the household sector, but much of it comes from internally generated funds in business. In addition, the foreign sector is of growing importance in closing the national saving/investment gap. Let us now dig further into private-sector saving, and the balance between household and business saving.

Table 4.6 Demographic and social factors influencing household saving

	Old age dependency ratio[a]	Young age dependency ratio[b]	Participation rate: > 65	Population growth	Participation rate: women
1962–1970					
United States	15.8	49.5	16.7	1.2	45.5
Japan	9.5	37.7	35.6	1.1	56.4
Germany	18.9	35.0	12.4	0.8	48.5
Finland	12.7	41.2	8.8	0.3	61.9
1971–1980					
United States	16.4	38.8	13.2	1.0	54.1
Japan	11.8	35.4	28.0	1.2	53.5
Germany	22.6	32.5	6.8	0.0	49.4
Denmark	21.0	34.7	n/a	1.7	63.6[c]
Finland	16.0	32.7	10.9	0.4	66.2
Norway	22.7	36.7	15.5	0.4	58.9
Sweden	23.6	31.8	7.5	0.3	67.5
1981–1991					
United States	18.2	33.9	10.9	1.0	64.8
Japan	15.5	30.5	24.6	0.5	58.0
Germany	21.8[d]	22.5[d]	3.4[d]	0.4	54.1[d]
Denmark	22.6	27.5	n/a	0.3	75.7
Finland	18.8	28.7	6.5	0.4	72.8
Norway	24.6	31.0	18.8	0.4	69.4
Sweden	26.9	28.3	8.0	0.4	78.5

[a] Population 65 years and over as a per cent of the working-age population.
[b] Population under 15 years as a per cent of the working-age population.
[c] 1971–79.
[d] 1981–90.

Source: Based on data from OECD, *Labor Force Statistics*, various issues.

Household versus business gross savings

A number of measurement problems are attached to the calculation of household saving rates, such as the standardization of the treatment of public and private pension and life insurance schemes, and the inclusion of saving by social security funds.[26] Such adjustments affect the level of the household savings ratio, sometimes substantially.[27] Households can be regarded as the ultimate owners of businesses. Accordingly, they may view retained business earnings as a close substitute for their own saving. More specifically, business earnings, or rather expectations about them, raise market valuations and household wealth. Earlier studies such as Denison (1958) and David and Scadding (1974) found evidence that changes in household saving in the United States were almost completely offset by changes in business saving. Recent studies such as Poterba (1987), Kotlikoff

Table 4.7 Business saving (as a percentage of GNP)[a]

	1960–70	1971–80	1981–90	1990	1991	1992
United States						
Before tax revenue[b]	11.9	11.9	13.0	13.3	12.4	11.9
Direct taxes	3.6	2.8	1.9	1.7	1.5	1.6
Other current payments	0.3	0.4	0.6	0.5	0.5	0.5
Interests	2.1	3.8	5.4	5.6	5.3	4.8
Dividends	3.3	3.2	3.3	3.7	3.1	3.1
Net saving	2.6	1.8	1.8	1.7	2.0	1.8
Net lending	−0.9	−1.7	−0.5	0.2	1.6	0.8
Japan						
Before tax revenue[b]	20.1	18.3	18.3	19.8	19.4	16.5
Direct taxes	3.4	3.6	4.4	5.0	4.6	3.9
Other current payments	0.9	1.2	1.1	0.6	0.7	0.6
Interests	8.3	9.9	8.8	9.6	10.4	8.6
Dividends	2.3	1.6	1.2	1.3	1.3	1.2
Net saving	5.2	2.0	2.7	2.7	1.7	1.5
Net lending	−9.2	−8.0	−5.6	−9.3	−8.4	−5.4
Finland						
Before tax revenue[b]	10.3	8.2	11.0	11.6	10.2	11.6
Direct taxes	2.1	1.4	1.3	1.4	1.8	1.6
Other current payments	1.0	1.4	1.5	1.0	0.9	1.4
Interests	3.4	5.3	7.0	9.7	10.7	11.5
Dividends	0.7	0.5	0.9	1.4	1.7	1.4
Net saving	3.2	−0.4	−0.1	−3.1	−6.2	−5.6
Net lending	−3.8	−6.4	−4.3	−8.5	−5.3	−3.7
Norway						
Before tax revenue[b]	–	12.8[c]	21.3	22.9	22.2	–
Direct taxes	–	4.1[c]	6.1	4.7	4.2	–
Other current payments	–	2.0[c]	2.3	2.0	2.0	–
Interests	–	5.9[c]	9.5	11.0	4.2	–
Dividends	–	1.1[c]	1.7	1.4	0.4	–
Net saving	–	−0.4[c]	2.5	2.9	3.0	–
Net lending	–	–	–	–	–	–
Sweden						
Before tax revenue[b]	–	7.0	12.0	14.2	11.1	15.5
Direct taxes	–	1.0	1.6	2.0	0.4	1.2
Other current payments		1.7	1.8	2.1	2.9	4.2
Interests	–	3.6	5.1	6.5	6.2	6.0
Dividends		0.9	1.7	2.5	2.5	2.6
Net saving	–	−0.2	−0.2	−3.3	−1.9	0.2
Net lending	–	−4.7	−4.5	−10.9	−5.5	−2.3

[a] For the non-financial corporate sector.
[b] 'Before tax revenue' means net operating surplus plus receipts of property income and current transfers.
[c] 1975–80.

Source: Calculations are based on OECD, *National accounts*, Vol. II, various issues.

(1988) and Schultze (1988) have indicated that this no longer holds: Poterba estimated that a fall in US corporate saving of $1 increases household saving by roughly 50–75 cents, while Schultze estimated a change of 55 cents.

The situation might be rather different in small open economies where domestic corporate assets are not all held by domestic households and where households possess a lot of foreign assets. This is the case in the Nordic countries, for instance.

Business saving, including depreciation, provides about half of private saving in most countries. The development of business savings follows profit developments very closely, differing from profits by the amount of dividends paid to shareholders. Further, the development of corporate saving relative to GNP mirrors the low profit shares as well as the low rates of return in the later 1970s and early 1980s. For the rest of the 1980s, it reflects the subsequent sharp rebound in these shares.

Household net saving shows a downward trend

As can been seen from Figure 4.3, net household saving as a percentage of GNP shows a weak downward trend which may be explained by the financial liberalization.[28] The trend was strongest in Japan among the major OECD countries. The Nordic countries, on the other hand, show a short, dramatic downturn at the end of the 1980s, which was later reversed.

Demographic factors may explain differences in national household savings ratios

The life-cycle hypothesis concerns the motives for household saving.[29] For the household sector as a whole saving may depend on demographic factors, current and expected wealth and on institutional or structural characteristics such as financial market opportunities, pension schemes and tax systems, which together interact with individual household saving behaviour to determine aggregate saving ratios.[30]

Demographic factors influencing household saving are shown in Table 4.6. The share of the elderly in the population affects saving. In most countries the old age dependency ratios have increased.[31] Further, the propensity to save seems to have changed. Many investigations show that the propensity is lower for young people as compared to their parents. Summers and Carroll (1987) argued that the increase in the relative well-being of the elderly was an important reason for the drop in the US household savings ratio in the 1980s. Bentzel and Berg (1983) argued that the introduction of the public social security systems, as in Sweden, had a significantly depressing impact on private saving. Generally speaking public pension expenditure rose substantially during the 1980s. This evolution has been even more pronounced in some of the smaller economies, the most striking example being

Sweden, where public pension expenditure represented 5 per cent of GDP at the end of the 1960s and almost 11 per cent by 1985.

According to the life-cycle hypothesis, households have some target as regards wealth needed to support their consumption throughout their lifetime, while according to the permanent-consumption approach, permanent consumption is defined as the amount that can be consumed while leaving net wealth unchanged. In either case, improvements in net worth reduce the need to save.

Changes in inflation often lead to real changes in saving as well as distorting its measurement, because at least in the short term nominal interest rates may not adjust so as to fully offset inflation.[32] Recent econometric studies suggest that inflation-induced wealth effects have had a positive impact on saving in most OECD countries.[33] The effect of interest rate movements on saving is, a priori, ambiguous, since they both have an income effect (via net interest payments) and a substitution effect. Dicks (1988) found a positive interest elasticity of saving for the UK, while Tullio and Contesso (1986) found the same thing for several other countries, among them Sweden.

In most of the OECD countries during the 1980s personal savings ratios fell, while the ratio of personal net worth or net financial wealth to personal disposable income rose significantly. Housing and equity generally accounted for much of the variation in household wealth. Expected capital gains boosted 'wealth' relative to household disposable income. Increases in the value of the houses and land stock have dominated changes in net worth over the past 20–25 years, and in most years were larger than the aggregated value of personal saving. Increases in the aggregated value of real estate were important in Sweden and Norway, too, up to the end of the 1980s. In most countries, the availability of credit through financial liberalization, or general monetary ease as in the case of Japan, is an important factor in explaining the rapid growth of mortgage and property prices. However, the 1987 stock market crisis and the financial and bank crisis that followed somewhat later, reversed the worldwide asset inflation and thus increased the incentives for household saving.

For a long time household savings ratios in the Nordic countries had been low in an international perspective. However, in the 1980s the net savings ratios as a percentage of disposable income showed a very clear picture of changed saving behaviour on the part of Nordic households. Except in Denmark the ratios were negative during the second half of the 1980s in all Nordic countries, as can be seen in Figure 4.4. A change in Nordic saving behaviour seems to have occurred simultaneously with the liberalization of the financial markets.[34] The rapid expansion of the credit stock, and the weaker emphasis on earlier bank savings, increased the household's opportunities for consumption. Consequently, saving, as measured by the OECD *National Accounts*, fell considerably. However, other variables also help to explain the changes in savings statistics. According to Koskela and Virén (1992) falling inflation rates and the

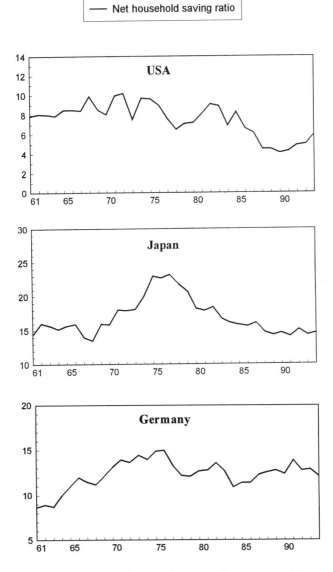

Figure 4.4 Net household saving ratios (percentage of disposable income)

rising real estate prices (and housing wealth) associated with the liberalization of the financial market, as well as a drop in real income growth, all contributed to the decline in the household savings ratios during the 1980s, although with some modifications in the case of Sweden.

Figure 4.4 (continued)

Source: Based on data from OECD, *Economic Outlook*, various issues.

The findings reported in Lehmussaari (1990), based on annual data for 1971–87, support the argument that household consumption and savings behaviour changed after the financial deregulation. In the case of Finland and Denmark, and to some extent Norway, the results indicate that earlier economic relationships appear to have broken down. Only in the case of Sweden does Lehmussaari find data suggesting that structural changes had not taken place since deregulation. He finds a possible explanation in the fact that a Swedish 'grey market' had already developed in the second half of the 1970s. However, the pattern revealed in Figure 4.4 suggests that the pattern of Swedish household savings has been affected as well.

A common feature in the Nordic countries as from 1987 was a noticeable rise in savings ratios. In the early 1990s all countries have returned to a pre-liberalization level of saving. The increase in savings ratios reflects the national appearance of the global financial crisis and the uncertainty about its duration and severity.

CONCLUDING REMARKS ON SAVING AND INVESTMENT

During the economic boom of the 1980s capacity pressure was often discussed as a serious problem in most OECD countries. Lack of funds due to inadequate saving was frequently claimed to be the root of the problem. Various distortions were also said to be hindering the achievement of nationally desired investment levels. But did gaps between desired investment levels at the aggregated firm level and at the national level really exist? If so, how large were they? To answer these questions properly we would have to know the actual level of real investment desired by companies. Unfortunately, we do not know these levels, and so the problem has to be discussed – as in our example of the Nordic countries – in terms of various restrictions on the supply of funds and in terms of the level of the cost of capital.

In this chapter we have discussed the supply of funds in terms of domestic savings. We have found indications, except in the case of Norway, that in the 1980s and at the beginning of the 1990s domestic savings still mattered to domestic investments. The role of domestic savings may be diminishing, but it was substantial in Denmark and Finland. Hence, the efficiency of the domestic financial markets in channelling savings does still matter to some market actors. The liberalization and deregulation have given many companies access to foreign capital, either direct or through banks, but some companies are hindered access to international savings. Without pre-empting the outcome of that discussion, it does seem likely that once the exchange controls were dismantled, obstacles would materialize in the form of information and cost barriers applying predominantly to small and medium-sized companies and to households. The fact that domestic savings seem most important to domestic investment in the case of Denmark, reflects the relatively high number of such companies in that country.

Private-sector saving fell when liberalization started in the different Nordic markets. However, when the financial crisis became apparent, it rose again. The pattern of reaction by savers in the different Nordic countries is so obvious that it can be used to trace the timetable of liberalization as well as the time when the financial crisis was first perceived in each individual country. As the pattern of net household savings shows, the liberalization occurred or gained credibility in Denmark and Norway in the period 1983–85 and in Finland and Sweden from 1987–88. The awareness of the financial crisis as a global phenomenon could be expected to have been contagious. However, this seems not to have been the case in the Nordic region, since the rise in Danish household saving, signalling such an awareness in Denmark, coincided with the downturn in net household savings in Finland and Sweden.

The idea that the very low household savings ratios observed in the Nordic countries represent a problem, is often said to be exaggerated. A more positive interpretation is then said to be that the low ratios can be explained to a large extent by the well-developed public social security systems in these countries and by very high levels of female participation in the labour force. However, even when adjustments are made for this, the savings ratios still seem rather low. A possible explanation may be found in tax disincentives.

An important observation concerns the strong negative correlation between government and private savings. This result is consistent with the Ricardian debt-neutrality hypothesis, which in turn implies that the way in which the governments of the three above countries finance their expenditures causes no crowding-out and has no effect on the interest rate. However, the classical Ricardian hypothesis is based on the private sector adjusting to expectations about future taxes. My interpretation does not subscribe to this view, but implies rather that the adjustment has been caused by regulatory changes and new taxes. Nordic history provides frequent examples of more or less mandatory policy measures influencing savings in the household sector, and of measures aimed at absorbing 'excess profits' from the business sector.

Another important observation is that changes like these have also made Nordic private-sector saving the most volatile relative to OECD standards. Hence the high degree of adaptability of private-sector saving is likely to be an enforced adaptability. Moreover, as will be shown in Chapter 9, the frequent changes in the saving rules imposed by governments signal a propensity to intervene that will lead to a higher relative cost of capital due to higher premiums for political risk. Consequently the investment level will be lower than it would otherwise have been. For existing investments this means – *ceteris paribus* – decreased international competitiveness. The policy-induced influence may differ among the Nordic countries due, among other things, to the way the deregulation process was handled in terms of its *timing*, its *credibility* and the *propensity of policy-makers to intervene*.

Nordic governments should worry not about the level of savings as such, but about whether their own activities – their own claims on resources and, more importantly, their ways of influencing the markets – are unduly distorting private-sector saving and investment decisions. On the positive side, the governments' claims on resources in terms of their need to issue bonds placed with the private sector paved the way for the development of national bond markets. A full assessment of the role of government should also include the interaction of taxation changes with financial liberalization and the effect of tax structures on the savings decisions of companies and households. The importance of the way policy-makers act and how this is reflected in political risk premiums, will be addressed in Chapters 6–9.

NOTES

1   It should be mentioned at an early stage in the chapter that the figures for savings are generally inaccurate. There are many alternative saving concepts, but which one should be chosen as the most useful depends on the purpose at hand. Here we will mostly use gross figures. Detailed definitions will then be given when the measure is used for the first time. Although net figures may often seem more interesting, the problems of measuring and interpreting depreciation and related issues represent a deterrent.

2   'Insiders' refers to people in the company, i.e. primarily management.

3   For a discussion on efficient markets, see Fama (1970).

4   This refers to both brokerage commissions and the spread between bid and offer prices.

5   The liquidity of bond markets will be discussed further in Chapter 12.

6   See Bergström and Södersten (1984).

7   Assuming no issues of new shares

8   See, for instance, Ando and Auerbach (1988). The rate of return on total capital before tax is defined by these authors as earnings after tax plus interest payments divided by the sum of total financial debt and the market value of equity. The return after tax equals earnings after corporate tax plus interest payment, less the imputed corporate tax deduction received for the interest payments divided by the same base.

9   For instance, inflation-related adjustments such as corrections for depreciations under inflationary conditions, corrections for net capital gains accrued to the net debtor, and adjustments for cost of inventory sold. Other adjustments involve institutional differences such as different accounting practices and asset composition.

10   A high Japanese debt/equity ratio as compared to international standards is discussed in Chapter 11.

11   Measured as a weighted average 'cash flow yields'.

12   See Meerschwan (1989) and Hoshi et al. (1989).

13   As discussed in Blinder (1987), for instance.

14   See, for instance, Greenwald and Stiglitz (1990) and Ford and Poret (1991).

15   See, for instance, Fazzari et al. (1988) and Hoshi et al. (1991).

16   See, for instance, Greenwald and Stiglitz (1988).

17   'More expensive' refers to risk-adjusted rates.

18   Feldstein and Horioka (1980) supported such a view by showing that for the

entire period 1960–74 as well as for subperiods, domestic savings passed into domestic investment almost on a one-to-one scale. Their approach has been criticized on many grounds. Obstfeld (1986) claimed that the coefficients simply reflected a missing variable – the growth rate of GDP or a combination of the GDP growth rate and labour's share of national income, while Summers (1988) found the budget deficit to be a plausible explanation of the observed relationship between saving and investment. Genberg and Swoboda (1992) claim that the equality between saving and investment domestically does not, *per se*, have any bearing on the degree of capital mobility. However, Feldstein and Bachetta (1992) reject this criticism. Dooley *et al.* (1987) support the observations of Feldstein and Bachetta and emphasize the need to analyse the extent to which expected returns on physical capital are equalized.

19 See, for example, Obstfeld (1986), Turner (1986), OECD (1990) and Feldstein and Bachetta (1992).

20 One explanation is that I, as opposed to the OECD study, have had to use annual data for individual countries. Feldstein and Bachetta (1992) emphasize that the close relationship between domestic saving and domestic investment is a long-term characteristic and does not hold from year to year. With time-series data, the saving retention coefficients are expected to be much lower than in cross-section analyses.

21 Constructed as an aggregate for the Nordic countries.

22 Surprisingly, considering Denmark's membership of the EU, and the fact that the country was deregulated fairly early. However, the high value is not so surprising if we consider the density of small and medium-size companies.

23 Nicoletti (1988) found very little support for the strict debt-neutrality hypothesis. However, this does not imply that fiscal action has no influence on private saving, since partial offsetting is still likely. Tax distortions are still important and changes in tax rules, even if they are deficit-neutral, can have a strong impact on private saving. In addition, expenditure programmes can change saving patterns.

24 Private-sector saving is the combined saving of the household and business sector.

25 The result does not just reflect a stable current account. Admittedly, by far the highest standard deviation in the current account deficit as a percentage of GDP was registered for Norway. But, of the other countries, Denmark showed the highest and the US the lowest standard deviation.

26 See Boskin (1988).

27 For example, the exclusion of consumer durables from consumption expenditures in the case of the United States, or the inclusion of pension fund saving in Sweden. Inflation adjustment may also change saving patterns.

28 Capital depreciation is difficult to measure, both within and across countries, which tends to make net saving ratios less reliable than gross ratios (depreciation is valued at historical cost or replacement cost).

29 See Ando and Modigliani (1963).

30 For a survey of the determinants of saving, see Sturm (1983).

31 For Japan, Horioka (1986) anticipates declining saving ratios after 1995 due to the changed age structure of the population.

32 See, for instance, Oxelheim (1990).

33 See, for instance, Richardson (1987).

34 Maybe less pronounced in Sweden than in the other Nordic countries.

REFERENCES

Ando, A. and A. Auerbach, 1988, 'The Corporate Cost of Capital in Japan and in the US: A Comparison', in Shoven, J. (ed.), *Government Policies towards Industry in the United States and Japan*, Cambridge University Press, London/New York.

Ando, A. and F. Modigliani, 1963, 'The Life Cycle Hypothesis of Saving: Aggregate Implications and Tests', *American Economic Review*, Vol. 53 (March), pp. 55–84.

Bentzel, R. and L. Berg, 1983, 'The Role of Demographic Factors as a Determinant of Saving', in Hemmings, R. (ed.), *National Saving and Wealth*, Macmillan, London.

Bergström, W. and J. Södersten, 1984, 'Do Tax Allowances Stimulate Investment?', *Scandinavian Journal of Economics*, Vol. 84, No. 2.

Bernanke, B. and M. Gertler, 1989, 'Agency Costs, Net Worth and Business Fluctuations', *American Economic Review* 79, pp. 14–31.

Bernanke, B. and M. Gertler, 1990, 'Financial Fragility and Economic Performance', *Quarterly Journal of Economics* 104, pp. 87–114.

Blinder, A., 1987, 'Credit Rationing and Effective Supply Failures', *Economic Journal*, Vol. 97, pp. 327–51.

Boskin, M., 1988, 'Issues in Measurement and Interpretation of Saving and Wealth', *NBER Working Paper No. 2633*, Cambridge, Mass.

David, A. and J. Scadding, 1974, 'Private Savings: Ultrarationality, Aggregation and Denison's Law', *Journal of Political Economy*, Vol. 82 (March–April), pp. 225–49.

Denison, E.F., 1958, 'A Note on Private Saving', *Review of Economics and Statistics*, No. 40 (August), pp. 261–7.

Dicks, M.J., 1988, 'The Interest Elasticity of Consumer's Expenditure', *Bank of England Working Paper*, No. 20 (December).

Dooley, M., F. Frankel and D. Mathieson, 1987, 'International Capital Mobility: What do Saving–Investment Correlations Tell Us?', International Monetary Fund, *Staff Paper 34*, pp. 503–30.

Fama, E.F., 1970, 'Efficient Capital Markets', *Journal of Finance*, Vol. 25, No. 2, pp. 383–416.

Fazzari, S., R. Hubbard and B. Petersen, 1988, 'Investment and Finance Reconsidered', *Brookings Papers on Economic Activity 1:1988*, Brookings Institution, Washington, DC, pp. 141–95.

Feldstein, M. and P. Bachetta, 1992, 'National Saving and International Investment', in Bernheim, B.D. and J.B. Shoven (eds), *National Saving and Economic Performance*, University of Chicago Press, Chicago, pp. 201–20.

Feldstein, M. and C. Horioka, 1980, 'Domestic Saving and International Capital Flows', *Economic Journal*, Vol. 90, pp. 314–29.

Ford, R. and P. Poret, 1991, 'Business Investment: Recent Performance and Some Implications for Policy', *OECD Economic Studies* 16, pp. 79–131.

French, K.R. and J.M. Poterba, 1991, 'Were Japanese Stock Prices Too High?', *Journal of Financial Economics*, Vol. 29, No. 2 (October), pp. 337–63.

Genberg, H. and A. Swoboda, 1992, 'Saving, Investment and the Current Account', *Scandinavian Journal of Economics*, Vol. 94, No. 2.

Greenwald, B. and J. Stiglitz, 1988, 'Examining Alternative Macroeconomic Theories', *Brookings Papers on Economic Activity 1:1988*, Brookings Institution, Washington, DC, pp. 207–60.

Greenwald, B. and J. Stiglitz, 1990, 'Macroeconomic Models with Equity and Credit Rationing', in Hubbard, R. (ed.), *Asymmetric Information, Corporate Finance, and Investment*, University of Chicago Press, Chicago.

Horioka, C.Y., 1986, 'Why is Japan's Private Saving Rate So High?', Mimeo, IMF, Washington, DC.

Hoshi, T., A. Kashyap and D. Scharfstein, 1989, 'Bank Monitoring and Investment: Evidence from the Changing Structure of Japanese Corporate Banking Relationship', in Hubbard, R.G. (ed.), *Asymmetric Information, Corporate Finance, and Investment*, University of Chicago Press, Chicago.

Hoshi, T., A. Kashyap and D. Scharfstein, 1991, 'Corporate Structure, Liquidity, and Investment: Evidence from Japanese Industrial Groups', *Quarterly Journal of Economics* 105, pp. 33–60.

Koskela, E. and M. Virén, 1992, 'Inflation, Capital Markets and Household Savings in Nordic Countries', *Discussion Paper*, No. 4/92, Bank of Finland.

Kotlikoff, L.J., 1988, 'Intergenerational Transfers and Saving', *Journal of Economic Perspectives*, No. 2 (Spring), pp. 41–58.

Lehmussaari, O.P., 1990, 'Why Saving Fell in the Nordic Countries', IMF Staff Paper, Vol. 37, No. 1 (March), pp. 71–93.

McCauley, R. and S. Zimmer, 1989, 'Explaining Differences in the Cost of Capital', *Federal Reserve Bank of New York Quarterly Review* (Summer), pp. 7–28.

Meerschwan, D., 1989, 'The Japanese Financial System and the Cost of Capital', in Krugman, P. (ed.), *The US and Japan in the '90s: Trade and Investment*, University of Chicago Press, Chicago.

Nicoletti, G., 1988, 'A Cross-country Analysis of Private Consumption, Inflation and the Debt Neutrality Hypothesis', *OECD Economic Studies*, No. 11 (Autumn), pp. 43–87.

Obstfeld, M., 1986, 'Capital Mobility in the World Economy: Theory and Measurement', *Carnegie-Rochester Conference Series on Public Policy*, North-Holland, Amsterdam.

OECD, 1990, *Liberalization of Capital Movements and Financial Services in the OECD Area*, Paris.

Oxelheim, L., 1990, *International Financial Integration*, Springer Verlag, Heidelberg.

Poterba, J., 1987, 'Tax Policy and Corporate Saving', *Brookings Papers on Economic Activity 2*, Brookings Institution, Washington, DC, pp. 455–503.

Richardson, P., 1987, 'Recent Developments in OECD's International Macroeconomic Model', *OECD Economics and Statistics Department Working Papers*, No. 46 (June).

Schultze, C.L., 1988, 'Setting Long-run Deficit Reduction Targets: the Economics and Politics of Budget Decision', Paper delivered to a meeting of the National Academy of Social Insurance, Washington (December).

Stonehill, A.I. and K.B. Dullum, 1981, *Internationalizing the Cost of Capital*, Wiley, Chichester.

Sturm, P., 1983, 'Determinants of Saving Theory and Evidence', *OECD Economic Studies*, No. 1 (Autumn), pp. 147–96.

Summers, L., 1988, 'Tax Policy and International Competitiveness', in Frenkel, J. (ed.), *International Aspects of Fiscal Policies*, University of Chicago Press, Chicago.

Summers, L. and C. Carroll, 1987, 'Why is U.S. National Saving so Low', *Brookings Papers on Economic Activity 2*, Brookings Institution, Washington, DC, pp. 607–42.

Tullio, G. and F. Contesso, 1986, 'Do After-tax Interest Rates Affect Private Consumption and Saving? Empirical Evidence for Eight Industrialized Countries: 1970–83', Commission of European Communities, *Discussion Paper No. 51*.

Turner, P., 1986, 'Savings, Investment and the Current Account: An Empirical Study of Seven Major Countries 1965–1984', *Bank of Japan Monetary and Economic Studies*, (October), pp. 1–58.

Chapter 5

On measuring the international dependence of national financial markets

In this chapter a framework will be presented for measuring the link between national and global markets, i.e. the degree of globalization. In Chapter 4 we looked at the saving–investment correlations as one way of measuring the international integration of national markets. Here we will go on to review the traditional options in measuring this type of integration, after which a possible approach for the present study will be proposed. Three forms of integration can be distinguished: *total*, *indirect* and *direct* financial integration.

POINT OF DEPARTURE

In Chapter 3 we found that small countries like the Nordic countries can be seen as approximate price-takers in a financial context. Consequently, the point of departure in this book is that the Nordic bond rates are determined to a large extent by forces outside the countries themselves. We have also noted that by October 1991 external deregulation had been completed in all four Nordic countries, i.e. *formal* integration had been achieved. The purpose of this chapter is to develop an adequate framework for analysing when *actual* integration came about.

My hypothesis is that actual Nordic credit market integration had been achieved prior to the establishment of formal integration, and that the gap between Nordic national and foreign interest rates – after risk premiums, transaction costs and exchange rate expectations have been eliminated – was gradually declining up to the moment of completion. This probably also applied to the case for the transmission time between foreign interest rate movements and the rates in the individual Nordic countries.

In discussing the factors determining national bond rates, let us leave behind any discussion of the Fisher Effect (Fisher 1930) and move straight on to the link between international markets.[1] This short-cut is motivated by the fact that the empirical evidence for the Fisher Effect is anyway not convincing, irrespective of whether or not tax effects are taken into account.[2] It is widely agreed that the relationship must be extended to include several more variables. This can be done either by adding new 'explanatory' variables to the relationship, or by accepting that the real interest rate is not constant but is a function of the investor's view of the investment environment and of the expectations based on this view. Thus, if investors believe that the chances of a higher return under similar risks are improved by going abroad, one can assume that the foreign return will be used as a benchmark and that the investors will adjust their return requirements upwards. An important item in the investors' evaluation will then concern their expectations regarding exchange rate movements. But, if the exchange rate is somehow to be allowed for in the domestic interest rate, we now come up against the question of the link with foreign markets.

Different forms of financial integration

Financial integration expresses the links between financial markets. It can be defined as total, direct or indirect; financial integration can also vary in strength along a scale from perfect integration to disintegration or segmentation. *Total* financial integration encompasses direct and indirect integration. Perfect (total) integration means that expected real interest rates are the same on the markets in question. Where total financial integration is not perfect, this may be due to imperfect direct and/or indirect financial integration.

Direct financial integration, which is also referred to as capital market integration, is expressed in deviations from 'the law of one price' for financial securities. Under perfect direct financial integration this law obtains, and an investor can expect the same risk-adjusted return on investments on different markets (and borrowers the same loan costs).

If the differential in expected risk-adjusted returns is greater than zero but less than, or the same as, the transaction cost, we can say that the markets are disintegrated but still efficient. The concept of efficiency then refers to the market actors, and means for example that these actors have not failed to exploit the possibility of achieving risk-free profits from covered interest rate arbitrage between markets in different countries. Deviations from this form of efficiency are known as general market inefficiency.

Another form of inefficiency or disequilibrium is caused by the controlling devices of economic policy. If a central bank imposes a relatively high cost on a transaction for deterrent purposes, the transaction cost represents an obvious inefficiency in this sense. If in the shelter of capital controls a central bank manages to keep the domestic interest rate low, and by doing so inserting a wedge between domestic and foreign interest rates, then this is another example of such an inefficiency. The transaction cost and the wedge are both examples of a central-bank generated inefficiency.

Indirect financial integration refers to a situation in which the return on an investment in one country is indirectly linked to the return on investments in other countries. The influence is exerted indirectly through other markets.

By way of disintegrated goods markets and foreign exchange markets, the capital markets are indirectly disintegrated. Perfect *total* financial integration presupposes perfect indirect integration, i.e. perfectly integrated goods and foreign exchange markets, and such a highly coordinated economic policy that the relative political risk premium is zero. If the perfect total integration is global, the world will consist of *one* financial market composed of perfectly linked national capital markets under strict purchasing power parity. Indirect segmentation can occur through foreign exchange markets, i.e. by 'monetary' disintegration. Thus, the degree of monetary integration affects the total financial integration indirectly. The presence of exchange risk can be seen as an expression of monetary disintegration.

The three measures of financial integration mentioned above will be used throughout the book since they are seen as more useful than the measures traditionally used – i.e. degree of capital mobility and degree of substitutability – in analysing the extent to which the disintegration of various markets adds to the gap between expected real interest rates, and to less than perfect total financial integration.

The concept of financial integration can be interpreted in many ways. One of these focuses on *geographical integration*. This form of financial integration, which is addressed in the present study, includes the international integration of national financial markets and the international integration of financial institutions/companies, i.e. cross-border cooperation and ownership relations between banks and between insurance companies. Another interpretation concerns *functional integration*, whereby is meant cross-functional integration, e.g. the extent to which banks add insurance services to their traditional offerings.

DIFFERENT WAYS OF ANALYSING DIRECT FINANCIAL INTEGRATION

In a discussion revolving around the concept of financial integration, the analytical alternatives – apart from the Feldstein–Horioka approach discussed in the previous chapter – are represented in Figure 5.1. The figure illustrates some major approaches in terms of certain key components, such as choice of dependent variable, inclusion of transmission effects, choice of method, choice of markets for comparison, etc.

Alternatives in choosing the dependent variable

According to Figure 5.1 there are three main paths to follow in analysing direct financial integration. The first goes via the *interest-sensitivity* of the capital flows. Here the capital flow is the dependent variable and the gaps between nominal interest rates – with or without forward cover – are among the explanatory variables. From the numerous studies already conducted one

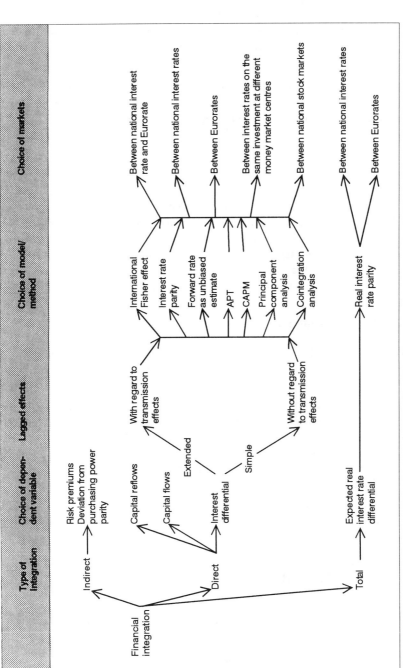

Figure 5.1 Choice of approach in analysing financial integration

Source: Oxelheim (1990).

Note: In addition to the approaches mentioned in Figure 5.1, we have the saving/investment approach suggested by Feldstein and Horioka (1980) and discussed in Chapter 4.

can learn very little about the role of capital flows in linking national markets together. The results from seemingly similar studies often contradict one another, simply because it is so difficult to measure capital flows appropriately. Apart from the general measurement problems mentioned in the introductory chapter, this approach is also problematic when it comes to:

- testing for causality;
- correctly dealing with the endogeneity of many of the most common explanatory variables;
- extending a limited two-country view in a meaningful fashion;
- distinguishing between endogenous and exogenous policy variables.

The second path goes via the *reflow of capital*, but the difficulties are the same. The third main path starts from the law of one price in financial markets. Here, the level of integration is derived from *comparisons of returns on securities*, which are similar in major respects and which are offered on markets in different countries or on the Euromarket. The dependent variable used here is the gap between domestic and foreign interest rates. By isolating an incentive for arbitrage in terms of opportunities for risk-free profits, or incentives for speculation in terms of excess profits, this suggests an approximation and alternative to the first two approaches mentioned above.

Choice of market combinations

If we want to compare the rate of return on a national market with that of another market, there are many alternatives we can choose from:

- comparing with a market in another country;
- comparing with the corresponding securities on the Euromarket;
- comparing securities in the same currency, but issued at different market centres, e.g. the return on a dollar investment in New York with that of an equivalent investment in London;
- using different assets, for instance shares, bank savings, bonds, etc.;
- comparing the cost of loans of various kinds.

The common denominator in all these studies is that the 'law of one price' must obtain on the financial side for the direct financial integration to be perfect.

WHAT DOES THE DIFFERENCE BETWEEN INTEREST RATES TELL US?

The difference between domestic and foreign interest rates can be written as follows:

$$r_d - r_{for} \simeq \hat{s}^* + \text{risk premiums} + \text{inefficiencies} \qquad (5.1)$$

where

r_d = domestic nominal interest rate;
r_{for} = foreign nominal interest rate;
$\hat{s}^*$ = expected relative change in exchange rate.[3]

Moreover, the expected change in the relative exchange rate change here can be expressed in terms of international purchasing power parity:

$$\hat{s}^* \simeq \hat{P}_d^* - \hat{P}_{for}^* + \hat{u}^* \tag{5.2}$$

where

$\hat{P}_d^*$ = expected domestic inflation;
$\hat{P}_{for}^*$ = expected foreign inflation;
$\hat{u}^*$ = expected change in the deviation from purchasing power parity.

By combining (5.1) and (5.2) we obtain the following formula as a basis for a discussion about total financial integration:

$$r_d^{R^*} - r_{for}^{R^*} \simeq \underbrace{\hat{u}^* + \text{risk premiums}}_{\text{indirect segmentation}} + \underbrace{\text{inefficiencies}}_{\text{direct segmentation}} \tag{5.3}$$

The left-hand side of (5.3) gives the difference between expected real interest rates. Expressed on the right-hand side is the level of segmentation – indirect and direct. If all the components on the right-hand side are zero, then the total integration is perfect. Moreover, if the values of $\hat{u}^*$ and the risk premiums deviate from zero, then we have *imperfect indirect financial integration*, while the presence of inefficiencies (values deviating from zero) indicates *imperfect direct financial integration*. The inefficiencies are of three kinds: transaction and information costs, general market inefficiency, and central-bank-generated inefficiency or more general inefficiency due to the implementation of economic policy. In measuring the level of financial integration, a distinction will also have to be made between *permanent* and *temporary* segmentation. By permanent segmentation is meant that the gap between bond rates is of a systematic kind. Temporary segmentation means that the adaptation to changes in the foreign interest level occurs after a certain time-lag.

THE CHOICE OF RATES OF RETURN FOR COMPARISON

In the analysis of integration three types of interest rates can be used: (1) real, (2) nominal, and (3) nominal with foreign rates covered on the forward market for foreign exchange. Starting from these types of interest rates we can distinguish five common expressions of financial integration, which are presented in Figure 5.2. The empirical results for the expressions will be discussed later in this book. A brief explanation only will be provided here.

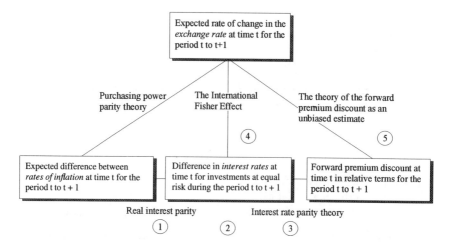

Figure 5.2 Equilibrium relationships[a] between changes in exchange rates, rates of inflation and interest differentials

[a]In approximate, but commonly used forms. For a more detailed description and empirical evaluation of these equilibrium relationships, see, for example, Oxelheim (1985).

Real interest rate parity (1)[4]

The level of (total) financial integration is expressed by real interest rate parity and possible deviations from such parity. Hence, the (total) financial integration of a country's financial market is perfect if the *expected* real interest rate at home is equal to the *expected* real foreign rate. If this is not so, and the financial integration is less than perfect, it is not possible to determine whether the imperfection is of a financial kind, or if it depends on the imperfect integration of other markets.

If the (total) financial integration is not perfect, we have to focus on the level of direct financial integration. As was previously noted, this type of integration should be studied in terms of the law of one price based on interest rates. Such a study can conform with one of the following alternatives.

Comparison between nominal interest rates (2)

This study can be based on an analysis of the difference and correlation between nominal interest rates. However, this alternative has obvious drawbacks in the case of volatile exchange rates, unless the analysis allows for the proposition of economic theory that interest differentials reflect the market's expectation of a movement in exchange rates during the period to which the interest rate refers. But allowing for expected exchange rate changes means that this alternative coincides with alternative (4).

Covered interest parity [5] (3)

One way of eliminating the problem of exchange rate expectations and the possibility of premiums for exchange rate risk, is to study the differential between Eurorates with the foreign interest rate covered on the forward market. An increase in direct financial integration will show up in the form of diminished deviations from international interest rate parity and a smaller flow of arbitrage across the national borders.[6] This also goes for the case of non-existent Eurorates, if the size of political risk premiums is assumed to be constant in the gap between the national and the foreign interest rates. If the size of the transaction cost is taken into account as well, this last alternative also reflects the efficiency of the market.

The International Fisher Effect (4)

A fourth alternative is to add the exchange expectations of the market actors to the alternative of comparing nominal rates only (2), and to study deviations from the International Fisher Effect. If the market actors are averse to risk, the analysis should be extended to consider their demand for risk premiums. The research literature contains relatively few examples of integration studies in which an extended approach of this kind, including premiums for exchange risk as well as political risk, has been adopted. However, there is much to suggest that such an approach provides the best conditions, theoretically and operationally, for determining the level of direct financial integration.

Unbiased forward rates (5)

A fifth alternative is to study the extent to which the forward rate is an unbiased estimate of the future spot exchange rate. The focus in this case is on the existence of an exchange risk premium.

THE LINK BETWEEN FINANCIAL INTEGRATION AND DIFFERENT MARKET IMPERFECTIONS

Table 5.1 provides a simple overview of the way in which total financial integration is linked to different markets. If financial integration is total and expected real rates of interest are equal, then international purchasing power parity and the International Fisher Effect must obtain. An increase in indirect integration, for example in the form of a reduction in risk premiums, will mean a higher level of total financial market integration. Furthermore, an increase in direct financial integration will also mean a higher level of total financial integration. However, it is important to note that a single observation of greater similarity between expected real interest rates cannot reveal

Table 5.1 Outline of total financial integration under different market assumptions

Form of integration	Market in country A		Market in country B	Effect on level of total financial integration if this form of integration does not prevail
Political and cultural integration	Politics and culture in country A	⟸⟹ ⇓	Politics and culture in country B	Political risk premium
Integration of goods market	Goods market in country A	⟸⟹ ⇓	Goods market in country B	Deviation from purchasing power parity
Monetary integration	Foreign exchange market in country A	⟸⟹ ⇓	Foreign exchange market in country B	Premium for exchange risk
Indirect financial integration				The above-mentioned premiums and deviation equal to zero
Direct financial integration	Capital market in country A	⟸⟹	Capital market in country B	Market inefficiencies
Total financial integration	Expected real interest rates the same in country A and country B			All above components equal to zero

Source: Oxelheim (1990).

whether the increased total integration is due to an increase in direct or indirect integration.

APPROACHING A MEASURE OF MARKET EFFICIENCY

Comparisons of prices on different markets coincide to a large extent with the analysis of market efficiency. These studies attract particular attention, since all – or almost all – classical theories in financial theory rest on the assumption of efficient markets.

Let us now adopt the investor's perspective. If we take the case for speculation as a point of departure in discussing possible demands regarding the gap between two prices so that market efficiency may prevail, we must complement the International Fisher Effect with demands from actors with risk aversion and re-write formula (5.3) as:

$$(r_i - r_j) - (\hat{s}_{ij}^* + \text{risk premium}) \leq \text{transaction cost} \qquad (5.4)$$

As long as formula (5.4) holds, there is no argument for speculation in terms of expected excess profits.[7] A special case of this formula is that of covered interest rate arbitrage. By replacing $\hat{s}_{ij}^{*}$ by the forward rate we can identify a potential pure arbitrage argument. This means that the future exchange rate in the arbitrage is known, and that there is consequently no exchange risk. A deviation between the domestic rate and the forward covered foreign rate indicates a segmented capital market. If the deviation is equal to or less than the transaction cost, the market can still be described as efficient. But even if we have eliminated the problem of exchange risk by adopting this approach, there still remains – unless the comparison refers to Eurorates – the question of pricing the political risk.

Efficiency is a prerequisite for interest rate parity. Efficient markets without transaction costs are a prerequisite for perfect direct financial integration. Thus, the money and bond markets can prove to be efficient without being perfectly integrated. If, on the contrary, international markets are inefficient in some way, this means that the integration is not perfect. In the real world this means that a market approaches the state of perfect direct financial integration only asymptotically.

A diminishing deviation from interest rate parity, given unchanged transaction costs, is not a sufficient condition for assuming an increase in direct financial integration. Before we can say anything about such an increase, we have to know whether the (relative) political risk premium has been constant; or, if it has changed, we need to know how much and in what direction.

MEASURING THE LEVEL OF DIRECT FINANCIAL INTEGRATION

We have now progressed to a point where it is reasonable to ask whether the level of international direct financial integration for a single country can be expressed empirically in a simple standardized measure. The answer, whenever such a question is raised, will usually be no, since there are both theoretical as well as empirical lacunae. However, it may be possible to formulate such a measure for individual sectors. A measure of financial integration for the whole financial market of a country thus has to be based on some form of subjective evaluation of all these measures together.

Individual measures for each sector should provide information about two things. First, it should express both permanent and temporary segmentation. Second, the measure should also allow for the possibility of comparison over time, thus providing further information about the development and growth of integration and interest rate transmission. In the next section, we will look at the design of such a measure.

APPLIED DEFINITION AND THE CHOICE OF MODEL

The empirical analysis in this book will be limited to *total* and *direct financial integration*, where direct financial integration is defined in the following way:

> Market A is perfectly (directly) financially integrated with market B if the interest rate on market A – after exchange rate expectations and risk premiums have been allowed for – is the same as the interest rate on market B at every moment in time, and if the politicians on market A have not themselves decided that this should be so.

The basic model for the analysis of direct financial integration in this study represents an extension of the International Fisher Effect,[8] as follows:

$$r_{d,t} - r_{for,t} = \beta_0 + \beta_1 \times (\text{expected exchange rate movement}) + \qquad (5.5)$$

$$\beta_2 \times (\text{exchange risk}) + \beta_3 \times (\text{political risk}) +$$

$$\beta_4 \times (\text{expression of institutional changes}) +$$

$$\beta_5 \times (\text{expression of lagged effects}) +$$

$$\in (\text{random term}).$$

The coefficient β_0 is an expression of *constant risk premiums, transaction costs, general market inefficiency,* and a *possible average (permanent) segmentation,* e.g. a result of interest rate policy autonomy.[9] If the transaction cost, and that part of the risk premium which is included here, remains constant, the comparison of β_0 for different subperiods will reveal whether the general market inefficiency and/or the central-bank-generated inefficiency have decreased. With this method it is difficult to distinguish between these two inefficiencies, and in order to get an idea of the magnitude of the inefficiencies resulting from the central bank manoeuvres, assumptions about the general market inefficiency have to be made.

Let us assume, for example, that a country's aim is a low interest rate, lower even than the comparative rate in the rest of the world, in order to promote more rapid economic growth, a higher rate of investment and lower unemployment than in other countries. Autonomy in the model will then give a negative intercept, once the transaction cost and constant risk premium have been eliminated.

Other β_i coefficients express the linear addition to the interest gap. The coefficient β_2 is the premium for exchange risk. For each unit of increase in the exchange risk, the interest gap increases by β_2 units, etc. The model we have now chosen exhibits certain similarities with an Arbitrage Pricing Theory model (APT model). In both models it is a case of identifying systematic risks and considering the sensitivity of the return on the respective risk factors.

Coefficients estimated in the model indicate the level of direct financial integration

The interest gap under perfect direct integration is always zero, if adjusted for risk premiums, transaction costs, and exchange rate expectations. In a study of imperfectly integrated markets, the analysis of changes in the level of integration must be based on an analysis of the gap and on the adaptation of the domestic interest rate to interest changes in the rest of the world. We can measure this propensity to adapt as expressed by covariation. Adaptation may not occur immediately, and we thus have to look at the strength of the covariation and at the pattern of time lags. For example, if it takes eighteen months before a change in a foreign interest rate makes its full impact on the domestic rate, while a later change of equivalent size needs only nine months before its impact is felt, then we have confirmation of increasing integration, unless the adaptability is an expression of a conscious policy. The shorter the time needed for an external change to reproduce itself on the domestic market, the higher the assumed level of integration between the markets.

The measure of direct financial integration consists of two parts

According to the approach derived from Oxelheim (1990), integration can be expressed by a combination of two parameter values (β_0, t). One of these parameters (β_0) expresses the size of the intercept from which the constant risk premiums have been eliminated. The other parameter (t) expresses the significant time-lag before a foreign interest rate movement reproduces itself in the domestic rate. Perfect direct financial integration is characterized by the parameter pair ($\beta = 0$, t = 0).

In the empirical analysis we may encounter a general analytical problem. While we calculate the β-values, we are also testing whether the model is true. Thus, non-significant parameter values could mean that the model is misspecified. However, by testing the autocorrelation in the residuals, we can get some idea as to whether such a misspecification has occurred. But if we find significant autocorrelation, we immediately face a new problem: we have to decide whether this autocorrelation depends on a misspecified model or on an improper choice of proxy variables. Table 5.2 shows the importance of different indicators of increasing direct financial integration generated by an empirical analysis along the lines suggested here.

PROBLEMS OF MEASUREMENTS AND STANDARDIZATION

Comparisons of international financial markets face many problems of measurement and standardization. The measurement of international capital flows is generally so unreliable that it is impossible to test a model in which the capital flow is a dependent variable. For this and other reasons

Table 5.2 Indicators in the empirical analysis of increasing direct financial integration

---

Factors indicating increased direct financial integration

- shorter time before foreign interest changes affect the domestic rate
- higher correlation between changes in foreign and domestic rates[a]
- the intercept $\bar{\beta}_0$ declines compared with previous periods.

Factors motivating greater belief in the above

- higher multiple coefficient of determination (R^2)
- lower standard error in estimated coefficients[b]
- better Durbin-Watson values[c] (D–W)

---

[a] Here we have the problem of interpretation discussed in Kenen (1976). Kenen emphasizes that strong correlation between interest rates tests market integration only after it has been adjusted for correlation which can be ascribed to underlying common factors. If the correlation is zero, this can be interpreted as a sign of segmentation. If this is not the case, the correlation must be 'purified'.
[b] If the standard errors are small, we can assume that the model contains less uncertainty as a result of multicollinearity, i.e. less linear dependence between the explanatory variables and less competition between these variables to express the same information.
[c] These values should be around two. If autocorrelation obtains, this is an indication among other things that important explanatory variables may have been left out of the model.

which were mentioned at the beginning of this chapter, the interest gap should be used as the dependent variable. But there are still difficulties, one of which concerns the comparability of the interest rates on the markets to be compared.

Another relevant issue in the assessment of integration concerns the elements that should be included in the cost of a financial transaction. In its narrowest form the transaction cost is defined as a function of the bid–ask spread. However, many researchers claim that the elusive cost of information search and the effect of controls should also be included. This disagreement about how to measure the transaction cost is unfortunate, since the existence of such a cost constitutes a sign of disintegration. For instance, one way for a government to segment the home market is by contributing to a high transaction cost and, consequently, to discourage the transaction.

Difficulty in finding comparable interest rates

To make sense, the comparison must involve interest rates that exactly reflect the same conditions regarding fundamental risks. Interest rates should be matched in every respect except the jurisdiction involved and the currency in which the loan is denominated or the investment is made.[10] The rates most frequently used are: day-to-day money rates, rates for treasury bills and treasury discount notes, prime rates, rates on bonds or the official discount rates. Potential sources of error must be considered when comparing interest rates in different countries, or the Eurorate with national market rates, or the interest rates on investments in different currencies on the Euromarket.[11] Moreover, the administrative regulation of interest rates can produce deviations from international rates in the long run on the national markets – deviations which are difficult to interpret. If the risks are not the same, the differences will have to be priced. In order to simplify the interpretation much effort should be spent on matching factors which are linked to a specific instrument, with a view to having the smallest possible difference for which a price has to be set. With this kind of matching it is possible to avoid such problems as differences in liquidity premiums, etc.

In so far as the risk premiums are not constant, the problem of finding unambiguous measures for them still remains. The source underlying the premium, i.e. the risk, thus has to be quantified. This problem will be addressed in the next four chapters and in Chapters 13 and 14, where an analysis of the Nordic bond markets will be presented.

Possible links between risk and return have to be considered. The size of the risk premium is conditional on the behaviour of the market actors. Are the actors steered by an aggregate-portfolio approach, for instance? If so, what form should this aggregate take in our empirical study? By examining published survey data about the corporate view, we can get some grounds for assumptions regarding the patterns of expectation and the attitude to risk of the most important group of market actors.

Bilateral or global comparisons?

The types of model described in the literature for different economies generally start, without further analysis, from the standard assumptions about the financial effects of markets on one another. A polarization occurs in that the financial quantities are assumed to be either exogenously or endogenously determined. Consequently it is often assumed that the United States is sufficiently large to be able to ignore influence from foreign markets. The interest rate in models of the US economy are endogenized. The Nordic countries, on the contrary, are assumed to be countries whose interest rates are wholly determined by influence from foreign markets. Thus, the bond rates are regarded as exogenously determined.

Aliber (1978) claims there are no countries small enough to justify the small-country assumption, and Hartman (1984) suggests that in fact there are probably no countries sufficiently large and dominant to remain unaffected by events in other parts of the world. Hartman also shows that international studies before the 1980s, in which the rate on US treasury bills was taken as given, failed to consider an important reverse chain of cause and effect, i.e. *from* events abroad *to* conditions on the US money market. In 1984, Hartman saw this mutuality as a relatively recent phenomenon. His study covers 1971–78, and it was not until the period 1975–78 that the mutual effects became significant. This can be partly explained by the diminishing importance of the US dollar as the benchmark for price-setting on the global foreign exchange markets.

Although there may previously have been a case for the *bilateral* analysis of the bond rate in a small open economy and the US rate, a broader measure of the 'global' bond rate than the US rate can provide, is now called for. Hartman's results (and those of others) leave the choice of a comparative rate open. The interest rate effect on small economies such as the Nordic can be envisaged in the following form:

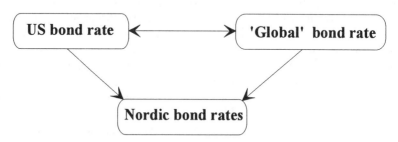

In the case of our present study it is possible that the US bond rate was the leader at the beginning of the study period, and the 'global' rate in the shape of an aggregate of bond rates was the leader in the later years. For this reason I will analyse the gap between the individual Nordic bond rates and both these bond rates in parallel.

How should we define the global bond rate?

One advantage of bilateral studies is that they provide an opportunity for investigating in detail the factors that distinguish markets from one another. For example, it is easier to model the transaction cost. However, an even more important advantage of the bilateral study is associated with the difficulty in finding a suitable definition of the 'global' bond rate. An aggregated bond rate of this kind can be created by combining the rates in the world's largest and economically most important countries, but we then encounter a weighting problem.[12]

The weighting of the different bond rates can be based on *trade weights* of some kind, on *net wealth* of different countries, or on *capital market weights*. Trade weights are to be preferred, since their correlation with bond rate movements can be assumed to be weaker than that of the capital market weights and net wealth weights. If the decision is to use trade weights, the next issue is to choose between bilateral or global weight systems. The weights used in traditional currency baskets are predominantly bilateral weights. IMF's MERM (Multilateral Exchange Rate Model) weights are an example of a system containing global weights. However, according to various studies in the foreign exchange field, where experience on these questions is greatest, the choice does not seem to have any major impact on the results or reliability of the analysis.

An analysis of the deviation from the global bond rate is motivated

On a perfectly functioning market it can be assumed that the investor has international options, i.e. when considering an investment the investor weighs the political risk in one country against the political risk in other countries. This makes for a further complication in the analysis, in that political risks in several countries have to be estimated, and the difference must be ascribed an explanatory value. The use of the global bond rate has a certain technical merit here, since we can assume that only the non-diversifiable political risk and exchange risk remain.[13] This effect, whereby our analysis begins to resemble an APT analysis, is definitely weaker in comparisons with individual countries than in comparisons with the global bond rate. The fact that the capital flows are global in character also speaks for using an aggregate bond rate for purposes of comparison rather than the rate of any individual country.

The transient nature of arbitrage causes measurement problems

In any analysis of the level of financial integration, the time aspect is of considerable importance. Arbitrage and speculation are a question of minutes and seconds. However, it is difficult to study such short-term transactions, at least in a structural model. Limited access to data represents a restriction. Obviously the timing aspect will be expressed less satisfactorily, the longer the period covered by the individual observations. This in turn adds uncertainty to the interpretation of observations of the level of financial integration. However, the use of market data and actual arbitrage situations may not eliminate but will at least reduce the drawbacks of having monthly or quarterly observations, rather than data observed every minute.

LESSONS LEARNT FROM A REVIEW OF THE RELEVANT LITERATURE

A survey of recent literature in this field shows that results about the level of financial integration are inconclusive. Big changes over the last few decades in the pattern of fluctuations in various real and financial variables might explain why there have been different conclusions about the level of financial integration. In some cases even comparisons referring to the same periods and securities have led to different results, depending on the choice of explanatory variables and methods of analysis. We thus have to ask ourselves: what is the situation in the mid-1990s and how robust are the results? From published articles and books it appears that the national financial markets of major industrial countries have approached a state where they constitute a common 'global market'. Hence, for these countries, direct financial integration is almost perfect. In some countries short-term markets (money markets) may still be segmented, whereas long-term markets (bond and stock markets) are perfectly integrated. Transaction costs and exchange risk presumably affect short-term investments more than long-term investments. In other countries, predominantly developing ones, the globalization process is still in its infancy.

In the mid-1990s integration appears to have reached a stage at which mutual causality prevails between US interest rates and the corresponding rates on the various national markets in Europe. This mutual influence can then be transmitted via the Eurorates. Generally speaking integration has gone so far that changes in a 'global' bond rate appear to have a significant effect in most countries. But even if the studied financial variables behave as though the market were largely integrated, no one denies that there is still some scope for a certain amount of domestic monetary autonomy. Admittedly the studies suggest that 'global effects' predominate, but country and regional effects exist as well.

One drawback of the studies published over the last few decades is that, with a few exceptions, they all concern single sectors of the financial market, and the grounds they provide for any inferences about the autonomy of national credit and monetary policies are weak. By focusing exclusively on bond markets the present study falls into the same category. The problem of estimating market expectations of future exchange rates is also frequently evaded and the value of the published results are thus impaired. Few studies have adopted the kind of extended Fisher approach which I have advocated here, and which may seem called for in an analysis of the market in a country lacking formal Euromarket quotations for its financial quantities. No published investigation has provided any indisputable quantitative measures of financial integration or of the changes in the level of integration over time. Moreover, few studies seem to have been devoted to the analysis of the behaviour of market actors.

Some general points arising from a review of recent literature are worth bearing in mind in connection with the empirical analysis of direct financial integration, reported in Chapters 10–14, namely:

- The analysis should be based on ex ante data.
- The influence of the global factor or 'global' bond rate needs to be examined.
- National US dollar interest rates should be used in preference to Eurodollar interest rates, whenever the dollar rate is used as a proxy for the global rate.
- It should be noted that in the 1980s the US dollar rate diminished in

importance as a global factor in comparison with an aggregate global interest level.

- The market's aversion to risk should be taken into account.
- An extension of the International Fisher Effect should be adopted, so that the price of exchange risk and political risk can be included in the model.
- A model of the formation of exchange rate expectations on the market is necessary.
- All compensation which the market can claim for uncertainty in the rules of the market should be included in the premium for political risk.

CONCLUDING REMARKS ON THE MEASUREMENT ISSUE

In this chapter a framework for analysing the integration and globalization of national bond markets has been developed. A model framework is called for in order to prove that the *actual* integration of the Nordic bond markets into the 'global' market, took place prior to their *formal* integration. An analysis of the components of the interest rate gap will show when and how actual integration occurred. For this reason the framework presented here contains a breakdown of the gap between the national and 'global' bond rate into its various components (see Table 5.3).

In this chapter I have emphasized the importance of finding a proxy for the 'global' bond rate in measuring the link between international markets. Some researchers argue that it is predominantly the United States which has affected the domestic bond rates on small national financial markets. However, it has also been found by other researchers that a 'global' rate, as a weighted average of bond rates in major industrial countries, has an effect on the bond rates. The analysis in Chapters 13 and 14 will therefore be not only bilateral but also multilateral.

Table 5.3 Elements of the interest rate gap

NATIONAL BOND RATE

Interest rate gap	Exchange rate expectations	Addressed in Chapter 8
	Exchange rate risk premium	
	Political risk premium	Chapter 9
	Transaction costs	The basis for inefficiencies in terms of regulations is discussed in Chapters 6 and 7, and in terms of market structure in Chapters 10, 11 and 12
	General market inefficiency	
	Central-bank-generated inefficiency	

'GLOBAL' BOND RATE

Since only one sector of the national financial markets – i.e. the bond market – will be empirically examined, Chapter 13 contains a brief analysis of the relation between bond rates and rates on the remaining sectors of the domestic market. International integration will then be measured and discussed in Chapter 14.

NOTES

1   According to the Fisher Effect:

$$r_t = r_t^{R*} + \hat{P}_t^*$$

where

r_t = nominal interest rate;
r_t^{R*} = expected real interest rate;
$\hat{P}_t^*$ = expected inflation.

Thus, Fisher assumed the nominal or money rate to be equal to the sum of an expected real interest rate and an expected inflation rate. Fisher's theory emphasizes that the real rate of interest depends on real phenomena. Since the influence of these phenomena probably changes slowly, the real rate is assumed to be constant in the short and medium terms.

2   The literature in this field is overwhelming. A summary of recent works can be found in Oxelheim (1990), and the main conclusion to be drawn from it, with implications for the present study, are given at the end of this chapter.

3   If the currency is managed within a semi-fixed exchange rate arrangement with a band for intervention, this component can be further decomposed into changes within the band and shifts of the band.

4   The numbers in parentheses refer to numbers in Figure 5.2.

5   Covered interest rate parity gives the following equilibrium premium on the forward market:

$$f = \frac{F_t - S_t}{S_t} = \frac{r_d - r_{for}}{1 + r_{for}}$$

where

f = forward premium in relative figures;
F_t = forward rate;
S_t = spot rate;
r_d = domestic rate of interest;
r_{for} = foreign rate of interest.

The interest rates refer to securities or loans which can be regarded as identical in everything except the choice of currency. Furthermore, the state of equilibrium is stable in the sense that all points that do not satisfy the relationship are assumed to activate market forces which result in a return to equilibrium. Taking transaction costs into account, covered interest parity should be represented by an interval rather than by a point.

6   Hence, the existence of economically exploitable risk-free profits can be interpreted as a lack of integration. By 'economically exploitable' is meant that

7   Excess profits refer to returns exceeding the sum of expected exchange rate changes, risk premiums and transaction costs.

8   The empirical analysis is based on an *assumption* of rational expectations. Provided this assumption is correct, we can concentrate on testing the other constituent of the theory for capital market integration, namely the process of making international financial transactions.

9   In a modelling context caution in the interpretation of the intercept β_0 is generally recommended. Here, however, it is a question of interpolation, i.e. the value 0 is included in the range of all the explanatory variables, and β_0 has an economic meaning.

10 Other risks, e.g. credit risk, liquidity risk, are matched.

11 One such source of error is the tax rates implicit in different rates. By assuming residence treatment we may disregard this source.

12 See, for example, Ingersoll (1987).

13 The political risk premium may be estimated by comparing national and Eurorates for the same currency whenever the latter rates prevail. As one major aim with the capital controls in the Nordic countries was to avoid the emergence of a Euro-equivalent to the domestic currency, such rates seldom exist for the entire period of our study.

REFERENCES

Aliber, R., 1978, 'The Interpretation of National Financial Markets: A Review of Theory and Findings', *Weltwirtschaftliches Archiv*, Vol. 114, No. 3, pp. 448–80.

Feldstein, M. and C. Horioka, 1980, 'Domestic Saving and International Capital Flows', *Economic Journal* [London], Vol. 90, pp. 314–29.

Fisher, I., 1930, *The Theory of Interest*, Macmillan, New York.

Hartman, D., 1984, 'The International Financial Market and US Interest Rates', *Journal of International Money and Finance*, Vol. 3, pp. 91–103.

Ingersoll, J.E., 1987, *Theory of Financial Decision Making*, Rowman & Littlefield, Yale.

Kenen, P.B., 1976, 'Capital Mobility and Financial Integration: A Survey', *Princeton Studies of International Finance*, No. 39, Princeton University.

Officer, L., 1982, *Purchasing Power Parity and Exchange Rates: Theory, Evidence and Relevance*, JAI Press Inc., Greenwich, Conn.

Oxelheim, L., 1985, *International Financial Market Fluctuations*, John Wiley & Sons, Chichester.

Oxelheim, L., 1990, *International Financial Integration*, Springer Verlag, Heidelberg.

Oxelheim, L. and C. Wihlborg, 1987, *Macroeconomic Uncertainty – International Risks and Opportunities for the Corporations*, John Wiley & Sons, Chichester.

Chapter 6

External bond market deregulation

The next four chapters focus on the interplay between economic policy-making and financial deregulation. The aim is to provide the background necessary for a better understanding of the transformation of national bond markets. Together these chapters will provide an insight into the degree of formal financial integration, i.e. the extent to which the national institutional and legal frameworks were harmonized on a global scale. In the discussion above I have suggested that non-financial companies in small national financial markets have to bear the cost of segmentation, in the shape of a 'thin' and insufficient supply of capital as well as a high cost of capital. A feature common to the Nordic markets is that they are all relatively small and, until recently, have been only loosely linked to the global financial market. Hence, by studying non-financial companies in the Nordic region I shall be looking for support for my suggestions. Chapters 6–9 will thus provide various types of information necessary to 'testing' them. The substance of these chapters will then be brought together and analysed in Chapter 14.

The deregulation involves policy coordination, which in turn has both an internal and an external dimension. The *internal dimension* refers to sectoral policy coordination to avoid wedges between sectors which provide opportunities for rent seeking, while the *external dimension* refers to the state at which the international harmonization of policies and laws has arrived on the way towards the complete abolition of capital controls. In this chapter I will address the external dimension and in Chapter 7 the internal.

In this chapter we will also look in more detail at the reasons for the existence of exchange controls in the individual Nordic countries, and how these reasons have varied between the countries and over time. In particular we will examine the reasons that prevailed most recently, i.e. the purpose during the ten years or so leading up to abolition. The different Nordic countries have gone about dismantling their exchange controls in general, and the regulation of bond operations in particular, in different ways, and I will pay special attention to certain distinctive features of their approaches. At the end of the chapter, the status of the deregulation in Finland, Norway and Sweden will be examined in light of the earlier completion of Denmark's external deregulation. In this context I will refer to EFTA (1989), looking at three groups of capital operations which, EFTA claims, correspond to the three stages of liberalization enacted in the EU. The three are:

- operations for trade in goods and services, personal transactions and direct investment;
- operations in the equity and bond market;
- operations in the monetary and exchange rate sphere.

EXCHANGE CONTROLS IN THE REGIONAL PERSPECTIVE

In the period since the Second World War many OECD countries have introduced exchange controls, citing the emergency clauses in the OECD's capital liberalization code regarding balance-of-payment problems.[1] However, as we noted in Chapter 2, few OECD countries were applying their controls by the mid-1990s. Those countries which still had exchange controls in force were generally hoping that these would help to prevent a high private-economy tax burden or general economic uncertainty from leading to the flight of capital.

Under their commitments as members of OECD and EFTA the Nordic countries followed the major European industrial countries in abolishing their exchange control systems at the end of the 1980s and the beginning of the 1990s. In the autumn of 1989 the finance ministers of the Nordic countries set up the common goal of liberalizing all capital movements by 1 July 1990.

Exchange controls in a fixed exchange rate environment

In a general context the paramount purpose of exchange controls is to provide the central bank with monetary autonomy. Every quantitative control measure has a theoretical tax equivalent with the same restrictive effect. Exchange controls on capital flows establish space for inserting a wedge between domestic and foreign interest rates without generating any inflow or outflow of capital. The point of applying the controls is that they should provide some degree of freedom for varying the monetary policy within reasonable limits, without letting exchange rates be affected by capital movements.

Exchange controls, together with a fixed exchange rate arrangement, leave room for autonomy as regards policy. Thus they signal to investors that market interventions can be expected. In view of the uncertainty which these possibilities imply, the risk-averse investor is expected to demand compensation. Consequently, exchange controls may give rise to premiums for political risk. Further, the mere existence of a legal framework of exchange controls – even if it is an inefficient one – also signals that there may be economic–political interventions to come. Hence, an inefficient exchange control may also trigger demands for risk premiums and cause social adjustment costs.

The isolation of a domestic credit market due to the imposition of exchange controls probably calls for considerable sacrifice on the part of some companies, while others are comparatively favoured. Companies with access to the international capital markets belong to this second category. They can escape some of the costs and risk premiums associated with the domestic market which have to be borne by companies that have access to the domestic credit market only.

The purpose of Nordic exchange controls

The role of exchange controls as a supplementary instrument of monetary policy in Nordic economic policy-making has varied over the years. During the 1970s and 1980s their purpose can be summarized as follows:

- To compel the private sector to help cover foreign borrowing needs – without dramatic interest effects on the domestic credit market – and to work for a stabilization of the private amount of debt in foreign currency.
- To reduce private capital movements, which could have given rise to systematic or random disturbances in the external value of the domestic currency.
- To provide arguments for keeping investments inside the country. One such argument – albeit not openly expressed – concerned employment. It was based on the idea that the investing company should perceive the factor price in its own country as more advantageous than the factor price plus the exchange uncertainty of a foreign investment.

Nordic exchange controls have focused on portfolio investments

OECD's capital liberalization code, in which a distinction is made between direct investment and portfolio investment, has been an important factor in the shaping of exchange controls in the Nordic countries. All these countries subscribed to OECD's definition of the two kinds of investment. A *direct investment*,[2] according to this definition, is an investment whose aim is to establish a permanent relationship between the investor and the investment object, particularly such a relationship as will create opportunities for exercising real influence over operations in the 'object', i.e. the company or other unit in which money has been invested. Investments that do not fit this description are classified as *portfolio investments*, and are assumed to have a portfolio purpose.

In the context of the Nordic exchange controls, the concept of foreign direct investment included such things as the acquisition of shares, loans from parent to subsidiary, a parent company's guarantee of a subsidiary's loan, and self-financing over and above the normal consolidation requirement.

The Nordic countries have often invoked OECD's emergency clauses

A fundamental principle underlying OECD's capital liberalization code is that a foreign direct investment should not be hampered by exchange policy or other controls. The Nordic countries undertook to adopt this code. Consequently, what had to be monitored was the genuineness of the direct investments. However, genuineness was not always easy to monitor; the boundaries were often blurred both as regards the original intention and by the changing nature of the investment over time. Under the exchange controls regime the reasons for a possible refusal had to be specified and reference made to the capital liberalization code.

From time to time the Nordic countries invoked the emergency clauses included in the code. One of these implies that the code can be set aside when a country has balance-of-payments problems. For instance, Sweden's position between 1969 and 1981 was that if an investment was to be permitted, it had to be favourable in a broader balance-of-payments context, and not just in light of its direct return. In 1969 a requirement was also introduced regarding the foreign financing of direct investment. This requirement was abolished in 1986.

Many features of the exchange controls were also based on other emergency clauses in the OECD capital liberalization code. One of these clauses stated that a direct investment could be stopped if it was of an exclusively financial kind and might be intended to provide entry to a country's foreign exchange market. Another clause provided for the prohibition of foreign direct investments aimed at circumventing tax regulations. Yet another clause allowed for stopping direct investments which might have serious effects on the national interest.

On certain points the Nordic countries had reservations about the freedom the code allows its member countries, particularly as regards portfolio investments. Nordic exchange controls were in fact aimed primarily at hindering portfolio investments, i.e. restricting over-the-border transactions in shares, bonds (and other securities) and loans. Thus, international sanction was obtained for the basic Nordic rule against this type of capital transaction.

NATURE AND SCOPE OF THE DANISH EXCHANGE CONTROLS

The recently abolished Danish foreign exchange regulations dated back to 1931. In Denmark the process of liberalizing capital movements was a gradual process starting at the beginning of the 1960s. The deregulation gained momentum in the early 1980s and was particularly far-reaching between 1983 and 1985. After the summer of 1985 only a few restrictions remained on the international capital transactions of individuals and private non-financial businesses, and the remaining restrictions were primarily related to capital exports. The distinction between private and corporate credit was difficult to uphold, however, and private consumption benefited directly and indirectly (e.g. by large-scale relending of foreign loans through investment institutions etc.) from the easy access to 'finance loans' without control over their use. In March 1986 restrictions were reimposed on the use of 'finance loans', but this move was not very effective in reducing the credit available for private consumption.

In compliance with both the OECD and the EEC agreements it was a policy objective in itself to integrate the Danish financial markets with the international markets, in order to improve their overall efficiency. In November 1987 the EEC Commission proposed that member countries should discontinue all restrictions on capital movements. The proposal was an element in the building-up of a framework for an integrated financial market in Europe.

Denmark's standpoint on the proposed directive, and thereby on full liberalization, was debated in the Folketing (Danish parliament) on 24 March 1988.[3] This debate provided a basis for the government's accomplishment of the liberalization. According to Danmarks Nationalbank (the Central Bank), the liberalization of the foreign exchange regulations was so far advanced that the few remaining restrictions at the beginning of 1988 had lost any importance in protecting foreign exchange reserves, since such transactions as were still covered by the restrictions could be accomplished by other means.[4] For this reason Danmarks Nationalbank supported the full liberalization of this area in October 1988, which also meant the termination of fifty-seven years of foreign exchange regulation.

Only reporting obligations remained after October 1988

At the end of August 1988, the Ministry of Industry issued a new Executive Order on Foreign Exchange Regulations which came into force on 1 October 1988, thus accomplishing the full liberalization of capital movements. Danish residents were allowed to hold positions in foreign currencies without any limitations on amounts, currencies or the instruments involved. However, some restrictions still remained. As a general rule, Danish private individuals and business enterprises had to file declarations with Danmarks National-bank, giving details of accounts held in banks abroad and the depositing of foreign securities abroad. In addition, private individuals who opened accounts with foreign banks had to authorize the Danish Ministry of Taxation and the Central Customs and Tax Administration to oversee the account and to obtain an undertaking from the foreign bank to file an annual report on the account with the Danish tax authorities. In the case of depositing foreign securities abroad, an undertaking also had to be given by the bank or financial institution abroad to submit annual details of the safekeeping account to the Danish tax authorities. The reporting requirement in this case applied to both private residents and business enterprises.

Danish external deregulation – a gradual process

The step-by-step removal of foreign exchange controls in Denmark appears to have followed roughly the same overall pattern as the Japanese deregulation, although extended over a longer period. Restrictions on commercial credits and loans were removed before the Code came into existence in 1961. For many years Denmark followed a liberal policy when it came to permitting inward direct investments in most sectors of trade and industry and, since the mid-1970s, also in the banking sector.

Whereas the process of liberalization of capital movements in Japan appears to have been closely linked to changes in the country's external economic situation, such links are less evident in the case of Denmark, although the progress of liberalization in general was most pronounced during periods of relatively favourable economic development. Thus the important liberalization measures for 1983–85, shown in Table 6.1, were introduced against the background of rapidly decelerating wage growth, a tight fiscal policy and increasing international confidence in the krone. The removal of capital controls during this period was an attempt to demonstrate the authorities' determination to correct economic imbalances, to strengthen the discipline of domestic wage and price setting, and to underline exchange rate commitments within the European Monetary System (EMS). However, important liberalization measures were also implemented during the second half of the 1980s, despite an initially unfavourable development in the economy.

The liberalization of cross-border bond operations

During the 1970s the gradual relaxation of the Danish rules on cross-border portfolio transactions was initiated, focusing primarily on capital inflows related to transactions in quoted securities. Accordingly, the purchase of Danish krone bonds by non-residents was gradually liberalized in the period 1971–73 and, as can be seen in Table 6.2, was fully deregulated in 1974. A

Table 6.1 A schematic description of the general Danish external deregulation

Direct investment	
Inward	*Outward*
• Largely liberalized before joining EC 1973.	• All deregulation steps applying to inward applies to outward as well.
• Formal permission for large investments required by the Ministry of Industry.	• Higher ceiling in 1983 for amounts involved in regulated transactions.
• Threshold for permission raised to DKK 10 million in 1985.	• Investment by financial institutions is still controlled.

Portfolio investments	
Inward	*Outward*

Equities

• Largely liberalized before joining EC in 1973, when non-residents were allowed to buy listed shares.	• Since January 1984 Danish residents may buy shares on foreign exchanges.
• Further deregulated in 1983, as purchases of non-listed shares were permitted.	• Since June 1985 Danish residents, upon application to Danmarks Nationalbank, may buy non-listed shares and invest in foreign unit trusts.

Bonds and money market instruments

• Largely liberalized, starting 1971.	• Starting in 1978, Danish residents could buy bonds listed in foreign exchanges issued by international organizations of which Denmark is a member.
• Temporary ban on non-residents' purchases of government krone-denominated bonds from February 1979 to May 1983.	• Since May 1983 Danish residents may buy exchange-listed foreign bonds with original maturity greater than two years.
	• Since January 1984 Danish residents may buy Danish bonds denominated in a foreign currency.
	• Since October 1988 foreign securities and Danish bonds issued abroad must be deposited.

Deposits and loans

• Restrictions on commercial credits and loans removed before 1961.	• Since October 1988 loans may be made to non-residents.
• In 1983 finance loans were allowed to be taken up without any qualitative restrictions or control on use of funds. Easing of rules for intra-company loans.	• In October 1988 residents became free to open accounts in foreign banks over and above the prevailing maximum limit for transfer abroad.
• Minimal maturity for 'finance-loans' reduced from five years to one in 1985.	
• In October 1988 it became permitted to settle debts abroad more than 30 days prior to the due date originally agreed. Also, private residents were allowed to raise foreign loans.	

Table 6.2 Danish external deregulation of bond issues and investment

| Character of transaction | Date | | Regulated by act: |
	Regulatory changes	No remaining restrictions from	
Resident Danish companies allowed to issue abroad in foreign currency.	As from June 1985 permitted to issue bonds in accordance with rules concerning financial loans	October 1988	
Resident Danish companies allowed to issue abroad in Danish kroner			
Non-residents allowed to issue in Denmark		October 1988	
Resident Danish investors allowed to invest in international bonds	As from June 1978 permitted to invest in bonds issued by international organizations	January 1984	The Executive Order on Foreign Exchange Regulations issued in pursuance of act No. 372 of 23 December 1964
Non-resident investors allowed to invest in Danish bonds denominated in foreign currency		December 1974	
Non-resident investors allowed to invest in Danish krone-denominated bonds	Ban on Danish government krone-bonds. 2 February 1979 to 1 May 1983	December 1974 (cf. the exception mentioned)	

temporary ban on non-residents' purchases of krone-denominated bonds applied between 2 February 1979 and 1 May 1983. On the outflow side, from the beginning of 1978 residents were permitted to purchase quoted foreign bonds, if they were issued by international organizations of which Denmark was a member. In 1983 the rules were further liberalized, and all restrictions on inward and outward investments in quoted bonds were removed at the beginning of 1984.

Between 1984 and 1988 the rules on the issuing of bonds abroad and on foreign issues in Denmark were substantially relaxed. As from 1 October 1988, the remaining exchange controls were abolished and foreign bonds were introduced on the Copenhagen Stock Exchange. From that date the Danish bond market was, *de jure*, internationally integrated.

NATURE AND SCOPE OF THE FINNISH EXCHANGE CONTROLS

Exchange control systems have been in operation in Finland at different times during the twentieth century. They were imposed in the period 1917–20 because of imbalances in foreign trade and a shortage of foreign exchange. Controls were reintroduced for a short period in the second half of 1931, with a view to supporting the external value of the Finnish markka. At the outbreak of the Second World War in the autumn of 1939, exchange controls were introduced again and remained in force until October 1991.

The main focus of the Finnish exchange control system has changed over time.[5] A great many amendments and revisions were made in the foreign exchange regulations in the early 1970s. A new Foreign Exchange Act was enacted in December 1972 and came into force at the beginning of 1973. It was amended many times over the next ten years or so. In the mid-1970s the emphasis in the authorization procedure of the Bank of Finland (Suomen Pankki) was on the relation of capital imports to the total supply of credit in the economy. In the 1980s exchange regulations were aimed primarily at protecting Finland from external disturbances and securing monetary policy autonomy. At the same time restrictions on investment and borrowing abroad were being gradually removed. A revised Foreign Exchange Act came into force at the beginning of 1985, and was further amended in December 1990. A simplified description of the external deregulation is presented in Table 6.3.

Extreme sluggishness of the Finnish external deregulation

In the government's 1990 bill on the amendment of the Foreign Exchange Act, it was suggested that the Bank of Finland's exchange control powers should be continued. The validity of the Foreign Exchange Act was extended by three years, until the end of 1993. According to the government's bill it was considered necessary at the time to retain the possibility of using exchange control powers in exceptional circumstances because of uncertainties associated with the integrated markets. These uncertainties, in turn, were seen as a result of disturbances caused by speculation. The right to use the exchange control powers 'in exceptional circumstances' was nevertheless restricted to cases in which some severe disturbance endangered the country's external liquidity and the stability of monetary conditions.[6]

All foreign exchange transactions were permitted at the beginning of 1991 unless the Bank of Finland specifically declared them subject to authorization. Thus short-term capital movements were also liberalized. However, the raising of foreign loans by individuals, and the channelling of foreign credit to individuals and comparable entities, continued to be subject to authorization until 1 October 1991. It was decided to continue to monitor the risks

Table 6.3 A schematic description of the general Finnish external deregulation

Direct investment	
Inward	*Outward*
• Restrictions since 1973 were largely removed in 1989 in conjunction with the easing of foreign exchange regulations. • All remaining restrictions were abolished at the beginning of 1991.	• Direct investment regulations from 1973 were removed in August 1988. • All direct investments were allowed for financial and insurance companies from June 1989 and for individuals from July 1990.

Portfolio investments	
Inward	*Outward*

Equities

• In 1973 non-residents became free to purchase shares through intermediaries. They were as of February 1990 no longer bound by this requirement. • Non-residents and residents were allowed to own 20 per cent of a Finnish company's equity in the form of non-restricted shares. In 1987 this figure rose to 40 per cent. • In February 1990 Finnish companies' share issues abroad were exempted from the requirement of prior authorization, which had been very liberal.	• Residents were not allowed to purchase foreign securities as of 1973. In April 1985 foreign companies were exempted. • In January 1986 residents became free to purchase securities quoted on foreign exchanges. • The upper limit on investments was raised from FIM 10,000 to FIM 50,000 in 1987, and to FIM 300,000 in 1988. • Almost all regulations for non-financial institutions were lifted in September 1989 and for individuals in July 1990.

Bonds and money market instruments

• The sale to non-residents of markka-denominated bonds was prohibited during 1985 to 1990. • Non-residents had to purchase Finnish bonds through an authorized bank.	• See description for equities above.

Deposits and loans

• In 1973 authorized banks became free to enter into forward contracts abroad and with residents. • From 1982 authorized banks could take part in foreign bank loan syndicates. • In 1986 the manufacturing and shipping industries became free to raise foreign credits (but not FIM bond debenture issues) of at least five years' maturity under the Central Bank's supervision. • In 1988 the onlending of foreign loans was prohibited to non-authorized agents. • In 1989 the Bank of Finland ceased to require approval for the terms of foreign financial credits for companies. • Further easing occurred for individuals and other companies in 1990 and 1991.	• At the beginning of 1973 the lending of domestic currency to non-residents for use in Finland became allowed without the Bank of Finland's permission up to FIM 50,000 per borrower. • From December 1984 loans to non-residents by authorized banks had to be refinanced using foreign credits. • Since September 1989 business companies are allowed to grant credit with a maturity of over one year to non-residents. • In July 1990 local authorities and some other institutions were also granted this right.

associated with the foreign operations (excluding direct investments) of authorized banks, mortgage banks and credit companies, by issuing licences to operate as an authorized bank or to engage in foreign exchange operations. Likewise, the channelling of credit by finance companies was monitored by this licensing system.

Access to the information needed for the compilation of balance-of-payments statistics was secured for the Bank of Finland by a special provision in the Foreign Exchange Act. Likewise, the monitoring of the risks of the authorized banks and other major financial institutions was based on powers conferred by the Act.

The liberalization of cross-border bond operations

The process of deregulating cross-border portfolio transactions in Finland has been gradual, not to say extremely cautious. However, in some respects – such as allowing non-residents access to markka-denominated bonds in the 1970s and the beginning of the 1980s – the market has been open. The liberal attitude shown by the Finnish authorities in some periods has primarily concerned inward investment, whereas outward portfolio investment remained heavily controlled until the late 1980s. As can be seen in Table 6.4, bond issues and investments, with a few exceptions, were heavily controlled until the beginning of the 1990s, when the Finnish bond market became *de jure* integrated with the global market.

NATURE AND SCOPE OF THE NORWEGIAN EXCHANGE CONTROLS

The basis in law for the Norwegian foreign exchange regulations is an Act of 14 July 1950 (the Currency Control Act), with subsequent additions. Detailed provisions on foreign exchange regulations have been issued by the Ministry of Commerce in pursuance of the Act.

The Norwegian external deregulation – a gradual process

The scope of the Norwegian exchange controls has shifted over time. In the case of foreign exchange regulations and capital controls, the aim in the 1970s was to ensure sufficient reserves to finance the import of indispensable items in case of a sharp drop in export revenues. The growing oil revenues in the late 1970s, and the emergence of more developed and less restricted international financial markets, reduced the need for capital controls for balance-of-payments reasons.

For most of the 1980s the Norwegian foreign exchange regulations and capital controls were aimed at strengthening the possibility of conducting an autonomous monetary and credit policy. To the extent that the regulations

Table 6.4 Finnish external deregulations of bond issues and investment

| Character of transaction | Date | | Regulated by act: |
	Regulated from	No remaining restrictions from	
Resident Finnish companies allowed to issue abroad in foreign currency	December 1948	August 1986[a] August 1990[b]	Bank of Finland foreign exchange regulations based on the Law on Foreign Exchange
Resident Finnish companies allowed to issue abroad in Finnish markka	December 1948	February 1990	
Non-residents allowed to issue in Finland	December 1948	February 1990	
Resident Finnish investors allowed to invest in international bonds	December 1948	July 1990	
Non-resident investors allowed to invest in Finnish bonds denominated in foreign currency	No regulation		
Non-resident investors allowed to invest in Finnish markka-denominated bonds	June 1985 (A temporary ban imposed)	February 1990	Bank of Finland foreign exchange regulations based on the Law on Foreign Exchange

[a] Manufacturing and shipping companies.
[b] All companies.

helped to reduce foreign capital movements, they were regarded as making domestic policy more effective.

The final phase in the external deregulation gained momentum at the end of the 1980s. In the Revised National Budget presented on 11 May 1990, the government proposed a comprehensive dismantling of foreign exchange controls as of 1 July 1990. The proposal was partly based on considerations of structural policy. It stressed the importance of being able to borrow from whatever source charged the lowest effective interest rate, and to be able to invest capital in projects providing the highest effective return. Growing foreign competition was expected to reduce interest margins and the cost of borrowing in the domestic credit system. A comprehensive dismantling of Norwegian foreign exchange controls should thus offer the prospect of efficiency gains.

An equally important prerequisite was that deregulation should facilitate tax control and statistics. As early as the autumn of 1989 the Ministry of Finance had appointed a working group consisting of representatives of the Ministry of Finance, the Directorate of Taxes and the Bank of Norway (Norges Bank), to consider tax control and statistical sources in the context of changes in the foreign exchange regulations. The group presented its report on 1 February 1990, and proposed certain concrete measures.

The 1990 revised national budget drew up a framework for the scope of the deregulation, and specified the foreign exchange controls that should be retained. This was approved by parliament (Storting) in June 1990. On this basis the Bank of Norway then prepared new foreign exchange regulations, which were adopted by the bank's executive board on 27 June 1990, replacing the previous foreign exchange regulations of 6 December 1989. Thus a formal legal basis remains, and the Currency Control Act of 14 July 1950 still provides the basis in law for foreign exchange controls. In conjunction with the deregulation on 1 July 1990, the Ministry of Finance rescinded by the regulation of 22 June 1990 the Ministry of Trade's regulations of 29 July 1955, and delegated the formulation of new provisions to the Bank of Norway.

The far-reaching deregulation of July 1990

The dismantling of foreign exchange controls as from 1 July 1990 was seen by the Bank of Norway as so far-reaching that it seemed most expedient to present it as a reversal of the rules.[7] After many years during which a comprehensive set of regulations had been applied on the principle that all transactions not explicitly permitted were forbidden, the new foreign exchange regulations introduced the opposite assumption, i.e. that all transactions are permitted unless explicitly forbidden.

A number of transactions that had previously been prohibited or subject to restrictive regulation, were now liberalized. From July 1990 Norwegian companies and private individuals were free (i.e. not subject to the Central

Table 6.5 A schematic description of the general Norwegian external deregulation

Direct investment	
Inward	*Outward*
• Prior to July 1990 restrictions applied on certain types of direct investments, e.g. real estate and insurance companies. • Until mid-1984 FDI in Norway had to conform with domestic legal requirements. A currency licence was required.	• FDI was subject to formal authorization, but after 1979 was seldom refused. • Since July 1990 no authorization is required.

Portfolio investments	
Inward	*Outward*

Equities

• Purchases of Norwegian shares by non-residents were progressively liberalized from 1973 onwards. • No restrictions since July 1990. However, some limitations apply to non-residents with a maximum ownership of 15 per cent for banks, 25 per cent for insurance companies, and 40 per cent for shipping companies.	• In June 1984 restrictions on purchases of foreign shares were relaxed. • Since July 1990 all transactions are free, but purchases of shares must be arranged through a Norwegian stockbroker.

Bonds and money market instruments

• In October 1979 non-residents were allowed to buy Norwegian bear bonds up to a value of NOK 1 million. • Non-residents' right to buy Norwegian krone-denominated bonds suspended in November 1984. • In July 1990 non-residents became free to buy krone-denominated bonds.	• In January 1985 restrictions on purchases of foreign bonds were relaxed. • Since July 1990 all restrictions have been abolished, but purchases and sales of foreign securities must take place through a Norwegian stockbroker. • In May 1989 foreigners became free to issue krone bonds in Norway.

Deposits and loans

• Foreign loans required a licence from the Bank of Norway up to July 1990, when this requirement as well as restrictions on household sector borrowing were lifted. • Since July 1987 import-competing manufacturing companies are permitted to finance real investments with foreign loans. • In December 1988 the rules on resident companies' borrowing in foreign currencies were eased. Incorporated companies with a share capital above NOK 500,000 could raise long-term loans in foreign currency without a licence. However, some companies were disqualified, e.g. those in the finance sector.	• Krone loans to other countries were allowed in 1986, but discontinued in 1987. • Restrictions on foreign loans in Norwegian kroner were lifted in July 1990.

Bank's licensing requirement) to make direct investments abroad, e.g. in the shape of purchasing or establishing companies (see Table 6.5). However, direct investment involving the purchase of shares must be done through a Norwegian stockbroker. This holds for other securities as well. The purchasing and establishing of companies abroad had previously been subject to a licensing requirement and a number of restrictions which depended on the structure of the Norwegian enterprise concerned (joint-stock company, limited partnership, etc.), on the country in which the foreign company was located (whether or not the country had a tax agreement with Norway), and on the purpose of acquiring the foreign company. Previous conditions regarding the licensing of direct investments such as the repatriation of profits, the annual reporting of accounts information and new licences due to a switch in the field of operations, ceased to apply as of 1 July 1990. Norwegian business and industry already enjoyed almost complete freedom to borrow in foreign currency before this date, although loans raised directly from a foreign source required a licence from the Bank of Norway. This requirement was annulled on 1 July 1990. At the same time restrictions on household sector borrowing in foreign currency were lifted.

However, the foreign exchange regulations of 27 June 1990 also imposed a few prohibitions and restrictions on residents' rights to conduct transactions with foreign countries or transactions in foreign currency in Norway. Residents still remained barred from taking out life and pension insurance policies with foreign insurance companies. The municipal sector was barred from carrying out transactions involving anything other than a negligible foreign exchange risk. Municipalities and municipal enterprises were thus forbidden to raise or grant financial loans in foreign currency or from underwriting such loans.

Pursuant to the foreign exchange regulations of 27 June 1990, payments and settlements between residents and non-residents have to be reported to the Bank of Norway. If a Norwegian foreign exchange bank is used, it is the bank's responsibility to report the transactions. In the event that a payment arrangement is established with a non-resident without using a Norwegian foreign exchange bank, for example if an account is opened with a foreign bank or a net settlement is arranged with a non-resident business correspondent, the resident is required to notify the Bank of Norway accordingly. Moreover, a resident who opens an account with a foreign bank is required to issue a declaration of consent to disclosure on a special form for this purpose. In the early 1990s, as before, the right to operate payment services in Norway on commercial grounds and to purchase and sell foreign means of payment was still confined to foreign exchange banks and their agents.

The liberalization of cross-border bond operations

As can be seen in Table 6.6, Norwegian regulations on cross-border bond issues and investment have been severe since 1950, although periods of temporary liberalization have occurred. For some years at the beginning of the 1980s, for instance, foreign investors were given access to krone-denominated bonds. Corporate bond issues abroad were subject to a

Table 6.6 Norwegian external deregulation of bond issues and investment

Character of transaction	Date		Regulated by act:
	Regulated from	No remaining restrictions from	
Resident Norwegian companies allowed to issue abroad in foreign currency	1950	July 1990	Law of Exchange Control[a]
Resident Norwegian companies allowed to issue abroad in Norwegian kroner	1950	July 1990	
Non-residents allowed to issue in Norway in NOK or foreign currency	1950	May 1989 July 1990[b]	Issuing control,[c] Law of Exchange Control
Resident Norwegian investors allowed to invest in international bonds	1950	January 1985 (limited access) July 1990	Law of Exchange Control
Non-resident investors allowed to invest in Norwegian bonds denominated in foreign currencies	1950	May 1989[d] July 1990	
Non-resident investors allowed to invest in Norwegian krone-denominated bonds	1950 A temporary liberalization between October 1979 and November 1984.	May 1989[d] July 1990	

[a] Law of 14 July 1950, No 10, concerning exchange control.
[b] In foreign currency.
[c] Law of 25 June 1965, concerning regulations on money and credit (Penge og kredittloven).
[d] Bonds listed with the Oslo Stock Exchange and registered with the Verdipapircentral.

licensing requirement until July 1990. Since 1 July 1990, the foreign exchange provisions include no restrictions on inward and outward portfolio investments in securities. However, residents' purchases and sales of foreign securities must be arranged through a Norwegian stockbroker.

NATURE AND SCOPE OF THE SWEDISH EXCHANGE CONTROLS

The Swedish exchange controls consisted of the Swedish Central Bank's (the Riksbank) application of the foreign exchange regulations based on the Foreign Exchange Act of 1939. Up to 1985, before the more substantial deregulations were initiated, the thrust of the exchange regulations can be summarized rather generally in the following terms:[8]

- Outgoing capital transactions resulting in portfolio investments were generally forbidden; the most important examples were the acquisition of foreign bonds and shares and bank deposits in foreign currencies in other countries.
- Outward and inward direct investments were free but subject to a test of 'genuineness'; in the case of outgoing investments there were financing conditions, and the Höganäs provisions applied.
- Trade-related transactions including the financing of loans were exempted from controls, provided the normal trading conditions were adhered to.
- Incoming portfolio investments in Swedish kronor were forbidden; in practice exceptions were allowed for the acquisition of Swedish stock-exchange-listed shares.
- Incoming portfolio investments in foreign currencies in the form of Swedish borrowing abroad were subject to liberal regulations; by and large this meant that the minimum term of the loan was two years.

Gradual removal of external controls from the mid-1980s

A schematic description of the Swedish external deregulations is given in Table 6.7. In January 1989 it was announced that the hard core of the Swedish exchange controls were to be abolished during the current year. The regulations were then abolished by 1 July 1989. However, some rules still remained which affected the freedom of investors, and which were motivated on grounds of tax control and national statistics. The liberalization of the hard core gave foreigners in particular the freedom to buy and sell interest-bearing securities in Sweden. Residents were free to trade in foreign currency and in interest-bearing securities and to hold accounts in foreign currency with authorized banks. The liberalization measures also covered short-term foreign borrowing, credits and loans in Swedish kronor and household

Table 6.7 A schematic description of the general Swedish external deregulation

Direct investment	
Inward	*Outward*

• FDI in Sweden was restricted before July 1989. However, some limitations still apply to non-residents, in which case permission has to be granted by the authorities. • In general up to 40 per cent of a company's equity capital and 20 per cent of the voting rights can be owned by foreigners in the form of non-restricted shares, which can also be owned by Swedes. • Investment in certain areas, such as real estate, transport and communication is controlled.	• Since January 1989 there are no restrictions on FDI abroad; some restrictions were imposed under the OECD Capital Liberalization Code between 1969 and 1981. Another requirement was introduced in 1969 such that FDI had to be financed abroad, but this was abolished in 1986.

Portfolio investments	
Inward	*Outward*

Equities

• In January 1989 foreigners became free to buy non-listed shares; previously they had been free to buy only listed shares on the stock exchange.	• Since January 1989 Swedes are allowed to buy unrestricted amounts of foreign shares. However, shares have to be deposited with an authorized resident bank or stockbroker.

Bonds and money market instruments

• In July 1989 non-residents became free to buy Swedish krona-denominated bonds; previous restrictions dated from 1939.	• In July 1989 Swedes became free to buy foreign bonds, in conjunction with the removal of foreign exchange restrictions.

Deposits and loans

• All restrictions were lifted in July 1989; previously loans were restricted, but legal entities could borrow in foreign currency for maturities exceeding one year. • The borrowing policy of 1974 was aimed at stimulating Swedish companies to borrow abroad, to help cover the deficits in the current account. Until 1977 the idea was that the government should not borrow abroad. • Between 1977 and 1979, the government was allowed to borrow abroad so long as the amount did not exceed the corresponding deficit in the current account. • In 1984 it was decided that if there is a deficit in the current account, it is to be financed by private foreign borrowing.	• In July 1989 the restrictions were lifted; previously foreigners' loans in Swedish kronor were very restricted.

borrowing abroad. The only remaining restriction was that transactions had to be made through authorized resident banks.

The liberalization of cross-border bond operations in greater detail

The Swedish exchange controls were aimed primarily at cross-border portfolio investment. Table 6.8 shows that cross-border bond transactions were severely restricted for almost fifty years, with a few exceptions. One such major exception was the deregulative step taken in 1974 as a result of the first oil crisis. Swedish companies were encouraged at that time to borrow abroad, to help the government to finance an emerging current account deficit. Resident Swedish companies were allowed to issue bonds in foreign

Table 6.8 Swedish external deregulation of bond issues and investment

Character of transaction	Date		Regulated by act:
	Regulated from	No remaining restrictions from	
Resident Swedish companies allowed to issue abroad in foreign currency	February 1940	1974	Exchange Control Ordinance
Resident Swedish companies allowed to issue abroad in Swedish kronor	February 1940	July 1989	
Non-residents allowed to issue in Sweden	February 1940	July 1989	
Resident Swedish investors allowed to invest in international bonds	February 1940	July 1989	
Non-resident investors allowed to invest in Swedish bonds denominated in foreign currencies	February 1940	1974	
Non-resident investors allowed to invest in Swedish krona-denominated bonds	February 1940	July 1989	

currencies. However, bond issues denominated in Swedish kronor were not allowed until July 1989, when the Swedish bond market became *de jure* integrated.

INTRA-REGIONAL COMPARISON OF THE PROCESS OF EXTERNAL DEREGULATION

The Finnish regulatory situation at the time the Danish deregulation was completed

As Denmark was the first of the Nordic countries to abolish exchange regulations, we can take that country as a Nordic reference case, and can examine the extent to which the Danish deregulations were contagious. At the time when Denmark completed its deregulation, Finland still had many restrictions in force. Most of them applied to long-term capital flows while the short-term flows on the money market remained fairly free, with the exception of financial transactions.

Many controls still remained for operations on the capital market, as regards issuing and trading in securities. Finnish collective investment securities could not generally be sold abroad, and a permit was required for the admission of foreign collective investment securities into the Finnish market. Long-term financial credits and loans were restricted, except for resident foreign exchange banks, parent companies and subsidiaries, which were all allowed to deal in such transactions with non-residents; companies which were engaged in business activity could (without permission) raise credits of at least five-years' maturity to finance their own operations.

Some restrictions were maintained on certain money market operations connected with the issuing and trading in short-term securities. Finnish residents, however, were free to trade in short-term securities abroad. Short-term financial credits and loans were restricted, but resident foreign exchange banks, parent companies and subsidiaries were free under certain conditions to deal in short-term financial credits and loans with non-residents. The issuing of Finnish negotiable instruments and claims on foreign financial markets were restricted, as was the admission of foreign counterparts into Finland. Operations in foreign exchange between residents and non-residents were almost unrestricted. Operations in deposit accounts were fairly free for non-residents, but for residents, apart from financial institutions, upper limits were imposed.

The Norwegian regulatory situation at the time of the completion of the Danish deregulation

Among EFTA's first group of capital operations (see the beginning of this chapter), the most highly controlled area was outward Norwegian direct investment. Operations in real estate and personal capital movements were also still restricted when Denmark became formally deregulated.

The second group was also fairly tightly controlled. Issuing and trading in securities on the domestic and foreign capital markets were heavily restricted, as was the admission of collective investment securities abroad and in Norway. Restrictions also applied to dealings in financial credits and to loans between residents and non-residents.

In the third group, Norway applied a number of controls. Issuing and trading in money market securities were severely restricted, e.g. non-bank residents were not allowed without restriction to issue short-term securities denominated in foreign currencies, nor were issues of foreign securities permitted on the domestic money market. Operations in negotiable instruments and non-securitized claims were restricted for non-bank residents not engaged in commercial practice. Exchange operations, when conducted through exchange banks, were quite free. Operations with deposit accounts were fairly free for non-residents, but generally restricted for residents other than financial institutions, especially if kroner were involved.

The Swedish regulatory situation at the time of the completion of the Danish deregulation

According to EFTA (1989) Sweden imposed controls on capital movements in the same areas as Finland and Norway, but with greater rigidity in practice with regard to the operation of deposit accounts. In the first group of EFTA's classification, the area subject to the most scrutiny was inward and outward direct investment, although applications were never refused in the end. Operations in real estate were fairly free, although there were some limitations for non-residents when it came to acquiring certain types of real estate. In addition, personal capital movements were restricted in some areas, e.g. loans, gifts and endowments.

In the second group, controls still restricted many operations in the capital market. Heavy restrictions applied to issuing and trading in interest-bearing securities on the domestic and foreign capital market, except that resident legal persons could issue such securities in foreign currency with maturities of at least one year. Operations in collective investment securities were fairly free, whereas operations in financial credits and loans between residents and non-residents were in general rather restricted, although resident legal persons could borrow in foreign currency for maturities of at least one year. Commercial credits were free and banks could extend foreign currency loans to non-residents without limit.

The restrictions in the third group referred mainly to money market operations and to operations in deposit accounts. Issuing and trading in short-term securities were heavily restricted, as they were in Norway, although legal persons could borrow against short-term foreign currency paper, provided the borrowing was maintained for at least one year. Operations in negotiable instruments and non-securitized claims were fairly free on the foreign financial market, while there were restrictions on operations in the domestic financial market. Foreign exchange operations could be carried out quite freely by non-residents, but non-bank residents were restricted in their exchange operations with non-residents. Swedes were not as a rule allowed to open foreign currency accounts, with the exception of authorized resident banks, insurance companies, certain shipping companies, importing and exporting companies and residents abroad.

Common features in Nordic external deregulation

Between October 1988 and October 1991 exchange controls in the Nordic countries were abolished, and most foreign transactions came to be allowed. However, restrictions still applied as regards the way such transactions were to be conducted. With few exceptions it was obligatory, for purposes of statistical registration and tax control, to use domestic authorized banks or brokers as intermediaries.

As matters stood before exchange controls were abolished, capital market regulation between the Nordic countries meant that it was easier for a company in any Nordic country to negotiate a business deal, a joint venture or a direct acquisition with a company outside the Nordic group, than with another company in the region. In the first case there was only one regulatory agency to contact and argue with, namely the one in the company's home country. A West German or US company, for example, was more or less free to pursue its part of the deal without consultation with any regulatory body. But if two Nordic companies spotted a mutually beneficial business combination involving capital market transactions, most notably equity arrangements, there were two regulatory bodies to deal with, and they might not be in agreement with another, or be prepared to move fast towards a decision. This situation, of course, made it tempting for Nordic companies to look outside for new business combinations, with the result that there was less intra-Nordic industrial cooperation than the extent of industrial activity in these countries might lead one to expect.

For the purpose of Nordic economic cooperation this was a very unhappy situation, because it may have slowed down or even prevented the building of efficient business combinations on a Nordic basis for which there was great potential. The regulatory framework of the Nordic capital markets prior to their external deregulation constituted a built-in bias in the allocation process which pushed direct industrial cooperation outward to companies in other countries.

The external deregulation may have provided motivation for increasing the share of intra-Nordic investment in individual companies. Small and medium-sized companies especially may have started their internationalization by investing in their Nordic neighbour countries. At the same time there may have been some increase in cooperation due to Nordic regionalism.

CONCLUDING REMARKS ON EXTERNAL DEREGULATION

The existence of a functioning system of exchange controls can be seen as a sign of financial segmentation. If we want to measure the efficiency of the controls, we can try to establish whether the volume of capital movements – given a certain interest differential – is different when exchange controls obtain and when they do not. The comparison is thus hypothetical, and the difficulties involved in measuring effectiveness in this way are obvious.

A 'softer' way of analysing effectiveness is to look at the way the controls were perceived by those who were subject to them. Such an analysis of the effects of the Swedish exchange controls appeared in Oxelheim (1990). It was reported there that the restrictions which the exchange controls imposed on corporate opportunities for acting to the best economic effect also led to corporate demands for compensation, i.e. a premium for political risk. The managers in an interview study, reported in Oxelheim (1990), declared that although they were seldom denied permission when they applied for it, the *mere existence* of an institutional framework compelling them to make such an application signalled uncertainty about the outcome of their next application. Thus, they used to claim premiums for repatriating their capital to Sweden, and for investing it within the sphere of influence of the Swedish government and the Swedish Central Bank.

We have already noted above that Nordic politicians made agreements setting goals for external deregulation. The timing for the completion of this external deregulation was not well coordinated, however, which may have generated a lot of extra tension in the slowest countries. In Denmark general external deregulation started in the 1960s, and was more or less complete by the mid-1980s, just about when the other Nordic countries were beginning. Sweden finished next, with all its remaining exchange controls lifted by mid-1989. Norway followed in mid-1990. At that time Finland still had some exchange controls in force, mainly concerned with short-term foreign borrowing. But by October 1991 Finland's external deregulation was complete, as was also the formal deregulation of the entire Nordic area. Denmark, Sweden and Norway all adopted a gradual deregulation approach, as did Finland – albeit at a considerably slower pace.

At the end of the 1980s Denmark had to stick to the EC-agreement of financial liberalization, and may have put pressure on its Nordic neighbours. At first glance the Danish deregulation appears to have generated spill-over effects among its Nordic neighbours. However, a closer examination of a 'calendarium'[9] covering most of the Nordic policy measures that may have affected capital flows, reveals that the dates when a decision was taken or, in some cases, when the implementation of a particular deregulatory measure occurred, do not fall into any convincing pattern for Nordic policy coordination, on either a week-by-week or a month-by-month basis.

Turning to the deregulation of the bond market, we find that the formal deregulative process in the Nordic countries diverged in the case of cross-border bond issues and investments. Danish external deregulation started on the inflow side as far back as the beginning of the 1970s. Non-residents were completely free to buy bonds in Danish kroner in 1974, but were temporarily banned between 1979 and 1983. On the outflow side, deregulation began at the end of the 1970s. The other Nordic countries followed very much later. However, non-residents were allowed to buy Finnish markka-denominated and Norwegian krone-denominated bonds during some periods in the 1970s and at the beginning of the 1980s. These countries then imposed a temporary ban on such transactions and – unlike Denmark – retained it until the final abolition of all exchange controls.

Corporate bond issues have been much more restricted. Issues abroad in the home currencies were not without restrictions until the end of the 1980s in Denmark and Sweden, and not until the beginning of the 1990s in Finland or Norway. Unlike the other Nordic countries the Swedish authorities gave companies domiciled in the country the right to issue abroad in foreign currencies as early as 1974. This permission meant the beginning of the erosion of the efficiency of the Swedish exchange controls. The Swedish authorities were very restrictive about krona-denominated issues, however, and the first krona-denominated issue did not in fact appear until 1988, when the World Bank issued a krona-denominated loan; a loan that was immediately swapped into US dollars.

NOTES

1   See Chapter 2 above or, for a broader discussion of the content, updating and implications of the code, see also OECD (1990).
2   The aim of a foreign direct investment, according to the IMF definition, is to 'acquire a lasting interest in an enterprise operating in an economy other than that of the investor, the investor's purpose being to have an effective voice in the management of the enterprise'. The common view of the practical minimum of equity for having an 'effective voice' in management is a 10 per cent ownership. However, several countries such as France, Germany and the UK use other definitions.
3   The EEC capital-liberalization directive was adopted on 24 June 1988 and came into force on 1 July 1990. Prior to its adoption, Denmark had achieved the fulfilment of a number of demands and requirements, including the retention of legislation on non-residents' acquisition of real estate in Denmark in respect of second homes. Furthermore, the directive provided an opportunity for the countries to find a solution to the tax-control problems, which might arise from the liberalization of foreign exchange.
4   See Danmarks Nationalbank (1988).
5   For a detailed description of the history of exchange control in Finland, 1917–1991, see Lehto-Sinisalo (1992).

6   See Government Bill No. 48/1990.
7   See Bank of Norway (1990).
8   See SOU (1985).
9   The calendarium (or diary), which is based on press releases and materials from governments and central banks in the Nordic countries, is too extensive to be published in this book. It will therefore be published separately.

REFERENCES

Bank of Norway, 1990, *Annual Report*, Oslo.

Danmarks Nationalbank, 1988, *Beretning og regnskab*, Copenhagen.

EFTA, 1989, *Consequences and Problems of Liberalizing Capital Movements in the EFTA Countries*, Report by the Working Group on Liberalization of Capital Movements, EFTA/EC 7/89.

Lehto-Sinisalo, P., 1992, 'The History of Exchange Control in Finland', *Discussion Paper*, No 3/92, Bank of Finland.

OECD, 1990, *Liberalization of Capital Movements and Financial Services in the OECD Area*, Paris.

Oxelheim, L., 1990, *International Financial Integration*, Springer Verlag, Heidelberg.

SOU, 1985, *Översyn av valutareglering*, No. 52, Stockholm.

Chapter 7

Internal bond market deregulation

It is assumed that a perfectly functioning financial market in a closed economy allocates savings in such a way that these will be used to the best economic effect. It is further assumed that this market apportions the risk-bearing in the economy in such a way that every actor (or actors) can carry the amount of risk they choose. As financial integration increases, the expression 'best economic effect' acquires a global dimension. History shows that different types of internal controls often prevent the market forces from finding the 'best' effect.

In the Nordic countries internal controls of various kinds were in force during the period studied here. In so far as they were effective, the countries' financial markets were unable to function altogether as described above. The actors on these markets were prevented to a greater or lesser extent from using their particular market to achieve a satisfactory trade-off – such as the free market forces permit – between risk and return. In this chapter we will examine the elimination of such internal controls in general and, in the case of bond markets, in some detail as well. Tax reforms will be treated as part of the general internal transformation.

THE EMERGENCE OF MARKETS

The 'new order' in the Nordic financial systems can be traced back to changes in the economic environment after the first oil crisis. The rise in inflation and the increasing volatility of both inflation and exchange rates generated a good deal of uncertainty, and economic growth in the industrialized countries slowed down. Another factor which altered the financial position of several sectors was the expansive fiscal policy that was adopted in many countries. Denmark, Norway and Sweden, for instance, pursued such policies. A deficit in the current account in Denmark and Sweden persisted with a large public sector deficit. In Norway the oil revenues began to balance the current account deficit inherited from the late 1970s, with a temporary shortfall in the second part of the 1980s. The fiscal policies in Finland were not as demand-orientated as those adopted by its neighbours, but here too the current account deficit remained at a constant low level, but with a large private sector deficit and a public sector surplus up to the beginning of the 1990s.

The international financial system also changed noticeably during the same period, with the wider adoption of flexible exchange rates and the expansion of the Euromarket. At the same time the growing internationalization of business and banking in the Nordic countries was creating a new demand for currency-related services. The financial behaviour of companies and banks became more closely linked to events in the leading financial centres of the world and, as internationalization continued to spread, businesses also learned more effective ways of handling the risks associated with the flexible exchange rates. Thus, the international economic integration of Nordic markets can be regarded as the single most important factor behind the changes that occurred in the financial markets of these small Nordic economies. Without the escalating internationalization of their business and banking sectors, the demand for financial market operations would probably have remained too small to make such changes necessary.

The focus in Nordic policy-making shifted over time

The general trend in foreign indebtedness, private and public, in the Nordic countries during the 1970s is shown in Figure 7.1. Except in Norway we can see a change in the economic policies, especially in the countries pursuing strong demand-orientated policies. Monetary and credit policy became more concerned with guaranteeing the financing of the current account deficit and ensuring the stability of the exchange rate. In all the Nordic countries monetary and credit policies were tightened to curb the growth of liquidity in the economy resulting from the 'permanent' state budget deficits.[1] In the 1970s economic growth was relatively strong in all the countries (and in Finland extraordinarily strong at the end of the 1970s), while at the same time the inflation rate was rising. This created further pressure to maintain a tight monetary policy, which was traditionally based on direct regulations.

However, because of changes in the financial environment and especially changes in the behaviour of companies, credit rationing was no longer effective. Liquidity in the economies grew apace. The credit expansion started in Norway and Denmark, appearing a little later in Sweden and Finland as well. Problems were also first noticed by the countries in that order, and can be regarded as *contagious*. Recognition of the problems and the propensity to take corrective action on the other hand, were not contagious. Banks continued lending on a grand scale, until the problems turned up in their own organizations. In the absence of any adequate control instruments, they went on manoeuvring their asset combinations to unsustainable levels up to the last possible minute, by exploiting off-balance-sheet opportunities.[2]

The low-interest-rate policy adopted in three of the Nordic countries (not

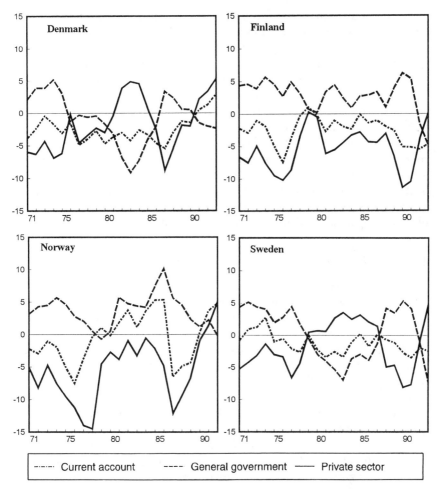

Figure 7.1 Net lending by sectors in the Nordic economies (percentage of GDP)

Source: OECD, *National Accounts*, Vol. II, various issues.

Note: Current account figures were taken from section 10 of the National Accounts, and net lending figures were adopted from sections 6, 7 and 8 under the capital accumulation account. If figures were not available for the private sector, these figures were calculated as the difference between the current account and the figure for the general government, since this provided a comparatively accurate view. Net lending corresponds to the excess of net acquisitions of financial assets by transactors over their net incurrence of liabilities, whereas the current account shows the receipts and disbursements of income. Overall, the accounts should balance, i.e. the general government plus the private sector should approximately equal the current account.

Denmark) by regulating the lending rate in credit markets, failed to clear the markets. Existing excess demand for loans was met by the unregulated markets that emerged in Sweden, Norway and Finland. For a period at the beginning of the 1970s a grey credit market also existed in Denmark.

History shows that the rationing of a financial market is efficient only until the actors learn how to circumvent the rules. And they do this as soon as the incentives to evade the rules are sufficiently strong. Regulative action thus induces innovations, aimed at getting around the rules. The process of liberalizing financial markets depends on the dynamic efficiency of the existing financial system. Mature conditions and competition, as in the US financial market for instance, continuously generate sophisticated innovations, while the kind of concentrated oligopolistic and rationed financial systems that were typical of the Nordic countries in the 1970s, are less conducive to innovation. How much less innovative the Nordic markets were, will be discussed in Chapter 12. More competition usually means that banks lose an inexpensive source of funding. The emergence of a grey market, as a parallel to the rationed market, added to the pressure for a Nordic deregulation and liberalization in the early 1980s.

Money markets were the first to reach a state of maturity

The borrowing requirement of 'general government', as designated in Figure 7.1, triggered the development of money markets in all the Nordic countries.[3] However, the emergence of such a market was also in the interest of the authorities as a prerequisite for pursuing policies based on open market operations.

Changes in the financial systems of the Nordic countries started in the short-term market as a natural consequence of the change in corporate financial behaviour. The tendency towards increasingly market-orientated systems, including the household market, was gradually growing. In the Nordic economies the financial surplus in the household sector led to a greater demand for securities and, as the cost of bank loans rose, equities and bonds as a source of corporate funding appeared increasingly attractive. This added to the pressure for further development of the equity markets and encouraged a growing international interest in the Nordic stock exchanges.

From rate or quantity regulations to open market operations

Rate or quantity regulations were applied extensively in the Nordic countries in the 1970s. The fact that the Nordic central banks returned to direct market operations during the 1980s must be considered in light of the evolving money market in the wake of the great budget deficit in these countries, as described above, and the new capital market prospects. As can be seen in Table 7.1, the abolition of Nordic rate and quantity regulations in the banking sector can be seen as an indication of the general attitude of politicians to deregulation. Particular issues connected with the deregulation of the bond markets will be addressed on pp. 162–6.

With the help of open market operations the central bank's aim is to influence the banking industry's cash liquidity and the general interest level.

Table 7.1 The abolition of rate and quantity regulations in the banking sector

Deregulatory action	Denmark	Finland	Norway	Sweden
Deregulation of banks' deposit rates	1981[a]	–[b]	–[c]	1978
Deregulation of lending rates by insurance companies	–[c]	–[d]	1985	1980
Banks granted permission to issue CDs	–[c]	1982	1985	1980
Liquidity ratios for banks are abolished	–[e]	–[f,g]	1987	1983
Deregulation of banks' lending rates	1981	1985/1986[h]	1985	1985
Loan ceiling on bank lending lifted	1980	–[f]	1987	1985
Marginal placement ratios for banks and insurance companies abolished	1987[i]	–[f]	1985	1986

[a] For some kinds of deposit 1984.
[b] Never in fact regulated, although the favourable tax treatment of deposits and bonds implied an informal link with the base rate of the Bank of Finland. It was changed in 1989 so as to intensify competition in financial markets. Since then deposits and bonds with market rates have substituted the traditional deposits and bonds with interest rates determined by the base rate of the Bank of Finland.
[c] No regulations in the postwar period.
[d] Only the interest rate on relending of pension funds has been linked – and, at the beginning of the 1990s is still to some extent linked – to the base rate of the Bank of Finland. The Bank of Finland gave 'recommendations' concerning lending rates by insurance companies prior to spring 1986. Otherwise no direct regulation.
[e] There has never been an obligation for Danish banks to hold certain securities.
[f] There have not been explicit quantitative restrictions (except occasionally, e.g. in the late 1950s and early 1960s).
[g] The cash reserve requirement was initiated in 1979 and, at the beginning of the 1990s, this instrument is still used.
[h] The Bank of Finland began to relax its interest rate controls in 1983, the upper limits on lending rates were abolished at the end of 1985 and the regulation on average lending rates was abandoned at the beginning of August 1986.
[i] During 1985–87 a system of marginal placement ratios was in force.

Banks' borrowing is thus of crucial importance to the effectiveness of market operations.[4] Several factors affect the extent of the banks' borrowing in the central bank. The foreign exchange inflow and the government expenditure surplus reduce bank borrowing, while government borrowing on the domestic market works in the opposite direction. Two techniques are employed by the central bank to reduce or increase bank borrowing from the central bank:

- direct buying or selling of government securities;
- repurchase agreements in government securities.

The central banks use repurchase agreements mainly to counteract the considerable fluctuations in cash liquidity in the banking system. This generally means that the central banks buy government securities from the banks and commissioning agents, with an agreement for their resale after a certain time, e.g. seven days.[5] The interest conditions for these transactions can be established either by the central bank setting a particular rate or by an auction procedure.

As a result of the direct buying and selling of government securities combined with repurchase agreements, the central banks hope to be able to retain a tighter grip on the extent of bank borrowing from the central bank and, thus, over the interest rate on the money market. In this way the central banks influence short-run financing costs of the banks and other borrowers, as well as corporate foreign exchange transactions. And when the central bank effects a change in short-term financing costs, this tends – if it is regarded as long-lasting – to make an impact on the interest rates for long-maturity financial assets as well.

As in the case of external deregulation, a calendarium has been kept, with entries and exits for the various internal policy measures in force in the Nordic countries between 1977 and 1991.[6] It gives the dates of changes in reserve requirements, interest rate ceilings, liquidity ratios, official discount rates, ceilings on bank lending in the central bank, call money rates, authorization requirements, etc. The calendarium shows no evidence of Nordic policy coordination as regards internal deregulations on a day-by-day, week-by-week or even month-by-month basis. Changes in the rules of the game have been frequent. Thus we can expect non-negligible political risk premiums to appear in the gap between the national Nordic interest rates and the global rate. I will return to this question in Chapter 9.

Key features of the general Nordic internal transformation

The internal *de jure* liberalization of the Nordic financial markets in the 1980s led to the following changes:

- the emergence of unregulated markets and a closer internal integration of the whole financial system within each individual country;
- the functional integration of financial submarkets, i.e. traditional institutions took over the activities of other existing institutions or moved into newly established activities and products;
- increased competition in financial markets, leading among other things to institutional adjustments such as mergers, exits and the creation of new types of financial institutions (often rather specialized);
- the gradual elimination of most monetary policy instruments of quantitative regulation in favour of market-orientated instruments.

Internal deregulation of the Nordic bond markets

Let us now move on from the general liberalization process to the deregulation of the Nordic bond markets. A cross-country comparison based on Tables 7.2–7.5 reveals that the Danish bond market has been

Table 7.2 Internal deregulation of the Danish bond market

Denmark	Date		
	Introduced	*Eased*	*Abolished*
Issuing controls (regulating who is allowed to issue)	1977	1981	1989[a]
Investment obligations (e.g. on pension funds)	No regulation[b]		
Reserve requirements (on banks)	No regulation		
Interest rate regulations (regulations on the rate of issue and on bond rates)	No regulation[c]		

[a] New credit law in 1989.
[b] Pension funds had to keep low-risk bonds.
[c] Enacted a minimum-interest level in 1989.

Table 7.3 Internal deregulation of the Finnish bond market

Finland	Date			Regulated by type of act:
	Introduced	*Eased*	*Abolished*	
Issuing controls (regulating who is allowed to issue)	1942	–	1993	Security Market Act
Investment obligations (e.g. on pension funds)	No regulation			
Reserve requirements (on banks)	1979, 1990	–	June 1993[a]	Cash Reserve Agreement
	1993	–	–	Minimum Reserve Law
Interest rate regulations (regulations on the rate of issue and on bond rates)	No regulation			

[a] The original agreement was replaced by a law on 30 June 1993; the reserve ratio had been 0 per cent since the end of May 1993. The new law – Minimum Reserve Law – requires deposit banks and foreign credit institutes to keep 2 per cent of their liquid deposits, 1.5 per cent of other deposits, and 1 per cent of their Finnish funds as an interest free reserve at the Bank of Finland. See Bank of Finland (1993) for further details.

Table 7.4 Internal deregulation of the Norwegian bond market

Norway	Date			Regulated by type of act:
	Introduced	Eased	Abolished	
Issuing controls (regulating who is allowed to issue)	March 1972	Oct 1980[a] May 1986 July 1987 July 1988 March 1989 April 1989 May 1989 July 1990 Nov 1990 April 1992	1995[b]	The law on Money and Credit (Penge og Kreditt-loven) §15, 25 June 1965
Investment obligations (e.g. on pension funds)	1969	1984	1985	–
Reserve requirements (on banks)[c]	1969 1969 1966	– – –	1987 1984 1987	Amendments to the Bank Law of 24 May 1961, No. 1 and 2.
Interest rate regulations (regulations on the rate of issue and on the bond rates)	1965	Oct 1977 Mid-1980s	Oct 1987	–

[a] The permission to issue private bonds was liberalized in October 1980.
[b] When this book was being written, it was claimed by the Financial Market Department at the Bank of Norway that the regulation was to be abolished sometime during the first half of 1995.
[c] The Norwegian reserve requirement system was divided into three parts – primary reserve requirements (primærreservekrav), deposit requirement (plasseringsplikt), and loan regulation (utlånsregulering). Primary reserve requirements on banks, life insurance companies and financial institutions were abolished in the first half of 1987. The remaining requirement (loan regulation) was abolished in October 1987 (Bank of Norway 1989).

comparatively liberal in a Nordic perspective. Issuing controls is the only tool of regulation that Danish policy-makers have used to influence the bond market; internal deregulation of this market was completed in 1989. Finnish policy-makers also employed issuing controls, but in addition imposed reserve requirements on banks. Issuing controls was abolished in 1993, but the earlier agreement concerning reserve requirements was replaced the same

Table 7.5 Internal deregulation of the Swedish bond market

| Sweden | Date | | | Regulated by type of act: |
	Introduced	Eased	Abolished	
Issuing controls (regulating who is allowed to issue)	January 1952	1980[a] 1985[b] 1988[c] 1991[d]	October 1991	Based on an agreement in January 1952 between the Swedish Central Bank and the market actors.
Investment obligations (e.g. on pension funds)	(January 1952), 1980	1984[e]	December 1986	Based on an agreement in 1969 between the Swedish Central Bank and the insurance companies involving the Postbank and Pension funds.
Reserve requirements (on banks)	1950, 1969	1952–1968	April 1994[f]	Since 1969 the Swedish Central Bank maintains reserve requirements based on the law of 1962 concerning liquid and cash ratios
Interest rate regulations (regulations on the rate of issue and on bond rates)	1952	1983–1984[g] 1988[h]	January 1991	Based on an agreement in January 1952 between the Swedish Central Bank and the market actors.

[a] Banks and housing institutions allowed to issue.
[b] Real estate companies and local governments allowed to issue.
[c] Requirements on maturity and size eased.
[d] Index bonds allowed.
[e] Investment obligations abolished for non-life insurance companies.
[f] As of this date the ratio was zero; the Central Bank may still impose reserve requirements.
[g] An issue rate less than 100 per cent was accepted.
[h] Depending on maturity the rates of issue were allowed to vary within a given interval.

year by a new law. In other words control over bank reserves was reinforced. Heavy internal regulation, of all the four kinds included in the tables, has been employed on the Norwegian and Swedish bond markets. This started to let up in the mid-1980s in Norway and, apart from issuing controls, was finally abolished in 1987. The easing of Swedish internal regulations also began in the mid-1980s, and except for the possibility for policy-makers to impose reserve requirements it was completed in 1991.

Thus the internal deregulation of the national bond markets has followed different routes in the individual Nordic countries. At one extreme the Danish market was exposed to few restrictions, and was a 'market' as early as the mid-1970s. At the other extreme we find the Finnish market, which did not achieve liberalization of the regulations previously in force until the beginning of the 1990s. In between, we find the Norwegian and Swedish bond markets, where in the Norwegian case the bulk of the deregulative measures were undertaken in the mid-1980s and in the Swedish case at the beginning of the 1980s with an auction-based bond market established in 1984. However, even in these two countries many parts of the liberalization process were not completed until the early 1990s.

TAX BURDEN IN THE REGIONAL PERSPECTIVE

Personal and corporate taxation have been highly influential in shaping the financial markets of the Nordic countries. As we have noted, these countries are among the five highest tax-paying countries in the world, with complex tax rules, differential treatment of legal entities, and frequent changes in the rules which encourage financial services for reducing or circumventing the payment of taxes by way of tax arbitrage etc.

Tax incentives may explain a low propensity to invest in production facilities. Generous tax deductions in the Nordic countries have generally been allowed on household interest payments. For long periods deductions were allowed not only on mortgage loans but also on consumer loans. Prior to the deregulation, low after-tax interest rates were mitigated by credit rationing. After the deregulation, however, a surge in the household demand for credit was not fully offset by an increase in nominal interest rates, since the fixed exchange rate policy meant that nominal domestic interest rates were largely determined by foreign rates. Because increases in nominal interest rates were limited, the logical alternative to depressing the demand for credit was to reduce the tax value of interest payments.

Concern that the tax system might deter saving was strengthened in the second half of the 1980s in the Nordic countries, where interest payments on consumer loans had hitherto been fully deductible. The deduction of interest payments often represented the largest single deduction for tax purposes: in Norway, for example, deductions rose from 3.25 per cent of GDP in 1976 to 5.5 per cent in the mid-1980s. This practice had adverse effects on the savings

Table 7.6 Main features of capital-income taxation in the first half of the 1980s

	Interest income	Capital gains	Dividends
Denmark	Taxed as income	Generally not taxed	Double taxation; withholding tax of 30 per cent
Finland	Taxed as income (except regulated rate income)	Long-term gains not taxed	Investment income not taxed below threshold
Norway	Taxed as income above threshold	Favourable	Exempt from local income tax
Sweden	Taxed as income	Long-term gains more favourable	Double taxation
Austria	Withholding tax	Not taxed below threshold	Double taxation; withholding tax of 20 per cent
France	Taxed as income	Not taxed below threshold	Not taxed below threshold
Germany	Taxed as income above threshold	Only short-term speculative gains on shares taxed as income	Taxed as income
Italy	Withholding tax	Not taxed	Tax credit in respect of taxes paid by companies
United Kingdom	Taxed as income	Not taxed below threshold	Tax credit in respect of corporate taxes paid
United States	Taxed as income	40 per cent of long-term capital gains taxed at marginal rate; all short-term gains taxed at marginal rate	Double taxation; dividends not taxed below threshold

Source: OECD (1985).

ratio (OECD 1987c). The need to introduce greater symmetry into the taxation of capital income was part of the rationale of the Nordic reform. In Denmark, for instance, in the reform of 1986, as part of a drive to increase savings, a 20 per cent tax on interest on consumer loans was introduced, and interest costs were made deductible only against capital income. In Sweden tax deductions for interest payments were also restricted, with the tax value being gradually reduced to 30 per cent.

The point of departure for the reform of Nordic capital–income taxation in the 1980s is given in Table 7.6, together with a corresponding exposition for some other OECD countries. The Nordic countries adopted a combination of a residence (or worldwide) principle and a source (or territorial) principle in taxing foreign-source income.[7] The Nordic countries were thus able to tax interest accrued within their borders on a territorial basis, and to tax their own residents on their income earned worldwide.

A change in the scope of tax reforms appeared in the mid-1980s

In the early 1980s concern was growing that economic distortions resulting from higher taxes imposed additional and unacceptably high efficiency costs on an economy. The pursuit of more economically neutral (i.e. less biased and discriminatory) tax systems became a budgetary force as it also reflects a desire to ease the overall burden of taxation. In principle this implied a movement towards a system of revenue-raising which minimizes the impact of taxation on economic behaviour. This movement resulted in tax reforms from the mid-1980s, whose main content can be summarized as follows:[8]

- A reduction in income tax rates linked to a broadening of the income tax base; a reduction in the number of marginal rates and a lowering of top rates relative to the standard rate. In some countries there have also been moves to integrate income and social security taxes.
- A rationalizing and broadening of the consumption tax base, through a switch to a general expenditure tax (usually value added tax, VAT).
- A trend towards broadening the base and achieving greater neutrality in the corporate tax system, often accompanied by a switch from household to corporate taxation and/or a better integration of corporate and personal income taxes (including capital gains).

The rationale behind these reforms was that high marginal tax rates threatened work incentives and aggravated problems of tax avoidance and evasion. The reforms were further motivated by the fact that accumulated tax concessions had rendered tax systems overly complex and inequitable, which distorted consumption/saving decisions as well as patterns of investment, corporate finance and production.

General features of the Nordic tax reforms

The Nordic tax reforms followed the pattern of international tax reforms as described in the previous section. The income tax base for the taxation of individuals was broadened, the value of deductions restricted and marginal rates reduced. The major features in the taxation of corporations were lower tax rates and reduced allowances, with a view to making the system neutral in competitive terms.

Taxes and the Danish financial market

In the mid-1990s, *individual taxpayers* in Denmark are subject to a national income tax and, usually, to two municipal income taxes – one for the local tax district and the other for the county tax district. In addition a church tax is imposed on the same basis as the municipal income taxes. A national tax on net wealth is also levied on individuals whose wealth exceeds a certain threshold. Certain capital gains and some types of non-recurring income are subject to a special flat-rate tax rather than the progressive rate for ordinary income.

Since 1987, a distinction has been made between personal income (including employment and business income) and income from capital; this distinction is relevant to the taxation of national income, since different rates of tax and different rules for deductibility of certain expenses, notably interest, apply. A third category, dividends from resident companies, was introduced in 1991, to be taxed separately from other income.

For long periods interest payments were fully deductible from the individual's taxable income (and interest earnings were taxable). This practice provided an incentive for household borrowing, which was in accordance with the political aim of helping households to acquire homes, i.e. it was a low incentive for financial saving. It proved administratively difficult to change such patterns and to impose general disincentives for household borrowing, since most of the electorate owned – and still own – private real estate financed through mortgage institutes. Nevertheless, a reform which gave households less incentive to borrow was implemented in March 1986.[9] The reform aimed at equalizing and reducing the subsidy element inherent in the tax deductibility of interest payments. The 'tax value' of interest payments was set at about 50–56 per cent for all income groups, i.e. irrespective of the marginal tax rate. Similarly, interest income was taxed like other capital income (dividends, rental value, etc.) at a flat rate of 50–56 per cent.

The 'potato diet' reform which was implemented in October 1986, further reduced the value of interest payments on consumer loans to 31–37 per cent. This diet was imposed retroactively and involved a 20 per cent tax on loans for consumption. A decision to lift the retroactivity in the consumption tax imposed by the potato diet was taken in the Folketing in November 1988. All loans raised before 11 October 1988 and which were in the process of liquidation, were made exempt from the consumption tax.

In the 1980s dividends were taxed as both corporate and personal income. This double taxation was generally considered detrimental to 'productive' investments, and in 1982 a minor tax credit had been introduced to reduce the personal taxation of dividends. In connection with the tax reform of 1991, however, double taxation was completely eliminated.

The taxation of private capital gains on bonds was introduced in 1985.

Capital gains were to be free of taxation if ownership had lasted three years or more. The new rules for bonds reduced the incentive to issue papers with nominal interest rates differing significantly from the market rate. Henceforth tax freedom on capital gains was to be granted only if the nominal interest rate of the bonds at the time of issuance met a minimum rate. This rate is continually specified by the monetary authorities.

The rates for the national income tax for 1994 were 14.5 per cent (22 per cent in 1992) on total taxable income, plus 4.5 per cent on any excess over DKK 234,900 in so far as it exceeded DKK 20,000, plus 5 per cent on any excess over DKK 173,100 of personal income only.[10] Personal income in 1992 was taxed at a marginal rate up to 68 per cent. For 1994 the figure fell to 65 per cent. For the income year 1994 (valuation at the end of 1993) a wealth tax of 1 per cent was charged on taxable wealth exceeding DKK 1,580,500 for a single taxpayer and DKK 3,161,000 for married couples.

In the mid-1990s, Danish *corporate taxpayers* are subject to a corporate income tax which, with the exception of a special hydrocarbon tax, is the only tax imposed on the profits of corporate bodies. Up to 1984 insurance companies and pension funds were exempt from taxation. However, the high real interest rates prevailing in the early 1980s (in 1982 about 10 per cent per annum) provoked the introduction of the *real-interest tax*, which ensured that yields on bonds and shares did not exceed 3.5 per cent per annum in real terms. This tax was introduced to reduce the large capital accumulations in these financial institutions, primarily in order to prevent disproportionally large pension payments after the turn of the century. An additional motive behind this taxation was the large public revenue to be tapped by the public sector. Extensions to this law were often called for, since the 3.5 per cent real interest allowed was seen as relatively high compared with the long-term growth potential of the economy. Perhaps even more important, however, were the distortions created by the uneven taxation of alternative investments, which tended to favour 'passive' and unproductive investments in real estate or bonds rather than in shares etc. The tax reforms implemented in 1986 and 1991 gradually broadened the tax base to cover foundations, societies, associations, mortgage institutions, and other hitherto untaxed financial institutions.

Between 1977 and 1991 Denmark had an imputation system for the taxation of corporate profits, whereby resident shareholders were entitled to a special tax credit, which in the final years of the system was equal to 25 per cent of the dividends. Following the tax reform implemented in 1991 the imputation system was abolished, to be replaced by a system under which the tax liability of resident shareholders with respect to dividends from Danish companies was restricted to 30 per cent or 45 per cent.

Annual depreciation allowances on all fixed assets other than buildings could be claimed under the diminishing-balance method at various rates up to 30 per cent. The depreciation base consisted of the cost of fixed assets less the sales proceeds of disposals and depreciation allowances previously claimed. Until the income year 1991, the depreciation base was adjusted for the general increase in consumer prices, but this rule was then abolished.

From the income year 1991 (assessment 1992–93) the income tax was 38 per cent of taxable income. Previously the rate was 40 per cent. There were no other corporate income taxes. Dividends, whether distributed to a resident or to a non-resident, were also subject to a withholding tax at the rate of 30 per cent. For non-residents the tax was final[11] and this was also the case for residents up to DKK 32,700 for single persons. Any excess of this amount was levied an extra 10 per cent tax. The *value added tax* (VAT) was 25 per cent as of 1 January 1992. Gains on the sale of bonds and other debt-claims were in general taxable only if the bonds carried a rate of interest which was below the minimum interest (as quoted on the stock exchange). Taxable capital gains were included in the company's total taxable profits.

Taxes and the Finnish financial market

A major tax reform was enacted in 1992 and came into effect on 1 January 1993. According to this new system *individual taxpayers* in the mid-1990s in Finland are subject to national income tax, municipal income tax and church tax. Residents are taxed at progressive tax rates for national tax purposes and at proportional rates for municipal, church and social security tax purposes. Legacies and gifts are not only subject to inheritance and gift taxes imposed by the state, but can also be regarded as taxable income for local tax purposes. In addition the state imposes a net wealth tax and an array of indirect taxes. The municipalities also imposed a real estate tax as from 1993.

For long periods interest payments were fully deductible from the taxable income of households and companies. Following the tax reform implemented in 1989, interest payments on housing loans in Finland were deductible up to FIM 25,000, and on consumer loans, up to FIM 10,000.[12] However, under the new reform, interest on debts incurred to finance private consumption ceased to be deductible. Interest became deductible only from income on capital. In the case of the interest revenues of residents on domestic bank deposits and loans, a withholding tax of 25 per cent applies (15 per cent in 1992). Interest paid by a person other than a bank or an issuer of bonds, however, are not subject to this tax (IBFD 1994).

Dividends used to be double taxed before the 'avoir fiscal' system was introduced in 1990, although some deductions could be made in personal taxes. The imputation system (avoir fiscal) began to affect the distribution of corporate profits as from that year. As from 1993 companies pay income tax on their profits at a rate of 25 per cent (the rate was 36 per cent in 1992). Resident shareholders include the dividends in their taxable income but are entitled to an imputed tax credit representing one-third (nine-sixteenths in 1992) of the grossed-up dividends.

Included in the capital category are capital gains from the sale of property. The capital category is subject to the national income tax at the flat rate of 25 per cent. To calculate the capital gain, the acquisition cost is deducted from the proceeds of the disposal. A deduction is allowed of at least 30 per cent of the proceeds (before 1989, 50 per cent).

As of 1994 no state income tax is due if the taxpayer's income is below FIM 41,000 (40,000 in 1992).[13] For income exceeding that amount that rate increases progressively from 7 to 39 per cent, with the 39 per cent rate applying to amounts exceeding FIM 280,000. In addition the taxpayer has to pay municipal tax (varying between 15 and 20 per cent), church tax (varying between 1 and 2 per cent), national pension premiums (1.55 per cent in 1994, plus another 4.87 per cent as an extra premium if employed), and sickness premiums (1.9 per cent of the first FIM 80,000 and 3.8 per cent of excess taxable income). The sum of national and local income taxes, net wealth tax, church tax and social security premiums payable by the insured must not exceed 70 per cent of the taxable income as assessed for national income tax purposes.

Corporate taxpayers in Finland were subject to a corporate tax of 25 per cent in 1994 (IBFD 1994). This rate stems from the major tax reform that was enacted in Finland in 1992 with effect from 1 January 1993. Corporations are not subject to any local taxes, although part of the revenue from the corporate income tax is shared by the state, municipalities, and the two state churches (the Evangelical-Lutheran Church and the Orthodox Church). Corporate taxpayers also have to make social security contributions and to pay real estate tax and value added tax (VAT). The payment of VAT was a precondition for joining the EU, and it replaced the turnover tax which had taken effect from 1 October 1991.

Prior to the tax reform of 1989 corporate profits were, in principle, subject to double taxation. However, steps were taken to assuage the total tax burden on profits and to promote broader share-ownership. As from 1990 the double taxation of corporate profits was replaced by the imputation (avoir fiscal) method. Under this system companies pay tax on their profits which are then credited to the (resident) recipient of dividends.

In the mid-1990s buildings can be depreciated only by the declining-balance method. The allowable rates of annual depreciation vary according to the main building material used and the type of building. For machinery and equipment normal depreciation is allowed on a collective (pool) basis, i.e. on the total book value of all assets at the end of the previous tax year less the cost of assets sold plus the cost of assets acquired during the year. The maximum rate of depreciation is 30 per cent. Special rules apply to cars. Items of machinery and equipment whose estimated useful life does not exceed three years can be fully written off in the year of acquisition.

Up to 1992 corporate taxpayers were subject to a municipal income tax, which was imposed at flat rates varying from 14.5 to 20 per cent, depending on the municipality. The rate for Helsinki, for instance, was 15 per cent. The church income tax was also imposed at a flat rate. Since the tax reform of 1992 corporate taxpayers pay these taxes indirectly in that a part of the total corporate income tax of 25 per cent is apportioned to the municipalities and the churches. The municipalities take up the greater part of these taxes (11.2 for the municipalities and 0.84 per cent for the churches). All capital gains are taxed as part of the corporate taxpayer's ordinary income.

Taxes and the Norwegian financial market

Prior to 1988 *individual taxpayers* in Norway were subject to three taxes on income: the national income tax, the municipal income tax (usually imposed at two levels of local government) and the tax on behalf of a 'tax equalization fund', the proceeds of which were divided among the municipalities. In addition, social security premiums and net wealth taxes were – and in the mid-1990s still are – payable. All these income taxes were imposed on the same taxable basis of net income, i.e. gross income less allowable deductions.

Since 1988, however, the national income tax has been split into two elements, one imposed on gross income, i.e. the same basis as social security premiums, and the other – like the municipal income tax and contributions to the 'tax equalization fund' – on net income.

Another significant change occurred when the tax reform of 1991 became effective on 1 January 1992. The major objectives of this reform were to reduce tax rates as such, while also abolishing various deductions, allowances and exemptions. There were to be two taxes on income:

- tax on general income, which is basically defined as net income, after allowable deductions, from all sources;
- tax on gross personal income, which is defined as all earned income (employment, personal services, the labour element of business income and pensions).

In Norway, too, there had been a long period when unlimited tax deduction on households' interest payments was allowed. Combined with relatively high marginal tax rates, this brought the real after-tax interest rate close to zero and generally strengthened the households' demand for credits. With credit quite easily available from banks there is reason to believe that households were inflating their financial asset-and-debt structure by making financial investments with borrowed funds in order to obtain an after-tax profit. The tax reform of 1986 meant a major step in the elimination of distorting tax incentives, by reducing the tax value of deductions: the top marginal tax rate for interest deductions was lowered from over 66 per cent in 1986 to around 48 per cent in 1988. The tax reform of 1991 should then be seen as part of a process of gradual adjustment. Personal income was taxed to an increasing extent on a gross basis, i.e. before various deductions. This made it less favourable for the household sector to borrow. Note that only real interest payments are deductible.

One major element of the 1991 tax reform was the introduction of a full imputation system for dividends distributed by Norwegian companies to shareholders (individuals or companies) who were resident in Norway. As the prevailing company income tax of 28 per cent was equal to the rate of tax applying to the general income of individuals, the imputation system implied that no income tax would be due on dividends received. This element in the new system has applied since 1993.

In the mid-1990s capital gains on the sale of movable or immovable property are generally taxable (and capital losses deductible), but subject to a number of exemptions and special provisions. Special rules apply in the computation of gains on the disposal of shares in Norwegian companies. In computing the gain, the shareholder's cost of acquisition of each share is increased annually by that part of the company's retained profits (after tax and dividend distributions) which is attributable to that share. Taxation of capital gains also takes place when a company is liquidated. In computing the (adjusted) cost of the acquisition of shares sold, the first-in-first-out method is used if the shareholder sells only part of his or her holding in a particular company.

At the present time yields on various financial assets are taxed in different ways. Interest payment on bank deposits and bonds is taxed at the same rates as ordinary earned income. Dividends on shares are taxed more favourably. Capital gains on shares are taxed favourably and according to how long the asset has been owned. Losses are tax deductible only with respect to capital gains. Capital gains on bonds are free of tax. The same applies to capital gains on life insurance saving, but changes are to be expected here. Household savings in banks and shares (through approved equity funds) give tax reductions within certain limits.

Since 1992 state tax on the income of individuals is no longer applicable. All the municipalities have become tax-raising authorities with a flat rate of 28 per cent (in 1994, 20.25 per cent municipal tax and 7.75 per cent equalization tax) on general income in excess of NOK 45,200 (NOK 43,400 in 1992) for persons with dependants (NOK 22,600 for a single person). An additional tax on earned income, including benefits-in-kind, is assessed. For class II taxpayers (i.e. taxpayers with dependants), the top tax in 1994 was 9.5 per cent of earned income in excess of NOK 252,000 and 13 per cent of earned income in excess of NOK 263,000.

Norwegian *corporate taxpayers* were also covered by the tax reform that came into force on 1 January 1992. The main objective of this part of the reform was to broaden the tax base and reduce tax rates, as well as to introduce a system of full imputation with regard to distributed corporate profits. The national and municipal net worth taxes were abolished for resident and non-resident companies, and corporate taxpayers were henceforth to be subject to one tax on income only. Among other things the broadening of the tax base for corporate taxpayers meant abolishing deductible allocations to the consolidation reserve, some reduction in allowable rates of depreciation, and less flexibility in the valuation of stock.

Traditionally it has been more favourable for the corporate sector in Norway to finance investments from loan capital than from equity because interest payments have been tax deductible while dividends to shareholders were paid from after-tax profits. The low interest rate policy also favoured loan capital at the expense of equity financing. However, various tax reliefs introduced in the 1980s made equity financing more competitive. The financial investments of actors in the corporate sector were generally taxed as ordinary corporate income.

Following the 1991 tax reform the Norwegian corporate tax system has become a full imputation system, i.e. dividends are increased by an imputation credit equal to the corporate income tax attributable to these dividends, and the shareholder's income tax liability on the aggregate of dividend and imputation credit is reduced by the amount of the credit. However, this system usually applies to resident shareholders only.

The 1991 tax reform has also influenced the system of depreciation, by altering the classification of business assets into a number of classes and by generally reducing the maximum rates of depreciation allowed. In 1994 the income tax for corporate taxpayers was 28 per cent, of which the municipal rate accounted for 11 per cent and the equalization tax rate 17 per cent. *Value added tax* that year was 22 per cent (20 per cent before 1993) and an investment tax of 7 per cent was also levied on most purchases for which VAT can be claimed as a deduction (credit) for refund, with the exception of goods for resale and capital assets used in production and mining activities.

Taxes and the Swedish financial market

In the mid-1990s *individual taxpayers* in Sweden are subject to income taxes raised by the state and the municipalities. In addition, the state imposes a net wealth tax and an array of indirect taxes. Legacies and gifts are subject to tax imposed by the state. A major reform of the Swedish tax system became generally effective from 1 January 1991. For purposes of harmonization in preparation for full membership of the EU (from 1 January 1995), Sweden further planned the revision of various tax laws to be phased in between 1991 and 1996.

At the beginning of the 1980s household interest payments were fully deductible in Sweden. A tax free return of a maximum SEK 800 per year on savings in banks and in shares (through bank funds) was introduced in 1982. However, the reform which was implemented from 1983–85 reduced the tax value of interest payments for many households to 50 per cent. Moreover, a deficit in one source of income could be used to offset net income from other sources. New tax rules allowed a person to deduct interest payments fully against positive capital income. In this case, the tax value of interest payments was equal to an individual's marginal tax rate. The tax value of interest payments was limited to 50 per cent only, if interest payments exceeded capital income. The new tax reform (effective as of 1 January 1991) meant that the tax value of interest payments was reduced further to 30 per cent.

For households and individuals all kinds of dividends and interests received are in principle taxable. Until the recent tax reform, capital gains on shares and bonds were taxed according to the number of years the items had been owned. Capital losses were tax deductible only in respect of capital gains. This deductibility has been gradually curtailed, however.

Since 1991 national income tax has been imposed on taxable earned income, i.e. employment and business income. In 1994 the first SEK 198,700 (in 1992 SEK 186,600) of earned income was exempt from that tax; on any excess, tax was levied at the rate of 20 per cent. Since a municipal income tax of about 31 per cent was imposed on earned income, the lowest aggregate rate of income taxes was about 31 per cent; the highest marginal rate was about 51 per cent.

Income from capital and capital gains is taxed separately at a flat rate of national income tax (without a tax-free amount); no municipal tax is imposed on such incomes. From 1991–93 the rate was 30 per cent. The capital gains tax on trade in equity was cut to 12.5 per cent for 1994, but put up to 30 per cent again in 1995. The double taxation of dividends was eliminated in 1994, with dividends becoming tax-free for shareholders that year. In 1995 double taxation was reintroduced.

The tax burden on the individual taxpayer who is a resident in Sweden for at least part of the tax year is reduced, provided the aggregate amount of national income tax, net wealth tax and municipal income tax exceeds a ceiling equal to 55 per cent of the sum of the taxpayer's earned income and income from capital. To arrive at the amount of the ceiling a reduction is made in the net wealth tax, the national income tax on income from capital and the national income tax on earned income, in that order. The municipal income tax is never reduced.

Swedish *corporate taxpayers* in the mid-1990s are subject to national income tax and certain payroll taxes and social security charges. No local income taxes are levied on corporate profits. The national net worth tax is not levied on resident companies. The major reform of the Swedish tax system that became generally effective on 1 January 1991 also affected corporate taxpayers. In principle corporate profits were still subject to double taxation. However, in 1994 various measures were taken to alleviate the total tax burden on such profits and to promote wider share-ownership, e.g. by giving total exemption for dividends received by shareholders and halving the tax on certain capital gains. As mentioned above, the total tax exemption for shareholders was abolished in 1995.

As a general principle machinery and equipment are depreciated according to the declining-balance method. For corporate taxpayers maintaining adequate accounting records, the maximum depreciation allowance following the tax reform is 30 per cent of the aggregate book value of all assets at the beginning of the tax year, plus the cost of assets acquired, less the amount received for assets sold or lost during the year. Should a straight-line depreciation of 20 per cent per annum on all assets result in a lower book value in any year, the annual depreciation allowance can be increased correspondingly. However, if the taxpayer can prove that the real value of machinery and equipment is lower than that resulting under the above-mentioned depreciation methods, depreciation can be allowed in an amount needed to get the book value to correspond to the actual value.

Since the assessment year 1992, i.e. from the financial year beginning 1 April 1990 onwards, most Swedish and foreign companies other than life insurance companies, investment companies and holding companies, have been allowed to make allocations to a tax-free tax equalization reserve. As from the income year 1994 (assessment 1995), corporate income tax has generally been imposed at a flat rate of 28 per cent (previously 30 per cent). For 1990 the rate was 40 per cent and, before that 52 per cent. From the fiscal year 1992 (assessment 1993) investment funds and life insurance companies have been subject to a lower tax rate of 25 per cent. As from 1 January 1992 the general *value-added tax* rate has been 25 per cent, although some lower rates have applied from time to time for foodstuffs and restaurant businesses and for service-related industries. Special capital gains rules apply to the sale of shares or other securities not classified as inventory.[14]

Nordic taxation in a global perspective

In the context of the globalization of Nordic financial markets we can say that *the* most important tax reforms in the individual countries occurred in 1986 in Denmark, in 1989 in Finland, in 1986 in Norway and in 1991 in Sweden. The purpose of Tables 7.7–7.9 is to provide a brief summary of the transformation of the Nordic tax systems in a global perspective. The tables show changes in personal and corporate tax rates, as well as corporate tax allowances. Nordic personal tax rates are high by international standards, whereas Nordic corporate taxes have on average been relatively beneficial to Nordic companies. Perhaps this last just reflects the fact that the Nordic countries are participating in the global 'race-to-the-bottom' of taxes[15] in order to attract inward investment.

However, as we have seen in the previous sections, Nordic tax reforms have also been aimed to some extent at largely harmonizing taxes with the EU standards. Hence, some tax-generated investment distortions may have been reduced or eliminated. In light of the high Nordic tax burden at the

Table 7.7 Changes in personal income tax rates

	Central government taxes				State and local tax	Overall top rate
	Lowest and highest marginal rates			Number of tax brackets[a]		
	1975	*1983*	*1988–89*		*1988–89*	
Denmark	19–44	19–44	22–40	3	28	68
Finland	10–51	6–51	11–44[b]	6	16	60
Norway	6–48	4–41	10–29[b,c]	3	25	54
Sweden	7–56	3–54	5–42[b,d]	3	30	72
Australia	20–65	30–60	24–49	3	–	49
Austria	23–62	21–62	10–50[b]	5	–	50
Belgium	17–60	17–72	25–55[b]	7	6–8	59
Canada	9–47	6–34	17–29	3	16	45
France	5–60	5–65	5–57	12	–	57
Germany	22–56	22–56	19–53[e]	Formula[f]	–	53
Greece	3–63	11–63	18–50	9	–	50
Iceland	–	25–50	28	1	7	35
Ireland	26–77	25–60	35–58	3	–	58
Italy	10–72	18–65	10–50[b]	7	–	50
Japan	10–75	10–70	10–50[b]	5	5–15	65
Luxembourg	18–57	12–57	10–56	24	–	56
Netherlands	20–71	17–72	35[g]–60	3	–	60
New Zealand	19–57	20–66	24–33	2	–	33
Portugal	4–80	4–80	16–40[b]	5	–	40
Spain	15–62	16–65	25–56[b]	16	–	56
Switzerland	1–13	1–13	1–13	6	5–34	47
Turkey	10–68	25–65	25–50	6	–	50
United Kingdom	35–83	30–60	25–40	2	–	40
United States	14–70	11–50	15–28/33	3	2–14	38

[a] Not including zero-rate band.
[b] From 1989.
[c] Including a surcharge of 6 per cent on income above SEK 180,000.
[d] The government has proposed to reduce the overall (central plus local) tax rate to a range of either 30 to 50 or 30 to 60 per cent by 1991.
[e] From 1990.
[f] The tax rate increases by linear progression.
[g] Including employee social security contribution of 28 per cent.

Sources: OECD (1987a, 1987b, 1989) and information supplied by the OECD Secretariat.

beginning of the 1990s and the old propensity of Nordic governments to impose taxes on new objects every now and then, investors will need some time before they allow the shift in national tax paradigms to affect their own investment decisions.

Table 7.8 Corporate tax allowances

	Normal depreciation method	Investment allowance or credit (1986)	Total allowance[a,b] in 1983	
			Equipment	Structures
Denmark	DB (M), SL (S)	–	22.2	12.9
Finland	DB	–	22.4	12.0
Norway	DB	–	36.7	20.6
Sweden	DB (M), SL (S)	IA (m)	34.5	22.4
Australia	SL or AD*	IA removed	38.3	7.7
Austria	SL or AD*	IA	47.3	31.3
Belgium	DB	IA	44.8	29.2
Canada	DB, AD	IC*	31.8	18.1
France	SL, DB (M)	–	34.5	22.2
Germany	DB or SL	–	48.4	27.5
Ireland	AD*	–	55.0	55.0
Italy	SL, AD	–	24.2	12.9
Japan	DB or SL	–	36.0	16.1
Netherlands	DB or SL	–	41.0	24.0
New Zealand	DB (M), SL (S)	–	24.1	5.4
Spain	DB or SL	IC	32.9	26.2
Switzerland	DB or SL	–	12.3	6.9
United Kingdom	DB or SL (S)	(AD abolished 1983)	52.0	41.4
United States	AD	(IC abolished 1986)	44.3	25.3

[a] At 'average' inflation per dollar of investment.
[b] The difference between the tax rate and allowances indicates the degree to which the system of capital allowances by itself is distortionary. Allowances smaller than the tax rate indicate that capital formation is *ceteris paribus* taxed; allowances greater than the tax rate imply that it is subsidized. The standard formulation of the neoclassical user cost of capital is:

$$c = q \, [(r(1-t) + d) \times (1 - k - t \times Z)]/(1-t)$$

where c = the real cost of capital per dollar of investment (which is equated in equilibrium with the present value of the net income stream generated by the asset); q = the relative price of capital goods; $r(1-t)$ = the after tax cost of funds; d = the true economic depreciation rate on new assets; k = the rate of the investment tax credit; t = the statutory corporate income tax rate; Z = the present discounted value (in dollars of the year of investment) of depreciation deductions stemming from the investment. The last term on the right hand side summarizes the effect of the corporate tax system, where $(k + t \times Z)$ is the value of the tax concession given by the government to the company. It can be seen that if $(k + t \times Z)$ equals the statutory corporate tax rate t then $(1 - k - t \times Z)/(1-t) = 1$ and the after-tax return is the same as the pre-tax one and the effective marginal tax rate is zero.

Sources: OECD (1987b, 1989), and McKee *et al.* (1986).
Note: SL = straight line; AD = accelerated depreciation; DB = declining balance; M = machinery; S = structures; * being cut back.

Considerable tax wedges in the investor perspective

In Table 7.10 we can see the tax wedges in the Nordic countries in 1991.[16] If we look at company taxes only, we find that the wedges were below the OECD average in all the Nordic countries except Norway. However, when

Table 7.9 Changes in corporate income tax rates

Country	1972	1983	1986	1988–89	Treatment of dividends	1993
Denmark	36	40	50	50	Imputation	34
Finland	58	59	50	45[a]	*Imputation[b]	25
Norway	51	51	51	51	*Imputation[b]	28
Sweden	54	52	52	52	Classical (p)	30
Austria	58	55	55	30	*Imputation[b]	39
Belgium	48	45	45	43	Classical	39
Canada[b]	50	51	53	44	Imputation	38
France	50	50	45	42	Imputation	33
Germany	52.5	56	56	56	Imputation	56
Iceland	–	65	51	51	Classical (p)	33
Ireland	50	50	50	43	Imputation	40
Italy[c]	44	46	46	46	Imputation	52
Japan[c,d]	47	53	53	50	*Classical[b]	38
Luxembourg	40	40	40	36	Classical	39
Netherlands	48	48	42	35	Classical	35
Spain	–	35	35	35	Classical (p)	35
New Zealand	45	45	48	28	*Imputation	30
United Kingdom	52	52	40	35	Imputation	33
United States	48	46	46	34	Classical	34

[a] From 1990.
[b] Formerly split rate system: lower tax rate on distributed income.
[c] Combined national and local tax rates.
[d] 40 per cent national tax in 1989, to be reduced to $37\frac{1}{2}$ per cent in 1990.
* Recent change.

Sources: OECD (1987b, 1989), Pechman (1988) and national sources. OECD (1991), Price Waterhouse (1993) and Ernst & Young (1993).
Note: Classical system: economic double taxation; (p): partial deduction for dividends paid. Imputation system: credit for company tax withheld.

Table 7.10 Nordic tax wedges in 1991

	Tax wedge		
	Company tax only	Company tax and personal income tax	Company tax: Official per cent tax
Denmark	0.9	2.4	38
Finland	0.6	4.4	39
Norway	1.8	2.5	50.8
Sweden	0.0	2.0	30
OECD average	0.9	2.0	–
EU average	0.7	1.8	–

Source: OECD (1991).
Note: The OECD calculation is based on assumptions about a common set of activities and financing, and an inflation of 4.5 per cent and a real interest rate of 5 per cent. The tax wedge in the column 'Company tax only' is based on a 0 per cent tax for the shareholder. When personal tax is considered in Column 2, it is used at its highest rate of marginal tax on capital gains/income.

personal (investing) taxes are also taken into account, we find that the wedges in all the Nordic countries were above both the OECD and the EU levels. Hence, we find that equity investments are discouraged in an international comparison. Moreover, the tax wedge as reported by OECD (1991) is larger for transnational than for domestic investments. This discrimination is on a par with or even below the OECD average.

SUPERVISORY STRUCTURES

Regulations imposed on financial market actors and aimed at improving the safety and soundness of the financial system, constitute another important part of the internal regulation system. However, the regulatory environment in a country can in itself create risks, as we noted briefly in Chapter 2, if different parts of the environment are pursuing inconsistent regulatory policies. This risk may vary between countries, in so far as their supervisory structures differ. The supervisory structures in the Nordic countries, as in most European countries in the early 1990s, were quite different from that of the United States, as Table 7.11 clearly reveals. Table 7.12 shows the supervision of banking and securities in terms of the number of authorities involved in the supervision at the end of the 1980s, and thus the exposure to potential inconsistencies between different supervisory authorities. We can see that in the early 1990s the Nordic countries – like many of the countries in the tables – had a single supervisory agency for both banking and securities companies, while most countries seem to have a special authority for supervising insurance companies. On that score, however, the Nordic countries are among the exceptions.

Nordic supervisory authorities

Finanstilsynet in Denmark (the Danish Financial Supervisory Authority), was established on 1 January 1988 as an amalgamation of the Supervision of Commercial Banks and Savings Banks and the Insurance Supervisory Authority. The supervision of mortgage–credit institutions (Kredittilsynet) was transferred from the Ministry of Housing to Finanstilsynet on 1 January 1990. Finanstilsynet answers to the Ministry of Industry, but like the seven other authorities answering to the Ministry, it has considerable freedom within its field of competence. Finanstilsynet cooperates closely with Danmarks Nationalbank (the Central Bank). Within the EU, however, it is more common that the central bank supervises the banks without the cooperation of any other authority as in the Danish case.

Finansinspektionen (the Financial Supervisory Authority) in Finland is in charge of supervising the banks, while the insurance department within the Ministry of Social Affairs and Health is the supervisor of the insurance

Table 7.11 Supervisory authorities for banking, insurance and securities in major OECD countries in the early 1990s

	Banks	Insurance	Securities
Denmark Finland Norway Sweden	Finanstilsynet Finansinspektionen Kredittilsynet Finansinspektionen	Finanstilsynet Socialdepartementet Kredittilsynet Finansinspektionen	Finanstilsynet Finansinspektionen Kredittilsynet Finansinspektionen
USA	Office of the Controller of the Currency, Federal Reserve System, Federal Deposit Insurance Corporation	Federal Insurance Inspection Authorities	Securities and Exchange Commission, Commodity Futures Trading
Japan Germany	Part of the Ministry of Finance Bundesaufsichsamt für das Kreditwesen	Part of the Ministry of Finance Bundesaufsichsamt für das Versicherungswesen	Part of the Ministry of Finance Bundesaufsichsamt für das Kreditwesen/Deutsche Bundesbank/Departement des Wirtschaft
France	Commission Bancaire	Direction des Assurances	Commission des opérations de bourse, Commission Bancaire, ministère des Finances et al.
Belgium	Commission Bancaire	Contrôle des Assurances	Caisse de garantie des agents de change, Commission de la bourse
Netherlands United Kingdom	De Nederlansche Bank Bank of England	Verzekeringskamer Part of Ministry of Trade	Stichting Toetzicht Effectenverkeer Securities and Investment Board, self-regulating organizations
Italy	Banca d'Italia	Instituto per la Vigilanza sulle Assicurazionni	Commissione nazionale per le societa e la borsa
Canada	Office of the Superintendent of Financial Institutions	Office of the Superintendent of Financial Institutions	Securities Commissions

Table 7.12 Major differences in regulatory segmentation and functional supervision

	Regulatory segmentation for banking and securities activities			Functional supervision for banking and securities activities
	One principal supervisor (one for both)	*Two principal supervisors (one for each)*	*Multiple supervisors*	*Degree of current or planned use*
Universal systems				
France	X[a]			Low[b]
Germany	X[a]			Low[b]
Italy	X			Low[b]
Netherlands	X			Low[b]
Switzerland	X			Limited[b]
Blended systems				
Belgium	X			Low
Denmark	X			High
Canada		X		High
Finland	X			High
Japan		X[c]		Limited
Norway	X			High
Sweden	X			High
United Kingdom		X		High
United States			X	Limited

[a] The Banking Commission, the principal bank supervisor, shares responsibility for supervising the securities activities of banks with the Stock Exchange Council.
[b] In countries with universal banking systems, banks are the principal providers of securities activities, so that the need to allocate supervisory responsibility has not spurred the development of functional supervision as it has in some blended system countries.
[c] The Banking and Securities Bureaux are both part of the Ministry of Finance, but they operate somewhat independently.
Source: Adapted from Cumming and Sweet (1988), revised for Sweden and extended to include the other Nordic countries.

business. The supervision of the securities business was included among the tasks of the Bankinspektionen from 1 November 1988 for the option market and from 1 August 1989 for the trade in securities in general. At the beginning of 1992 the question of creating a joint authority and designating it Finansinspektionen was being discussed. However, no such joint authority was created. Nevertheless, Bankinspektionen changed its name to Finansinspektionen on 1 October 1993. It should be noted that its structure is not the same as that of the Swedish Finansinspektionen, which includes the Banking and Insurance Commissions.

The Norwegian Kredittilsynet (The Norwegian Banking, Insurance and Securities Commission) was established in 1986 as a merger between the

Table 7.13 Nordic supervisory authorities (and dates of changes in authority)

Date	Denmark			Finland			Norway			Sweden		
	Banking	Insurance	Securities	Banking	Insurance	Securities	Banking	Insurance	Securities	Banking	Insurance	Securities
Authority in charge at the beginning of 1976	Tilsynet med Banker og Sparekasser	Försäkringstilsynet	Tilsynet med Banker og Sparekasser	Bankinspektionen	Socialdepartementet		Bankinspektionen	Forsikringsrådet	Handelsdepartementets meglingskontroll	Bankinspektionen	Försäkringsinspektionen	Bankinspektionen
24 March 1986							Kredittilsynet	Kredittilsynet	Kredittilsynet			
1 January 1988	Finanstilsynet	Finanstilsynet	Finanstilsynet									
1 November 1988						Bankinspektionen (options)						
1 August 1989						Bankinspektionen (securities in general)						
1 July 1991										Finansinspektionen	Finansinspektionen	Finansinspektionen
1 October 1993				Finansinspektionen		Finansinspektionen						

Banking Commission and the Insurance Commission. A change in the law on 7 June 1985 paved the way for this merger. Although it was formally established on 24 March 1986 it was not fully operative until mid-1987. Kredittilsynet cooperates closely with the Bank of Norway and, like the Bank of Norway, is accountable to the Ministry of Finance. Meetings between Kredittilsynet and the Ministry of Finance also take place at least once a month. A substantial reorganization of Kredittilsynet was undertaken and was completed by 1 April 1991.

Finansinspektionen (the Financial Supervisory Authority) in Sweden is accountable to the Swedish Ministry of Finance. It was established in July 1991 as a merger between the Banking and Insurance Commissions. The regulatory body that was established in 1991 for the activities of the Finansinspektionen included the supervision of some thirty laws dating from 1934 onwards. A new regulation came into force in April 1992. A schematic description of major changes in the Nordic supervisory authorities is presented in Table 7.13.

Deposit insurance in the Nordic region

In the mid-1990s, all the Nordic countries with the exception of Sweden have formal deposit guarantee schemes. However, their genesis differed between the countries.

In Denmark the tradition used to be that banks which ran into financial difficulties were taken over by other banks, so that the depositors incurred no losses. Between the end of the Second World War and 1987, only one bank suffered bankruptcy. In 1987, however, there were problems in the Danish banking industry, and several political parties began to call for a scheme whereby small depositors would be secured in the event of bankruptcy. When the Ministry of Industry at the end of October 1987 proposed a bill for a Deposit Guarantee Fund, it was also complying with the recommendation of the EC Commission of 22 December 1986 that member countries who had not yet introduced a deposit guarantee scheme in any form should establish one. Subject to minor amendments the Danish bill was passed on 16 December 1987. The scheme consists of a fund organized as an independent private institution. Holders of deposits with banks (commercial banks, cooperative banks and branches of foreign banks in Denmark) and certain credit institutes with special authorization (banking houses) are granted cover for losses on deposits in the event of bankruptcy. The fund's financial base comes from deposits and in some cases contributions from the institutes themselves. No maximum figure for the total loss is specified, but in the comments attached to the bill it is stated that should one of the largest banks or several of the institutes at a time get into serious financial difficulties, intervention by the public authorities will be considered. The institutes' annual contribution to the fund may amount to a maximum of 0.2

per cent of total deposits. The fund can also raise loans guaranteed by the Ministry of Industry to meet its commitments.

Deposits in Finnish banks are insured by law in the form of bank guarantee funds. Banks pay into these funds a fixed sum each year which is based on their total assets. At the beginning of the 1990s, for instance, commercial banks paid the compulsory premium of 0.0001 per cent of their total assets. Members of the guarantee fund are jointly responsible for the ability of the members to meet their commitments, and the size of the premium can be adjusted in light of the general situation. An obvious weakness is that the sum which has to be paid into the guarantee fund does not depend on the riskiness of a bank's loan portfolio. Hence, banks financing risky investments may benefit at the expense of other more prudent banks. The Bank of Finland has also been forced to exercise a 'lender of last resort' function, and to come to the rescue of some banks.

In Norway depositors have effective guarantees against losses through the Banking Security Fund, established collectively by the banks and guaranteed as a last resort by the government. In addition the Government Bank Insurance Fund was established on 15 March 1991 with an initial capital of NOK 5 billion, to underpin the soundness of the banking system as well as securing depositors' interests by granting loans on special terms (support loans) to the Commercial and Savings Banks Guarantee Funds, to facilitate the infusion into the banks of risk capital from the guarantee funds.

CONCLUDING REMARKS ON INTERNAL LIBERALIZATION AND TAX HARMONIZATION

Various institutional characteristics of the Nordic financial markets have developed in rather different ways. At the beginning of the 1980s Finland, Norway and Sweden had broad-based credit controls combined with low interest rate policies, while Denmark had relatively high domestic interest rates compared with many other countries. Credit rationing was used most extensively in Finland and Norway. The role of credit rationing then diminished rapidly, and since the beginning of the 1990s the view of Nordic markets as being undeveloped and strongly regulated, has no validity any longer.

The timing of the general internal deregulation also differed between the Nordic countries. Whereas the liberalization gained momentum in Denmark as far back as the 1970s and the beginning of the 1980s, the process started much later in the other Nordic countries. The Danish *de jure* internal deregulation of the bond markets was almost complete by the beginning of the 1980s, followed by the other Nordic countries ten years later. In Norway and Sweden the bulk of the deregulative measures occurred in the second half of the 1980s, while in Finland most of the deregulations took place from the beginning of the 1990s onwards.

On the tax front there were also differences between the Nordic countries in the timing as well as the content of the main tax reforms. The Danish and Norwegian authorities managed to get to grips with distortional incentives in 1986, while Finnish and Swedish authorities did not achieve any fiscal changes of equal significance until 1989 and 1991. However, in 1991 a tax wedge above the OECD average appeared not only for Finnish investors, but also for Danish and Norwegian.

The timing of the tax reforms relative to the timetable for the rest of the internal deregulation was also different. Although all the Nordic countries began to introduce radical tax reforms from the mid-1980s onwards, only in Denmark was the major reform undertaken before *de jure* external and internal deregulation had been completed. In the other Nordic countries the tax reforms were undertaken after *de jure* deregulation was completed, and taxes in these countries may thus have contributed to significant distortions in investment patterns.

The effects of the internal deregulation were felt on the demand side as well as on the supply side of the bond markets. A general effect that benefited both sides was the greater transparency that resulted. The timetable for deregulative measures may make a noticeable impact on the way a market evolves and continues to develop. Internal regulation may provoke changes in the size of the market shares of different sectors in the national financial market.

As regards supply factors, we have seen that during the 1980s Nordic policy-makers attempted to eliminate incentives that favoured loans rather than equity. The double taxation of dividends was abolished in all the Nordic countries in the early 1990s, making it less interesting for companies to issue bond loans – which would also have reduced the supply of bonds. In 1995, however, double taxation was reintroduced in Sweden, but the effects were somewhat mitigated in that only a low percentage of the gains were taxed. A measure that probably helped to increase the supply of bonds was the changeover from credit rationing to a virtual market by the abolition of issuing controls, which were lifted in Denmark in 1989, in Sweden in 1991, in Finland in 1993 and in Norway in 1995.

Deregulative measures affecting the demand for bonds – apart from those that just increased transparency in a general way, making it easier for investors to assess different investment opportunities – included the dismantling of the investment obligation. The lifting of this regulation, which was never in force in Denmark and Finland, probably had a negative effect mainly on the demand for government bonds. In Norway the regulation was abolished in 1985 and in Sweden in 1986. One measure that influenced demand in the Nordic countries, but in different directions, is the way the tax on bond rate income and capital gains from trading in bonds has been treated. Capital gains have generally been taxed in the Nordic countries at a higher rate than trading in stocks. Special rules have applied to the computation of the tax and the gains have been taxed as ordinary income.

In most countries the global financial crisis of the 1990s led to a reconsideration of supervisory structures and to far-reaching changes. The possibility that serious problems or systemic risk might arise from the multiplicity of institutions – official and private – involved in the surveillance, has been reduced in most instances by assigning the whole supervisory responsibility to a single authority. This may prove effective, as it eliminates the risk of inconsistencies. But on the negative side, it may also weaken the flexibility of the financial system.

NOTES

1   Norway was the exception here.
2   The UK economy, which was constrained by a credit crunch caused by the banks' problems, provides a parallel here. The combination of potential capital constraints and increased risk-aversion impaired the willingness or ability of banks to meet a projected upswing in the demand for bank credit.
3   The need for domestic borrowing varied among the Nordic countries, as some of them borrowed heavily from abroad.
4   Market operations are effective only in periods when the banking system is not borrowing at penalty rates from the central bank or investing surplus liquidity with the National Debt Office.
5   The buying and selling activities may also be more general, as in Finland, and involve certificates of deposit issued by different sectors.
6   This calendarium, like the one for external deregulation, is based on press releases and other types of published material from central banks and ministries of finance. It shows on a daily basis the date a decision was taken (or in some cases implemented). The calendarium, which will be published in a separate book, is aimed at providing opportunities for an assessment concerning Nordic policy coordination.
7   According to the residence principle, the home country taxes its residents on their worldwide income, i.e. irrespective of where it has been earned. When the source principle applies, the government only taxes income earned inside its borders, regardless of the nationality of the income recipient.
8   For a more complete description see OECD (1987b) and OECD (1989).
9   It was actually adopted by a substantial majority in the Folketing in June 1985.
10   In the period 1987–91 there were some transitional rules to mitigate the effect of the new system of differentiating between personal income and income from capital. In 1987 income from capital was treated as personal income, to the extent that it exceeded DKK 50,000. As from 1991, the amount of income from capital so treated was reduced by DKK 100,000.
11   A reduced rate may apply to certain countries. See IBFD (1994).
12   Depending on the family size.
13   Except for the source: tax on interest income.
14   See, for example, IBFD (1994) for further information about the rules for the taxation of bonds.
15   See Oxelheim (1993).
16   A tax wedge may be calculated on a basis of the company tax and on the tax of the investors' rate of return. When this last is 0 per cent, the tax wedge is thus a result of company tax only. Assume that inflation is 3 per cent and the nominal

bond rate is 10.2 per cent, then the real rate of the bond investment is 7 per cent before tax. Hence, the investor requires at least a 7 per cent rate of return on an equity investment. The requirement on the corporate rate of return may then be calculated for a Danish company, for instance, as $[10.2/(1 - 0.38)] = 16.5$ per cent. This implies a requirement of a real rate of return of 13.1 per cent. The difference between the real return on investment before company tax and the real rate of return for the investor after company tax is the tax wedge. In this example it is $13.1 - 7 = 6.1$ per cent. A negative tax wedge implies that the investment is subsidized by the company tax.

REFERENCES

Bank of Finland, 1993, *Yearbook*, Helsinki, pp. 23–4 and 60–2.

Bank of Norway, 1989, *Norske Kreditmarkeder – Norsk Penge- og Kredittpolitikk*, No. 17, Oslo.

Cumming, C.M. and L.M. Sweet, 1988, 'Financial Structure of the G-10 Countries: How Does the United States Compare?', *Quarterly Review*, Federal Reserve Bank of New York, Winter.

Ernst & Young, 1993, *Worldwide Corporate Tax Guide*, New York.

IBFD, 1994, *Supplementary Service to European Taxation*, Amsterdam.

McKee, M.J., J.J.C. Visser and P.G. Saunders, 1986, 'Marginal Tax Rates on the Use of Capital and Labour in OECD Countries', *OECD Economic Studies*, No. 7 (Autumn).

OECD, 1985, *Banking and Monetary Policy*, Paris.

OECD, 1987a, *The Tax-Benefit Position of Production Workers 1983–1986*, Paris.

OECD, 1987b, *Taxation in Developed Countries*, Paris.

OECD, 1987c, *Economic Survey of Norway*, December, Paris.

OECD, 1989, *Economies in Transition – Structural Adjustments in OECD Countries*, Paris.

OECD, 1991, *Taxing Profits in a Global Economy*, Paris.

Oxelheim, L., 1993, 'Foreign Direct Investment and the Liberalization of Capital Movements', in Oxelheim, L. (ed.), *The Global Race for Foreign Direct Investment: Prospects for the Future*, Springer Verlag, Heidelberg.

Pechman, J.A. (ed.) 1988, *World Tax Reform: A Progress Report*, Brookings Dialogues on Public Policy, Washington, DC.

Price Waterhouse, 1993, *Corporate Taxes: A Worldwide Summary*, London.

Chapter 8

Monetary integration

In this chapter we will be looking at monetary issues which have an impact on the demand and supply of bonds. In the earlier chapters, we have noted that for long periods the governments in all the Nordic countries have opted for corner (1) in the monetary policy triangle (Figure 1.1). They have used capital controls combined with fixed exchange regimes to achieve monetary policy autonomy. We have also seen that all the Nordic countries lifted their controls during the period 1988–91, thus moving to corner (2) in the triangle. However, for some of the countries the move was presumably only a formal acknowledgement of the fact that efficiency had already been eroded. The extent to which this was so will be further discussed in Chapter 14. In 1992 Finland, Norway and Sweden moved to corner (3) in the triangle by adopting a floating exchange regime. Denmark in the mid-1990s was still somewhere between corners (2) and (3), with the krone inside the ERM but with a very broad fluctuation band (±15 per cent).

In the bond market perspective the monetary issues will appear in comparisons between international bond rates. Such comparisons need an assessment of future changes in exchange rates and of the size of the exchange-risk premiums. The theory for determining the size of the premiums has not yet been fully agreed upon. However, demands for premiums are probably motivated on the grounds of the volatility in nominal or real exchange rates. The lack of success in pegging the exchange rate is shown in Table 8.1, as manifest in the necessity to devaluate. To complete the picture of parity changes, some revaluations also occurred during the period, all of them small and all of them in Finland (1–2 per cent). Hence, although exchange rates have been fixed for long periods, the deviations from purchasing power parity have been substantial.

The choice of exchange rate regime affects the level of indirect bond market integration, via the level of monetary integration. Perfect monetary integration means that the exchange rate strictly follows purchasing power parity. If perfect monetary integration prevails, then the premium for exchange risk is zero[1] and the expected exchange rate movement is derived from the purchasing power parity relationship. Imperfect (total) financial

Table 8.1 Devaluations in the Nordic countries (official changes in central parities, per cent)

	Denmark	Finland	Norway	Sweden
April 1977	3.0	5.7	3.0	6.0
August 1977	5.0		5.0	10.0
September 1977		3.0		
February 1978		8.0	8.0	
September 1979	5.0			
November 1979	5.0			
September 1981				10.0
October 1981	5.5			
February 1982	3.0			
June 1982	4.25			
August 1982			2.5	
September 1982			3.0	
October 1982		10.0		16.0
March 1983	2.5			
July 1984			2.0	
April 1986	1.98			
May 1986			12.0	
January 1987	3.0			
November 1991		12.3[a]		
September 1992		Floating		
November 1992				Floating
December 1992			Floating	

[a] Not really a devaluation, since the currency for some hours was allowed to float on November 15.

Note: For Denmark, a devaluation of the Danish krone is registered against the Deutschmark.

integration, when perfect monetary integration obtains, is caused by possible political risk premiums and/or inefficiencies.

An exchange rate regime implying a permanently *fixed* exchange rate between two countries would mean that the two countries must also have coordinated policies, an equal level of inflation and, *de facto*, also the same money. But if the exchange rate is not to be regarded as permanently fixed, which is a realistic assumption, the risk premium for currencies in such a system, e.g. with an adjustable peg, may very well be greater than in a system of freely floating exchange rates.

The chapter opens with a survey of Nordic exchange rate arrangements since the mid-1970s. This is followed by an empirical analysis of nominal and real exchange rate fluctuations,[2] and, in conclusion, a discussion about the impact of monetary issues on the demand and supply of bonds.

DANISH EXCHANGE RATE ARRANGEMENTS

Denmark has a history of exchange rate cooperation, first within the Bretton Woods system and then within Europe. An important factor in the case of the Danish situation has been the ambition to stabilize the exchange rate of the Danish krone (DKK). This goal led Denmark's government to participate in the European joint float, and as of 13 March 1979 in the exchange rate arrangement of the European Monetary System (EMS).

During the 1980s the declared goal of the Danish government to pursue a policy involving a stable Danish krone within the EMS enhanced the credibility of the Danish economic policy, and by the beginning of the 1990s paid off in the shape of fairly good results in the balance of payments, inflation and interest rates. It gave the Danish krone in the mid-1990s a position among the hard-core currencies in the European currency system. However, on the way to achieving this position, Denmark's policy of fixed exchange rates imposed strict limits on the scope of the country's fiscal policy actions. According to the close connection between the currencies of the EMS countries, and later also to the conditions of the European Monetary Union (EMU), each individual country is supposed to give very high priority to the attainment of equilibrium in government finances. Hence, in the mid-1980s a tight fiscal policy became a necessity, after several years when deficits had been piling up to a record high level of public debt, as we saw in Figure 3.1.

In the early 1990s Denmark participated – together with Belgium, France, Germany, Ireland, Italy, Luxembourg, the Netherlands, Spain, the United Kingdom and Portugal – in the exchange rate mechanism (ERM) of the EMS. In accordance with this agreement Denmark maintained the spot exchange rates between the Danish krone and the currencies of the other participants within margins of 2.25 per cent (in the case of some currencies 6 per cent) above or below the cross rates based on the central rates expressed in European Currency Units (ECUs). The foreign exchange turbulence from 1991–93 brought on by a Danish referendum opposed to the European Union on 2 June 1992, became too fierce for the EMS; some countries left the system, and for some of the others, including Denmark, the margins were extended to ±15 per cent in August 1993.

Intervention praxis

Danmarks Nationalbank (the Central Bank) has undertaken to intervene on the Danish foreign exchange market only at the intervention rates agreed upon within the EMS. This obligation implies that Danmarks Nationalbank stands ready to buy or sell the currencies of the other countries participating in the EMS in unlimited amounts at these specified rates. Middle rates (average of buying and selling rates) for 20 foreign currencies (including the

ECU) are officially fixed daily, reflecting the going rates at the time of the fixing.

Danmarks Nationalbank also intervenes for the purpose of smoothing out fluctuations in krone-related exchange rates. This smoothing out occurs only with respect to movements in the EMS currencies, predominantly the Deutschmark. Interventions may technically be executed in any currency included in the official fixing of exchange rates, and the US dollar is often used as the intervention currency.

Danish market rules

Denmark formally accepted the obligations of Article VIII, sections 2, 3 and 4 of the International Monetary Fund Agreement, as from 1 May 1967. The Executive Order on Foreign Exchange Regulations, effective from 1 October 1988, allowed Danish residents to hold positions in foreign currencies, with no limitations on the amounts, currencies, or instruments involved. However, the regulations also contained restrictions, and payments between residents and non-residents had to be reported to Danmarks Nationalbank for statistical purposes if the payments exceeded DKK 60,000. After 1 October 1988 there were no restrictions on foreign exchange dealing. However, foreign exchange dealers (banks) were obliged to keep their net foreign exchange position (spot plus forward) against the Danish krone within a range equal to ±10 per cent of their capital. There were no taxes or subsidies on purchases or sales of foreign exchange.

FINNISH EXCHANGE RATE ARRANGEMENTS

During the post-war period, apart from a few recent exceptions, Finland has followed a policy of fixed exchange rates. At first the exchange rate was fixed under the Bretton Woods system. In mid-1973, when this system had collapsed, the Bank of Finland (the Central Bank) started to calculate different types of currency basket to provide guidelines for its foreign exchange policy, but the basket concept was not formally and legally adopted until 1977. It was then of the traditional Nordic type, with an exchange rate index based on foreign trade shares. In the wake of the Norwegian and Swedish currencies, the Finnish markka (FIM) was pegged to the ECU on 7 June 1991.

Until June 1991 the external value of the markka was defined in terms of an index reflecting a weighted average of the exchange rates of the convertible currencies most important to Finland's foreign trade. These were defined as the convertible currencies of countries which accounted for not less than 1 per cent of Finland's commodity imports and exports in each of the three preceding calendar years. The value of the currency of an individual country could theoretically change, without limitations, in relation to the Finnish markka. However, a median point was determined for the currency index around which the markka could fluctuate by ±3 per cent. The Bank of Finland was bound to keep the exchange rate index of the markka within these boundaries.

Finland's decision to link the markka to the ECU was unilateral and aimed at enhancing credibility. Abolishing the ECU linkage required legislative changes. However, a change in the average exchange rate did not require such a move. In practice the Bank of Finland and the government were committed to the policy of a stable markka. The idea of winning additional international credibility through the ECU linkage failed. The pressure on the markka became too intense in November 1991, and the markka was allowed to float for a few hours until the new parity with the ECU was fixed on 15 November 1991. The pressure continued and, in the general foreign exchange market turbulence of mid-1992, on 8 September 1992 the markka was allowed to float again. Finland had thus moved to corner (3) in the policy triangle exhibited in Figure 1.1.

Finnish intervention praxis

Until June 1991 the value of the exchange rate index was maintained by the Bank of Finland within a margin established by the State Council. Between 1 January 1984 and 29 November 1988 the range was 101.3–106.0 (1982 = 100). On 30 November 1988 it was widened to 100.5–106.8, and as of 17 March 1989 it was lowered by about 4 percentage points to 96.5–102.5. The weights used in the index were adjusted quarterly and the base year was changed annually. The Bank of Finland calculated and published the currency index on a daily basis and quoted daily (noon) buying and selling rates for the US dollar, the intervention currency. Buying and selling rates for the rouble were based on the rates of the State Bank of the USSR for the US dollar against the rouble. Quotations for other currencies were based on market cross rates.

Theoretically the markka could fluctuate freely within its fluctuation band. However, the Bank of Finland sometimes set target areas within the fluctuation range, in which it held the markka's value. Until the mid-1980s the markka's index was not effectively allowed to move within the fluctuation band. However, from the end of that decade and especially after the abolition of the currency controls, the central bank allowed the markka to fluctuate more freely within its fluctuation range. When it was necessary, the Bank of Finland influenced the exchange rate of the markka on the currency market by spot or forward interventions. With the help of spot interventions the Bank of Finland fine-tuned the exchange rate of the markka within its fluctuation range.

The EMS currencies dominated the trade-weighted index (constituting 45 per cent of the index). But, since Sweden and Norway used the same type of indices based on foreign trade shares, and since the Norwegian and Swedish currencies were also in practice tied to the EMS currencies, Finland's actual EMS linkage was somewhat more extensive than its formal linkage. Before the pegging of the Norwegian krone and the Swedish krona to the ECU, the EMS currencies accounted for about 80 per cent of the Finnish basket, when indirect effects are also taken into account. After the linkage, the proportion rose to 85 per cent. In the trade-weighted index, the remaining portion was made up of the US dollar and the Japanese yen.

The value of the ECU against the FIM on the day the Finnish markka was pegged to the ECU was 4.87580. It was calculated on a basis of the average rates on 6 June 1991. At the time of calculation the old exchange rate index was exactly at the mid-point of its fluctuation range. Hence, the ECU/FIM exchange rate of 4.87580 became the central rate of the ECU against the FIM. The markka's fluctuation range remained at ±3 per cent, identical to the range allowed by the old index. The ECU/FIM exchange rates were thus allowed to float between FIM 4.72953 and FIM 5.02207.

The ECU-pegged system differed from the previous arrangement in that the markka could no longer fluctuate without limit in relation to individual ECU currencies, because the ERM restricted the movement of currencies in relation to each other. Thus, maximum bilateral fluctuation boundaries could also be calculated for the markka. For example, against the Deutschmark the fluctuation range was ±5.29 per cent.

Since Sweden and Norway had also tied their currencies to the ECU, it was possible to calculate bilateral fluctuation ranges against them as well. Against the Norwegian krone (NOK) the markka could fluctuate by ±5.25 per cent, and against the Swedish krona by ±4.5 per cent. The pegging of the Finnish markka to the European currencies was thus clearly more binding than before.

Another essential difference was that the US dollar and the Japanese yen were no longer included in the basket. Consequently the markka's fluctuations against these currencies could be greater than before, while fluctuations against currencies within the ERM decreased.

On 15 November 1991, after a few hours float, the new mid-point became 5.55841. The markka's fluctuation range remained unchanged at ±3 per cent. The lower limit was thus 5.72516 and the upper limit 5.39166. After a period of several speculative attacks against the Finnish currency, the markka was allowed to float freely as from 8 September 1992.

Finnish market rules

Finland formally accepted the obligations of Article VIII, sections 2,3 and 4 of the International Monetary Fund Agreement as from 25 September 1979. In the early 1990s authorized banks were able to deal among themselves, and with residents and with non-resident banks in US dollars and other convertible currencies. There were no taxes or subsidies on purchases or sales of foreign exchange.

NORWEGIAN EXCHANGE RATE ARRANGEMENTS

For most of the 1970s the Norwegian krone was part of the European joint currency float. On 12 December 1978 the Norwegian authorities withdrew the krone from the float and decided to peg it to a basket of currencies which were of special importance to the country's trade in goods and services. The value of the krone was then fixed against a weighted average of 14 currencies. The weights were selected with a view to stabilizing the competitiveness of Norwegian exports of raw materials and manufactured goods. Hence, in principle, Norway's export competitiveness should not be affected by international exchange rate fluctuations. On 2 August 1982, the Bank of Norway (the Central Bank) decided to replace bilateral trade weights by MERM (Multilateral Exchange Rate Model) weights. A further modification came about on 2 July 1984, when a new index based on a geometric average of changes in individual exchange rates from their base values replaced the arithmetic average.

In the 1990 national budget the government announced that it would be in Norway's best interest to increase the country's cooperation with the European exchange rate system. On 19 October 1990 the external value of the Norwegian krone was pegged to the ECU. Linking the krone to the ECU was seen by the government at that time as being advantageous, in light of the prospective European monetary union and Norway's position in an integrated Europe. The decisive factor behind the decision to follow the ECU appeared to be that Germany was the exponent of a tough exchange rate policy, placing heavy emphasis on price stability in its monetary and credit policy. Further, the evident drop in the level of inflation in Norway and surpluses in the current account paved the way for the decision to change the exchange rate regime. By linking the krone to the ECU, the government indicated that price and cost levels were to remain low. A disciplined exchange rate policy was seen as providing a basis for a lower interest rate level than would otherwise have been possible.

The unilateral peg made the value of the Norwegian krone dependent to a large extent on movements in the Deutschmark, as this currency had the highest weight in the ECU. As a result, however, the Norwegian krone was subject to uncontrollable fluctuations against currencies such as the US dollar and the Japanese yen. Following the demise of the fixed Finnish markka and Swedish krona, the Norwegian authorities also had to yield to the powerful forces behind the European exchange turbulence in 1992 and allow the Norwegian krone to float as of 10 December 1992.

Norwegian intervention praxis

The external value of the Norwegian krone was pegged to the ECU at NOK 7.9940 per ECU, which corresponded to 112.0 in the former exchange rate index from 11 May 1986. The exchange rate was managed in order to allow only limited fluctuations (±2.25 per cent) around its central value.[3] This meant that the krone's value against the ECU could vary between 7.8141 and 8.1739 NOK/ECU. The bilateral fluctuation margins between the Norwegian krone and the EMS currencies were thus restricted by the EMS currencies' fluctuation margin against the ECU, plus the Norwegian krone's fluctuation margin against the ECU (about 9 per cent). The exchange rate of the krone for the US dollar, the principal intervention currency, is quoted daily, together with those of eighteen other currencies (and the ECU) on a basis of the market rates.

Norwegian market rules

Norway formally accepted the obligations of Article VIII, sections 2, 3 and 4 of the International Monetary Fund Agreement as from 11 May 1967. In the early 1990s, residents (Norwegian companies and private individuals) could freely enter into forward and interest rate contracts with Norwegian foreign exchange banks and non-residents, for protection against exchange rate risk. There were no taxes or subsidies on purchases or sales of foreign exchange. Residents were allowed to open accounts denominated in Norwegian kroner with foreign banks without restriction, but they had to notify the central bank of Norway.

SWEDISH EXCHANGE RATE ARRANGEMENTS

From March 1973 until 29 August 1977 Sweden was a member of the European joint float, known as the currency snake. During that period the Swedish krona (SEK) was devalued twice against the Deutschmark, 3 per cent in October 1976 and 6 per cent in April 1977. In August 1977, Sweden left the snake and devalued another 10 per cent. The krona was fixed against a basket with weights based on foreign trade. This index was arithmetic and similar to the ECU index. The system of trade weights was designed to keep competitiveness – as opposed to the price level – stable. In September 1981 the krona was devalued by 10 per cent against the basket and in October 1982, shortly after the election returning the Social Democrats to power, the krona was devalued 'aggressively' by 16 per cent.

Invoking the need to create credibility for the price stability goal, the Swedish authorities decided to peg the Swedish krona unilaterally to the ECU on 17 May 1991. The peg was set against the theoretical ECU. The exchange rate was set at SEK 7.40054/ECU and the band of ±1.5 per cent was kept from the previous basket arrangement. This meant that the Swedish krona was more restricted in its movements against the ECU than the majority of ERM currencies and the other Nordic currencies pegged to the ECU. The ECU link was unilateral, and the central banks of the EMS countries were not obliged to help the Swedish central bank to keep the krona within the limits of the band.

After a period of heavy speculative attacks on the Swedish krona, as part of the general foreign exchange market turbulence which followed the negative outcome of the Danish referendum on the EU and fuelled by the surrender of the Bank of Finland in its defence of the markka's ECU peg, the Swedish Central Bank had to give up its defence of the krona's ECU peg on 19 November 1992, and allow the krona to float. This surrender came only after a firm and aggressive defence action, with increases in the marginal rate on the banks' lending in the Swedish Central Bank to a peak of 500 per cent on 16 September 1992.

Swedish intervention praxis

In managing the exchange rate of the krona the Swedish Central Bank was guided up to May 1991 by a trade-weighted index based on a basket of the fifteen currencies of Sweden's most important trading partners. In constructing the index the Swedish authorities established two criteria which had to be met by every country and currency included in the basket:

- the country had to have accounted for at least 1 per cent of Sweden's total foreign trade (exports plus imports) during the previous five-year period, and
- each currency had to be quoted daily on the foreign exchange market in Stockholm.

The weights were proportional to Sweden's foreign trade with the countries whose currencies were included in the index, except that the weight of the US dollar was doubled and the other currencies adjusted accordingly. In order to take account of changes in average trade shares, the weights were adjusted each year (on 1 April) on a basis of the trade statistics for the last five calendar years.

The index value of 132 represented the benchmark for the effective value following the devaluation on 8 October 1982 (29 August 1977 = 100). The exchange rate was managed in order to allow only limited fluctuations around this benchmark. Beginning in June 1985, fluctuations in the spot rate were limited to within 1.5 per cent on either side of the given benchmark. The previous unofficial band width was ±2.25 per cent. An average of daily index values was published weekly by the central bank. The US dollar was the intervention currency. Spot rates for other currencies were established on a basis of cross rates in international markets. Forward market rates were left to the interplay of market forces.

The ECU link established in May 1991 led to a couple of major changes in intervention praxis. Definite limits as to how much the krona was allowed to fluctuate against the ERM currencies and the other currencies pegged to the ECU were introduced. Even though there were no official bilateral limits, these could be computed by adding ±1.5 per cent to the maximum movement within the ERM grid for a certain currency. The limits were maximum values, assuming that the Greek drachma and the Portuguese escudo were within the 6 per cent fluctuation band. The implicit theoretical limits, however, were narrower, taking into account the bands of the Dutch guilder and the Belgian franc against the Deutschmark.

Swedish market rules

Sweden formally accepted the obligations of Article VIII, sections 2, 3 and 4 of the International Monetary Fund Agreement as from 15 February 1961. In the early 1990s authorized banks were able to buy from and sell to other authorized banks and Swedish residents any foreign currency on a spot or forward basis against another foreign currency or Swedish kronor. Authorized banks could also purchase (sell) foreign currencies, spot or forward, from (to) foreign banks and other non-residents against any foreign currency or Swedish kronor credited (debited) to an account denominated in Swedish kronor. Currency option contracts could also be concluded freely with both residents and non-residents. There were no taxes or subsidies on purchases or sales of foreign exchange.

As a safety precaution limits were placed on the net foreign exchange positions (spot, forward, options) of banks in individual foreign currencies and on the total net position in all foreign currencies. The limit for each foreign currency and for the total net position was equal to 10 per cent of a bank's capital base. For a bank that was an authorized dealer, this second limit was equal to 15 per cent of its capital base. Banks could grant overdrafts to non-residents and also incur foreign exchange net liabilities for which the same limits applied. This enabled the banks to borrow foreign currency from non-residents for lending to foreign banks or other non-residents or to residents. Lending abroad in Swedish kronor was also freely permitted. Swedish banks were able to borrow abroad freely, while observing their limits on net foreign exchange holdings, in order to sell the proceeds against Swedish kronor in the market.

AN INTRA-REGIONAL COMPARISON

At the beginning of the 1990s Denmark was a member of the EMS, whereas Finland, Norway and Sweden were not, but for a short period these countries did peg their currencies unilaterally to the ECU. In principle EMS membership and the old exchange rate regimes of the Nordic EFTA countries were both variants of a fixed but adjustable exchange rate system. They created medium-term exchange rate stability, which was regarded as crucial to the creation of a favourable environment for foreign trade and capital movements. Until the beginning of the 1990s, the exchange rate arrangements of the Nordic EFTA countries were based on currency baskets, and differed from the EMS in four main respects.[4]

- The EMS countries were not able to change their exchange rates unilaterally, since a common decision was required, whereas Finland, Norway and Sweden could devalue or revalue at will.
- The composition of the national currency basket differed, while the ECU basket was common to all EMS countries. Shares of different currencies in the Nordic baskets were based on the economic importance of the respective countries. In Finland, Norway and Sweden the composition of the basket was determined in a way that was aimed at minimizing variations in the competitiveness of the economy. The weights are shown in Table 8.2.
- Inside the ERM of the EMS the bilateral exchange rates of the participating currencies are 'fixed but adjustable'. In the currency basket exchange rate regimes, this was the case only in relation to the currency index.

Table 8.2 National baskets weights before pegging to the ECU

	Finland	Norway	Sweden	ECU[a]
US dollar	8.7	11.0	21.0	–
Deutschmark	19.1	17.7	17.6	30.1
Pound sterling	12.9	14.7	10.1	13.0
French franc	6.8	9.2	5.4	19.0
Netherlands guilder	4.8	4.6	4.7	9.4
Italian lira	5.1	3.3	4.3	10.15
Belgian franc	3.1	2.4	3.7	7.6
Japanese yen	6.0	6.0	3.9	–
Swiss franc	2.4	1.2	2.2	–
Spanish peseta	2.0	–	1.8	5.3
Austrian schilling	1.6	1.5	1.4	–
Canadian dollar	–	3.6	1.2	–
Danish krone	4.5	6.8	7.3	2.45
Finnish markka	–	3.0	7.0	–
Norwegian krone	4.0	–	8.4	–
Swedish krona	19.0	15.0	–	–
Other EMS-currencies	–	–	–	3.0
Total	100.0	100.0	100.0	100.0
Weights for EU-countries (direct)	56.3	58.7	53.1	100.0

[a] Weight at the beginning of the 1990s.

• In the ERM both countries will intervene at the margin to keep the bilateral exchange rate inside the exchange rate band. However, in practice the main responsibility to intervene has been on the part of the weaker currency country. The country whose currency is under pressure can borrow from the intervention funds of the EMS.

As we have seen, Finland, Norway and Sweden all pegged their currencies to the ECU without being members of the EMS and thus without enjoying the advantage of having access to intervention funds. To some extent this was compensated by bilateral borrowing agreements with European central banks.

The Nordic art of pegging the currency to the ECU

On 19 October 1990 the Norwegian krone was pegged to the ECU. On 17 May 1991 the Swedish krona was linked to the ECU, followed by the Finnish markka on 7 June 1991. All three countries chose the technical solution of expressing the international value of their respective currency units in the form of one theoretical ECU. However, as can be seen from Table 8.3, the margins of fluctuation for the Norwegian, Swedish and Finnish currencies around the central value differed somewhat, reflecting the differences between the three currencies' margins of fluctuation prior to the linkage.

All three currencies were unilaterally pegged to the ECU. After the linkage was established, Norway and Sweden entered into swap agreements with the central banks of the EU, whereas just before the markka was allowed to float in September 1992 Finland entered into some swap agreements (at least with the German Bundesbank). None of the three countries changed the exchange rate of their currencies at the time of the linkage, thereby stressing their adherence to a fixed exchange rate policy.

Table 8.3 Central value and margin of fluctuation for the currencies of Norway, Sweden and Finland

	Norwegian krone	Swedish krona	Finnish markka	
			6 June 1991– 14 Nov 1991	15 Nov 1991– 8 Sept 1991
Central value vis-à-vis ECU	7.9940	7.40054	4.87580	5.55841
Lower limit (weakest value)	8.1739	7.51155	5.02207	5.72516
Upper limit (strongest value)	7.8141	7.28953	4.72953	5.39166
Swing margins	±2.25%	±1.5%	±3.0%	±3.0%

The interest rate reaction to the ECU linkage

The interest rate differential between the ECU and the Norwegian krone, as shown in Figure 8.1, displayed a tendency to narrow after the pegging. In Sweden interest rates fell markedly around the time of the linkage, but increased slightly a few days later, albeit to a lower level than before. The Finnish interest rate level also fell because of the economic prospects following the ECU linkage. However, the Finnish interest rates did fluctuate widely later on, reflecting a difficult economic situation in Finland with a slowdown in exports and negative GDP growth, which reinforced the demand for the 'devaluation' that did eventually take place. The Swedish rates (not shown in the figure) also increased dramatically in 1992 before the time when the Swedish krona was allowed to float.

What are the potential gains from membership of the EMU?

On 1 January 1995 Finland and Sweden became members of the European Union. Norway, however, elected not to join. None the less cooperation with the other Nordic countries will continue and no major difference will be

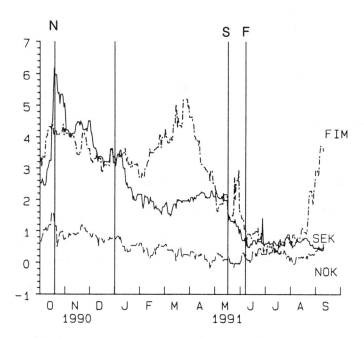

Figure 8.1 Interest rate differential between the ECU and the Norwegian krone, the Swedish krona and the Finnish markka, respectively (three-month money market rates)

Source: Based on Bank of Norway (1991).

noticeable in the immediate future, because of the EEA agreement or a modified version of it. For Finland and Sweden an association with the existing EMS and a commitment to the second and third stages of the Delors plan are presumably on the agenda.

In the mid-1990s Finland and Sweden have floating currencies. The main argument in favour of their association with the EMS is the added credibility it could give to their efforts to achieve price stability. This gain, however disputable, would materialize in both the short and the medium term. In the *short term* the intervention responsibility of the other participating countries and the possibility of getting short-term financing for interventions, would make it easier to defend the existing exchange rate against speculation. An association with the EMS in the *medium term* would put pressure on policy-makers and labour market participants to avoid inflation. This increased credibility, in turn, could reduce interest rate differentials.

On the question of the credibility-increasing effect of association, it can be argued on the other hand that the EMS is neither a necessary nor a sufficient condition for credibility.[5] Credibility can also be increased by means of internal measures. An independent national central bank, 'a conservative central banker' to use the jargon in current economic literature, can also create the needed credibility.[6] The EMS, as a guarantee for medium-term credibility, is in fact based on the same idea, with the German Bundesbank operating as a conservative banker. In Chapter 3 it was shown that the Finnish and Swedish central banks, and to some extent the Danish as well, could be described as fairly independent in comparison with the Norwegian. Nor is the EMS as it stands in the mid-1990s a sufficient condition for credibility, because of the width of the band and because exchange rate realignments are not excluded. Expectations of exchange rate changes also create interest rate differentials inside the ERM. High interest rates can persist for a long time, if the necessary exchange rate realignments are delayed. Speculative crises are not excluded inside the EMS either.

A frequent argument in favour of EMS membership has been that it reduces the costs of disinflation by increasing the credibility of the economic policy. However, some empirical studies have suggested the opposite. Disinflation in the EMS has been accompanied by a bigger increase in unemployment and heavier decline in output growth rates than have been obtained on average in the other OECD countries.[7] None the less it can be argued that the EMS might help in *maintaining* low inflation rates, because it makes it more costly for the authorities to create surprise inflation.

Another argument against association with the EMS concerns the composition of the optimal currency basket. An optimal basket is derived in accordance with some economic objective. Examples of objectives are a minimization of changes in competitiveness, production, prices, current account, foreign reserves, etc. The official currency baskets of Finland, Norway and Sweden have put the main emphasis on the minimization of changes in competitiveness. The major Nordic argument for adopting the ECU basket of the EMS, which is the same for all participating countries, was price stability. If the ECU basket differed substantially from the various optimal baskets, a substitution of national baskets for the ECU basket would incur a cost to the economies. A comparison of the Nordic baskets and the ECU basket shows rather clearly that adopting the ECU basket would entail such a cost, at least if measured according to the competitiveness criterion. The most obvious difference between the baskets is a high weight for the dollar in the Nordic baskets and no weight at all in the ECU basket (see Table 8.2). How big the cost would be, and the extent to which it would be compensated by the benefits of association with the EMS as part of the EMU, remains an open question.

BEHAVIOUR OF EXCHANGE RATES

The foreign exchange markets in the Nordic countries are relatively small in a global context in terms of average daily turnover. Of the Nordic markets the Swedish was the largest in April 1992, with an average daily turnover of USD 22 billion, i.e. around 2 per cent of the global market.[8] In terms of growth in this particular respect the Swedish market has grown fastest among the top fifteen markets. Between 1989 and April 1992 the daily average rose by 64 per cent. The Norwegian market was number two in the Nordic area with an average turnover of USD 7 billion per day in April 1992, and a growth of 20 per cent since 1989. Let us now turn to an analysis of the behaviour of nominal and real Nordic exchange rates in order to understand their importance in explaining the gap between domestic and foreign bond rates.

Nominal exchange rate fluctuations

The prices of major currencies expressed in Nordic currencies are exhibited in Figures 8.2–8.5. As can be seen, the prices of US dollars in Nordic currencies resemble the progress of a roller-coaster. Moreover, the bilateral exchange rates fluctuate substantially, despite the fact that all the Nordic countries had adopted 'fixed' exchange rate regimes. However, as we have noted, for most of the period 'fixed' refers to a basket and not to individual currencies. All the Nordic currencies have experienced a trendwise decline in value since 1977. The depreciation has been substantial against CHF and JPY, and even against DEM. In a Nordic perspective these have been 'hard' currencies. Among the Nordic currencies the depreciation in value of an individual currency has been most considerable in the case of the Swedish krona. Since value changes in Nordic currencies have been substantial, we assume that expectations about exchange rate changes play an important role in explaining the gap between Nordic national bond rates and their foreign equivalents.

In this section we are also interested in the intrinsic elements of exchange-

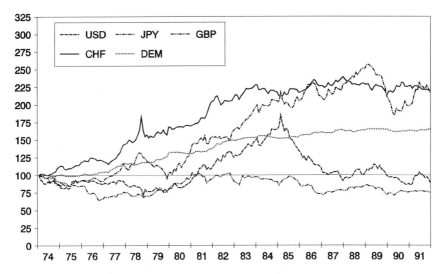

Figure 8.2 Exchange rate index DKK/foreign currency, 1974 to December 1991
(nominal rates, monthly data, end of period; index: 1974:01 = 100)

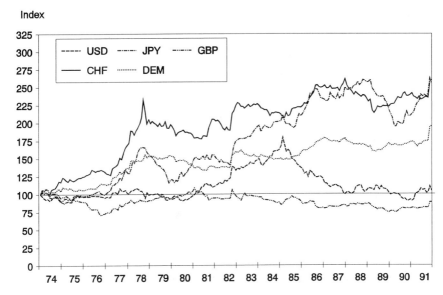

Figure 8.3 Exchange rate index FIM/foreign currency, 1974 to December 1991
(nominal rates, monthly data, end of period; index: 1974:01 = 100)

Index

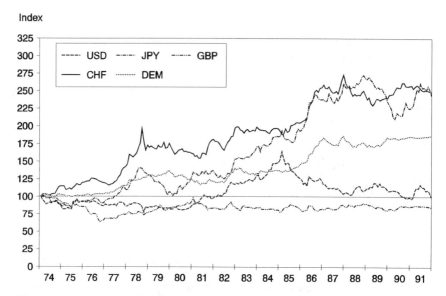

Figure 8.4 Exchange rate index NOK/foreign currency, 1974 to December 1991
(nominal rates, monthly data, end of period; index: 1974:01 = 100)

Index

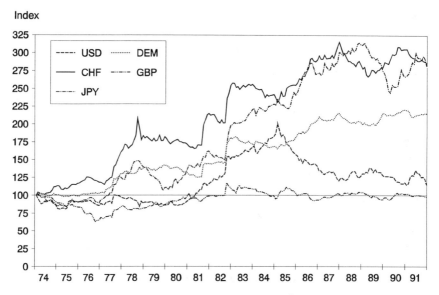

Figure 8.5 Exchange rate index SEK/foreign currency, 1974 to December 1991
(nominal rates, monthly data, end of period; index: 1974:01 = 100)

rate risks as the basis for claims for a risk premium. Risk is an expression of unanticipated fluctuations in some target variable. Exchange-rate risk can be based on unanticipated fluctuations of nominal or real exchange rates. Fluctuations can be measured in many ways. However, the most frequently used measure in the context of risk calculation is the standard deviation.

The standard deviations in various nominal exchange rates are shown in Tables 8.4–8.7. The currencies in the tables are those which have been most frequently used in international bond issues. The split into subperiods is aimed at facilitating longitudinal comparisons. The guideline for the split has been intraperiod homogeneity in an institutional perspective. Having the same subperiods for all the Nordic countries means, however, that the split is a compromise. Standard deviations for changes in the price of a particular foreign currency were roughly the same for the different Nordic currencies. This is most obvious in the case of the Japanese yen, where the range in standard deviations for the whole period under investigation was 2.82–2.96.

Table 8.4 Mean and standard deviation as monthly percentage change in the spot rate DKK/foreign currency, 1974–92

Currency	Number of observations	Minimum	Maximum	Mean	Std Dev
1974–92					
GBP	215	−9.6	8.7	−0.1	2.70
USD	215	−10.8	11.6	−0.0	3.39
DEM	215	−1.9	4.3	0.2	0.79
CHF	215	−10.8	11.2	0.4	2.01
JPY	215	−7.6	8.3	0.4	2.96
1974–76					
GBP	35	−8.3	4.3	−1.1	2.55
USD	35	−6.6	8.5	−0.4	2.78
DEM	35	−1.9	2.2	0.1	1.00
CHF	35	−4.1	4.3	0.5	1.67
JPY	35	−5.3	8.3	−0.3	2.44
1978–89					
GBP	144	−9.6	8.7	0.0	2.82
USD	144	−10.8	11.6	0.2	3.58
DEM	144	−1.7	4.3	0.2	0.73
CHF	144	−10.8	11.2	0.3	2.15
JPY	144	−7.6	8.3	0.5	3.05
1989–92					
GBP	36	−4.6	3.9	−0.3	1.98
USD	36	−6.6	10.6	−0.4	3.61
DEM	36	−0.7	0.7	0.0	0.36
CHF	36	−2.7	3.2	−0.1	1.32
JPY	36	−6.0	5.4	−0.4	2.93

Table 8.5 Mean and standard deviation as monthly percentage change in the spot rate FIM/foreign currency, 1974–92

Currency	Number of observations	Minimum	Maximum	Mean	Std Dev
1974–92					
GBP	215	−6.6	12.7	−0.0	2.50
USD	215	−6.6	13.5	0.1	2.90
DEM	215	−5.2	13.0	0.3	2.00
CHF	215	−8.4	12.6	0.5	2.65
JPY	215	−6.3	10.4	0.5	2.82
1974–76					
GBP	35	−6.6	3.9	−0.9	2.40
USD	35	−3.6	6.2	−0.1	1.96
DEM	35	−5.2	5.2	0.4	2.05
CHF	35	−5.4	6.3	0.8	2.43
JPY	35	−5.5	6.0	0.0	2.24
1978–89					
GBP	144	−6.5	12.7	−0.1	2.39
USD	144	−6.6	13.5	0.0	2.97
DEM	144	−4.6	13.0	0.2	1.83
CHF	144	−8.4	12.6	0.2	2.66
JPY	144	−6.3	10.4	0.4	2.84
1989–92					
GBP	36	−3.7	9.3	0.1	2.27
USD	36	−5.9	8.7	0.0	3.29
DEM	36	−4.0	11.0	0.5	2.20
CHF	36	−6.5	10.3	0.3	2.38
JPY	36	−4.9	8.7	0.0	2.94

In the same period the range was the greatest for the DEM-related exchange rates (0.79–2.04). In the most recent period in the table the DEM-related exchange rates still exhibited the greatest range. In fact the range even grew (0.36–2.20), with the DKK/DEM rate showing the lowest volatility and the FIM/DEM the highest.

The lowest standard deviation in the table appears for DKK/DEM for the period 1989–92 (0.36), whereas the highest appears for DKK/USD in 1989–92 (3.61). These figures underline the fact that EMS membership reduces volatility in exchange rates among currencies participating in the EMS, but increases the volatility in exchange rates with currencies outside the system.

Generally speaking, the USD-related exchange rates have consistently exhibited the highest standard deviations. The only exceptions were the FIM/USD rate from 1974–76 and the SEK/USD rate from 1978–89. The standard deviations in USD-related exchange rates increased over time in the case of all the Nordic currencies except SEK. In general, the standard

Table 8.6 Mean and standard deviation as monthly percentage change in the spot rate NOK/foreign currency, 1974–92

Currency	Number of observations	Minimum	Maximum	Mean	Std Dev
1974–92					
GBP	215	−8.6	8.0	−0.1	2.43
USD	215	−9.9	11.9	0.0	3.00
DEM	215	−3.5	7.1	0.3	1.50
CHF	215	−9.9	11.6	0.5	2.40
JPY	215	−5.7	10.5	0.5	2.84
1974–76					
GBP	35	−8.6	5.3	−1.2	2.59
USD	35	−6.8	9.6	−0.4	2.87
DEM	35	−2.0	2.3	0.1	1.05
CHF	35	−4.3	4.2	0.5	1.85
JPY	35	−4.6	9.4	−0.3	2.66
1978–89					
GBP	144	−7.1	8.0	0.1	2.44
USD	144	−9.9	11.9	0.2	3.02
DEM	144	−3.5	7.1	0.3	1.72
CHF	144	−9.9	11.6	0.4	2.67
JPY	144	−5.7	10.5	0.6	2.87
1989–92					
GBP	36	−2.9	3.1	−0.1	1.49
USD	36	−6.5	10.4	−0.2	3.22
DEM	36	−2.1	2.2	0.2	0.86
CHF	36	−3.5	2.8	0.1	1.35
JPY	36	−5.0	5.3	−0.2	2.58

deviations of all the other exchange rates except the DEM-related rate increased between 1974–76 and 1977–89, after which they declined. Norway exhibits a slightly different pattern in having registered an increase in the DEM-related rate and a drop in the GBP-related exchange rate between the two periods. This probably reflects factors connected with the position of Norway and the United Kingdom as oil-producing countries. Tables 8.4–8.7 provide a basis for evaluating nominal exchange risks, to the extent that we can assume that nominal fluctuations do matter and that they are unanticipated. The large size of the maximum and minimum changes in the tables reminds us of the probable importance of expected rate changes in explaining the gap between domestic and foreign bond rates.

Table 8.7 Mean and standard deviation as monthly percentage change in the spot rate SEK/foreign currency, 1974–92

Currency	Number of observations	Minimum	Maximum	Mean	Std Dev
1974–92					
GBP	215	−8.2	17.1	0.0	2.68
USD	215	−7.2	18.0	0.1	3.03
DEM	215	−3.1	17.5	0.4	2.04
CHF	215	−8.0	17.0	0.5	2.79
JPY	215	−6.1	14.7	0.5	2.92
1974–76					
GBP	35	−8.2	4.4	−1.2	2.41
USD	35	−5.5	8.6	−0.4	2.69
DEM	35	−2.4	2.3	0.1	0.99
CHF	35	−3.5	4.4	0.5	1.74
JPY	35	−4.6	8.4	−0.3	2.49
1978–89					
GBP	144	−5.9	17.1	0.1	2.56
USD	144	−7.2	18.0	0.2	2.99
DEM	144	−3.1	17.5	0.4	2.26
CHF	144	−8.0	17.0	0.4	3.03
JPY	144	−6.1	14.7	0.6	2.91
1989–92					
GBP	36	−2.9	3.9	−0.2	1.67
USD	36	−6.9	8.0	−0.2	2.90
DEM	36	−2.7	2.7	0.2	1.11
CHF	36	−3.9	3.2	0.0	1.45
JPY	36	−5.5	5.4	−0.3	2.52

Real exchange rate fluctuations

As we noted at the beginning of this chapter, real exchange rate fluctuations are another ingredient in any consideration of exchange risk. Purchasing power parity is also frequently mentioned whenever the future value of a currency is being debated.

Any deviations from purchasing power parity (PPP) tell us something about the degree of over- or undervaluation of a currency. The openness to international trade, as shown in Table 3.1, and the elasticity in a country's foreign trade determine the persistence of a deviation from parity. Transactions on the financial markets can then serve to reinforce it. Some deviations may also appear as speculative bubbles. Figures 8.6–8.9 show the development of real effective exchange rate indices or purchasing power parity indices for the Nordic countries. Index 100 is the parity level. Values over 100 indicate the extent of an overvaluation, while values under 100 refer to

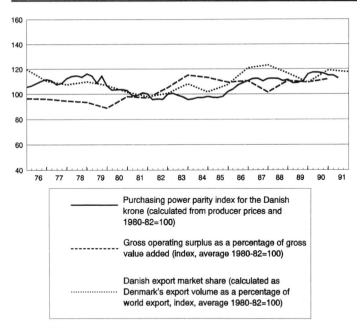

Figure 8.6 Real effective DKK rate and the global competitiveness of Danish goods and services, 1976–91 (quarterly data)

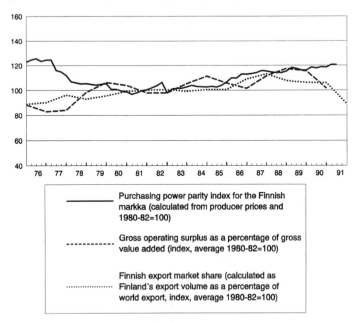

Figure 8.7 Real effective FIM rate and the global competitiveness of Finnish goods and services, 1976–91 (quarterly data)

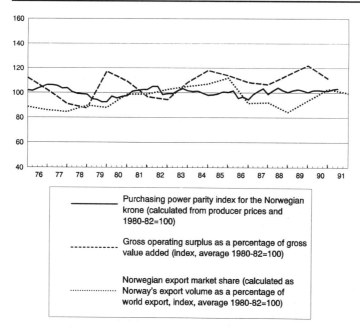

Figure 8.8 Real effective NOK rate and the global competitiveness of Norwegian goods and services, 1976–91 (quarterly data)

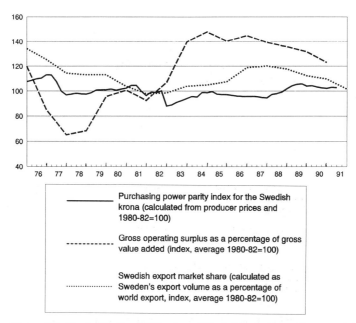

Figure 8.9 Real effective SEK rate and the global competitiveness of Swedish goods and services, 1976–91 (quarterly data)

undervaluation. The choice of reference point and index affects the calculation of the deviations and can always be debated. Here we have used the producer price index and trade weights in our calculations.[9]

Table 8.8 displays corporate aspects of deviations from purchasing power parity. As pointed out in Oxelheim and Wihlborg (1987), these deviations are of operational as well as strategic concern to the company. In dealing with the deviations the company faces two main options:

- adjusting the price in foreign currency to a change in PPP, thus experiencing a shift in the export market share, or
- setting the foreign price without considering the change in PPP, thus experiencing a change in gross margin.

Figures 8.6–8.9 show that shifts in export market shares and operating profits as a percentage of value added reflect fluctuations in the real effective exchange rate. For Sweden, in particular, the relationship emerges clearly.

At the corporate level the implications of a fixed exchange rate policy are obvious. If the authorities in a country have pegged the nominal rate without being able to pursue an adequate policy, the results will appear in substantial deviations from PPP. In Table 8.8 we can imagine the size of the costs in terms of operating surplus (as a fraction of gross value added) experienced by the industrial managers in their efforts to keep the export market share constant, when the real effective exchange rate index changes by one percentage point.[10] The estimated models in the table differ across countries in terms of lag structure and the size of the coefficients. Danish industry, for instance, will experience a 0.35 per cent decrease in the gross operating surplus as a percentage of gross value added in the year following the increase of one percentage point in the real effective rate. Swedish industry seems to have the highest sensitivity, and will experience a drop of 1.7 percentage points altogether in its operation surplus as a percentage of gross value added, in the two years following an increase of one percentage point in the real effective exchange rate. No acceptable model was found for Norway which probably

Table 8.8 Gross operating surplus in Nordic manufacturing and deviations from purchasing power parity, 1976–91 (annual data)

Country	Profit coefficients	adj R^2	D-W
Denmark	$b_2 = -0.35^*$	0.56	1.45
Finland	$b_1 = -0.12$	0.53	1.36
Sweden	$b_1 = -0.79^*, b_3 = -0.94^*$	0.81	2.11

Note: The comprehensive model tested was $X_t = a + b_1 Y_t + b_2 Y_{t-1} + b_3 Y_{t-2} + C_1 Z_t + C_2 Z_{t-1}$, where X_t = gross operating surplus as a percentage of gross value added, Z_t = export market shares of a particular country computed as export volumes as a percentage of world export, and Y_{t-1} = average purchasing power parity index in period $t-1$ to t. * means significant at the 5 per cent level.

reflects the special characteristics of Norway as an oil producer.

Most companies are to some degree averse to risk. Thus, the dramatic shifts in corporate cash flows following changes in the real effective exchange rate can be expected to be reflected in corporate claims for risk premiums.

A way of measuring the currency risk is to measure the volatility of real effective exchange rates. Table 8.9 shows a measure based on squared deviation from PPP. Thus, instead of basing the measure on squared deviations from the average PPP value as in the standard deviation, we have measured the squared deviation from parity. In calculating this measure we assume that the market actors incorporate in their risk expectation a potential bias in terms of a systematic long-term under- or overvaluation of a currency. However, this choice of measure makes the delicate task of identifying an adequate equilibrium more important.

The size of the observed squared deviations in Table 8.9 reflects the

Table 8.9 Mean and average squared deviation from purchasing power parity, January 1976 to June 1991 (monthly data, percentage points)

	DEM	JPY	USD	DKK	FIM	NOK	SEK
January 1976–June 1991							
Maximum	9.9	37.6	29.7	21.0	25.8	6.8	13.2
Minimum	–6.0	–14.9	–18.8	–4.7	–3.2	–8.0	–11.9
Number of observations	186	186	186	186	186	186	186
Mean	2.9	8.0	–2.2	6.6	9.5	0.4	0.0
Average squared deviation	4.2	12.6	11.9	7.0	8.0	3.1	5.1
November 1982–June 1991							
Number of observations	104	104	104	104	104	104	104
Mean	2.4	11.0	0.3	6.7	10.8	0.4	–1.8
Average squared deviation	4.5	14.1	14.0	7.4	6.9	2.1	4.5
July 1989–June 1991							
Number of observations	24	24	24	24	24	24	24
Mean	6.3	8.5	–12.1	15.1	18.7	1.4	3.8
Average squared deviation	1.4	5.9	4.0	3.1	1.6	0.8	1.0
January 1976–December 1979							
Number of observations	48	48	48	48	48	48	48
Mean	5.9	6.6	–8.8	10.9	13.2	0.6	3.5
Average squared deviation	1.5	9.3	3.4	3.6	8.4	4.5	5.8
January 1976–June 1989							
Number of observations	138	138	138	138	138	138	138
Mean	1.9	9.1	0.1	4.7	6.0	–0.4	–2.1
Average squared deviation	4.4	14.0	12.8	6.8	5.8	3.0	3.7

(inverted) openness to trade, showing the lowest value for Norway and the highest for the USA and Japan. The high level of openness to trade should also explain the low range between maximum and minimum deviations for Norway compared to the other Nordic countries. Ranges derived from Table 8.9 differ somewhat from those that can be derived from Figures 8.6–8.9, since monthly data is used in the former and quarterly data in the latter. The squared deviations should provide us with an additional impression of exchange rate risk, but to be able to evaluate the measures based on volatility in nominal or real exchange rates in terms of risk we have to compare them with corresponding measures in other countries.

A measure of exchange rate risk

We have now calculated the volatility of nominal as well as real exchange rates that involve Nordic currencies. The next stage is to transform the volatility into risk premiums. The first question revolves around the actual source of risk. Do the nominal exchange rate fluctuations constitute the source, or is it real exchange rate fluctuations that count? The next question concerns the link between the source and the premium. How should the source be transformed into a premium? The utility function may play an important part here. What then is the character of the risk premium? Is it constant or does it vary with time? Finally, in one way or another the premium should be relative in scope. How can that feature be captured?

I shall not go into great detail here regarding the theory of exchange rate risk and risk premiums. The theory actually consists of a number of competing theories and the empirical results are inconclusive. However, we can note that there are two main approaches to the empirical determination of the risk premium. One turns on the analysis of the portfolio balance, in which incomplete substitutability creates a wedge between expected net return on domestic and foreign investment, and gives rise to a premium. The second approach uses intertemporal asset pricing models, based on discrete points in time. In neither case have the empirical analyses yet produced any convincing results.

As regards the character of the exchange risk premium, the results are ambiguous. Tests for constant risk premiums have produced mixed results. Frenkel (1978), for example, found a statistically insignificant constant premium, while Frenkel (1982) reports significance in the case of certain currencies. Many researchers have also used variable risk premiums in their models. Thus, within the framework of a balance portfolio model Frankel (1979, 1982) and Dornbusch (1982), for example, found support for a premium varying with time.

In the presence of obvious analytical problems, however, there is some comfort in recognizing that the premium for exchange rates is probably small relative to the size of the expected change in exchange rates.[11] It can be

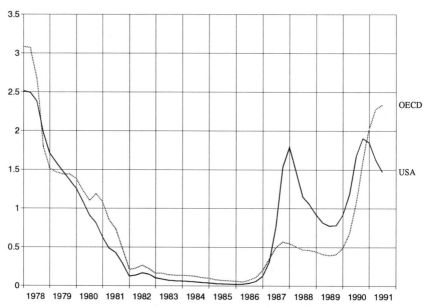

Figure 8.10 Relative exchange rate risk attaching to the Danish krone

Note: Calculated as the ratio between the squared deviation in fluctuations of the Danish krona around purchasing power parity and the corresponding squared deviations for the USD (bilateral studies) and for the USD, DEM and JPY as a weighted average.

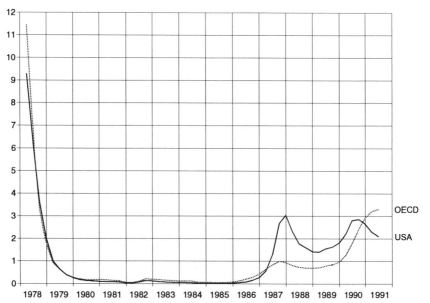

Figure 8.11 Relative exchange rate risk attaching to the Finnish markka

Note: Calculated as the ratio between the squared deviation in fluctuations of the Finnish markka around purchasing power parity and the corresponding squared deviations for the USD (bilateral studies) and for the USD, DEM and JPY as a weighted average.

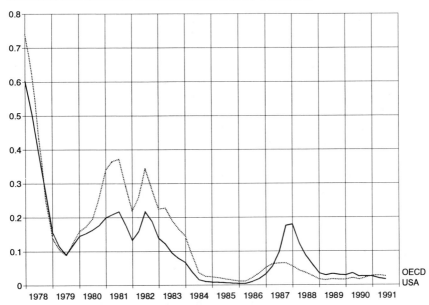

Figure 8.12 Relative exchange rate risk attaching to the Norwegian krone

Note: Calculated as the ratio between the squared deviation in fluctuations of the Norwegian krona around purchasing power parity and the corresponding squared deviations for the USD (bilateral studies) and for the USD, DEM and JPY as a weighted average.

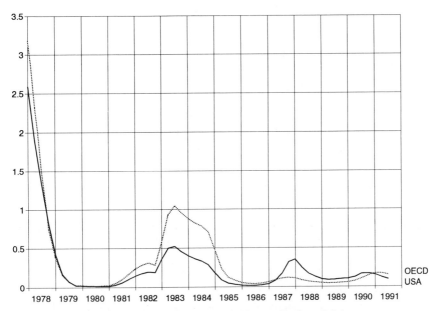

Figure 8.13 Relative exchange rate risk attaching to the Swedish krona

Note: Calculated as the ratio between the squared deviation in fluctuations of the Swedish krona around purchasing power parity and the corresponding squared deviations for the USD (bilateral studies) and for the USD, DEM and JPY as a weighted average.

assumed that precision in estimating the premium is of minor importance when compared with the uncertainty which dogs the evaluation of the expected exchange rate movement.

Finally, let us focus on the relative character of the risk. It seems appealing to assume that whenever international investors assess the riskiness of different countries, they apply an international perspective, comparing the volatility in the different currencies concerned – in which case the risk premium should reflect relative volatility. One way of capturing this relative aspect is to assume that claims for exchange risk premiums are based on relative volatility in the deviation from purchasing power parity.[12]

To illustrate the relative risk we can here construct a proxy for exchange risk, computed as the ratio between the average squared deviation in deviations from PPP for a particular Nordic country and for the US. In studies including comparisons between national rates and the global rate, the risk has been calculated as the ratio between the average squared deviation in deviations from PPP in the particular country and a weighted average of the corresponding squared deviations in the United States, Germany, and Japan. In constructing the weighted average, relative GDP size has been used.

The risk variables are based on the assumption that the investor remembers the risk, i.e. the volatility in this respect over the last twenty-four months. The weights attached to each observation can be of equal size or exponentially decreasing, assuming that the memory fades away. In Figures 8.10–8.13, which show the exchange risk profiles of the Nordic countries, I have used equal weights. The calculations are based on monthly data. It should be noted, though, that the length of time during which the investor's memory stores the volatility and the weighting system has been chosen at my own discretion.

According to the risk profiles exhibited in Figures 8.10–8.13, the highest exchange risk attaches to the Danish krone and the Finnish markka, while the risk in Norway and Sweden has been low. In the latter cases the volatility in real exchange rates has been considerably below that of the USA and of the weighted average of the major OECD currencies.

Correlation between currencies

Tables 8.10–8.17 show correlations between exchange rates – patterns which can be helpful in the decision to adopt a portfolio approach. However, for the period under investigation explicit portfolio models were probably rarely used. According to Oxelheim (1990), explicit portfolio models were at any rate not being used in Swedish multinationals for the greater part of the period. In view of this we may assume that the premiums for risk are additive in the investor's calculations of required returns. There are two tables for each Nordic country. The first shows the correlation pattern for the whole period without corrections for major parity changes. In the case of Denmark

Table 8.10 Correlations between monthly changes in the spot price of different currencies in DKK, 1974–91

	GBP	USD	DEM	FRF	BEC	CHF	NLG	SEK	NOK	ITL	ATS	JPY	FIM
GBP	1.00												
USD	0.39	1.00											
DEM	0.14	0.04	1.00										
FRF	0.29	0.20	0.21	1.00									
BEC	0.15	0.00	0.53	0.21	1.00								
CHF	0.19	0.01	0.42	0.17	0.22	1.00							
NLG	0.29	0.10	0.78	0.35	0.61	0.37	1.00						
SEK	0.40	0.51	0.13	0.13	0.03	0.05	0.10	1.00					
NOK	0.45	0.48	0.24	0.23	0.15	0.08	0.24	0.58	1.00				
ITL	0.35	0.41	0.19	0.49	0.18	0.22	0.32	0.26	0.23	1.00			
ATS	0.15	0.08	0.91	0.28	0.54	0.43	0.76	0.15	0.23	0.25	1.00		
JPY	0.39	0.41	0.12	0.21	0.09	0.27	0.14	0.37	0.34	0.29	0.12	1.00	
FIM	0.50	0.56	0.14	0.27	0.05	0.10	0.14	0.76	0.60	0.37	0.19	0.40	1.00

Table 8.11 Correlations between monthly changes in the spot price of different currencies in DKK, July 1989 to December 1991

	GBP	USD	DEM	FRF	BEC	CHF	NLG	SEK	NOK	ITL	ATS	JPY	FIM
GBP	1.00												
USD	0.12	1.00											
DEM	0.07	−0.06	1.00										
FRF	0.37	0.20	0.24	1.00									
BEC	0.26	0.05	0.73	0.40	1.00								
CHF	0.57	0.22	−0.04	0.07	0.20	1.00							
NLG	0.08	−0.01	0.95	0.27	0.81	0.05	1.00						
SEK	0.51	0.79	−0.11	0.26	0.06	0.45	−0.10	1.00					
NOK	0.73	0.52	0.23	0.35	0.41	0.57	0.30	0.75	1.00				
ITL	0.49	0.49	−0.05	0.38	0.18	0.12	−0.02	0.60	0.56	1.00			
ATS	−0.06	−0.08	0.94	0.19	0.67	−0.16	0.86	−0.16	0.09	−0.18	1.00		
JPY	0.50	0.55	0.17	0.31	0.12	0.31	0.14	0.61	0.64	0.36	0.08	1.00	
FIM	0.67	0.63	−0.03	0.41	0.14	0.53	−0.04	0.72	0.65	0.65	−0.16	0.67	1.00

and Sweden all the coefficients are positive, i.e. the prices of different currencies as expressed in DKK and SEK all developed in the same direction. On an average the two currencies have grown successively weaker compared to all the other currencies involved in the analysis. In the case of FIM and NOK there are some negative coefficients. The second set of tables referring to the subperiod are constructed in such a way as to exclude the most substantial parity changes, in order to show correlation within 'basket' arrangements. Here we find a strong negative correlation between the price

Table 8.12 Correlations between monthly changes in the spot price of different currencies in FIM, 1974–91

	GBP	USD	DEM	FRF	BEC	CHF	NLG	DKK	NOK	ITL	ATS	JPY	SEK
GBP	1.00												
USD	0.17	1.00											
DEM	0.22	−0.03	1.00										
FRF	0.28	0.04	0.74	1.00									
BEC	0.25	−0.02	0.92	0.75	1.00								
CHF	0.25	−0.04	0.69	0.55	0.63	1.00							
NLG	0.30	0.01	0.96	0.78	0.93	0.68	1.00						
DKK	0.20	−0.01	0.91	0.76	0.91	0.62	0.90	1.00					
NOK	0.30	0.17	0.62	0.52	0.61	0.40	0.62	0.62	1.00				
ITL	0.28	0.21	0.58	0.68	0.59	0.49	0.63	0.58	0.36	1.00			
ATS	0.21	−0.02	0.98	0.76	0.92	0.70	0.95	0.91	0.61	0.60	1.00		
JPY	0.27	0.25	0.23	0.24	0.23	0.33	0.24	0.22	0.23	0.26	0.22	1.00	
SEK	0.07	0.11	0.24	0.11	0.22	0.12	0.22	0.25	0.32	0.11	0.23	0.14	1.00

Table 8.13 Correlations between monthly changes in the spot price of different currencies in FIM, July 1989 to December 1991

	GBP	USD	DEM	FRF	BEC	CHF	NLG	DKK	NOK	ITL	ATS	JPY	SEK
GBP	1.00												
USD	−0.30	1.00											
DEM	−0.15	−0.44	1.00										
FRF	−0.17	−0.44	0.92	1.00									
BEC	−0.12	−0.45	0.97	0.94	1.00								
CHF	0.32	−0.28	0.19	0.14	0.24	1.00							
NLG	−0.15	−0.42	0.99	0.93	0.98	0.22	1.00						
DKK	−0.22	−0.44	0.94	0.95	0.95	0.21	0.95	1.00					
NOK	0.34	−0.17	0.69	0.64	0.70	0.38	0.70	0.63	1.00				
ITL	−0.14	−0.24	0.76	0.81	0.81	0.00	0.78	0.82	0.67	1.00			
ATS	−0.18	−0.40	0.99	0.91	0.96	0.16	0.98	0.92	0.66	0.74	1.00		
JPY	0.21	0.38	−0.34	−0.41	−0.42	−0.15	−0.36	−0.45	−0.04	−0.43	−0.33	1.00	
SEK	0.09	0.38	0.25	0.28	0.27	0.16	0.26	0.30	0.62	0.44	0.26	0.07	1.00

of EMS currencies and of the US dollar in FIM, NOK, and SEK.

The coefficients of correlation between exchange rates when only FIM, NOK or SEK are involved are consistently high and fairly constant throughout the period. This may express some cooperation in exchange rate policies in the countries concerned. According to Feldt (1991), some cooperation did in fact exist up to the moment of the devaluation of the Swedish krona in 1982. The timing of Nordic devaluations prior to that date clearly supports this view. However, the intra-Nordic correlation coeffi-

Table 8.14 Correlations between monthly changes in the spot price of different currencies in NOK, 1974–91

	GBP	USD	DEM	FRF	BEC	CHF	NLG	SEK	DKK	ITL	ATS	JPY	FIM
GBP	1.00												
USD	0.22	1.00											
DEM	0.12	−0.08	1.00										
FRF	0.23	0.05	0.65	1.00									
BEC	0.15	−0.08	0.88	0.66	1.00								
CHF	0.20	−0.05	0.65	0.47	0.56	1.00							
NLG	0.20	−0.04	0.94	0.70	0.89	0.62	1.00						
SEK	0.22	0.30	0.23	0.18	0.20	0.14	0.20	1.00					
DKK	0.11	−0.04	0.86	0.69	0.86	0.55	0.84	0.26	1.00				
ITL	0.29	0.27	0.53	0.66	0.53	0.44	0.59	0.28	0.54	1.00			
ATS	0.12	−0.05	0.97	0.68	0.88	0.65	0.93	0.24	0.87	0.56	1.00		
JPY	0.30	0.30	0.18	0.22	0.17	0.30	0.18	0.27	0.18	0.29	0.17	1.00	
FIM	0.33	0.36	0.25	0.32	0.23	0.21	0.24	0.67	0.29	0.40	0.29	0.31	1.00

Table 8.15 Correlations between monthly changes in the spot price of different currencies in NOK, July 1989 to December 1991

	GBP	USD	DEM	FRF	BEC	CHF	NLG	SEK	DKK	ITL	ATS	JPY	FIM
GBP	1.00												
USD	−0.23	1.00											
DEM	−0.47	−0.39	1.00										
FRF	−0.36	−0.29	0.84	1.00									
BEC	−0.46	−0.38	0.94	0.89	1.00								
CHF	0.23	−0.10	−0.09	−0.06	−0.01	1.00							
NLG	−0.51	−0.38	0.99	0.86	0.96	−0.06	1.00						
SEK	−0.06	0.68	−0.25	−0.04	−0.21	0.04	−0.26	1.00					
DKK	−0.47	−0.33	0.89	0.91	0.91	0.01	0.90	−0.04	1.00				
ITL	−0.24	−0.04	0.53	0.70	0.61	−0.20	0.54	0.21	0.69	1.00			
ATS	−0.49	−0.35	0.99	0.82	0.93	−0.12	0.97	−0.21	0.86	0.49	1.00		
JPY	0.27	0.43	−0.40	−0.38	−0.50	−0.08	−0.44	0.24	−0.46	−0.32	−0.38	1.00	
FIM	0.22	0.34	0.08	0.30	0.12	0.24	0.06	0.44	0.21	0.46	0.05	0.28	1.00

cients, albeit high, were not as high as the correlation coefficients involving the price of EU currencies as expressed in Nordic currencies.

CONCLUDING REMARKS ON MONETARY INTEGRATION

The exchange rate policies in the Nordic countries have been firmly aimed at avoiding devaluations, which in practice means a policy of fixed exchange rates with respect to an average exchange rate between the domestic

Table 8.16 Correlations between monthly changes in the spot price of different currencies in SEK, 1974–91

	USD	GBP	ATS	BEC	DKK	FRF	DEM	ITL	NLG	NOK	CHF	JPY	FIM
USD	1.00												
GBP	0.29	1.00											
ATS	0.13	0.36	1.00										
BEC	0.12	0.38	0.93	1.00									
DKK	0.13	0.35	0.93	0.92	1.00								
FRF	0.20	0.43	0.82	0.81	0.82	1.00							
DEM	0.11	0.36	0.99	0.93	0.92	0.80	1.00						
ITL	0.34	0.43	0.69	0.68	0.68	0.76	0.68	1.00					
NLG	0.15	0.43	0.96	0.94	0.92	0.83	0.97	0.72	1.00				
NOK	0.30	0.45	0.69	0.68	0.69	0.65	0.69	0.53	0.70	1.00			
CHF	0.09	0.37	0.75	0.69	0.69	0.64	0.75	0.59	0.74	0.51	1.00		
JPY	0.31	0.37	0.32	0.32	0.32	0.35	0.32	0.37	0.33	0.34	0.41	1.00	
FIM	0.27	0.44	0.52	0.50	0.54	0.57	0.51	0.53	0.52	0.58	0.46	0.30	1.00

Table 8.17 Correlations between monthly changes in the spot price of different currencies in SEK, July 1989 to December 1991

	USD	GBP	ATS	BEC	DKK	FRF	DEM	ITL	NLG	NOK	CHF	JPY	FIM
USD	1.00												
GBP	−0.50	1.00											
ATS	−0.65	−0.00	1.00										
BEC	−0.69	−0.08	0.96	1.00									
DKK	−0.66	−0.01	0.93	0.96	1.00								
FRF	−0.72	−0.09	0.91	0.95	0.97	1.00							
DEM	−0.69	0.04	0.99	0.97	0.95	0.92	1.00						
ITL	−0.64	0.15	0.75	0.84	0.86	0.85	0.79	1.00					
NLG	−0.67	0.04	0.98	0.98	0.96	0.93	0.99	0.80	1.00				
NOK	−0.71	0.45	0.72	0.77	0.71	0.70	0.75	0.64	0.77	1.00			
CHF	−0.39	0.42	0.31	0.40	0.35	0.34	0.35	0.21	0.38	0.55	1.00		
JPY	0.17	0.25	−0.29	−0.37	−0.37	−0.37	−0.29	−0.40	−0.32	−0.10	−0.04	1.00	
FIM	−0.41	0.42	0.43	0.48	0.50	0.51	0.47	0.54	0.47	0.43	0.49	0.08	1.00

currencies and other currencies. Since the end of the 1970s the target has been to keep the currency index (set by the central bank) unchanged, although the exchange rate between individual currencies has all the time been allowed to change. However, finding an adequate parity to defend proved to be a delicate task. The failures are expressed in big deviations from purchasing power parity in all four Nordic countries and in great swings in the measures of relative volatility, at least in Denmark and Finland. The chapter thus provides many indications that in the early 1990s the monetary integration of the Nordic countries was far from perfect. Our observations also support the view that, on average, a substantial expected exchange-rate change and to some extent a premium for exchange-rate risk can be expected to appear in the gap between Nordic and global bond rates.

As we noted earlier, financial liberalization has been followed by overvalued currencies on a global scale. In Denmark, Finland and Sweden the immediate aftermath of the completion of *de jure* deregulation also witnessed overvalued currencies, whereas no such reaction has been found in the case of the Norwegian krone. When the Finnish markka and the Swedish krona were allowed to float in 1992 a dramatic depreciation followed, implying an undervaluation of these currencies in a PPP sense of about 5 to 10 per cent, an undervaluation that is still there in the mid-1990s.

The intervention-prone policies pursued by the Nordic governments with a view to defending the existing exchange-rate goals are probably also reflected in corporate charges for political risk premiums. Hence, there may be some overlapping between the political and the exchange risk. In the next chapter, we will turn to a discussion of political risks.

NOTES

1   Assuming that only volatility in real exchange rates gives rise to claims for an exchange risk premium.
2   A calendarium giving the dates of the main measures with implications for Nordic exchange rate arrangements was kept, but will be published separately. The calendarium has provided opportunities for assessing the extent to which such measures have been coordinated with measures in the Nordic neighbour countries, and the extent to which policy measures in one country have spurred similar policies in adjacent countries.
3   The fluctuation band remained unchanged when the krone was pegged to the ECU.
4   See Etla *et al.* (1990).
5   Except in the third stage of the EMU.
6   An inflation objective can be set for the monetary policy conducted by the bank.
7   See, for example, de Grauwe (1989) and Dornbusch (1988).
8   According to BIS (1992) and their calculation based on national central bank reports.
9   For a discussion of these choices, see Oxelheim (1985).
10 During the 1970s and 1980s, companies have outlocated production which sometimes has meant reduced export market shares at the national level. However, such structural shifts should appear in our estimation as a general compensating increase in the profit measures.
11 See, for example, Frankel (1985).
12 Fama and Farber (1979) and others argued at an early stage that the premium for systematic risk must be regarded as a function of differences between currencies with regard to the variance in the deviations from purchasing power parity.

REFERENCES

Bank of Norway, 1991, *Economic Bulletin*, No. 3, Oslo.

BIS, 1992, *Recent Developments in International Interbank Relations*, October, Basle.

de Grauwe, P., 1989, 'The Cost of Disinflation and the European Monetary System', *CEPR Discussion Paper*, No. 326, London.

Dornbusch, R., 1982, 'Exchange Risk and the Macroeconomics of Exchange Rate Determination', in Hawkins R. *et al.* (eds), *The Internationalization of Financial Markets and National Economic Policy*, JAI Press, Greenwich, Conn.

Dornbusch, R., 1988, 'Credibility, Debt and Unemployment: Ireland's Failed Stabilization', *NBER Working Paper No. 2785*, Cambridge, Mass.

Etla *et al.*, 1990, *Growth and Integration in a Nordic Perspective*, Helsinki.

Fama, E.F. and A. Farber, 1979, 'Money, Bonds and Foreign Exchange', *American Economic Review*, September, pp. 327–48.

Feldt, K.-O., 1991, *Alla dessa dagar*, Norstedts, Stockholm.

Frankel, J.A., 1979, 'The Diversifiability of Exchange Risk', *Journal of International Economics*, Vol. 9, September, pp. 379–93.

Frankel, J.A., 1982, 'In Search of the Exchange Risk Premium: A Six-Currency Test Assuming Mean-Variance Optimization', *Journal of International Money and Finance*, Vol. 3, pp. 319–38.

Frankel, J.A., 1985, 'International Capital Mobility and Crowding Out in the US Economy – Imperfect Integration of Financial Markets or of Goods Markets?', *NBER Working Paper*, No. 155, Centre for Economic Policy Research, Australian National University, Canberra.

Frenkel, J.A., 1978, 'A Monetary Approach to the Exchange Rate: Doctrinal Aspects and Empirical Evidence', in Frenkel, J.A. and H.G. Johnson (eds), *The Economics of Exchange Rates: Selected Studies*, Addison-Wesley, Reading, Mass.

Frenkel, J.A., 1982, *Interest Rates, Exchange Rates and the Emerging Strength of the US Dollar*, University of Chicago Press, Chicago.

Oxelheim, L., 1985, *International Financial Market Fluctuations*, John Wiley & Sons, Chichester.

Oxelheim, L., 1990, *International Financial Integration*, Springer Verlag, Heidelberg.

Oxelheim, L. and C. Wihlborg, 1987, *Macroeconomic Uncertainty – International Risks and Opportunities for the Corporations*, John Wiley & Sons, Chichester.

Chapter 9

Political risk

The importance of political risk has been mentioned several times above, but so far we have said very little about the way this type of risk can be adequately defined or measured. Our brief definition of political risk as risk attaching to *changes in the market rules*, however, goes a long way towards capturing its essence. But, as we found in Chapter 8, the borderlines between political risk and exchange risk are blurred, and the very brevity of our definition may add to the confusion. For instance, is a change in the exchange regime to be seen as adding to the exchange rate risk or the political risk? According to our definition, the answer has to be that it adds to them both.

The evolution of financial markets has been accompanied by new policy challenges. On a global scale the 1980s and early 1990s brought a new set of basic economic problems, confronting policy-makers with the need for new policy options. Shifting market conditions altered the effectiveness of traditional policy instruments, and restricted access to new ones. The changes particularly affected the field of monetary policy, putting more emphasis on the role of fiscal policy, incomes policy and so on.

In the Nordic region the liberalization of the financial markets, combined with a fixed exchange rate regime, highlighted the question of the autonomy of monetary policy. Although this type of autonomy had in fact long been limited in the Nordic countries, due to variously substantial external and fiscal deficits, the autonomy issue did not receive much attention until the external *de jure* deregulation appeared on the agenda and, finally, was implemented, implying a move from corner (1) to corner (2) in the monetary policy triangle in Figure 1.1. However, the *de facto* deregulation that, as we will see in Chapter 14, preceded this stage generated such a move much earlier, limiting or extinguishing any policy choice in rate-setting on the domestic market and in making credit available. By deciding to let their currencies float, Finland, Norway and Sweden then moved on into corner (3) of the triangle in 1992. This move meant regaining monetary autonomy, although this was devoted almost exclusively to curbing inflation.

The character of the Nordic countries as political economies, i.e. political-sector-dominated economies, means that policy-makers in these countries are forced to offset domestic effects from shocks and disturbances in the world economy, mainly by changing the tax bases or the tax rates. Consequently, given our definition of political risk, we would expect the Nordic countries to be exposed to high risks of this kind. The emergence of different policy regimes during the period of financial market transition can also be expected to reveal itself in political changes of varying frequency, which in turn affect the uncertainty of non-political actors about the stability of the market rules. Accordingly, we have good grounds to assume that the political risk fluctuates over time.

Studies[1] of corporate decision-making show that managers are greatly averse to political risk, and such risk commands a price. If managers undertake an investment that is exposed to political risk, they will demand a premium in the form of a higher expected return. This incremental element in the return is the political risk premium. To some extent the premium may be traded off against the exchange risk premium since, as we have noted, we can expect some covariation between political risk and exchange rate risk. For instance, the defence of a fixed nominal exchange rate and a desire to keep domestic inflation in line with inflation in the country or group of countries to which the currency is pegged, calls for extensive fiscal policy measures. In the early 1990s the transition towards a single currency in Europe has clearly revealed the importance of supportive fiscal policies. Accordingly, we can assume that the political risk premiums, at least as a temporary phenomenon, will increase; they are the price for the reduction or elimination of the exchange risk premium.

The chapter opens with a discussion of the concept of political risk. This is followed by an empirical analysis of the two major sources of risk. We will look first at the development of the relative indebtedness of a country, and second at the policy measures actually adopted. In conclusion, the impact of political risk on bond market performance is discussed.

THE ELEMENTS OF POLITICAL RISK

Political risk is not a clear-cut concept. It is often used synonymously with country risk, although it should rather be seen as a subset of that risk. Country risk encompasses all risks that an investor encounters in a country,[2] i.e. not only the risk of policy-induced changes but also the risk of strikes, riots etc. Political risk thus constitutes that part of the risk which is caused by politicians in the form of changes in the rules applying on that country's market. It comprises risks manifest at the company level as an involuntary loss of control over assets due to such things as expropriations, confiscations, etc., or as an increase in volatility in the expected returns due, for instance, to a tax change or a policy measure which sets the market forces out of action. Some political risks can be described as macro-risks, since they affect all companies or investors in a country, while others are specific to an industry or a company.[3] It should be noted, too, that political risks according to our definition do not apply only to foreign companies or investors as is the case in many other definitions, but to domestic companies and investors as well.

Much of the literature concerned with country risk adopts a narrower definition than the one I have given above, placing this risk on an equal footing with what is traditionally known as the risk of national suspended payments. A good deal of this literature emphasizes the link between the international debt crises of the 1980s and 1990s, and devotes much attention to the question of whether international interest rates reflect the risk of national suspension of payments, i.e. whether the interest rate is a positive function of the size of the debt.[4] The debt–service ratio,[5] the ratio between external reserves and imports, and the ratio between capital inflow and payments on the debt, are then taken as expressions of the country risk.

Oxelheim (1984b) adopts a broader view, which also means giving greater weight to the political risk elements in the country risk. It is argued there that since industry is slow to adapt to change, the present level and development of the industrial structure foreshadows future risks of intervention and changes in the rules in the country concerned. Consequently, a good proxy for country risk should include such things as measures of the size, concentration, internationalization and ownership structure of the country's industry and the diversification of its exports.

Another strand in the literature[6] emphasizes relative indebtedness as an important source of political risk. Oxelheim (1990) looks at the use of a country's relative indebtedness (net foreign assets as a ratio of GDP) and finds it to be a good proxy for political risk in an economic–political environment characterized by capital controls. The logic behind the choice of proxy is that the existence of capital controls signals the authorities' *propensity* to intervene, since as a rule capital controls are imposed to guarantee policy autonomy.[7] It is then assumed that in this environment the indebtedness signals the *need* for interventions, since a high net foreign debt reduces the free scope for policy-making, thus making more likely the appearance of new taxes or similar measures affecting the corporate returns on investments. Oxelheim (1990) reports that during the period 1977–84 relative indebtedness represented an important reason for the gap between Swedish and foreign interest rates.

The choice of proxies for political risk

In this book we are looking for proxies for political risk with good forecasting value. Since the period under investigation involves a dismantling of capital controls in all the Nordic countries, we have to consider a modification of the proxies used in Oxelheim (1990) as described above. A new proxy has to be found for the propensity of national authorities to intervene. Thus, in the present book I have chosen a proxy based on the past intervention record of the politicians in a particular country. I have used a cumbersome but appealing way of describing their record by keeping an *ex post* calendarium[8] of relevant policy changes. 'Relevant' refers here to policy devices whose effect means an increase in the uncertainty of a market. Consequently I have removed from the calendarium all policy measures aimed at deregulation or at securing the financial infrastructure. What remains are measures such as new taxes or tax rate changes on securities, withholding taxes, capital gains taxes, as well as such devices as changes in the investment obligations imposed on banks and insurance companies, changes in liquidity ratios, and so on. I admit that the choice of policy measures to be included may seem rather subjective. Nevertheless, they do provide information about the authorities' propensity to intervene. The forecasting value of the information has of course to be continuously assessed. If an entirely new policy regime is established, the forecasting value may be disputed and the proxy may have to be revised.

In its most elaborate form we can envisage the proxy as encompassing all relevant policy changes, with weights reflecting their individual importance, as expected according to some utility measure. However, in practice, such weighting is not feasible, and the only way to proceed is to take some kind of short cut. Here our short cut is in the form of a measure of the number of days showing policy changes that affect the uncertainty of the markets in a particular country. I thus pay no attention to the number or the importance of the changes occurring on the individual days. In other words it is assumed that a day showing ten changes in the market rules is sending the investor the same signal about the authorities' propensity to intervene as a day when only one such change is registered. A similar shortcoming concerns the importance of different policy changes, since I equate a 30 per cent increase in capital gains tax, for instance, with a 1 per cent increase in the banks' investment obligations. It goes without saying that the numerous measurement problems may reduce the value of the proxy, but it can still be regarded as having substantial 'signalling value'.[9]

The arbitrariness involved in selecting the policy changes which add to the uncertainty of a market, means that the chosen set of changes can sometimes be questioned. Different groups of investors may have diverse opinions about the value of a signal sent by any one change. For instance, a policy measure undertaken with a view to stabilizing the market in the long run, will be seen by investors in real capital as something that reduces uncertainty, and by short-term investors or investors in fixed income securities as something that increases the risks. In screening the policy changes for their contribution to greater uncertainty, I have adopted the view of this second category.

Finally, as regards a proxy for the authorities' need to intervene, I will retain the national relative indebtedness as suggested in Oxelheim (1990). Since the forecasting value of our proxies depends on the representativeness of the recent past relative to the future, in any estimate of the political risk over time the proxies will have to be appropriately modified whenever there is a change in policy regime. An example of such a change was the dismantling of the capital controls and the consequent move from corner (1) to corner (2) in the policy triangle (Figure 1.1).

Political risk premiums

The political risk premium is a form of compensation for the systematic component in political risk. Premiums are often estimated in terms of the difference between the domestic and the Eurorate, with both rates having similar characteristics in all relevant aspects except jurisdiction.[10] By comparing the premiums for two countries – let us say Finland and the USA – involved in a financial transaction, we can obtain a measure of the relative risk premium required if an investor is to treat the two countries as offering equal potential for an investment. Unfortunately, i.e. in terms of our need for data, one of the aims of Nordic policy-makers has been to avoid using their own domestic currencies in international transactions and thus to prevent them from becoming Eurocurrencies. This means that our time series of Eurocurrency rates are not long enough to allow an interest rate comparison over the whole period under investigation. In addition a somewhat puzzling feature often emerges, namely the diminutive size of the risk premium when it is derived from the difference between the Eurorate and the domestic rate. The premiums seem small, in view of the potential impact a new tax or a similar change in policy can have on an investment.

Another way of estimating the relative political risk premium would be to start from the covered interest rate arbitrage, based on the national interest rates which are standardized in all respects except currency and jurisdiction. However, since this procedure also calls for a proxy for political risk and does not offer a short cut, there are no alternatives left but to estimate the premium as a function of the proxies we have identified: foreign indebtedness and policy-makers' propensity to intervene. Next we turn to a description of the way these two sources of the risk premium have developed over time.

RELATIVE INDEBTEDNESS AS AN INDICATOR OF POLITICAL RISK

As we have noted above, many researchers have largely agreed about the use of indebtedness as a proxy for political risk. As became apparent in the 1980s a country's indebtedness can lead to payment difficulties which seriously reduce that country's scope for economic–political manoeuvring. Consequently, there is a greater likelihood that restrictions and controls will be imposed, which in turn implies a greater political risk. Indebtedness has been measured here as a country's net foreign assets as a percentage of GDP, (NFAGDP).[11] The standardization with GDP is introduced in order to obtain an expression which indicates any change in the risk in 'real' form.

How, then, should indebtedness be interpreted in terms of the need for intervention? Is it the level of indebtedness, or changes in it, or a combination of the two that sends signals about such a necessity? And should the need for intervention be based solely on the indebtedness situation in one country, or should it be related to the situation in other countries? Since we have adopted the international investor's perspective here, the underlying assumption in using the indebtedness of one country only is in fact that the indebtedness of the rest of the world is negligible. However, the justification for this is questionable, and it could be argued that the risk should be in some sense relative. This is most obvious if the investor is comparing and evaluating two investment alternatives only. Assume, for instance, that the investor is deciding between investment in Finland or the USA, then the political risk in Finland should of course be compared with the corresponding risk in the other country. Let us look at both the ways suggested above for using the indebtedness in the calculations. The indebtedness of an individual

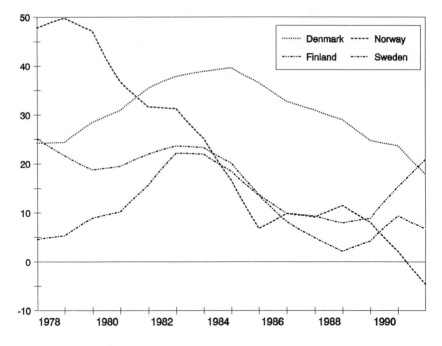

Figure 9.1 Nordic foreign indebtedness in relation to US foreign indebtedness

Sources: Based on data from OECD, *National Accounts*, Vol. 1, 1992; Danmarks Nationalbank, *Annual Yearbook*, various issues; Bank of Finland, *Database*; Bank of Norway, *Database*; The Swedish Central Bank, *Statistical Yearbook*, 1985, and *Sveriges tillgångar och skulder mot utlandet*, 1992:1.
Note: Calculated as the difference between Nordic national indebtedness (net foreign debt as a percentage of GDP) and US indebtedness. An increasing value means higher indebtedness for the Nordic country as compared to the USA.

country is shown in Figure 3.1, while indebtedness in a comparative form is
shown in Figure 9.1 (Nordic indebtedness relative to the USA) and second
in Figure 9.2 (Nordic indebtedness relative to the weighted indebtedness of
the USA, Germany and Japan).[12]

Figures 9.1 and 9.2 show a trendwise decline in Nordic indebtedness *vis-
à-vis* the USA. For Denmark and Finland the decline started in 1984, for
Norway in 1978 and for Sweden in 1982. In the case of Finland and Sweden,
however, the development changed direction in 1986 and 1988 respectively.
The Norwegian decline was halted for some years at the time of the dramatic
decrease in the price of crude oil in the mid-1980s. In a comparison between
Nordic foreign indebtedness and that of the major OECD countries, we find
a fairly gradual Nordic increase during the 1980s except in the case of
Norway, where relative indebtedness was falling.

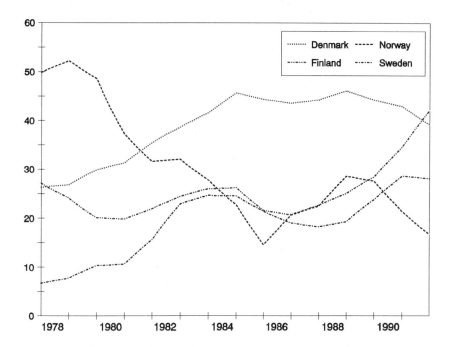

Figure 9.2 Nordic foreign indebtedness in relation to the weighted foreign
indebtedness of major OECD countries

Sources: Based on data from OECD, *National Accounts*, Vol. 1, 1992; Danmarks
Nationalbank, *Annual Yearbook*, various issues; Bank of Finland, *Database*; Bank of Norway,
Database; The Swedish Central Bank, *Statistical Yearbook*, 1985, and *Sveriges tillgångar
och skulder mot utlandet*, 1992:1.
Note: Calculated as the difference between Nordic national indebtedness (net foreign debt
as a percentage of GDP) and weighted indebtedness of USA, Germany and Japan. The size
of GDP has been used as weight.

The risk premium reflects relative risk in bilateral comparisons

In a repayment perspective it is easy to understand intuitively that someone providing a loan to a country as debt-ridden as Sweden, for instance, would demand a risk premium. However, it is not this credit aspect that concerns us here; rather we are considering the premium as a compensation for uncertainty about the rules of the market in a particular country. The higher the value of the net foreign debt variable, the more imminently can economic–political interventions and regulations be expected. It may become more difficult for investors to get their money out of the country (cash flow lag), or in extreme cases it may be impossible for them to get the whole investment out at all (the confiscation case). Consequently we can expect a positive relationship between the proxy and the premium, such that in terms of the configurations in Figures 9.1 and 9.2, and other things being equal, the higher the value in the figures the greater the interest gap.

THE HISTORICAL RECORD OF CHANGING MARKET RULES AS A SOURCE OF POLITICAL RISK

In this section we will look at the proxy for the authorities' propensity to intervene, in order to get additional information for an assessment of the size of the political risk premiums. Figures 9.3–9.6 illustrate this propensity in the individual Nordic countries. The basic logic here is that the market participants perceive the risk as associated with recent experience (the last twenty-four months) regarding changes in market rules. My suggested estimate of the risk is based on the assumption that the investors or market participants have a 24-month-memory. They base their view of the risk on adaptive expectations, thus recalling what has happened during the last twenty-four months in the way of changes in the rules, which have increased the uncertainty attaching to business operations in the country concerned.

To construct the profiles I screened all policy measures – fiscal and monetary – that appeared in the period 1974–91. Political changes connected with deregulations were excluded. The result was then transformed into a variable, with a '1' for each day containing changes in the rules and a '0' elsewhere. Admittedly recollection is a purely subjective affair, but as a paradigm individual memory can be modelled in one of two ways: as a weighted or unweighted aggregate of historical events. Most people, however, seem to remember recent events more accurately. Here we assume that memories fade away, which means that exponentially diminishing weights are attached to policy changes undertaken during the last twenty-four months. The number of days during the last month when changes in the rules occurred is allotted a weight equal to 1, while the number in the month before is allotted a weight of 0.9, then 0.9^2, 0.9^3 and so on. Thus recollection of the number of changes twenty-four months ago is assumed

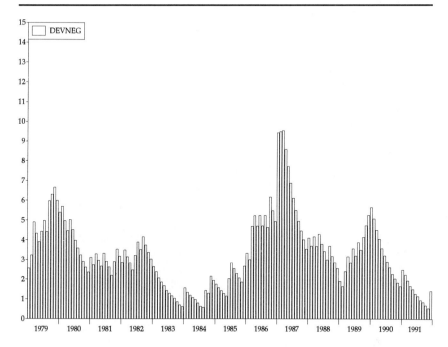

Figure 9.3 Political risk in Denmark (number of days during the last twenty-four months when changes in the rules occurred, which increased uncertainty; exponential weights)

to be weak, and is allotted a weight of $0.9^{24} = 0.08$.

From Figures 9.3–9.6 we can identify periods marked by a considerable propensity on the part of policy-makers to intervene, and by great political turmoil. In Denmark such a period is seen at the time of the 'potato-diet' in 1986 to 1987, in Finland at the beginning and end of the 1980s, in Norway at the time of the dramatic drop in the price of crude oil in 1986, and in Sweden on the occasions of the devaluations of the Swedish krona in 1981 and 1982.

Here, as in the case of indebtedness, it can be argued that the investors' claims for risk premiums due to a governmental propensity to intervene, should be based on a relative assessment, i.e. the propensity of the authorities in one country should be compared to the corresponding propensity in other countries. Involving a large number of countries would be a very demanding task, given the enormous amount of data that would have to be gathered, and it may not even be necessary since the propensity of the individual country concerned seems to have a high explanatory power to the emergence of gaps between the domestic and foreign rates.[13]

Even in the case of the seemingly similar Nordic countries, measurement problems arise, making comparisons between these countries difficult. The

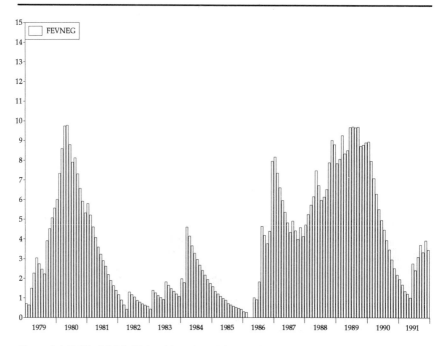

Figure 9.4 Political risk in Finland (number of days during the last twenty-four months when changes in the rules occurred, which increased uncertainty; exponential weights)

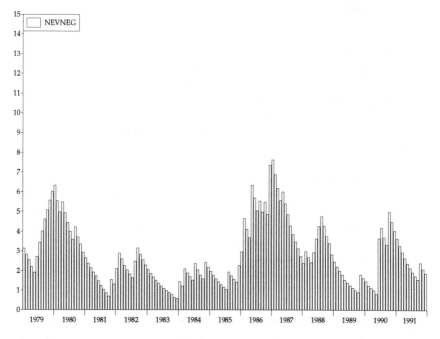

Figure 9.5 Political risk in Norway (number of days during the last twenty-four months when changes in the rules occurred, which increased uncertainty; exponential weights)

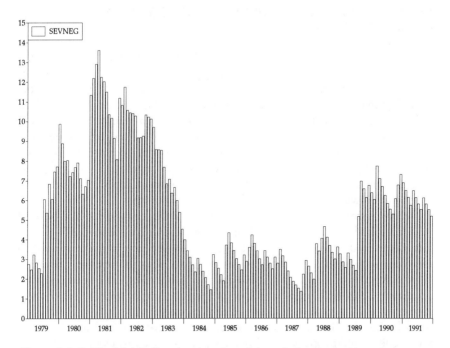

Figure 9.6 Political risk in Sweden (number of days during the last twenty-four months when changes in the rules occurred, which increased uncertainty; exponential weights)

different profiles displayed in Figures 9.3–9.6 are therefore not fully comparable, since to a large extent they reflect the reporting traditions of policy-makers in the different countries and their assessment of what the market needs to know. Similarly, unchanging reporting traditions over time have to be assumed in intra-country comparisons. Although with the exception of Sweden the peaks are almost the same size in the different countries, they should not be interpreted as carrying the same risk; rather, it is the market's way of interpreting the information that matters. For instance, in mid-1989 the memory of a potential investor in Finland of having experienced about ten days when policy changes occurred during the last twenty-four months (measured in accordance with a fading memory), may mean a demand for a lower risk premium than a potential investor in Denmark at the same time might demand on a basis of recollecting only four policy changes.

POLITICAL RISK AND INDIRECT SEGMENTATION – CONCLUDING REMARKS

This chapter has highlighted the problems involved in identifying the sources of systematic political risk, and of finding ways of converting these sources into a risk premium. We have also found clear indications that in Nordic terms the market rules have been far from stable. The risk profiles based on political changes which affect the uncertainty of a market differ across countries, but seem to have in common that they satisfactorily reflect the occurrence of economic turbulence in the individual countries. The two political risk proxies used here both strongly indicate that, given risk-averse actors, there are good grounds for assuming a non-negligible risk premium in the gap between Nordic national and global bond rates.

The two proxies for political risk identified in this chapter can also be used in a combined form. If we establish a simple dichotomy between high and low values in the two variables, we can identify the case of a strong need to intervene and a high propensity to do so, as the most interesting. The other three combinations, i.e. strong need and low propensity, little need and high propensity, and little need and low propensity, are of minor importance. However, if we assume a gradual increase in the variables as a relevant basis for risk, then the alternative of constructing a new total proxy by multiplying indebtedness and propensity to intervene, should be considered.

If we subscribe to a threshold-view of indebtedness of a country in an elaboration of the dichotomized approach and decide (arbitrarily) that a need to intervene appears at indebtedness of over 25 per cent, then starting from Figure 3.1 we would find a need in Denmark from 1980–93, in Finland from 1990–93, in Norway from 1978–81 and in Sweden from 1991–93. If we establish a similar dichotomy in our proxy for the authorities' propensity to intervene, and assume that this propensity is important whenever more than three days (according to the fading-memory principle) during the last twenty-four months have witnessed a change in the market rules, then we can identify a substantial propensity in Denmark in the periods 1979–80, 1986–87 and 1989–90; in Finland in the periods 1980–81 and 1986–90; in Norway in the periods 1979–80, 1986–88 and 1990–91; and in Sweden in the periods 1979–83 and 1988–91. When the two measures are combined in order to identify periods of high political risk in terms of a strong need and a high propensity to intervene, we find periods of such risk in Denmark in 1980, and 1988–91 1986–87 and 1989–90, in Finland in 1990 and 1988–91, in Norway in 1979–80 and in Sweden in 1991.

If instead we use indebtedness measured in relation to the OECD, and decide to use an excess Nordic indebtedness of 20 per cent as a high risk signal, we can identify periods of high political risk in Denmark in 1979–80, 1986–87 and 1989–90 (the same as in the previous case), in Finland in 1980–81 and 1986–90, in Norway in 1979–80, 1987–88 and 1990, and in Sweden from

1982–83 and 1988–91. When indebtedness is measured relative to indebtedness in the USA and with the same risk limit as was used in the OECD case, the risk period is reduced in the case of Finland to a single year, 1981, in Norway to 1979–80 and in Sweden to 1983. Generally speaking, when the proxies for need and propensity are combined, they give much shorter high-risk periods than either of the individual proxies on their own.

The findings presented in Chapters 6–9 regarding institutional features of the Nordic financial markets thus provide empirical indications of indirect segmentation, i.e. of deviations from PPP and of the existence of political and exchange risks. We have also found that the strength of all these elements has varied from country to country, and that consequently total international financial integration of the four financial markets in these countries does not obtain. In Chapter 14 we will look further at the extent to which these risks have been reflected in the gaps between Nordic and international bond rates, and in Chapter 15 at the extent to which they have been induced by inconsistent policies in the course of the transformation of the Nordic financial markets.

Before embarking on an analysis of differences in the cost of capital (or rather in bond rates), let us examine some institutional characteristics of the development of the Nordic bond markets and look at some relevant numerical facts, noting at the same time the presence of various forms of inefficiency such as market inefficiency or inefficiency generated by the central bank.

NOTES

1 See Aharoni (1966), Basi (1963), Kobrin (1979), Kobrin *et al.* (1980) and Oxelheim (1984a).
2 See, for example, Leavy (1984).
3 See, for example, Kobrin (1982) and Oxelheim and Wihlborg (1987).
4 See, for example, Frank and Cline (1971), Feder and Just (1977), Feder and Ross (1981), Edwards (1984) and, from a theoretical angle, Dufey and Giddy (1978).
5 Interest payments and amortizations as a percentage of the country's export earnings.
6 See, for example, Lessard (1983) and Dooley and Isard (1986) for the argument that a country's international relative indebtedness constitutes the fundamental source of the country risk for the country concerned, and that this source applies to LDCs as well as to industrial countries.
7 An interview study reported in Oxelheim (1990) confirms that even if the capital controls are inefficient there will still be a risk premium, since the mere existence of the legal framework for such controls 'signals' the government's belief in the successful exercise of an autonomous policy.
8 The calendarium embraces the different calendariums discussed in Chapter 6 containing the timetable for external deregulative measures, in Chapter 7 containing dates for internal deregulative measures including tax changes, and in Chapter 8 containing dates of changes in exchange regimes and related issues.
9 For future use the value of the proxy may be enhanced by the implementation

of weighting schemes applicable to the different policy changes and to the number of such changes in a day.

10   See, for example, Edwards (1984) for the use of the interest differential *vis-à-vis* LIBOR as the premium for country risk. Empirically, however, as is shown in Brewer (1983) for example, the determination of the premium is often more complex than this.

11   Which can also be interpreted in terms of underlying budget deficits.

12   In fact calculated as the difference between the indebtedness of an individual Nordic country and a weighted industrial world indebtedness.

13   See, for example, Oxelheim (1995).

REFERENCES

Aharoni, Y., 1966, *The Foreign Investment Decision Process*, Harvard University, Boston.

Basi, I., 1963, *Determinants of United States Private Direct Investment in Foreign Countries*, Kent State University, Ohio.

Brewer, T., 1983, 'Political Sources of Risk in the International Money Market', *Journal of International Business Studies*, Vol. 14, spring/summer, pp. 161–4.

Dooley, M.P and P. Isard, 1986, *Country Preferences and Exchange Rate Determination*, IMF, Washington, DC.

Dufey, G. and I. Giddy, 1978, *The International Money Market*, Prentice-Hall Foundations of Finance Series, Englewood Cliffs, New Jersey.

Edwards, S., 1984, 'LDC Foreign Borrowing and Default Risk: An Empirical Investigation 1976–80', *American Economic Review*, Vol. 74, pp. 726–34.

Feder, G. and R.E. Just, 1977, 'A Study of Debt Servicing Capacity Applying Logit Analysis', *Journal of Development Economics*, Vol. 4, pp. 23–58.

Feder, G. and S. Ross, 1981, 'Project Debt Servicing Capacity of Developing Countries', *Journal of Financial and Quantitative Analysis*, December, pp. 651–69.

Frank, C. and W. Cline, 1971, 'Measurement of Debt Servicing Capacity: An Application to Discriminant Analysis', *Journal of International Economics*, Vol. 1, No. 1 (March).

Kobrin, S., 1979, 'Political Risk: A Review and Reconsideration', *Journal of International Business Studies*, Vol. 10, spring/summer, pp. 67–80.

Kobrin, S., 1982, *Managing Political Risk Assessment: Strategic Response to Environmental Change*, University of California Press, Berkeley.

Kobrin, S. *et al.*, 1980, 'The Assessment and Evaluation of Noneconomic Environments by American Firms: A Preliminary Report', *Journal of International Business Studies*, Vol. 11, spring/summer, pp. 32–47.

Leavy, B., 1984, 'Assessing Country Risks for Foreign Investment Decisions', *Long Range Planning*, Vol. 17, No. 3, pp. 141–50.

Lessard, D.R., 1983, 'Comments on Buiter', in Hawkins, R., R. Lewich and C. Wihlborg (eds), *Research in International Business and Finance*, JAI Press, Greenwich, Conn.

Oxelheim, L., 1984a, *Exchange Risk Management in the Modern Company – A Total Approach*, Scandinavian Institute for Foreign Exchange Research, Stockholm.

Oxelheim, L., 1984b, 'Country Risk and Industrial Structure in a Nordic Perspective', *Unitas*, Helsinki.

Oxelheim, L., 1990, *International Financial Integration*, Springer Verlag, Heidelberg.

Oxelheim, L., 1995, 'On the Measurement of Political Risk', Mimeo, Lund University.

Oxelheim, L. and C. Wihlborg, 1987, *Macroeconomic Uncertainty – International Risks and Opportunities for the Corporation*, Wiley, Chichester.

Chapter 10

Development of primary bond markets

In this chapter we turn to the development of the Nordic primary markets, starting with a discussion of the different categories of bonds issued on these markets and the different categories of issuers operating there. This will be followed by a closer look at the development of primary markets in each of the Nordic countries included in this study. Background data on institutional changes are then summarized in timetables based on information from Chapters 6, 7 and 12, to provide a clearer picture of the course of the transition. Next the role of Nordic issues on international markets will be addressed. The status of the Nordic bond markets in an international perspective will also be analysed, and the chapter concludes with a discussion of differences in the development of the individual Nordic primary markets and of the role these markets have played in meeting corporate funding requirements.

MAJOR TYPES OF BONDS AND ISSUERS

Among capital market segments as a whole, the bond market generally exhibits the widest range of choices. Figure 10.1 shows the menu in an oversimplified form which none the less succeeds in revealing the multiplicity of alternatives.

The classic bond has a fixed rate of interest, and matures on the date set at the time of issue. The importance of fixed-rate straight bonds has grown over time, and in 1990 the size of such issues on the Euromarket was almost twice that of all other kinds of Eurobond issue.[1]

The main types of bonds issued and traded on the Nordic markets are the following:

- *Government bonds* are debt instruments issued by governments (national treasuries) to finance fiscal deficits. These instruments were initially held by financial institutions in the Nordic countries, but since the beginning of the 1990s they are also frequently in the hands of corporations or households, as well as being held by foreigners. With a

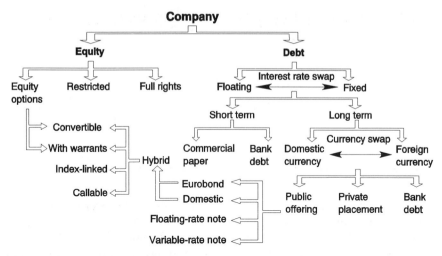

Figure 10.1 Major financing alternatives

few exceptions Nordic bonds are issued with maturities of five to twenty years, and the bulk with maturities up to ten years. The Nordic governments issue bonds either with fixed rates (paid annually) or with floating rates (generally paid quarterly). Most of the bonds are issued as tap issues.[2]

- *Municipal bonds* are debt instruments issued by local governments to finance investment in such things as infrastructure and human capital (e.g. schools).
- *Mortgage bonds* are debt instruments issued by Nordic mortgage institutions to provide loans to individuals and corporations for the purchase of housing, land and other real assets, where the asset or land serves as collateral for the loan. With a few exceptions Nordic mortgage bonds are issued with maturities of two to thirty-five years, with Danish bonds occupying the upper end of the range. Mortgage bonds are issued predominantly on a tap basis.
- *Bank bonds* are debt instruments issued by banks. During the 1980s Nordic banks were increasingly involved in this kind of funding. Bank bonds are predominantly bullet bonds[3] on a tap issue basis with fixed coupon and maturities less than five years.
- *Non-bank financial institution bonds* are debt instruments issued by financial institutions of a non-bank character and outside the mortgage sector. Issues by finance companies dominate this kind of bond.
- *Corporate bonds* are debt instruments issued by companies. In practice this way of raising capital is open only to businesses with strong credit ratings. Corporate bonds can be divided into two categories, *industrial bonds* and *other bonds*. The holder of a typical Nordic industrial bond

receives interest payments once or twice a year and the face value of the bond when it matures. Some industrial bonds are *convertible*, which means that the holder is allowed to convert them into a specified number of shares during a specified period before the maturity date.[4] In the mid-1990s the principal buyers of Nordic industrial bonds are pension funds, insurance companies, households and foreigners.

- *Premium bonds* are debt instruments issued by national debt offices. They are fixed loans on which no interest is paid to the bondholders. Instead, the holders receive their returns as premiums distributed as prize money in a lottery. The bonds are redeemed at par value at maturity date. In the mid-1990s the main holders of premium bonds are households.
- *Mass-debentures* are debt instruments employed primarily by Finnish and Swedish corporate issuers. These loans carry a somewhat higher credit risk than other bonds, to which they are subordinate in case of bankruptcy.

Issuers in the Nordic bond markets

The aim of this chapter, as mentioned above, is to highlight the role of bond markets – in particular Nordic national markets – in the funding of domestic non-financial companies over the last twenty years. Since statistics do not lend themselves easily to a comparison across countries even in a homogeneous region of the Nordic kind, various issuers have been divided into three main groups. In the first group – the *central and local governments* – we find the National Treasury, the Debt Office and the municipalities, which account for government, municipal and premiums bonds. The second group consists of the *financial sector*, mortgage institutions and financial institutions, accounting for mortgage bonds and bonds issued by banks and non-bank financial institutions. Finally, the *non-financial sector* constitutes the third group, i.e. non-financial companies issuing corporate bonds and mass-debentures.[5] The three groups represent three different parts which bond markets can play in corporate funding:

- making *no contribution* to the funding;[6]
- making an *indirect contribution* in that the financial institutions lend funds borrowed on the bond market;
- making a *direct contribution*.

THE DEVELOPMENT OF PRIMARY BOND MARKETS – A COUNTRY-BY-COUNTRY PRESENTATION

In this section we will discuss developments since the 1970s, focusing on primary bond market activities in the Nordic countries.

Public borrowing needs were the driving-force in some Nordic countries

Previous chapters have described the Nordic economies as heavily indebted, with the indebtedness spinning off in the 1970s following the first oil crisis. From the mid-1970s Denmark and Sweden were both facing serious problems in financing their public sectors, and state borrowing assumed enormous proportions. The public deficit (excluding oil revenues) was also substantial in Norway, but the oil revenues saved the Norwegian financial markets from the same severe difficulties as in the other countries. In Finland the public sector deficit led to some government borrowing, but this remained at a much lower level than in the rest of the Nordic region.

During the second half of the 1970s debt financing in all the Nordic countries was effected predominantly by bond issues in domestic markets. The authorities in Finland, Norway and Sweden imposed quantitative regulations, paving the way for low-cost government issues, while the Danish policy was based on open-market operations by the Central Bank. In the 1980s the central government deficits in the Nordic countries – and therefore also the need to borrow – gradually declined. The private sector, however, became increasingly interested in issuing bonds.

Generally speaking the Nordic governments have varied considerably as regards their own role in influencing market conditions. In Denmark alone of the four Nordic countries, the bond market was governed by market forces at a very early stage, that is to say supply and demand were balanced by the interest rate. We have seen in Chapter 7 that there was no investment obligation on the part of financial institutions, and government bonds had to compete with private sector bonds. In the 1980s internationalization and integration forced a change of attitude on policy-makers in Finland, Norway and Sweden as well. A market in the real sense began to develop in these countries in the early 1980s, but it was not until the middle of the decade that more determined efforts were made to become an integrated part of the global financial market. To begin with the change in attitude towards cross-border portfolio investment was asymmetrical, favouring the import rather than the export of capital. At the beginning of the 1990s symmetry in this respect was achieved.

Issues by different groups

Table 10.1 shows issues by Nordic borrowers in 1980 and 1990. The purpose is to reveal changes in issuing patterns (i.e. the size of the issues by different groups), and changes in investor patterns (i.e. the kind of investors with whom the issues are placed). Unfortunately, the statistical conventions differ as between the Nordic countries, and there are no accessible sources on which to base comparisons of the role of domestic markets only.[7] This means that Nordic issues on international markets have to be included.

Table 10.1 Bond issues by Nordic borrowers (end of period)

	Danish[a] 1980	Danish[a] 1990	Finnish[b] 1980	Finnish[b] 1990	Norwegian[c] 1980	Norwegian[c] 1990	Swedish[d] 1980	Swedish[d] 1990
	Units of national currency (bn)							
Total circulating bonds at nominal values	483	1,409	33	215	142	434	372	1,223
Share issued by:				*% shares*				
State	22	36	47	24	44	23	45	29
Mortgage institutions	70	54	32[e]	28[e]	21[e]	38[e]	44	57
Banks, municipalities and others	} 8	} 10	4	30	25[f]	28[f]	3	8
Non-financial companies			17	18	10	11	8	6
Shares placed with:[g]				*% shares*				
Banks[h]	17	11	26	20	34	17	32	15
Insurance companies	23	22	3	6	12	} 20	16	17
Pension funds	15	15	1	0	12		31	26
Foreigners	} 45	} 52	45	42	40	38	8	20
Others			25	32	2	25	13	22

[a] Including treasury bills.
[b] Bonds and debentures.
[c] Bearer bond debt.
[d] Bonds and debentures.
[e] Including private credit enterprises and private financial companies.
[f] Including state banks and non-listed bonds.
[g] For Finland, Norway and Sweden the figures include foreign bonds issued in these countries.
[h] Including the Central Bank.

Sources: Based on data from Danmarks Nationalbank, *Quarterly reports*, various issues; Central Statistical Bureau of Denmark, *Statistical Yearbook*, various issues; Central Statistical Bureau of Finland, *Financial Market Statistics* and *Statistik över masskuldebrev*, various issues; Central Statistical Bureau of Norway, *Credit Market Statistics*, and *Bank- of Kredittstatistikk*, various issues; Bank of Norway, *Pengar og Kreditt*, various issues; Central Statistical Bureau of Sweden, *Database* and *Financial accounts*, various issues. The Swedish Central Bank, *Statistical Yearbook*, various issues; Bank for International Settlements, *Database*; and own estimates.
Note: Domestic and international issues included.

Table 10.2 helps to interpret the nominal figures regarding changes in the size of the issues in Table 10.1, by showing the relative importance of issues undertaken by borrowers from the different Nordic countries.

In 1990 the stock of Danish issues (at par value) was by far the largest in terms of relative size, amounting to about 1.7 times the size of the Danish GDP. This figure was also high relative to international standards that year. The relative size of the outstanding stock of issues made by the US, Japanese,

Table 10.2 Relative size of outstanding stocks of Nordic bonds (nominal values, percentage of GDP, end of year)

Borrower from	1975	1980	1985	1990
Denmark	95	123	166	166
Finland	14	17	30	41
Norway	38	50	44	66
Sweden	60	71	96	91

Sources: Based on data from Nordic Statistical Secretariat, *Yearbook of Nordic Statistics*, various issues; Danmarks Nationalbank, *Quarterly Reports*, various issues; Central Statistical Bureau of Denmark, *Statistical Yearbook*, various issues; Central Statistical Bureau of Finland, *Financial Market Statistics* and *Statistik över masskuldebrev*, various issues; Central Statistical Bureau of Norway, *Credit Market Statistics*, and *Bank- of Kredittstatistikk*, various issues; Bank of Norway, *Pengar og Kreditt*, various issues; Central Statistical Bureau of Sweden, *Database* and *Financial Accounts*, various issues; The Swedish Central Bank, *Statistical Yearbook*, various issues; Bank for International Settlements, *Database*; and own estimates.
Note: Domestic and international issues included.

UK and German borrowers corresponded that year to about 1.0, 0.9, 0.4 and 0.6 times national GDP respectively. The stock of Finnish issues was the smallest: less than half the size of Finland's GDP. However, between 1975 and 1990 the stock of Finnish issues showed the highest growth of any of the Nordic countries. As a percentage of GDP the Finnish stock of bonds increased by 200 per cent, to be compared with a growth of about 50–75 per cent in the relative size of the outstanding stock of bonds issued by borrowers from the other Nordic countries.

An assessment of the relative significance of bond issues in relation to different kinds of issuer reveals considerable differences among the Nordic countries. The greater part of the bonds issued by Danish borrowers in the 1980s were issued by mortgage institutions. Although their relative share fell slightly in the course of the decade, in 1990 these institutions still accounted for about half the total outstanding Danish stock. Issues by the Danish government increased during the first half of the period, and accounted for about one-third of the stock in 1990.[8] For the period as a whole the remaining 10 per cent consisted of issues by all other borrowers, including non-financial companies. Sweden exhibits a similar pattern in terms of the size distribution, although the development over time shows the reverse pattern, i.e. an increase in the relative importance of issues by mortgage institutions at the expense of the relative importance of government issues. As the 1980s proceeded, the relative size of the stock of Swedish mortgage bonds approached the size of the Danish stock. In 1990 the stock of Swedish mortgage bonds was ahead of the relative size of the Danish stock by some percentage points.

The patterns for Finnish and Norwegian issues were similar to the

Swedish, in that the relative importance of government issues declined; in all three countries these issues accounted for almost half of the total outstanding stocks in 1980 and for about a quarter in 1990. However, the resemblance stops here, since taking the period as a whole we find that issues by Norwegian banks and non-governmental public sector borrowers together accounted for a large relative share of the total, or about one quarter. In Finland the relative drop in the share of government issues as a percentage of total issues was more than compensated by a rise in the share of issues by banks (on the international market) and by municipalities. The relative importance of corporate issues remained more or less unchanged in all four Nordic countries. In 1990 the biggest relative share of corporate issues – nearly one-fifth – was reported for Finland and the smallest for Denmark.

In the early 1990s a large proportion of Danish, Finnish and Norwegian bonds were in the hands of foreign investors, while Swedish bonds were evenly distributed between banks, insurance companies, pension funds, foreigners and others. The drop in the share of issues placed with banks reflects the diminishing use or final abolition of reserve requirements. The relaxation or lifting of investment obligations could thus have been expected to reduce the share of bonds held by insurance companies and pension funds. In the case of these investors, however, investing in bonds is part of their business, which means that a lower investment obligation may not necessarily mean a smaller share of bonds in their portfolios. Rather, what may ensue from relaxed regulations is a portfolio adjustment in favour of non-restricted bonds traded on the market. Hence, since the issuing of restricted bonds stopped more or less concurrently with the easing of investment obligations, a gradual adjustment ensued. At the beginning of the 1990s most restricted loans had either matured or been converted, and the case for a further change in holding strategies of insurance companies and pension funds was not present any longer.

Development of the Danish primary bond market and Danish issues

The financial sector in Denmark has traditionally distinguished itself from those in the other Nordic countries by being more market-orientated. A sophisticated bond market has long existed, and monetary policy has long been market-orientated. Quantitative restrictions have been imposed to a limited extent only. A summary of institutional changes is provided in Table 10.3. At the beginning of the 1990s the Danish bond market encompasses all types of bonds, from fixed-income to floating rate and index-linked bonds. Further, the bonds no longer exist physically, they only appear as book-entry securities registered with the Danish Security Centre. Electronic trading started in September 1987.

Bonds occupy the central position in the credit stock as a whole. The outstanding debt in the 1980s amounted to 1.2–2.0 times GDP. It increased

Table 10.3 Timetable for institutional changes relating to the Danish bond market

1974 – Non-residents are allowed to invest in Danish bonds, both krone-denominated and foreign-currency-denominated.
     – Convertible bonds are offered.

1978 – Residents are allowed to buy bonds issued by international organizations of which Denmark is a member. Bonds have to be purchased and sold through, and deposited with, authorized Danish foreign exchange dealers.

1979 – Sale of krone-denominated bonds to non-residents is suspended.

1982 – Index-linked bonds are introduced.
     – Registration of bond loans begins.

1983 – Suspension of foreign sales of krone-denominated bonds is lifted.
     – Residents may freely buy foreign bonds, provided that the original maturity exceeds two years.
     – Listing of bond loans begins.
     – A book-entry securities system is introduced.

1984 – Residents are allowed to invest in international bonds.
     – Floating rate notes are introduced.
     – Residents are permitted under open general licence to issue Danish bonds by placing a public sale on a foreign capital market.

1985 – Residents' purchases of unlisted international bonds are still subject to approval from the central bank, but this is administered in a more liberal way.
     – Bonds with warrants are offered over the counter (OTC).
     – Interest rate futures are offered over the counter.
     – Eurokronebonds are introduced.

1986 – Interest rate options are offered over the counter.

1987 – Reporting of trade in bonds begins.

1988 – Issuing control of mortgage credit is abolished.
     – Stockbrokers may trade in bonds from their own offices.
     – A market for futures and options (FUTOP) is launched.
     – Interest rate swap agreements are offered over the counter.
     – Interest rate options are offered on the stock exchange.
     – Interest rate futures and forwards are offered on the stock exchange.
     – Forward rate agreements (FRAs) are offered over the counter.
     – The Danish Financial Supervisory Authority (Finanstilsynet) is established to supervise the banking, insurance and securities sectors.
     – Resident companies may issue abroad in foreign currency and Danish kroner.
     – Non-residents are allowed to issue in Denmark.
     – All other remaining cross-border restrictions are abolished, but trade in international bonds has to take place through authorized domestic banks or brokers. Danish bonds issued abroad must be deposited.

1989 – Issuing controls are abolished.
     – A foreign currency denominated bond (apart from ECU), issued by non-residents, is quoted on Copenhagen Stock Exchange for the first time.

1990 – A system is established to ease the settlement of payments in connection with trading in foreign-currency-denominated bonds registered with the Danish Security Centre.
     – Bonds with warrants are offered on the stock exchange.

from somewhere in the range of 1.3–1.5 times GDP in the first half of the 1980s to about twice GDP in 1986, following the rapid credit expansion associated with the economic upswing that year. In 1990, however, total bond credit was back at slightly less than 1.7 times GDP.

Traditionally the bond market has been dominated by private institutions issuing bonds with collateral in real estate or other real assets. At the beginning of the 1990s more than 2,000 such series were issued. They are generally issued on a tap basis at maturities of ten, twenty, thirty or thirty-five years. Mortgage institutions traditionally possess a monopoly in issuing bonds with collateral in real estate. The regulations governing mortgage credit (ceilings on lending per property, restrictions on purpose, etc.) are politically determined and have often been utilized as instruments of economic policy, as was evident on several occasions in the mid-1980s.[9] Also, the regulations set limits on the maximum amount of the mortgages and control the currency used.

At the beginning of the 1970s some twenty-five mortgage institutions were responsible for most issues of mortgage bonds. During the 1980s five mortgage credit institutions accounted for most mortgage credit lending. In addition to these institutions two new mortgage credit institutions were approved in 1990 and 1991 respectively. More structural changes occurred in the early 1990s in the shape of a merger between IRF Industrial Mortgage Banking Holding A/S – consisting of IRF Industrial Mortgage Banking A/S and IRF Erhvervsfinansiering A/S – and Tryg Nykredit.

From the 1980s onwards the bond market became increasingly dominated by new government issues. In 1982 the government bond share in the net growth of the bond debt reached the 75 per cent level, which brought the government bond share of the total stock to one-third. From the mid-1980s on, issues of treasuries declined – a reflection of the dramatic reduction in public sector deficits. The government started to issue bullet loans in 1987. At the beginning of the 1990s the sale of government bonds was being effected on a tap basis through Danmarks Nationalbank. Generally speaking these bonds pay one coupon a year, except for bullet loans which pay the coupons quarterly. Government bonds, unlike mortgage bonds, are not callable.[10]

The outstanding stock of bonds issued by the Danish financial sector increased considerably in the second half of the 1980s, as can be seen in Figure 10.2, while the stocks of government bonds and non-financial-sector bonds remained more or less unchanged. Mortgage institutions accounted for most of the bonds in the financial sector. As a result of the major liberalization that occurred from 1980–84, these institutes increased their lending to industry from an average of about DKK 4 billion in the first half of the 1980s to an average of about DKK 20 billion in the second. Industry's average share of the total lending of the mortgage institutions rose from about 11 to about 26 per cent.[11]

Non-financial companies have raised capital on their own account on the

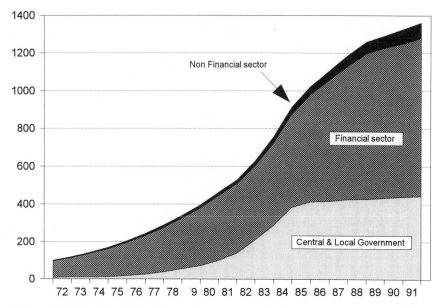

Figure 10.2 Total circulating Danish bonds, 1971–91 (nominal values, stock at end of period, bn DKK)

Sources: Based on data from Danmarks Nationalbank, *Quarterly Reports*, various issues; Central Statistical Bureau of Denmark, *Statistical Yearbook*, various issues; and own estimates.
Note: Domestic and international issues by Danish borrowers included. The figures differ somewhat from those presented in Table 10.1 since we do not need to compromise here or to include treasury bills.

Danish bond market to a limited extent only. In 1990 corporate bonds represented only a small percentage of the total Danish domestic credit stock, while the total stock of bonds represented about 47 per cent. However, funds have been raised through mortgage institutions and, above all, through the IRF Industrial Mortgage Banking A/S. Danish non-financial companies have thus benefited indirectly from the domestic bond market in terms of fund-raising.

Danish tax legislation has offered different incentives at different times to different groups of investors. Banks and other investors who are liable to tax on yields on a gross basis, constitute one category. Another group consists of pension funds which are exposed to tax rules that encourage the purchase of long-term bonds to be held until maturity. This group is mainly interested in index-linked bonds. Finally, private investors taxed solely on the coupon rate have a high propensity to buy bonds paying a low coupon rate.

A notable feature of the Danish bond market is the scale on which krone-denominated government bonds are sold abroad. These sales started in the mid-1970s and expanded rapidly after 1983, when the temporary suspension of sales imposed in 1979 was lifted. In 1990 about 50 per cent of Danish bonds were held by foreigners. At the same time the outstanding stock of krone-denominated bonds issued abroad represented only a small percentage of the total stock of krone-denominated bonds. There has thus been a substantial export of Danish krone-denominated bonds.

Development of the Finnish primary bond market and Finnish issues

Up to the beginning of the 1990s the Finnish bond market was heavily regulated (see Table 10.4).[12] Government and private-sector bond rates and other issue terms were controlled by the authorities. Permits to issue bonds were granted by the government. Debentures and other bonds, however, were only registered with the Bank of Finland. The government granted tax-free status for bonds on an individual basis. For long periods regulated and unregulated rates were to be found side by side on the Finnish market, thus allowing for interest arbitrage between the two segments. As well as the state, the mortgage banks – which grant loans for energy and other infrastructural investments – also issued tax-free bonds. However, the only way for companies to approach a bond market was to go via the taxable bond market. A gradual relaxation of restrictions on the bond market occurred in the late 1980s. In January 1991 all markka-denominated bonds became available to foreign investors.

As was shown in Table 10.2, the outstanding stock of Finnish bonds was small in comparison with the stocks in the other Nordic countries. In 1975 the Finnish stock represented only about 14 per cent of Finland's GDP, whereas in Denmark the stock was almost equal to GDP. Although the Finnish market grew fast in the 1980s, in 1990 it was still less than half the country's GDP. The relative strength of the Finnish banks and the country's strict regulations are the main reasons for the modest size of the Finnish bond market.

Up to the mid-1980s the Finnish domestic bond market was dominated by government bonds, and the rapid development of the bond market was mainly a result of an increase in government bond issues, with maturities generally ranging from three to five years. The demand for these bonds was encouraged by the fact that the yield was tax-free. However, in October 1987 the government issued the first taxable government bond loan. Following the introduction of a new withholding tax on interest income in 1991, the Finnish government decided to stop issuing tax-free government bonds. The issue of tax free government bonds in August 1989 was thus proved to be the last of its kind. In the case of tax-free mortgage bonds the last issue was in September 1990. At the beginning of the 1990s two basic types of government bonds were being issued: yield bonds to private investors and other bonds to institutional investors. In the case of Finnish bonds the coupon is generally paid annually. Government bonds are sold at so-called

Table 10.4 Timetable for institutional changes relating to the Finnish bond market

1970	– Registration of bond loans is made compulsory.
1981	– Authorized banks' rights to act as intermediaries in selling Finnish bonds and debentures to non-residents is extended to include new issues.
1982	– Convertible bonds are introduced.
1985	– Temporary ban on non-residents' purchase of markka-denominated bonds and debentures is imposed.
1986	– Ban on non-residents' purchase of markka-denominated bonds and debentures is eased.
	– Bonds with warrants are introduced.
	– Floating rate notes are offered over the counter (OTC).
	– Zero-coupon bonds are offered over the counter.
	– Interest rate options are offered over the counter.
	– Manufacturing and shipping companies allowed to issue abroad in foreign currency.
1987	– First issue of taxable government bonds.
	– Forward rate agreements (FRAs) are offered over the counter.
	– Interest rate futures and forwards are offered over the counter.
1988	– Legislation enabling trading in standardized options and futures is introduced. The Finnish Options Market Ltd starts trading in standardized options and futures on shares.
	– Floating rate notes are introduced.
	– Computerized bond trading is introduced.
1989	– Listing of bond loans begins.
	– The issuing of tax free government bonds ceases.
1990	– Non-residents are permitted to purchase new markka-denominated bonds.
	– Non-residents are allowed to issue markka-denominated bonds in Finland.
	– Finnish companies are allowed to issue bonds denominated in any currency abroad without special permission from the Bank of Finland.
	– Interest rate swaps are offered over the counter.
	– Eurobond issues allowed.
	– The issuing of tax free mortgage bonds ceases
1991	– A withholding tax on interest income is introduced.
	– Zero-coupon bonds are offered on the stock exchange.
	– All remaining cross-border restrictions are abolished. However, trade in foreign bonds has to take place through authorized domestic banks or brokers.
	– A book-entry securities system is introduced.
1992	– A primary dealer system is introduced to improve the liquidity and transparency of the secondary market.
	– An attempt is made to bring the trade in bonds to the stock exchange, but this proves to be a failure.
1993	– Issuing controls are abolished.
	– The Financial Supervisory Authority (Finansinspektionen) is established to supervise the banking and the securities sectors. The Ministry of Social Affairs and Health (Socialdepartementet) still controls the insurance sector.
1994	– Forward contracts based on government benchmark bonds are introduced on the stock exchange.

Dutch auctions.[13] Options and futures were being offered in 1988 when Finnish Options Market Ltd launched its operation, but in the early 1990s options and futures on bonds were not available.

With the introduction of a property income deduction, the demand for taxable securities grew. This applied particularly to corporate debentures. In the first half of 1985 the growth in bond and debenture issues by non-financial and financial companies was especially rapid, as foreign investors began to show an interest in these loans on account of their high, fixed interest rates. Foreign portfolio investment in these securities was quite high until the Bank of Finland banned this type of capital import at the end of June 1985. The stock of Finnish bonds held by foreigners was still high in the early 1990s.

As Figure 10.3 shows, the stock of Finnish bonds issued by the financial sector was booming from the 1980s onwards. Finnish banks were the main issuer in this sector. The share of bonds in bank funding increased in 1990, and a record high number of issues, including both foreign currency and markka-denominated bonds, was registered. Most of the markka-denominated bonds were placed with foreigners.

At the beginning of the 1990s Helibor bank bonds were the main kind of

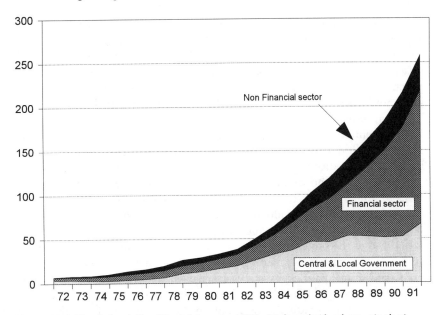

Figure 10.3 Total circulating Finnish bonds, 1971–91 (nominal values, stock at end of period, bn FIM)

Sources: Based on data from Central Statistical Bureau of Finland, *Financial Market Statistics* and *Statistik över masskuldebrev*, various issues; and own estimates.
Note: Domestic and international issues by Finnish borrowers included.

bond being issued. They were issued as bullet bonds on a tap basis with fixed coupons and maturities of between one-and-a-half and five years. Mortgage bank bonds, issued by subsidiaries of Helibor banks with maturities of three to ten years, were the other main type of bond being issued. The stock of bonds issued by the government and the non-financial sector had remained more or less unchanged since the mid-1980s.

Although by US standards the importance of bonds in corporate funding has been low in Finland as in the other Nordic countries, the stock of outstanding Finnish corporate bonds and debentures did increase slightly from the beginning of the 1980s on. An examination of Table 10.2 shows that the stock increased from about FIM 6 billion in 1980 to almost FIM 40 billion at the end of the decade. Corporate bonds constituted about 2 per cent of the total domestic credit stock in 1990, with the domestic bond market altogether representing about 13 per cent of the total. New types of loan construction, such as convertible bonds and bonds with warrants, were occasionally employed during the second half of the 1980s.

Development of the Norwegian primary bond market and Norwegian issues

Up to 1980 the bond market in Norway was heavily regulated on both the supply side (by issuing regulations[14]) and the demand side (by quota allocations in the Credit Budget); it was also regulated as regards the terms attached to the securities. Non-residents were not allowed to issue or purchase bonds on the Norwegian market, as can be seen in Table 10.5. The government was able to control both demand and supply in the bond market. Trade in bonds on a voluntary basis was more or less non-existent. Government regulation in the 1970s, resulting in lower bond yields than market conditions would have allowed, meant that the bond market share of the domestic credit supply fell in the late 1970s to around 6–10 per cent.

The liberalization of the Norwegian bond market began in the period 1980–82, but it really took off in 1985. The requirement that banks and insurance companies should hold a certain proportion of their capital in bonds was also completely abolished that year. Issuing regulations were liberalized at the same time, but some sectors were still denied unrestricted access to the market. Remaining restrictions applied to foreigners, households and municipalities, as well as to banks, finance companies and loan associations engaged in the housing sector. The restrictions imposed on these institutions were gradually removed in the second half of the 1980s. Mortgage institutions were the first to receive permission to issue bonds, followed by banks and finance companies. By 1985 the general deregulation had triggered a booming interest in bond issues on the part of Norwegian borrowers, as can be seen in Figure 10.4.

The process of deregulation led to the rise of new categories of investors

Table 10.5 Timetable for institutional changes relating to the Norwegian bond
market

1979	– Non-residents are allowed to buy bearer bonds up to a value of NOK 1 million.
	– Eurokrone-denominated bonds are introduced.
1980	– Bond issuing controls are relaxed.
	– Convertible bonds are introduced.
1981	– Listing of bond loans begins.
	– Reporting of trade in bonds begins.
1982	– Issuing control is tightened up.
1983	– Interest rate swaps are offered over the counter (OTC).
1984	– Non-residents' right to purchase Norwegian bonds (including government bonds) is suspended.
	– Bonds with warrants are introduced.
	– Parts of the reserve requirements are abolished.
1985	– Bond investment obligations are abolished for all financial institutions.
	– Loan associations are allowed to issue bonds freely in order to grant loans to the business sector.
	– The Norwegian Register of Securities (Verdipapirsentralen) is established and begins to register bond loans as of 1986.
	– Eurobonds may be traded freely in the secondary market.
	– Interest options are offered over the counter.
	– Interest rate futures and forwards are offered over the counter.
1986	– A book-entry securities system is introduced.
	– The Norwegian Banking, Insurance and Securities Commission (Kredittilsynet) is established to supervise the banking, insurance and securities sectors.
1987	– Remaining reserve requirements are abolished.
	– Interest rate regulations are abolished.
	– Forward rate agreements are offered over the counter.
1988	– Restrictions on bond issues to finance housing, the primary sector and power plants removed. Municipal borrowing in the bond market is still subject to control.
1989	– The Norwegian bond market is reopened to foreign investors.
	– Non-residents are given the right to issue krone-denominated bonds in Norway.
	– An electronic trading system, decentralized to the broker's offices, is introduced.
1990	– All remaining cross-border restrictions are abolished, but trade in international bonds has to take place through authorized domestic banks or brokers. The issuing regulations mainly contain provisions designed to secure a transparent and efficient bond market and to meet certain tax and statistical requirements.
1991	– Floating rate notes are offered.
1992	– Index-linked bonds are offered.
1993	– Interest rate futures and forwards are offered on the stock exchange.
	– It is permitted to offer interest rate options on the stock exchange.
1995	– Issuing controls are abolished.

in bonds, namely financial institutions, the corporate sector and to some degree households. These investors were further encouraged by favourable taxation arrangements for capital gains on bond investments. At the beginning of the 1990s all bonds were registered in book-entry form with the Norwegian Registry of Securities, and an electronic trading system was in use. Although the Monetary and Credit Act exercised some control over new issues, it applied mainly to procedures and structures.

The relative size of the outstanding stock of Norwegian bonds almost doubled between 1975 and 1990 (See Table 10.2). The main increase – about 50 per cent – occurred between 1985 and 1990 in response to the deregulative measures introduced during that period. However, in 1990 the stock was still small in comparison with the relative size of the Danish stock of bonds, but was comparable, for instance, to the relative size of the outstanding stock of German bonds.

The Norwegian bond market is made up of government and government-guaranteed bonds and bonds issued by municipalities, banks, the corporate sector and various loan associations such as mortgage institutions. Bank bonds are a recent phenomenon, since banks were not allowed to issue bonds until the late 1980s.

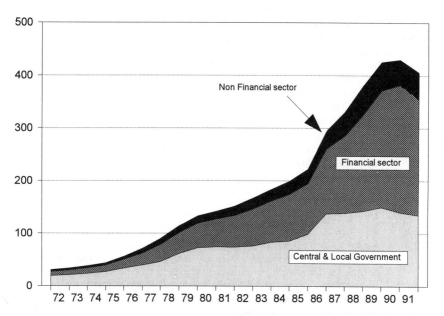

Figure 10.4 Total circulating Norwegian bonds, 1971–91 (nominal values, stock at end of period, bn NOK)

Sources: Based on data from Bank of Norway, *Economic Bulletin*, 1993, No. 2; Central Statistical Bureau of Norway, *Credit Market Statistics* and *Bank- og Kredittstatistikk*, various issues; and own estimates.
Note: Domestic and international issues by Norwegian borrowers included.

As a rule Norwegian bonds in the early 1990s had a fixed coupon (annual payment), and consisted for the most part of bullet loans on a tap issue basis and with maturities not exceeding five years. Loans which did not have maturities of over five years usually had an adjustable interest rate combined with put or call options. Bond market institutions in Norway did not lend money to the household sector as was the case in Denmark and Sweden.

As can be seen in Figure 10.4, growth in the stock of Norwegian bonds after the mid-1980s was due primarily to new issues from the financial sector. However, during this period the stock of bonds issued by the non-financial sector also increased substantially. In 1990 the stock of corporate bonds expanded from about NOK 15 billion in 1980 to almost 50 billion, predominantly through new issues on the international market. The greater part of the new issues were placed with foreigners. At the beginning of the 1980s this investor group's holdings were almost exclusively in government bonds, whereas a decade later two-thirds of their portfolios of krone-denominated bonds consisted of corporate issues. The share of new issues placed with banks also declined substantially as a result of the abolition of the liquidity requirements imposed on the banks, according to which they had to hold a proportion of their balances in certain types of liquid assets, among them government bonds.

Norwegian non-financial companies have been increasingly using the bond market to raise capital. However, by the beginning of the 1990s 80 per cent of the outstanding stock was being issued on international markets. In addition, Norwegian companies were able to rely indirectly on the domestic bond market, by borrowing considerable funds raised by mortgage institutions as loans to industry alongside their loans to the housing and public sectors. Corporate issues of convertible bonds and bonds with warrants were small.[15]

Development of the Swedish primary bond market and Swedish issues

In 1952 the authorities introduced tight controls. Up to the 1980s the Swedish bond market was then strictly regulated and was entirely dominated by a small number of participants, on both the issuer and the investor side. On the supply side the regulations applied to issuing, and on the demand side to investment obligations and liquidity requirements, which compelled pension funds (the AP fund), insurance companies and banks to stick to low-return government bonds (priority bonds). In addition, the Swedish Central Bank imposed restrictions on the price at which bonds could be issued. Companies were allowed to issue bonds, but only after the government and the housing sector had satisfied the main part of their needs. Banks were forced to absorb large amounts of fixed-interest government and housing bonds. The bond share of total bank-sector assets increased from about 20 per cent around 1970 to more than 25 per cent at the beginning of the 1980s.

In 1983 the requirement that banks should acquire priority bonds was abolished, and the bond share of total bank sector assets then fell by almost 50 per cent over the next few years.

In general the restrictions on the Swedish financial markets were relaxed somewhat in the mid-1970s, as a result of the growing fiscal deficit. For instance, as is shown in Table 10.6, foreign borrowing by Swedish companies was encouraged by certain legislative changes. None the less, the revival in the bond market was due mainly to the stimulating effects of the money market. When the government started issuing long-term market-rate bonds in late 1983, these were immediately traded and quoted along with the money market instruments. In addition, some of the corporate bonds were quoted, and new forms of housing bonds were marketed in smaller denominations aimed at households and small-scale institutions. The final step in the deregulation was taken later, with the abolition of all restrictions on cross-border portfolio investment in 1989 (although Swedish bonds were not allowed to leave the country, but had to be deposited in a custody account), and with the lifting of regulations on bond issue prices in 1991.

Between the mid-1970s and the mid-1980s the outstanding stock increased by about 60 per cent as a percentage of GDP. During the second half of the 1980s it fell by about 5 per cent. In 1990 the relative size of the outstanding stock of bonds was the second highest in the Nordic countries, albeit remaining much lower than the equivalent Danish figure. The relative size corresponded to that of the US stock of bonds.

A shrinking budget deficit during the second half of the 1980s meant that the role of the central government as an issuing body declined in importance, and the housing mortgage institutions became the biggest borrowers. With the exception of the largest of them – the Urban Mortgage Bank of the Kingdom of Sweden – these institutions were owned predominantly by banks. Since the 1970s government bonds and mortgage bonds have constituted about 90 per cent of the stock of Swedish bonds.

In November 1983 a new kind of treasury bond was issued, and as from April 1984 these bonds have been issued by auction. As the old type of government bond was still being issued up to 1986, this meant that for a couple of years two kinds of government bond were being used at the same time. The new treasury notes are issued with maturities of two to ten years, while the maturities of the old-styled government bonds had usually been longer. Mortgage bonds also carry maturities of two to ten years, the standard being five years. These bonds are sold on a tap basis and, like treasury notes, are straight bonds repaid in full at maturity. Coupons are generally paid annually. Auctions are also used by the mortgage institutions, while other bonds are mostly sold under fixed commitment underwriting. All government and mortgage issues are registered with the Stockholm Stock Exchange. Corporate bonds represent a minor share of the bond market only, partly because the bond market is only open to large companies which can

Table 10.6 Timetable for institutional changes relating to the Swedish bond market

1968 – Convertible bonds are offered.

1974 – Residents are allowed to issue abroad and non-residents are allowed to invest in Swedish bonds denominated in foreign currencies.

1978 – Regulations on banks' deposit rates are abolished.

1980 – Ceilings on interest rates on private-sector bond issues are abolished.
– Banks are allowed to issue bonds with a maximum maturity of seven years.
– New permits to hold bonds in foreign currency are to be issued upon application, with a stipulated maximum amount for each bank.
– Investment obligations for insurance companies are introduced.

1981 – Bonds with warrants are offered over the counter (OTC).

1982 – Ceilings on new bond issues from private companies are abolished.
– Bonds with warrants are offered on the stock exchange.

1983 – Issuing controls are liberalized.
– New form of government bond (treasury note) is introduced.
– Obligation of banks to acquire priority bonds is abolished.

1984 – Government bonds issued by auction.
– Investment obligations on insurance companies are altered from a net to a gross basis, i.e. investment obligations for current issues only; the obligation to hold on to them is discontinued.
– Bonds aimed at households are issued by mortgage houses.
– An OTC market for forward, futures and options on government bonds is established.
– Restrictions on the benchmark rate for industrial bonds are eased.

1985 – Investment obligations on insurance companies (except life-insurance) are lifted.
– Stockholm Option Exchange (OM) is opened.

1986 – Banks' placement obligations for priority housing bonds are abolished.
– Issues of the old type of government bond cease.
– Standardized options on bonds are offered by OM.
– Forward contracts on premium bonds are introduced.
– Interest rate options are offered.
– Interest rate swaps are offered over the counter.
– Floating rate notes are offered.

1987 – Forward rate agreements (FRAs) are offered over the counter.

1988 – Intermediary institutions are permitted to issue floating-rate notes.
– Bonds denominated in Swedish kroner are issued abroad for the first time.
– The minimum maturity of bonds is reduced to one year.
– Interest rate futures and forwards are offered on the stock exchange.
– Intererest rate swaps are offered on the stock exchange.
– Forward rate agreements are offered on the stock exchange.
– Variable rate notes are introduced.

1989 – All cross-border restrictions are lifted, but trade in international bonds has to take place through domestic authorized banks or brokers.
– A turnover tax on interest bearing securities is introduced.

Table 10.6 Continued

	– An electronic trading system called SAX (Stockholm Automated Exchange) is introduced. – Mortgage Benchmark Bonds (MBB) are introduced.
1990	– The turnover tax on interest bearing securities is relaxed.
1991	– All remaining restrictions on bond issuing rates are abolished. Restrictions on the use of index clauses in the pricing of bonds are also lifted as the last part of the issuing controls. – Interest rate regulations are abolished. – Index-linked bonds are offered over the counter. – Zero coupon bonds are issued. – Taxation is changed in a way that influences bond holdings. – The Stockholm Bond Exchange (SOX) is opened.
1992	– Index-linked bonds are offered on the stock exchange.
1993	– The Financial Supervisory Authority (Finansinspektionen) is introduced to supervise the banking, insurance and securities sectors. – A book-entry securities system is introduced.
1994	– Reserve requirements ratio is set at zero.

afford to obtain ratings of their long-term credit worthiness.[16]

The Stockholm Stock Exchange introduced an automatic dealing system for the trading of bonds and premium bonds in 1989. Since then there has been no trading on the floor of the exchange. In the early 1990s bond trading was taking place over the counter and prices were quoted on a yield-to-maturity basis.[17]

Although the role of the Swedish National Pension Insurance Fund declined during the 1980s, it remained the largest investor in Swedish bonds in the early 1990s. The Swedish insurance companies constituted another important group of bond investors, while the banks' share fell, as it did in all the other Nordic countries, as a result of the lifting of investment obligations. By international standards Swedish households hold a small proportion of the total stock, except for the lottery bonds issued by the government. Foreigners increased their holdings of Swedish bonds from 8 per cent in 1980 to 20 per cent in 1990, but in comparison with the other Nordic countries this was still a small proportion. Since 1989 foreign investors have been allowed to invest in krona-denominated bonds.

Figure 10.5 shows the development of Swedish bonds in circulation. Issues by central and local governments have fallen, as have issues by the non-financial sector. New issues by the financial sector contributed to the substantial growth in the stock of Swedish bonds since the beginning of the 1980s. Issues by banks and mortgage institutions thus more than compensate for the declining role of government issues.

The Swedish non-financial sector increased its stock of outstanding bonds from about SEK 30 billion in 1980 to almost 75 billion in 1990.[18] In the early

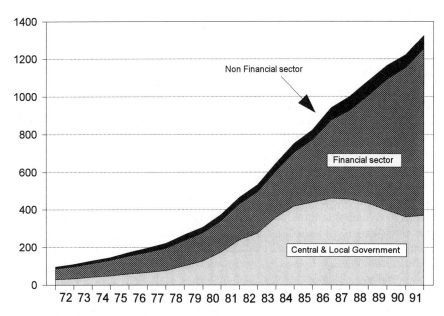

Figure 10.5 Total circulating Swedish bonds, 1971–91 (nominal values, stock at end of period, bn SEK)

Sources: Based on data from Central Statistical Bureau of Sweden, *Database* and *Financial Accounts*, various issues; The Swedish Central Bank, *Statistical Yearbook*, various issues; and own estimates.
Note: Domestic and international issues by Swedish borrowers included.

1990s about half the corporate bond issues took place on the international market. Corporate domestic bonds represented only a small percentage of the total domestic credit stock, of which the total domestic bond market constituted more than 20 per cent. Yet, the Swedish non-financial sector may have benefited from the bond market indirectly, due to the increased stock of mortgage issues.

ISSUES ON INTERNATIONAL BOND MARKETS

When the Nordic markets were heavily regulated, external issues (i.e. on the international bond market) offered Nordic borrowers an alternative. But Eurobonds[19] and foreign issues are only open to borrowers with a high credit rating and a reputation in the financial markets, or to borrowers seeking a limited quantity of funds.[20] A borrower who does not fit this picture has to consider the use of private placements, medium-term notes or syndicated credits. Nordic issuers have borrowed substantial amounts on the international markets. In 1990 about 10–25 per cent of the total outstanding stock of international issued bonds for each respective country were issued by non-financial companies.[21] In this section we will look at the way Nordic borrowing operations on international markets have developed over time.

Nordic external bond offerings in 1980 represented 13 per cent of the world offerings; in 1990 the figure fell to 8 per cent (see Table 10.7). The annual growth of Nordic external issues between 1980 and 1990 was about 14 per cent, while world external issues grew about 20 per cent annually. Finnish and Swedish issuers were very active at the end of the 1980s and at the beginning of the 1990s. The size of Finnish external issues increased gradually over the period, while the two large Swedish devaluations in the early 1980s caused a jump upwards in the propensity of Swedish borrowers to raise capital by external issues. In Sweden the nominal level attained then remained more or less stable throughout the decade. In nominal terms the highest annual amount registered for Nordic borrowers in the 1980s appears for Swedish borrowers in 1980 when this group represented more than 7 per cent of all external issues in global terms. In a Nordic comparison Danish borrowers were the most active in 1986, when they borrowed 4 per cent of the total amount issued globally.

Nordic currencies have been used only rarely in international bond issues. During the 1980s, the Nordic governments worked actively to prevent their currencies from becoming Eurocurrencies, although the Danish government had a slightly more liberal view and the Danish krone was sometimes used. Table 10.8 shows the development of the use of different currencies in Nordic external issues over time. For instance, we see that Nordic issues constituted a substantial share of all US dollar-denominated external issues in 1984. Their share was about 14 per cent, of which more than half was accounted for by Swedish borrowers. About 17 per cent of all ECU-denominated bond issues in 1986 were undertaken by Nordic, predominantly Danish, issuers. The Danish borrowers also accounted for 8 per cent of all yen-denominated external issues in 1982. In addition to the major currencies reported in Table 10.8, Swedish borrowers often used Luxembourg francs in issuing foreign bonds in the 1980s. Towards the end of the 1980s these issues amounted to 5–10 per cent of the total external issues in that currency.

Intra-Nordic bond issues

Intra-Nordic bond issues have been difficult to arrange in the past, on account of the powerful government regulations described above. However, it is not difficult to think of reasons why actors in one Nordic country might be interested in issuing a bond loan in one or more of the others. One reason could be the geographical and cultural proximity and the similarity of the markets, with all the advantages this implies on the information front. Another reason could be the importance of intra-Nordic trade, and the need to match the trading patterns with financial flows in order to reduce risks. All

Table 10.7 External bond offerings from three major borrowers and Nordic borrowers[a] (billions of US dollars)

Borrowers	1973	1980	1981	1982	1983	1984	1985	1986	1987	1988	1989	1990	1991	1992	January–August 1992	January–August 1993
Denmark	0.2	1.2	0.8	1.1	2.4	3.8	2.9	9.1	4.1	4.3	4.9	4.3	1.3	4.6	3.6	10.0
Finland	0.1	0.3	0.6	0.8	0.8	1.4	1.4	3.3	3.0	4.8	5.4	7.0	9.5	14.2	8.5	8.2
Norway	0.1	0.8	0.6	0.8	0.6	1.1	2.3	5.8	4.1	5.4	2.8	0.9	3.3	4.7	4.4	3.9
Sweden	0.1	2.8	1.7	2.5	4.1	6.4	6.2	5.8	4.6	8.4	6.1	6.6	6.5	13.3	6.7	16.0
Japan	–	3.8	4.9	8.3	13.6	17.0	21.6	34.4	44.4	51.3	97.5	55.4	72.1	56.2	37.7	40.4
United Kingdom	1.3	1.6	1.4	1.3	2.1	5.0	15.6	19.6	12.7	26.5	20.3	20.0	30.9	33.7	20.4	26.8
United States	1.3	5.8	6.6	14.8	7.4	23.0	39.6	43.1	21.5	17.3	15.8	21.8	21.1	17.6	11.1	15.6
Total – OECD	5.6	32.0	39.2	63.6	67.0	96.8	147.2	212.3	166.6	213.4	240.4	208.4	282.9	296.9	200.0	281.0
Total – World	8.6	38.0	47.8	75.5	77.1	109.5	167.8	227.1	180.8	227.1	255.7	229.9	308.7	333.7	223.7	320.9

[a] Excluding bonds classified as 'special placements'.
Source: Based on data from OECD, Financial Market Trends, various issues.

Table 10.8 External bond issues by currency

Borrowers and currency	1982	1983	1984	1985	1986	1987	1988	1989	1990	1991	1992	1992 Jan–Aug	1993 Jan–Aug
Dollar bond issues (bn USD)													
Denmark	0.5	1.7	2.6	1.4	5.3	0.8	0.9	1.2	1.7	–	1.4	0.6	2.8
Finland	0.3	0.3	1.0	0.5	1.5	1.0	1.6	3.0	0.9	1.7	4.5	2.0	2.6
Norway	–	–	0.9	1.6	3.6	0.8	2.2	0.5	0.2	1.4	1.8	1.4	0.7
Sweden	1.7	3.0	5.3	4.0	2.8	1.6	3.2	1.7	1.9	2.1	5.7	3.1	6.4
Total (world)	48.2	43.9	69.6	102.2	124.7	65.9	84.7	127.1	79.9	96.0	126.3	78.8	118.1
Yen bond issues (bn JPY)													
Denmark	78	35	50	100	216	148	112	270	209	61	–	–	35
Finland	–	–	–	48	159	120	152	185	368	137	181	10	180
Norway	–	–	15	31	143	246	176	109	59	10	150	150	–
Sweden	–	–	32	80	218	155	197	170	298	80	15	15	436
Total (world)	967	969	1,447	2,843	3,947	3,786	2,821	3,281	4,399	5,516	5,201	3,168	4,194
DEM bond issues (bn DEM)													
Denmark	0.3	0.5	0.9	1.0	1.3	0.5	0.9	0.2	0.6	0.2	1.2	1.2	2.0
Finland	–	–	0.3	0.7	0.7	–	1.1	–	1.5	1.8	3.5	2.2	3.0
Norway	–	–	–	0.3	0.2	0.6	0.8	0.3	–	–	1.5	1.5	1.5
Sweden	–	0.3	0.5	2.0	0.5	0.3	0.7	0.2	1.2	0.5	3.4	0.8	–
Total (world)	13.0	16.8	19.3	32.4	37.5	27.0	41.4	30.9	30.0	34.2	53.1	30.2	60.1
Foreign bond issues in Switzerland (bn CHF)													
Denmark	–	–	–	0.2	0.1	0.7	1.1	0.3	0.2	0.2	0.5	0.4	1.5
Finland	–	–	0.3	0.3	0.1	0.5	0.3	0.3	0.3	0.8	0.9	0.2	0.4
Norway	–	–	0.2	0.2	0.4	1.1	1.0	0.1	–	–	–	–	0.2
Sweden	–	–	0.9	0.9	0.4	0.7	1.0	0.3	0.6	0.6	0.9	0.5	1.4
Total (world)	23.1	28.2	30.4	35.6	41.6	36.5	38.1	30.6	32.2	29.0	25.2	11.6	24.9
ECU bond issues (bn ECU)													
Denmark	–	–	0.2	0.3	0.7	0.6	0.2	0.2	–	–	1.3	1.3	0.3
Finland	–	–	–	0.3	0.2	0.1	0.4	0.3	0.4	1.9	1.5	1.5	0.5
Norway	–	–	–	0.1	0.1	–	–	–	0.1	1.2	0.3	0.3	–
Sweden	–	–	0.1	–	0.3	0.1	0.7	0.4	0.3	1.1	0.9	0.9	0.6
Total (world)	–	2.5	3.9	9.6	7.6	6.5	9.5	11.4	14.1	26.0	17.1	17.0	3.3

Source: Based on data from OECD, *Financial Market Trends*, various issues.

this means we might expect to see more intra-Nordic issuing activity once the markets open up.

In October 1988 non-residents were allowed to issue in the Danish market. In 1989 NOK- and SEK-denominated loans were issued for the first time in this market, and loans in FIM appeared in 1990. At the end of 1991 the stock of bonds issued in SEK constituted almost 80 per cent of the total stock issued in a foreign currency in the Danish market. In Finland, during the first two years following the invitation to non-residents in 1991, only one issue was offered by another Nordic borrower, namely a small issue in 1992 by Swedish Export Credit. The Norwegian market was opened to foreign borrowers in May 1989. Four loans were issued during 1990, all by Nordic borrowers: the Nordic Investment Bank, OKO Bank, the Scandinavian Airlines System and Swedish Export Credit. No issues by borrowers from the other Nordic countries appeared on the Swedish market in the first few years after the abolition of Swedish capital controls in July 1989.

With hindsight we can conclude that geographical and cultural proximity appears to be less important than we might think in a world of advanced information technology. Moreover, Nordic capital controls have left Nordic borrowers better informed about the Euromarket and large non-Nordic national markets than about capital markets in their neighbouring countries, which suggests that the sequential approach often seen in Nordic trade and investment arrangements does not apply to this case. The second reason suggested above for a wave of intra-Nordic issuing may be rejected, on the grounds that the degree of diversification demanded was already being achieved by other means.

AN INTRA-REGIONAL COMPARISON OF THE STATUS OF PRIMARY MARKETS AT THE BEGINNING OF THE 1990s

The rapid development of the Nordic national bond markets during the 1980s resulted in their being ranked among the twenty largest markets in the world at the beginning of the 1990s. Table 10.9 shows that in terms of currency sectors and outstanding stocks the Danish krone market, the largest of the Nordic currency sectors, was ranked tenth, while the Finnish markka market, the smallest Nordic sector, was ranked seventeenth. If the comparison were to take the size of the countries – e.g. their GDP – into account, then the ranking would be even more flattering to the Nordic group. Measured in this way, the Danish market was the largest of any of the industrial countries.

In the early 1990s the Nordic national markets diverged from the general pattern of the public sector being the biggest issuer in the domestic sector of the bond market (See Table 10.9). In all the Nordic countries the non-bank financial-sector issues represented 50 per cent of the total amount borrowed in the domestic sector. The domestic part of the Danish non-bank financial sector was one of the largest in the world, second only to the corresponding part of the US market, with the Swedish non-bank financial sector ranking fourth.

Moreover, domestic issues from the non-financial sector – mainly companies – represented only a small proportion of total private-sector issues on the domestic markets in all the Nordic countries. This contrasts with the patterns on the US market, where non-financial issues constituted the bulk of domestic private-sector issues. If the US domestic bond market represents one extreme case, the German domestic market represents the other, with almost no issues by non-financial companies. However, German non-financial companies have certainly benefited indirectly from the domestic bond market as a result of their close interaction with the banking sector and the large issues by that sector.

In the Nordic countries the domestic bond markets provided financial support for domestic industry on a scale somewhere between the two extreme cases. Further, Nordic non-financial companies may have benefited indirectly from the substantial funds raised by the non-bank financial sector on the bond market. The use of Nordic currencies in international issues was still rather uncommon at the beginning of the 1990s, be it foreign activities on Nordic markets (foreign issues) or issues in Nordic currencies abroad (Euromarket issues).

Table 10.10 shows that the volume of international issues by Nordic borrowers has generally been substantial. In terms of the total nominal amount outstanding at the end of 1990, Swedish borrowers were ranked ninth, while Norway, in fourteenth place, borrowed least of the Nordic countries. Together Tables 10.9 and 10.10 provide us with an opportunity to assess the total amount of issues by sector. It can be seen that issues by the public sector constituted almost two-thirds of the nominal value of the total global bond market. However, the predominance of the public sector, particularly governments, disappears when we look at the pattern of international issues. Table 10.10 shows private-sector borrowers to be the major issuers on the international bond market, with Denmark representing an exception to this rule. About one-fifth of total private sector bond issues outstanding at the end of 1990 appeared on the international market. Among borrowers from individual countries, US and German issuers fell below that average, as did the Danish. In this group of countries the proportion was about one-tenth. At the other extreme, about four-fifths of the total issues of UK borrowers appeared on the international market. Finnish and Norwegian private sector issues were in the region of two-fifths to three-fifths, while Swedish issues registered average figures.

The overall impression from an examination of Table 10.9 is that Nordic non-financial companies have made little direct use of bond issues. However, since the table covers only issues denominated in the currency of the country in which the companies are located, one alternative remains to be investi-

Table 10.9 The largest currency sectors in the global bond market at the end of 1990 – a selective view (nominal value outstanding, expressed in billions of US dollars[a])

Bond market	Total publicly issued			Domestic sector						International sector	
				Public sector			Private sector				
	Rank	%	Nominal value	Central government	Agency	State and local	Non-financial	Bank	Non-bank financial	Foreign	Euro
US dollar	1	(44.9)	5,984.9	(34.5) 1,653.4	(65.7) 1,413.5	(59.3) 596.0	(70.3) 1,187.6	(8.1) 109.2	(48.3) 417.6	81.7	525.9
Japanese yen	2	(19.3)	2,576.9	(24.3) 1,163.6	(18.0) 387.2	(14.3) 143.3	(12.6) 212.0[b]	(37.2) 502.8	–	52.1	115.9
Deutsche Mark	3	(8.4)	1,123.8	(6.2) 295.3	(2.3) 49.3	(2.7) 27.0	(0.1) 1.7	(44.6) 603.1	–	147.4	
Danish krone	10	(1.6)	212.6	(1.4) 66.5	–	–	(0.6) 9.6	–	(15.2) 131.3	0.2	5.0
Swedish krona	12	(1.3)	174.7	(0.9) 40.9	–	(0.1) 0.9	(0.6) 10.4	(0.3) 4.6	(13.4) 115.8	0.1	2.0
Norwegian krone	16	(0.4)	49.7	(0.3) 13.1	(0.2) 4.0	(0.6) 5.9	(0.1) 1.7	(0.1) 1.1	(2.7) 23.2	0.2	0.5
Finnish markka	17	(0.3)	33.3	(0.2) 7.9	–	(0.0) 0.5	(0.4) 6.5	–	(1.9) 16.5	0.2	1.7
Total (21 largest)		(100)	13,321.3	(100) 4,787.0	(100) 2,151.4	(100) 1,004.4	(100) 1,689.1	(100) 1,352.9	(100) 865.1	1,471.4	

a All local currency figures are converted at end-1990 exchange rates.
b Includes some issues made by financial sector entities.

Source: Based on data from BIS (1991).

Table 10.10 Composition of borrowing on the international bond market (billions of USD, end-1990)

Borrower's country of residence	Rank	Total outstanding Nominal amount	Breakdown by type of borrower Central govern- ment	State- owned corpor- ation	Other govern- ment	Bank	Other financial institu- tions	Other borrowers
Japan	(1)	317.7	–	0.7	3.5	52.2	15.7	245.5
US	(2)	170.2	–	0.2	0.5	26.0	38.6	105.0
UK	(3)	127.8	4.0	0.6	–	31.6	49.0	42.6
Sweden	(9)	40.7	12.0	0.6	0.7	7.5	11.0	9.0
Denmark	(11)	32.2	17.4	0.3	1.9	5.8	3.3	3.5
Finland	(12)	28.2	5.9	1.1	–	13.0	3.7	4.5
Norway	(14)	22.4	2.8	–	1.5	8.8	3.6	5.7
Global total		1,472.5				321.1	175.8	574.0

Borrower's country of residence	Breakdown by type of currency Domestic currency	USD	Japanese yen	Deutsch- mark	Swiss franc	ECU	Other
Japan	18.5	205.8	*	11.2	69.2	5.7	7.3
US	105.3	*	15.9	5.9	16.8	6.1	20.2
UK	70.8	36.5	4.3	4.0	5.7	1.5	5.0
Sweden	0.8	12.8	9.5	2.4	4.3	2.9	8.0
Denmark	1.6	9.0	7.8	3.7	2.2	2.6	5.3
Finland	1.3	8.1	8.2	2.8	1.7	2.3	5.1
Norway	0.4	7.8	5.9	1.5	2.7	0.4	3.7
Global total	–	607.6	168.0	147.4	175.3	74.6	299.6

* Not strictly applicable.

Source: Based on data from Bank for International Settlements, *Database*.

gated: these companies may have borrowed on the international bond market through issues denominated in other currencies. Table 10.10 shows the extent to which this occurred in a breakdown of the amount of issues on the international bond market by type of borrower's country of residence and currency in different countries.

A closer look at the international issues by the private sector, as shown in the table, reveals that for the two major countries of borrower residence, Japan and the United States, 'Other borrowers', i.e. largely non-financial companies which are not state-owned, accounted for the majority of the issues. This contrasts with the pattern of international issues by the private sector in the Nordic region, where banks and financial institutions are the major issuers.

By combining Tables 10.9 and 10.10 we can find the relative importance of the international market for issues by non-financial companies. As a global average about one-quarter of non-financial bond issues occurred on the international market, whereas the US and German non-financial sectors represent the extreme cases with 8 and 90 per cent respectively.[22] In the Nordic countries international issues were the most popular with Norwegian companies (77 per cent), and least popular, but albeit still above the global average, in Denmark (27 per cent). This is quite consistent with our findings in Chapter 4, namely that domestic savings were of great importance to domestic investment in Denmark and of no importance to domestic investment in Norway.

There are a number of reasons why Nordic non-financial companies used the international bond market relatively more than US companies. First, for long periods Nordic investors were forced to finance their foreign direct investment from funds raised abroad because of the exchange regulations. The high frequency of issues denominated in currencies other than that of the home country is explained by the Finnish, Norwegian and Swedish governments' efforts to prevent their currencies from becoming Eurocurrencies.[23] Second, Nordic markets have been characterized by a general scarcity of capital and, for long periods, by a rationed supply of funds. Third, price considerations may have encouraged issuers to approach international markets, since the Nordic economies – as public-sector-dominated economies – are characterized by frequent government (or regulative) intervention, which in turn leads investors to charge a political risk premium for investing there.[24] Finally, the international issues by Nordic borrowers have been a necessary part of a signalling programme intended to pave the way for equity issues in prestigious markets such as the US market at a later date. The first three of these explanations stem from the Nordic national bond markets' history of segmentation and inefficiency, whereas the fourth explanation reflects the segmentation of the stock markets.

CONCLUDING REMARKS ON PRIMARY BOND MARKETS

In all the Nordic countries the bond markets have been regulated on both the supply side (by issuing controls) and the demand side (by investment obligations[25] and reserve requirements). However, in Denmark the degree of regulation has been distinctly lower than in the other countries. Traditionally, demand-side regulation has served the purpose of controlling banks and pension funds, etc. For a while the investment obligations proved useful in providing relatively inexpensive domestic sources of credit for the public sector. The different regulative modes may also account for some of the differences in the distribution of the total stock of bonds across the Nordic countries in 1990.

The authorities have also provided differentiated incentives, in order to promote a satisfactory placement of bond issues among investors. These incentives, which have steered different groups of investors towards different types of bonds, have been largely created by the regulations and tax policies pursued in the Nordic countries. In Sweden, for example, the bond market was divided into a priority[26] and a non-priority sector, of which the first was subsidized in the sense that priority bonds could be issued at low rates and still be placed with investors, thanks to the prevailing investment obligations. For many years a similar segmentation was to be found in Finland, since tax exemption was granted for bonds such as government bonds, while industrial bonds and debentures were generally taxed. Furthermore, the government could grant tax free status to issuers. In Denmark incentives generated by asymmetries in taxation have divided investors into three main groups.

The major driving-force behind the development of the individual Nordic primary bond markets has been the public-sector deficit and borrowing requirement. This was especially pronounced in Finland from 1978–85, in Norway from 1972–79 and in 1986 and in Sweden from 1977–86, whereas growth in the Danish bond market was already quite substantial in the ten-year period before a heavy public borrowing requirement appeared in the years 1981–84. The development of a government bond market also encouraged the emergence of a financial sector and a corporate bond market, since liquidity in bonds in general provided opportunities for bargaining and speculation in interest rate development. In all the Nordic markets the stock of central and local government loans remained more or less constant in nominal terms between 1985 and 1991, while the importance of financial sector bonds increased dramatically. The biggest increase occurred in issues from the financial sector. The stock of bonds issued domestically by the non-financial sector also took off during this period, albeit much more slowly.

The Norwegian non-financial sector was the most active among the Nordic countries in raising funds in international bond markets, with Danish companies at the other extreme. The low level of international issues by the Danish non-financial sector may mean that the deregulated Danish market has been successful in supplying funds to domestic companies via mortgage institutions. However, the small amounts issued by Danish companies abroad may also reflect the fact that on average Danish companies are small, which does not make them good candidates for a successful international bond offering.

NOTES

1 See *Euromoney*, May (1991).
2 Issued on an 'as-required' basis, often in irregular amounts.
3 In bullet bonds there is no payment of the principal until maturity. The alternative to bullet bonds is sinking fund bonds, implying an annual part repayment so that only a small amount remains outstanding on maturity.
4 Convertible bonds consist of an ordinary bond and a call option on the company's share.
5 Including issues by state enterprises.
6 This first group contributes indirectly to funding by channelling its loans into the corporate sector as subsidies, soft loans (and occasionally as loan on ordinary terms) and shareholder stakes. Although soft loans have been frequently employed in Denmark, for instance, the group as a whole can be regarded as a small contributor to the funding of non-financial corporations. See Oxelheim (1993).
7 The table is to be interpreted as the only way of creating comparability among the Nordic countries. Figures for 1990 differ somewhat from those that can be derived later by combining Tables 10.9 and 10.10, primarily due to a slight difference in the definitions used (in terms of maturities).
8 However, issues by mortgage institutions recaptured their dominating role in the second half of the 1980s.
9 Regulations are handled by the National Housing Agency. Important legislative acts are the Mortgage Credit Act of December 1989 with supplementary ministerial decrees. The mortgage institutions are supervised by the Supervision of Mortgage Credit Institutions except in the case of the Mortgage Credit Fund of Danish Agriculture, where the Danish Ministry of Agriculture is the supervisor.
10 Callable bonds can be called in by the borrower from the investor at a predetermined price.
11 See Danmarks Nationalbank, *Beretning og regnskap*, various issues.
12 The 1969 Act on Bonds, Debentures and Other Bonds regulated liquidity requirements and registration. Since 1989 the Security Market Act has been the main piece of legislation governing the bond market.
13 At a Dutch auction the price paid is that of the lowest accepted tender.
14 Monetary and Credit Act, §15.
15 Bonds with equity warrants resemble convertibles except that the warrant can be traded separately.
16 A rating institute – Nordisk Rating (initially a joint venture between Standard & Poor's and the Stockholm School of Economics) – was established in Sweden in 1987.
17 Assuming that each coupon can be invested at the internal rate of return of the loan.
18 Channels like commercial paper programmes were more important to their funding, however. In 1990 the entire stock of international bond issues by Swedish non-financial companies was only 50 per cent larger than the average annual amount raised by commercial paper programmes by these companies. In the period 1988–90 Swedish companies borrowed about 10 per cent of the global amount raised by commercial paper programmes. Borrowing by companies from other Nordic countries was considerably smaller.
19 The very first Eurobond issue took place in July 1963. The loan was denominated in US dollars and the issuer was Autostrada, an Italian motorway corporation (Fisher 1988). In 1990 the Eurobond market accounted for more

than three-quarters of all outstanding international bonds.

20   In the early 1990s an upper limit of around USD 500 million was being discussed.

21   As can be seen in Table 10.10.

22   The difference between the two tables in terms of the treatment of state-owned enterprises does not influence these conclusions. In 1990 German international issues by the non-financial sector amounted to USD 14.7 billion.

23   Opportunities for US investors to use the US dollar in international issues should point in the other direction, i.e. that US corporations should have been relatively more active issuers abroad, since for them an international issue did not involve exchange risk.

24   See Oxelheim (1990).

25   Except for Finland.

26   Issuers of priority bonds were the Swedish Debt Office and the mortgage institutions.

REFERENCES

BIS, 1991, *International Banking and Financial Market Development*, Basle.

Fisher III, F.G., 1988, *Eurobonds*, Euromoney Publications PLC, London.

Oxelheim, L., 1990, *International Financial Integration*, Springer Verlag, Heidelberg.

Oxelheim, L., 1993, *The Global Race for Foreign Direct Investment – Prospects for the Future*, Springer Verlag, Heidelberg.

Walmsley, J., 1991, *Global Investing*, London, Macmillan.

Chapter 11

Bond markets in a corporate perspective

In assessing the role of bond markets in a corporate perspective we are faced with the problem that neither in theory nor practice are there any simple norms for corporate financial structures. When it comes to choosing the 'best' mix of equity and debt, various approaches do exist. Also, on the debt side, we find a set of alternative approaches to determining the 'best' composition as regards fixed versus floating rates, short-term versus long-term borrowing, secured versus unsecured debt, and the mix of currencies and markets on which to raise funds. To be able to assess adequately what is the 'best' solution for an individual company, it is also necessary to consider the motives for turning to the financial markets. The main reasons why companies use the bond market are:

- fund raising;
- cash management;
- risk management;
- marketing: financial and commercial;
- access to price information;
- signalling.

Having examined the development of the Nordic bond markets in Chapter 10, we can now ask ourselves what these markets have meant to Nordic companies. Although we found that the proportion of corporate bonds relative to the total stock of bonds was fairly small in all four countries, corporate bonds may still have played an important part in financing the corporate sector. However, in our attempt to discover how well the needs listed above have been met by the domestic market, we come up against a measurement problem: due to the way corporate reporting is traditionally organized, it is difficult to distinguish between domestic and international bonds in the companies' balance sheets. Consequently, in discussing bonds in this chapter I will refer to the role of bonds in general rather than bonds from the domestic market only. But with the figures presented in Chapter 10 fresh in our minds, we do at least have some idea about the proportion of international issues relative to the total amount issued by the Nordic industrial sector, and this will give us some guidance in interpreting the empirical observations.

When we turn to the empirical classification of the six corporate motives for using the bond markets, we face yet more problems. In order to classify corporate bond activities under one of these headings we need detailed information about the incentives behind the actions. Since this information is not available, all we can do is to analyse the appearance of bonds in corporate balance sheets, and assume that when they appear on the *liability side* they have met a corporate need for funds and a desire to signal, to manage risks or to market the company to a financial or commercial audience, or a combination of some or all of these motives. Whenever international bond issues appear in the analysis, the last two of these motives are likely to be particularly important. When we find bonds on the *asset side*, we may assume that the bond market has met a corporate need to manage cash and/or risks.

In this chapter we will start with a brief discussion of the non-tax forces which determine capital structure. Although the complexity of financial issues in the real world sometimes makes it difficult to draw a clear line between debt and equity, debt ratios are none the less often used as condensed indices of the structure of the claims on a company. Empirical evidence on the development of such ratios will be provided below. I will then turn to some empirical evidence regarding the role of different sources in the funding of investments, and will follow this with an analysis of the empirical relevance of bonds in Nordic non-financial companies. The concept of securitization is used here as a measure of the importance of bonds in the corporate perspective. Two measures will be discussed, one that applies to the asset side and expresses the proportion of bonds on that side in non-financial companies, and another that applies to the liability side and expresses the proportion of bonds on that side of the balance sheet. These measures are in contrast to more traditional ways of measuring securitization, such as the alternative introduced in Chapter 1 whereby credit market securitization is measured as the money and bond markets' share of total credit stocks. According to that measure, the Danish credit market was by far the most highly securitized market in the Nordic region in the 1980s. The chapter concludes with a summary of the empirical evidence on the importance of bonds and Nordic bond markets to Nordic non-financial companies.

ASPECTS OF CAPITAL STRUCTURE – THE CHOICE BETWEEN EQUITY AND DEBT

The modern theory of capital structure begins with the 'irrelevance theorem' of Modigliani and Miller (1958). According to this theorem the debt-to-equity ratio is irrelevant to the company's market value. In the world of

Modigliani and Miller the value of the company is determined exclusively by its investment decisions, which can thus be separated completely from its financing decisions. Their claim is based on strong assumptions about taxation and the way capital markets function, and leaves the commercial side of the company out of account. However, in the real world we have to modify their strong assumptions about no taxes or transaction costs, as well as paying attention to the interaction of a company's capital structure with the structure of its labour and product markets. The last ten years have also brought us other more 'realistic' theories on this particular point. When the costs of taxation and information and the costs connected with the monitoring and control of managers are introduced, then financing decisions have been found to have a significant influence on the value of the company to its shareholders.

The double taxation of corporate income and the tax deductibility of interest payments provide an incentive to favour debt financing. The greater the 'tax shield', the more a company should reduce its tax burden by financing with the help of tax deductible debts. Higher leverage, however, will increase the probability of the company getting into financial trouble in times of economic turbulence. The direct and indirect costs of this distress and of potential bankruptcy are naturally arguments on the other side. The search for the best debt-to-equity ratio should thus involve a trade-off between the tax shield provided by additional debt and the higher expected costs of financial distress.

The company's information flow is another important factor to consider in designing the 'best' capital structure. In general corporate managers are better informed about the performance and prospects of their company than outside creditors and shareholders. The way managers inform or 'signal' to outside stakeholders is therefore of crucial importance to their company's opportunities for getting a bond issue successfully placed on the market, for instance.

A third important factor is the extent to which creditors and shareholders are able to exercise control over the managers. The cost of financial distress is assumed to be less, the stronger the relationship between stakeholder groups and management. It is often claimed that the higher debt-to-equity ratios in Germany and Japan relative to those in the United States and the United Kingdom, have arisen as a result of the close relationship between banks and industry in the first two countries, which gives their banks a good deal of influence over managerial decisions.

Determinants of the optimal debt ratio

There are many theories about the factors that determine the optimal debt ratio.[1] In general these theories are based on the various reasons why companies sometimes seek to keep equity to a minimum. The explanations given above are only a few examples, albeit important ones. While the implications for the debt ratio of different tax considerations are fairly obvious, other factors that influence the capital structure need to be examined more closely. They can be grouped under five headings.[2] Each one of the five, which are not mutually exclusive, is characterized by the main cost involved, as follows:

- direct costs;
- cost of bankruptcy;
- costs due to interaction between capital markets on the one hand and product and labour markets on the other;
- incentive or agency costs;
- costs due to adverse selection or inefficient allocation.

In the following brief review of the different categories let us start with the most transparent of them, the *direct cost* of an issue. As generally described in its narrowest definition, this cost encompasses only fees directly linked to the issues such as stamp duty, commission fee, underwriters' fee, etc., whereas a more elaborate cost estimate should include information costs such as road show costs, costs for the development, printing and distribution of promotional material, etc. In motivating the capital structure, the direct cost of equity issues has to be compared with the direct cost of bond issues. Many studies have reported that the direct costs of *equity issues* can be substantial. In the first part of the 1980s, for instance, they were in the region of 3–10 per cent of the total amount issued.[3] Thus at that time only fairly large companies could opt for equity issues. Mayer (1990) reaches a similar conclusion, and finds that small and medium-sized companies are at a disadvantage, since a large part of the costs are independent of the amount issued.

The transaction costs of international public equity offers have been discussed in Oxelheim and Andrén (1995), among others. Their figures provide a general cost indication based on the direct costs of equity and bond issues by Swedish companies between 1980 and 1993. Oxelheim and Andrén found that the transaction costs of equity issues in 1983 lay somewhere between 2.8 and 6 per cent of the value of the issue. The total number of issues that year was nine, while twenty-four international public issues were offered during the period as a whole. Ericsson, for instance, paid USD 2.44 per share in commission in 1983, plus USD 640,000, or roughly 2.8 per cent of the value of this issue in New York;[4] the same year, a much smaller company, PLM, had issuing costs[5] amounting to about 5 per cent on its issue in Copenhagen, and Gambro had issuing costs of about 6 per cent on its issue in New York. The high cost of the Gambro issue may reflect the fact that the international issue occurred at more or less the same time as the initial listing in the domestic market.

In 1992–93, at the end of the period under investigation, three international public equity issues were made. Securitas, which was already listed in London at the time, accounted for one of these issues. As the only Swedish company making an international public equity offer in 1992, Securitas had a transaction cost of 5.9 per cent of the value of the issue. In 1993 one issue was undertaken by Svedala for which the commission fees amounted to 3.5 per cent, and another by Frontline involved a cost of 4.75 per cent. Common to these two companies was their fairly small size and the fact that they were not listed abroad prior to the issues. The cost of the two issues was thus probably somewhere near the upper limit of the cost spectrum.

The development described by Oxelheim and Andrén suggests that the transaction cost of international equity issues fell somewhat between 1980 and 1993. Allowing for differences between markets and borrowers, it was concluded that the decrease was a result of the pressure from greater competition on transaction costs. However, since transaction costs were measured according to the narrower definition, the decline may have been outweighed by a need for more information, which in turn would have led to higher information and marketing costs of a less transparent kind.

The direct cost of equity issues should thus be compared to the direct cost of *bond issues*. Rutterford (1985) shows that in the early 1980s in Germany the cost of bond issues was about 3.3 to 4.3 per cent of the amount issued. Thus, in the German experience as reported by Rutterford, the cost of equity issues exceeded that of bond issues.

Oxelheim and Andrén (1995) provide information regarding bond issues abroad, based on the issuing costs of Swedish companies. In 1981 Aga and Ericsson's transaction costs – selling-group concession, underwriting commission and management fees – for bond issues undertaken on the international market amounted to about 2.5–3 per cent of the value of the issue. In 1983, when Volvo undertook an issue on the international bond market, the equivalent transaction cost had dropped to 1.875 per cent, and for Electrolux in 1986 it had fallen to a mere 1.5 per cent. Electrolux had to pay direct costs of almost the same size in 1992 for their issue in US dollars and Luxembourg francs, whereas direct costs for Ericsson in 1992 and SKF in 1993 were below one per cent of the value of the issue. Oxelheim and Andrén find that for Swedish companies in the period 1980–93, the cost of international equity issues have exceeded that of international bond issues.

To sum up: studies of direct issuing costs provide arguments in favour of bond rather than equity financing,[6] and direct-cost considerations consequently motivate high debt ratios.

Our second cost category focuses on *bankruptcy costs*, which can take the form of direct costs, indirect costs or losses due to the inefficient liquidation of a company. American studies show that in the 1980s direct bankruptcy costs corresponded to about 3.5 per cent of the market value.[7] Indirect bankruptcy costs, on the other hand, seem to be much higher.[8] They are caused by inefficient action on the part of management due to their involvement in the process of bankruptcy. Replacing managers is an expensive business.[9] The third type of bankruptcy cost is related to the efficiency of the actual liquidation. Lengthy negotiations with creditors are very costly.[10] To sum up: high bankruptcy costs incline the company towards acquiring enough equity to reduce the probability of bankruptcy; bankruptcy-cost considerations will motivate a lower debt ratio.

A third group of explanations of capital structure encompasses arguments based on new capital market theories, which take up the effects of interaction between *capital markets* on the one hand and *product and labour markets* on the other. The point of departure here is a group of market actors with a stake in the company and in the way it is run. It is further assumed that the employees have invested in certain specific competencies which will be wasted if they are laid off. Among these people there must thus be a kind of trust or confidence that management does consider the interests of its customers and employees.[11] In this context the debt ratio is important, and it will affect the propensity of the company to consider the interests of these groups.

A higher debt ratio, for instance, will give managers who hold equity in the company the scope to undertake transactions which pay off in the short run, at the cost of the long-run sustainable profit potential. Managerial equity-holders will benefit from high short-term profits at the expense of stakeholders with longer-term interests such as employees, creditors and customers.

Managers might thus choose to increase their own wealth through their own equity and/or through career signalling. In an already highly leveraged company this would mean that management was cutting back on the quality of products, R&D expenditure, internal training programmes and other activities which could be expected to have positive long-term effects. This behaviour may affect other companies, and high debt ratios may open the way for price wars in the product markets,[12] as well as for the entry of new companies.[13] Companies already in the market may try to keep their debt ratios at a moderate level, in order not to trigger new entries. Hence, the debt ratio reflects imbalances between different stakeholder groups when it comes to the influence they exert, with a strong manager aiming for a high debt ratio and other stakeholders for a more moderate one.

Models involving product and/or input characteristics show that oligopolists tend to have higher debt ratios than monopolists or companies in competitive industries,[14] and that their debt will tend to be of a long-term kind.[15] Further, companies which are highly unionized, and those whose workers possess easily transferable skills, will be apt to have high debt ratios.[16]

A fourth cost category is built up around *agency costs*, i.e. costs due to conflicts of interest. These costs arise from the principal–agent problem, in that insiders and outsiders have contradictory interests.[17] Research in this area was initiated by Jensen and Meckling (1976) and built on earlier work by Fama and Miller (1972).[18] The agency problem has many dimensions. For instance, since the insiders' portfolios are generally less diversified, they will put greater emphasis on reducing operational risk than the outsiders – who have limited portfolio shares in the company – would want. Further, management also has an interest in extending the activities of the company into areas where they have comparative advantages, because this increases their own value to the company. They may also be interested in increasing the size of the company, since greater size usually means higher status and prestige, higher salaries and more power. In addition there may be a management interest in exploiting opportunities for transferring resources from the company they are leading and into other companies in which they are stakeholders.

Jensen and Meckling (1976) identify two types of interest conflict. One is between shareholders and managers and the other between shareholders and debt-holders. The first type arises because managers hold less than 100 per cent of the residual claim. As a result they do not get the full gain from their profit-enhancing activities, but they do carry the full cost. For example, the managers bear the entire cost of refraining from buying a corporate jet, but capture only a fraction of the gain. Hence, managers can be assumed to overindulge in these pursuits relative to the level that would maximize the value of the company. However, since this inefficiency will be smaller, the greater the fraction of the company's equity that is owned by the managers, one way of reducing the loss from the conflict between managers and shareholders would be to increase the managers' share of the net wealth created by their own activities. This can be done, while holding the managers' absolute investment in the company constant, by increasing the fraction of the company financed by debt, i.e. by increasing the debt ratio.

Debt financing also helps to mitigate the conflict in another way. Large cash inflows which are not matched by good investment prospects create resources which can be used by management for fringe benefits, empire-building and so on. This was the case, for instance, in many of the Nordic countries in the early 1980s, when profits in mature industries generated by huge devaluations were locked in as a result of capital controls and double taxation. Empires were created by cross-company shareholdings that reinforced the power of management at the expense of shareholder influence. In this connection another benefit of debt financing can be mentioned, in that a bigger debt reduces the amount of 'free cash' and increases the managers' traditional ownership of the residual claims. In accordance with the 'free cash' argument, Jensen (1989) predicts that industries like steel, the chemical industry, breweries, and wood and paper products are likely to be characterized by high leverage. Further, if bankruptcy is costly for managers, another benefit of debt financing will be the incentive for them to work harder and consume fewer perquisites.[19] Shareholders and creditors both have reason to opt for a fairly high debt ratio, in order to avoid the potential cost of incentives for strategic management action.[20]

The second type of conflict, i.e. between shareholders and debt-holders, arises because the debt contract gives shareholders an incentive to invest suboptimally. The loss in equity value from a poor investment is expected by shareholders to more than offset the gain in equity value captured at the expense of debt-holders. However, to the extent that debt-holders correctly anticipate the shareholders' future behaviour, shareholders will bear this cost to the debt-holders. Hence, in this case shareholders carry the cost of the incentive to invest in value-reducing projects created by the debt they have issued. This asset-substitution effect is an agency cost of debt financing which has to be traded off against the benefits of debt.[21] Since agency costs in this case are a result of the creditors' fear that value-reducing investments will be reflected in the terms of the loans, it is in the interest of shareholders and management to send out a signal, i.e. to take some action prior to the actual fund-raising, indicating that they will act properly.[22] In the case of bond loans, Green (1984) suggests the issuing of convertible bonds and warrants as one way of mitigating this agency cost. Another way is to include in bond contracts certain features aimed at preventing asset-substitution, such as interest coverage requirements, prohibition against investments in new and unrelated lines of business, etc. As a result of conflict between shareholders and debt-holders we can expect that, *ceteris paribus*, industries with very limited opportunities for asset-substitution will have high debt levels.

The fifth cost category is built up around the cost of *asymmetric information*[23] and *adverse selection*.[24] Asymmetric information is to be interpreted as an informational disadvantage for outsiders relative to insiders. The greater the conflict of interest between insiders and outsiders, the lower the share price which the outsiders are willing to pay and, consequently, the higher the cost of equity for the insider. Consequently, the insiders have to bear these agency costs. When insiders decide the size of an equity issue, they incorporate expectations about the price which outsiders are willing to pay for shares in the company. The insiders then calculate how much they will gain or lose themselves. Thus, corporate decisions will be dependent on insiders' expectations about the outcome of such calculations. This gives rise to an allocation loss which, like the agency costs mentioned above, has to be absorbed by the insiders.[25] Also, creditors have limited information and do not know how to design the loan contract. Consequently, the creditors will limit the individual company's access to capital and ask for collateral.[26] If creditors are able to rank companies and group them according to expected profitability and risks, some groups of companies will get no loans at all.[27]

In order to reduce the costs arising from asymmetric information, companies will use internal funds and/or risk-free debt, instead of new equity issues. Even debts carrying limited risk will be preferred to equity. The mispricing that arises from asymmetric information will lead to under-investment, which the company tries to avoid by using a security that is not too severely undervalued by the market. This ranking of different sources of funds for the financing of a new investment is referred to as the 'pecking order'.[28] It is not, however, the only way of mitigating underinvestment. Another way of resolving the problem goes through signalling with a richer set of financing options.[29]

The extra cost of issuing equity compared with using retained earnings will depend on the severity of the information problem. In practice it is hard to furnish the outsider with a 'complete' set of information, as some information has to be kept secret from the company's competitors.[30] The choice of financing in itself sends certain useful signals to potential shareholders.[31] Informational asymmetry suggests that a company is not likely to seek external finance if it has surplus funds to invest, which in turn suggests that its debt ratios are low or moderate.

The various cost arguments that have been discussed thus provide mixed evidence as regards capital structures. Consideration of taxation and direct costs will often provide a company with an incentive to maintain a high debt ratio, whereas consideration of bankruptcy costs would motivate the opposite. The other three cost categories discussed above, on the other hand, provide arguments both for and against high debt ratios. In these cases we have found that bonds can play a role in mitigating the various conflicts of interest.

When it comes to the empirical testing of the different arguments, two approaches are most commonly used. One is based on studies of the reaction of security prices to changes in corporate capital structure, and the second on a cross-sectional analysis of corporate debt ratios. Both support the view that there is a gap between the cost of capital raised internally and the cost of external funds. It is found that equity issues generally mean a reduction in equity prices and losses for the insiders.[32] It is further found that the debt ratio is negatively correlated with profitability.[33] This means that companies accumulate funds by retaining their earnings in periods of prosperity, to avoid using external equity issues in periods of recession.

Several empirical studies[34] show that capital structures resemble one another more within than between industries. There seems to be agreement that drugs, food and the electronic instrument industries are characterized by low debt ratios, whereas airlines and the brewery, cement, chemicals, paper and wood, steel and textile industries are characterized by high debt ratios. The most highly leveraged companies are found in regulated business sectors such as the telephone, electricity and gas utilities.

Empirical studies[35] of the specific characteristics that determine the debt ratio of companies and industries generally agree that leverage increases with fixed assets, non-debt tax shields, simultaneous outside holding of equity and debt claims, and debt concentration. The debt ratio is found to decrease with increasing growth opportunities, company size, volatility, advertising expenditures, R&D expenditures, bankruptcy probability, profitability, dispersed outside ownership and the uniqueness of the product.

A comparison of international debt ratios[36]

In global terms the ratio of total debt to total liabilities was converging in the 1980s and the beginning of the 1990s. However, the convergence was due mainly to an increase in the debt ratios of US companies, while the debt ratio in all the other major OECD countries remained more or less unchanged (see Table 11.1). During the period 1983–90 companies generally tended to rely heavily on retained earnings coinciding with rising profitability. Generally speaking, issues of debt securities appear to have increased in connection with the purchase of similar financial assets. It is interesting to note, as an illustration of the problem of separating equity and debt, that in France the falling debt ratios in French companies were a result of an increase in equity financing by share issues giving limited or zero voting rights.[37]

Although this kind of international comparison is affected by measurement problems, the dispersion in 1992 was clearly below that in 1980. A comparatively early development of the US stock market is often mentioned as an explanation of the low leverage of US companies. However, in the 1980s debt ratios in the US increased sharply. From the early 1980s onwards US companies relied heavily on debt security issues for their financing. In the period 1983–87, 18 per cent of total sources of US net financing consisted of securities, whereas minus 17 per cent consisted of equity issues, i.e. shares were being bought back. A growing proportion of the debt was in the form of junk bonds. Between 1982 and 1988 the junk bond share of outstanding corporate bonds rose from less than 7 per cent to over 20 per cent. These shares came to play a crucial role in the financing of highly leveraged transactions by US companies. 'Strip financing', whereby the same investor holds equal proportions of debt and equity, was another feature conducive to high debt ratios. However, the strongest driving-force behind the rising US debt ratios was probably the expectation of greater profitability.

The big increase in debt in US non-financial companies reflects a high volume of debt-financed take-over activity. In the second half of 1988 equity withdrawals on the part of these companies, related either directly to the take-over of other companies or to the withdrawal of equity capital to reduce the risk of hostile take-overs, rose to a level of 3.5 per cent of GDP.[38] The early 1990s saw a return to small net equity issues.

When we compare the debt ratios of Nordic non-financial companies with those of companies in major OECD countries, we find the Nordic companies more or less in the middle of the debt ratio spectrum, i.e. well above the US, UK and Canadian debt ratios, but – at least from the mid-1980s on – well below the Japanese. However, using a demarcation line of 60 per cent debt in separating high from low leverage (see Borio 1990), we find that Finnish, Norwegian and Swedish non-financial companies are highly leveraged, while since the beginning of the 1980s Danish companies have belonged to the low leveraged category.

Many reasons for the high degree of Nordic leverage can be found. A fairly close relationship between banks and non-financial companies is one reason for the Nordic companies' position in the upper part of the leverage spectrum. However, since banks have only recently been allowed to own shares in these companies, the relationships are not as strong as they are in Germany and Japan, for instance.[39] The intermediaries' simultaneous holding of equity and debt claims provides an environment more favourable to leverage, as we have noted, by reducing the scope for conflict between shareholders and debtholders. One reason for the US ratio increase was that equity was being bought back – an operation of which there is little evidence in the Nordic region. Taxation and 'thin' national equity markets have also favoured a debt approach.

In an intra-Nordic comparison we find that the debt ratios of Danish non-financial companies are lower than the ratios of most companies in the other Nordic countries. One explanation of this could be the large number of food-processing companies in Denmark, which are associated with low leverage.[40] However, the large number of small and medium-sized companies should have had a counteracting effect here. Many empirical studies show higher leverage for small companies compared with large ones.[41] The high proportion of breweries and chemical industries among the industrial top twenty Danish companies also argues for higher debt ratios.

Differences in industrial structure may also explain the dissimilarities in the early 1980s between Norway (oil-based) and Finland (paper, pulp and wood) on the one hand, and Sweden (R&D-intensive engineering) on the other, since we have found above that companies with a high level of tangible assets tend to have high debt ratios. The average debt ratio then dropped between 1980 and 1992 in all the three countries. At the end of the 1980s and the beginning of the 1990s Finnish, Norwegian and Swedish non-financial companies exhibited a similar degree of leverage.[42] Increased similarities in industrial structure may partly account for this.

Table 11.2 provides us with an opportunity to compare the debt ratios of non-financial companies with those of manufacturing companies, and those of small companies with those of large. The debt ratios of Nordic manufacturing companies are considerably higher in general than those of non-financial companies as reported in Table 11.1 – an observation quite consistent with the greater extent of tangible assets in manufacturing companies. Generally speaking the debt ratios of manufacturing companies in Denmark and Sweden are almost the same, and are much lower (about 10 percentage points) than the debt ratios in Finland and Norway, which have both developed in a fairly similar manner. The tentative conclusions we drew

Table 11.1 Debt ratios in non-financial companies in some OECD countries (total debt as percentage of total liabilities)

Country	1980	1982	1984	1986	1988	1990	1992
Denmark	63	63	57	58	58	58	56
Finland	80	81	72	71	65	63	63[a]
Norway	80	85	84	79	67	64	62[a]
Sweden	67	67	65	65	64	67	65[a]
Japan	84	83	82	81	81	80	80
Germany	60	60	57	55	61	61	61
France	68	72	72	75	66	61	58
UK	53	53	52	51	51	52	52[b]
Canada	46	49	48	47	47	48	51
USA	32	32	36	40	44	47	51

[a] 1991.
[b] estimate.
Source: Based on data from OECD, *Financial Statistics, Part 3, Non-financial Enterprises, Financial Statements*, various issues; and own estimates.

Note: For some countries, a change in the treatment of tax-conditioned depreciation has occurred over time.

Table 11.2 Debt ratios in Nordic manufacturing companies, 1979–90 (total debt as a percentage of total liabilities, ISIC 2–3)

Number of employees	Denmark[a]		Finland		Norway		Sweden	
	20–49	200–	20–49	100–	50–99	200–	20–49	200–
1979	62.9[b]		84.4	77.7	85.2	80.2*	72.1*	66.9
1980	63.5[b]		86.2	78.6	86.4*	79.0	68.8	67.0
1981	63.8[b]		87.7*	78.8	86.1	79.4	71.7	67.3*
1982	63.1[b]		87.1	80.0*	83.8	80.1	70.7	66.0
1983	59.2[b]		85.1	79.0	81.3	77.3	69.8	62.5
1984	65.3	57.5	85.2	77.7	78.3	75.2	67.7	57.2
1985	65.1[t]	57.5*	79.9	70.9	78.9	74.2	67.5	56.6
1986	65.3	54.9	79.3	69.3	79.2	73.6	65.0	56.2[t]
1987	65.6	55.1	76.0	67.5	74.7	70.5	68.0	56.6
1988	66.7	54.5	76.4	63.6[t]	73.6[t]	68.5	68.1	56.4
1989	66.9	54.2	71.6[t]	64.3	74.3	68.1	68.9	59.2
1990	69.3*	53.5[t]	73.9	66.0	74.5	67.9[t]	63.5[t]	59.9

[a] Account statistics for all non-financial companies in 1984/85 and for industrial joint-stock companies from 1986–90.
[b] 20 or more employees.

Sources: Calculations are based on data from Central Statistical Bureau of Denmark, *Industrial Accounts Statistics*, various issues; Copenhagen Stock Exchange, *Annual Report*, various issues; Central Statistical Bureau of Finland, Database – Enterprises (unpublished data); Central Statistical Bureau of Norway, Database (unpublished data 1979–86) and *Statistics of Account*, various issues (1987–90); Central Statistical Bureau of Sweden, *Enterprises*, various issues (1979–87) and Database (unpublished data 1988–90).
Note: * indicates max value and [t] min value for the period 1978–90.

from Table 11.1 obtain further support here. As a general trend debt ratios fell between 1979 and 1990 in all the Nordic countries, with a question mark hanging over the small and medium-sized Danish companies. The reason for the general decrease may lie in the elimination of tax incentives in favour of debt and the gradual reduction in corporate taxes, which were both discussed in Chapter 7.

Government policy has played a major role, through a variety of channels, in influencing the development of Nordic debt ratios. Taxation has been one instrument and the regulation of the operations of the financial system another. Regarding the second of these, three factors which favour debt financing can be distinguished: impediments to the development of stock markets, the extent to which financial and non-financial companies are owned by the government, and the granting of financial assistance to companies in the way of various subsidized credit facilities.

In the highly leveraged G-7 countries in Table 11.1, the Japanese and French governments have owned the most substantial fractions of their respective financial systems. The governments of these countries have also used their fraction as a channel for providing assistance to companies through soft loans, subsidized credits and government guarantees. The governments of the highly leveraged G-7 countries have tended to hinder securitized channels for debt financing. Typical mechanisms are the provision of assistance to companies through credit institutions, controls which discourage credit financing in international markets (France), restrictions on conditions for issuing and on the range of permissible instruments (especially Japan) and the design of the tax regime (Japan, Germany and France). All these conditions apply also to Finland, Norway, Sweden and, to some extent, Denmark.[43]

In the 1980s, as can be seen in Table 11.2, the gap between the debt ratios of small and large companies within the same country was largest in the case of Danish manufacturing companies at 10–15 percentage points and increasing, whereas in Finland it was small and fairly stable at around 8–9 percentage points and in Norway at 3–6 percentage points. At the beginning of the 1980s the debt ratio in small Swedish manufacturing companies was a mere 2 percentage points higher than the debt ratio in large companies. The gap increased, however, and reached about 12 percentage points in 1987 and 1988, due to growing debt ratios in small companies and falling ratios in large ones. At the beginning of the 1990s the gap returned to 3.5 percentage points.

Measures of indebtedness show that small and medium-sized Nordic manufacturing companies rely on debt to a greater extent than large Nordic companies. Since these companies cannot use the security markets, they have to rely on bank loans. Further, small companies are more heavily indebted in Finland and Norway than in Denmark and Sweden. The indebtedness of small Danish companies, however, is increasing and approaching the level in the Finnish and Norwegian small companies.

THE FINANCING OF NEW INVESTMENTS

There is consensus in international studies that the primary source used by non-financial companies for funding their investments is *retained earnings*, although Masulis (1988) shows a trendwise decline in the use of retained earnings in the funding of new investment. None the less in the early 1990s retained earnings were still by far the most important source, followed by *loans* and then by *new issues*.

The pattern displayed in Table 11.3 underlines the importance of internal funds – of which retained earnings account for the main part – as a general source of funding in companies in eight major OECD countries. Capital raised from equity issues directed to insiders (predominantly management) is usually scarce. It is limited by considerations of the risk carried by the insider as being on the corporate pay-roll list. Hence, issues of new equity are generally directed at outsiders. But even in total, new issues have never been a major source of funding. Although varying between countries, this source accounts at most for around 10 per cent of an investment.[44] Italian and French companies are at the upper limit, while US, British and German companies are at the other extreme. The Nordic countries are in the middle of the range, with Sweden exhibiting the highest average figure.

The direct cost argument discussed above indicates that the freedom of small and medium-sized companies is restricted when it comes to funding new investment.[45,46] Whenever retained earnings are insufficient these companies have to arrange for loans through a financial institution. In doing so they are limited for reasons of cost to using domestic institutions, which means that despite a formally high degree of direct integration in the particular financial market in which they are working, they are dealing with a segmented market. As a result of being locked in financially in this way, they have to bear many extra costs, for instance for the risk premiums that are typical of such markets. These include premiums for a possible loss of general creditworthiness regarding the banks in the country where they are

Table 11.3 Sources of funds: non-financial companies in some OECD countries (period averages as a percentage)

	Sweden[a] 1983–88	Canada 1983–88	France 1983–87	Germany 1983–87	Japan 1984–88	Netherlands 1983–87	UK 1983–88	USA 1983–88
Internal sources	70	64	89	105	64	89	84	79
External sources	30	36	11	–5	36	11	16	21

[a] All companies.

Source: Based on Mayer (1990) and, regarding Sweden, on data adapted from Gandemo (1990).

based and, in the case of small national financial markets, also possible oligopoly costs. Due to these various costs we might expect small and medium-sized companies to have a higher cost of capital on an average than large companies.

The financing of Nordic investments

Table 11.4 shows that investments undertaken by small Finnish companies in the first part of the 1980s were considerable, both in a Nordic and in a Finnish long-term perspective.[47] In the second part of the 1980s, the investment activity of small companies was on much the same level in the four Nordic countries, and was more or less consistently above the investment rate of large companies in their respective home countries. The largest systematic gap appears in Sweden, where small companies have invested at a fairly constant rate of 7 per cent as compared to 3.5 per cent in the case of large companies.

The average investment ratios for 1988–90 in almost all the Nordic countries were below the average investment ratios for 1979–87.[48] However, there is no clear indication that the investment activity of small companies has suffered more than that of large companies. The biggest decline in investment activity between 1979–87 and 1988–90 is registered for small manufacturing companies in Finland (from 9.7 to 6.1 per cent) and for large companies in Norway (from 8.9 to 3.8 per cent). In Sweden the activity has fallen off, but only slightly (0.3 per cent for both small and large companies).

Since no data is available to match the data set in Table 11.4, the ranking between the different sources of funds available to non-financial companies of different sizes has to be illustrated by the example of Sweden (see Table 11.5).[49] During the period 1980–86 loans were also a very important source of funds – alongside retained earnings – for financing the investments of fairly small Swedish companies (20–49 employees). In the case of really small companies (0–19 employees),[50] the table shows a dramatic change as a result of the economic boom. From having been the main source of funds in the period 1980–83, loans yielded place to retained earnings in the period 1984–86. The role of bonds in this financing-by-loans will be discussed below. Table 11.5 also indicates that fairly small companies (20–49 employees) relied on new issues of stocks to a lesser extent than larger companies (with more than 200 employees).

Another way of illustrating the importance of retained earnings in the investment operations of Nordic non-financial companies is shown in Figure 11.1. Although the matching is not perfect between the companies for which we have retained earnings and those for which we have investment figures, the figure suggests that annual retained earnings for the whole corporate sector correspond quite well to the annual amount invested by that sector.

Assuming that new issues are placed on the market during the same year

Table 11.4 Nordic net manufacturing investment, 1979–90 (net fixed annual investment as a percentage of total assets, ISIC 2–3)

Number of employees	Denmark		Finland		Norway		Sweden	
	20–49	*200–*	*20–49*	*100–*	*50–99*	*200–*	*20–49*	*200–*
1979	5.6[a]	n/a	8.4	6.0	10.7	7.2	7.1	3.7
1980	5.8[a]	n/a	14.3	7.3	6.7	5.0	9.5	4.7
1981	5.0[a]	n/a	16.2	7.7	5.7	9.5	7.6	4.3
1982	5.1[a]	n/a	8.0	7.1	5.3	9.6	6.8	3.0
1983	4.8[a]	n/a	10.4	6.4	2.9	4.6	6.4	3.4
1984	5.6[a]	n/a	10.5	6.4	7.1	9.0	7.1	3.6
1985	6.5[a]	n/a	5.6	5.9	7.8	11.9	7.4	4.0
1986	10.0	8.3	6.3	6.0	7.8	15.4	6.4	3.2
1987	8.5	5.6	6.5	6.3	10.1	8.1	6.1	2.9
1988	8.6	5.4	6.3	2.4	7.7	0.8	7.3	3.0
1989	6.9	4.9	6.5	5.6	6.4	9.9	7.9	3.8
1990	6.9	5.2	5.7	4.2	7.9	0.6	5.6	3.1

[a] 20 or more employees.

Sources: Calculations are based on data from Central Statistical Bureau of Denmark, *Industrial Accounts Statistics*, various issues; Copenhagen Stock Exchange, *Annual Report*, various issues; Central Statistical Bureau of Finland, Database – Enterprises (unpublished data); Central Statistical Bureau of Norway, Database (unpublished data 1979–86) and *Statistics of Account*, various issues (1987–90); Central Statistical Bureau of Sweden, *Enterprises*, various issues (1979–87) and Database (unpublished data 1988–90).

Table 11.5 Sources of funds: Swedish companies (as a percentage)

Source of fund	All companies		0–19 employees		20–49 employees		More than 200 employees	
	80–83	*84–86*	*80–83*	*84–86*	*80–83*	*84–86*	*80–83*	*84–86*
Retained earnings	61	68	49	76	58	61	66	67
New share issues	9	9	3	5	3	5	13	11
Loans	30	23	48	19	39	34	21	22
Total	100	100	100	100	100	100	100	100

Source: Adapted from Gandemo (1990).

in which the investment is made, a ratio between the issued amount and the amount of investment provides a good proxy for the role of new issues in investment. As a point of departure, Table 11.6 shows the relative size of new equity issues. In the case of the Norwegian companies the table reveals a somewhat complex pattern, with heavy fluctuations from year to year. In Sweden issues by large companies have been consistently bigger relative to

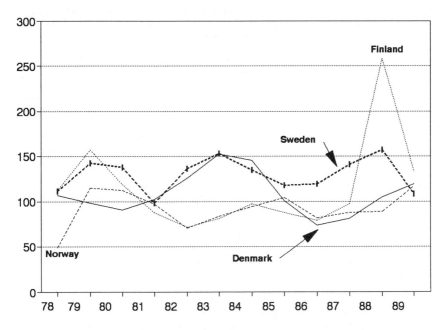

Figure 11.1 Annual retained earnings (as a percentage of manufacturing investments, 1978–1989)

Sources: Based on data from OECD, *Non-Financial Enterprises, Financial Statements*, various issues; Central Statistical Bureau of Denmark, *Industrial Accounts Statistics*, various issues.
Note: The earnings figures are gross (retained income before depreciation and provisions). For Denmark the data encompasses industrial joint-stock companies, for Finland private and public enterprises in manufacturing, for Norway a sample of companies in the mining and manufacturing industries (from 1981 the sample was extended to include all oil extraction companies regardless of the number of persons employed), and for Sweden the corporate part of the non-financial sector. The corporate part of the sector is defined to include joint-stock companies, partnerships, co-operatives, associations and foundations, i.e., all companies split up into legal entities.

issues by small companies. The large companies, except in Norway, also seem to some extent to have exploited the stock-market bubble leading up to Black Monday in October 1987, and to have financed their investments from new equity issues. In 1988 a temporary reaction occurred and the figures were almost halved.

Table 11.7 relates the equity issues to the size of contemporary investments. It is obvious that a very small proportion of the investments undertaken by small companies were funded by issues of new shares. Further, the figures for the small companies differ substantially from those of the larger ones. In the Swedish case the pattern is the same throughout the 1980s, when equity issues were more important to the investments of the large companies than to those of the smaller ones. In the Norwegian case

Table 11.6 New equity issues in Nordic manufacturing industries, 1979–90 (the value of the issue as a percentage of equity at the beginning of the year, ISIC 2–3)

	Denmark: number of employees 20–	Finland: number of employees		Norway[a]: number of employees		Sweden: number of employees	
		20–49	100–	50–99	200–	20–49	200–
1979	n/a	0.0	2.3	4.1	4.4	0.5	5.7
1980	n/a	0.0	3.3	1.7	7.0	1.0	3.3
1981	n/a	0.0	1.9	0.5	5.3	3.0	7.7
1982	n/a	0.0	3.1	1.9	14.8	1.9	4.5
1983	n/a	0.1	4.0	6.8	7.1	4.0	9.0
1984	2.2	0.2	3.1	11.0	11.4	5.3	5.6
1985	0.5	n/a	3.7	6.0	6.3	3.1	2.5
1986	2.4	n/a	2.4	15.4	18.1	2.4	5.6
1987	0.6	n/a	5.4	8.2	3.4	3.5	6.6
1988	1.6	n/a	3.2	2.8	12.8	2.2	3.0
1989	2.1	n/a	2.5	11.0	2.4	3.9	4.2
1990	1.0	n/a	5.1	19.1	5.7	1.3	1.9

[a] Excluding oil drilling.

Sources: Based on data from Central Statistical Bureau of Denmark, *Industrial Accounts Statistics*, various issues; Copenhagen Stock Exchange, *Annual Report*, various issues; Central Statistical Bureau of Finland, Database (unpublished data); Central Statistical Bureau of Norway, Database (unpublished data); and Central Statistical Bureau of Sweden, *Företaget*, various issues.

Table 11.7 The role of new equity issues in financing Nordic manufacturing investments (as a percentage of net investments undertaken the same year, ISIC 2–3)

	Denmark: number of employees 20–	Finland: number of employees		Norway[a]: number of employees		Sweden: number of employees	
		20–49	100–	50–99	200–	20–49	200–
1979	n/a	0.0	7.8	3.5	8.3	1.0	34.0
1980	n/a	0.0	8.6	2.0	19.4	1.4	15.0
1981	n/a	0.0	4.5	0.8	7.7	4.4	38.2
1982	n/a	0.0	7.5	3.2	19.3	3.3	34.6
1983	n/a	0.1	11.0	22.7	23.4	7.3	60.2
1984	14.6	0.2	8.9	17.4	20.2	8.0	33.6
1985	2.7	n/a	10.7	8.2	9.4	4.9	14.0
1986	11.4	n/a	7.7	18.7	19.8	4.7	40.2
1987	3.1	n/a	18.3	7.6	6.9	6.4	51.7
1988	9.1	n/a	33.9	4.1	271.2	3.4	24.9
1989	12.9	n/a	11.4	17.6	4.3	6.4	25.3
1990	6.9	n/a	29.8	22.4	158.8	5.3	15.0

[a] Excluding oil drilling.

Sources: Calculations are based on data from Central Statistical Bureau of Denmark, *Industrial Accounts Statistics*, various issues; Copenhagen Stock Exchange, *Annual Report*, various issues; Central Statistical Bureau of Finland, Database Enterprises (unpublished data); Central Statistical Bureau of Norway, Database (unpublished data 1979–86); and *Statistics of Account*, various issues (1987–90); Central Statistical Bureau of Sweden, *Enterprises*, various issues (1979–87) and Database (unpublished data 1988–90).

Table 11.8 Sources and uses of capital in Swedish companies, 1980–86 (capital flows as a percentage of business revenues)

Capital flows	Number of employees[a] 0–19		Number of employees[b] 20–49		Number of employees[c] 50–199		Number of employees[d] > 200	
	1980–83	1984–86	1980–83	1984–86	1980–83	1984–86	1980–83	1984–86
Internal	4.34	4.38	3.37	3.84	3.84	3.40	4.66	5.24
Issues	0.26	0.27	0.16	0.31	0.39	0.50	0.92	0.89
Long-term debt	4.24	1.15	2.29	2.16	1.65	0.90	1.47	1.67
Total capital provided	8.84	5.80	5.82	6.31	5.88	4.80	7.05	7.80
Fixed real investment	4.31	4.19	3.54	4.06	2.26	3.11	3.67	3.49
Financial investment	1.00	0.61	0.84	0.58	0.73	0.51	2.06	3.90
Total capital used	5.31	4.80	4.38	4.64	2.99	3.62	5.73	7.39
Net	3.53	1.00	1.44	1.67	2.89	1.18	1.32	0.41

[a] 113,100 companies (about 91 per cent of the total number of Swedish companies) in 1986.
[b] 7,200 companies (about 6 per cent of the total number of Swedish companies) in 1986.
[c] 3,100 companies (about 2 per cent of the total number of Swedish companies) in 1986.
[d] 1,000 companies (about 1 per cent of the total number of Swedish companies) in 1986.

Source: Based on data from Gandemo (1990).

the pattern is a mixed one. The extremely high values for Norway in 1988 and 1990 may reflect the fact that the issued amount was meant for future investments as well.

Once again we have to rely on data about Swedish companies to illustrate the reliance on long-term debt as a way of funding an investment. Table 11.8 shows that this dependency is less strong the larger the company. The table also reveals that in companies with up to 199 employees, internal flows covered real investments and sometimes not even that, while in the larger companies internal flows between 1980 and 1986 also provided scope for extensive financial investments. The table thus suggests that whenever access to long-term debt is blocked for small and medium-sized companies, their scheduled real investments have to be postponed. Since the capital market is usually closed to these companies for cost reasons, all that remains to them is bank loans. They have no alternative capital sources, since the opportunities for using new issues as a way of financing an investment are limited. Consequently, whenever the domestic credit market is distorted, small and medium-sized companies will run into financial trouble. Since these companies rely on bank loans, any distortions affecting the banking industry will hit them. To the extent that financial market transformations give rise to such distortions, small and medium-sized company growth will be impeded.

THE EMPIRICAL ROLE OF BONDS IN NON-FINANCIAL COMPANIES – THE LIABILITY SIDE

Tables 11.9–11.12 provide the basis for a comparison between the Nordic countries as regards the development of capital structures in their non-financial companies during the process of transition. The tables show the size of different sources of funds in a balance-sheet perspective. When it comes to the equity element on the liability side of Nordic companies, the four countries seem to be drawing closer to one another. However, at the end of the 1980s there was still a difference of approximately 8 percentage points between Denmark (with the highest proportion of equity) and Sweden (with the lowest). As we saw in Table 11.1, the Nordic figures are similar to the German figures – below the US and UK figures but above the Japanese. But, as the tables also reveal, the overall composition of the liability side of Nordic non-financial companies differs a good deal between the countries: Denmark and Sweden exhibit fairly stable proportions of equity and of short-term and long-term liabilities, unlike Finland and Norway.

Danish and Swedish companies are similar when it comes to the share of short-term and medium-term liabilities relative to total liabilities. The share of short-term liabilities in these companies was almost twice that of the long-term liabilities, whereas in Finland and Norway the share was nearly equal to that of long-term debt. The proportion of short-term and medium-term

Table 11.9 Liabilities of Danish non-financial companies (bn DKK)[a]

	1977	1980	1985	1989	1990	1991	1992
Total liabilities	67.4 (100)	90.6 (100)	167.8 (100)	217.2 (100)	229.0 (100)	241.2 (100)	247.7 (100)
Equity	26.3 (38.9)	33.1 (36.5)	71.0 (42.3)	91.4 (42.1)	95.8 (41.9)	101.6 (42.1)	108.9 (44.0)
Share capital	8.3	11.5	n/a	n/a	n/a	n/a	n/a
Reserves and provisions	17.9	21.6	n/a	n/a	n/a	n/a	n/a
Short and medium-term liabilities	28.0 (41.5)	39.6 (43.7)	70.8 (42.2)	90.8 (41.8)	93.5 (40.8)	98.2 (40.7)	97.9 (39.5)
Short-term bills and bonds	n/a	n/a	n/a	n/a	n/a	n/a	n/a
Short-term borrowed funds	n/a	n/a	n/a	n/a	n/a	n/a	n/a
Loans from affiliates	n/a	n/a	n/a	n/a	n/a	n/a	n/a
Loans from banks	6.6	7.9	n/a	n/a	n/a	n/a	n/a
Others	n/a	n/a	n/a	n/a	n/a	n/a	n/a
Trade credits received[b]	21.4	31.7	n/a	n/a	n/a	n/a	n/a
from affiliates	n/a	n/a	n/a	n/a	n/a	n/a	n/a
others	n/a	n/a	n/a	n/a	n/a	n/a	n/a
Other accounts payable	n/a	n/a	n/a	n/a	n/a	n/a	n/a
to affiliates	n/a	n/a	n/a	n/a	n/a	n/a	n/a
others	n/a	n/a	n/a	n/a	n/a	n/a	n/a
Long-term liabilities	13.2 (19.6)	17.9 (19.8)	26.0 (15.5)	35.0 (16.1)	39.7 (17.3)	41.4 (17.2)	41.0 (16.5)
Long-term bonds	n/a	n/a	n/a	n/a	n/a	n/a	n/a
placed with affiliates	n/a	n/a	n/a	n/a	n/a	n/a	n/a
others	n/a	n/a	n/a	n/a	n/a	n/a	n/a
Long-term borrowed funds, n.e.c.[*]	n/a	n/a	n/a	n/a	n/a	n/a	n/a
owed to affiliates	n/a	n/a	n/a	n/a	n/a	n/a	n/a
owed to banks	n/a	n/a	n/a	n/a	n/a	n/a	n/a
others	n/a	n/a	n/a	n/a	n/a	n/a	n/a

[a] Manufacturing industries.
[b] Total debt less otherwise specified items, 1977 and 1980.

Source: The tables are based on data from OECD, Financial Statistics, Part 3, various issues.
Note: * n.e.c. = not elsewhere classified.

Table 11.10 Liabilities of Finnish non-financial companies (bn FIM)

Total liabilities	1977 83.9 (100)	1980 117.7 (100)	1985 226.1 (100)	1989 362.0 (100)	1990 403.4 (100)	1991 424.5 (100)
Equity	16.1 (19.2)	23.8 (20.2)	62.8 (27.8)	137.6 (38.0)	147.4 (36.5)	155.1 (36.5)
Share capital	7.5	10.0	16.4	30.1	35.7	39.4
Reserves and provisions	8.6	13.8	46.4	107.5	111.7	115.7
Short and medium-term liabilities	38.4 (45.7)	53.0 (45.1)	89.1 (39.4)	103.6 (28.6)	111.8 (27.7)	107.1 (25.2)
Short-term bills and bonds	4.6	5.0	8.0	5.2	4.2	3.1
Short-term borrowed funds	10.1	12.9	27.2	29.0	35.0	40.7
Loans from affiliates	n/a	n/a	n/a	n/a	n/a	n/a
Loans from banks	n/a	n/a	n/a	n/a	n/a	n/a
Others	n/a	n/a	n/a	n/a	n/a	n/a
Trade credits received	19.4	28.4	42.2	49.7	49.1	39.7
from affiliates	n/a	n/a	n/a	n/a	n/a	n/a
others	n/a	n/a	n/a	n/a	n/a	n/a
Other accounts payable	4.3	6.8	11.7	19.7	23.6	23.6
to affiliates	n/a	n/a	n/a	n/a	n/a	n/a
others	n/a	n/a	n/a	n/a	n/a	n/a
Long-term liabilities	29.4 (35.1)	40.9 (34.7)	74.2 (32.8)	120.8 (33.4)	144.2 (35.8)	162.3 (38.2)
Long-term bonds	2.0	1.9	4.6	17.7	18.8	20.4
placed with affiliates	n/a	n/a	n/a	n/a	n/a	n/a
others	n/a	n/a	n/a	n/a	n/a	n/a
Long-term borrowed funds, n.e.c.*	27.4	38.9	69.6	103.1	125.4	141.9
owed to affiliates	n/a	n/a	n/a	n/a	n/a	n/a
owed to banks	9.0	14.1	26.8	40.3	48.5	52.1
others	n/a	n/a	n/a	n/a	n/a	n/a

Source: See Table 11.9.
Note: The figures have to be interpreted with caution over time since statistical changes were made in 1978, 1980, 1983, 1984, 1986 and 1989. *n.e.c. = not elsewhere classified.

Table 11.11 Liabilities of Norwegian non-financial companies (bn NOK)

	1977	1980	1985	1989[a]	1990	1991
Total liabilities	85.8 (100)	105.0 (100)	256.1 (100)	364.8 (100)	395.8 (100)	387.4 (100)
Equity	16.5 (19.2)	21.1 (20.0)	50.4 (19.7)	128.8 (35.3)	141.7 (35.8)	148.8 (38.4)
Share capital	5.9	7.7	17.2	27.3	27.8	26.3
Reserves and provisions	10.6	13.4	33.2	101.5	113.9	122.5
Short and medium-term liabilities	35.0 (40.8)	42.1 (40.1)	102.8 (40.1)	117.3 (32.1)	133.9 (33.8)	126.0 (32.5)
Short-term bills and bonds[b]	n/a	n/a	n/a	n/a	n/a	n/a
Short-term borrowed funds	5.2	6.7	8.7	10.9	10.4	7.9
Loans from affiliates	n/a	n/a	n/a	n/a	n/a	n/a
Loans from banks	4.6	5.7	6.7	9.1	8.7	6.3
Others	0.7	1.0	1.9	1.8	1.7	1.5
Trade credits received	18.0	19.1	28.3	34.5	36.1	32.7
from affiliates	n/a	n/a	n/a	n/a	n/a	n/a
others	n/a	n/a	n/a	n/a	n/a	n/a
Other accounts payable	11.8	16.3	65.8	71.9	87.4	85.5
to affiliates	n/a	n/a	n/a	n/a	n/a	n/a
others	n/a	n/a	n/a	n/a	n/a	n/a
Long-term liabilities	34.4 (40.0)	41.9 (39.9)	102.9 (40.2)	118.8 (32.6)	120.2 (30.4)	112.5 (29.0)
Long-term bonds	5.0	5.8	15.0	32.8	32.0	28.4
placed with affiliates	n/a	n/a	n/a	n/a	n/a	n/a
others	n/a	n/a	n/a	n/a	n/a	n/a
Long-term borrowed funds, n.e.c.*	29.4	36.1	87.9	86.0	88.1	84.1
owed to affiliates	6.6	7.1	38.4	35.0	36.9	29.8
owed to banks	n/a	n/a	n/a	n/a	n/a	n/a
others	22.7	29.0	49.5	50.9	51.2	54.4

[a] There is a break in the time series in 1987 because of change in the treatment of extraordinary tax-conditioned depreciation, which since 1987 is no longer deducted from the amounts of fixed assets but instead transferred to equity under the item 'Reserves and provision'.
[b] Included in 'Trade credits received'.

Source: See Table 11.9.
Note: *n.e.c. = not elsewhere classified.

Table 11.12 Liabilities of Swedish non-financial companies (bn SEK)

	1977	1980	1985	1989	1990	1991
Total liabilities	490.5 (100)	627.1 (100)	1,086.7 (100)	1,534.2 (100)	1,764.4 (100)	1,741.9 (100)
Equity	151.1 (30.8)	203.5 (32.5)	378.2 (34.8)	515.1 (33.6)	580.8 (32.9)	605.4 (34.8)
Share capital	78.5	60.3	95.2	121.0	136.9	141.8
Reserves and provisions	72.6	143.2	283.0	394.1	443.9	463.5
Short and medium-term liabilities	186.2 (38.0)	243.0 (38.7)	434.6 (40.0)	677.3 (44.1)	809.9 (45.9)	732.8 (42.1)
Short-term bills and bonds	n/a	1.2	1.4	0.9	1.1	n/a
Short-term borrowed funds	127.7[a]	67.7	145.8	303.3	378.3	222.1
Loans from affiliates	n/a	33.4	78.7	195.7	256.4	116.2
Loans from banks and others	n/a	34.4	67.1	107.6	121.9	105.8
Trade credits received	n/a	96.1	148.3	175.9	197.2	166.7
from affiliates	20.9[b]	n/a	n/a	n/a	n/a	n/a
others	106.8[b]	96.1	148.3	175.9	197.2	166.7
Other accounts payable	58.6	77.9	139.1	197.2	233.3	344.0
to affiliates	n/a	n/a	n/a	n/a	n/a	124.0
others[c]	58.6	77.9	139.1	197.2	233.3	220.0
Long-term liabilities	153.2 (31.2)	186.6 (28.8)	273.9 (25.2)	341.7 (22.3)	373.6 (21.2)	403.7 (23.2)
Long-term bonds	n/a	30.6	53.7	80.4	78.1	71.8
placed with affiliates	n/a	n/a	n/a	n/a	n/a	n/a
others	n/a	n/a	n/a	n/a	n/a	n/a
Long-term borrowed funds, n.e.c. *	153.2[d]	150.0	220.3	261.3	295.5	331.9
owed to affiliates	22.5[d]	28.6	49.0	101.8[d]	118.4[d]	129.6[d]
owed to banks	n/a	n/a	n/a	n/a	n/a	n/a
others	130.7[d]	121.4	171.2	240.0[d]	255.3[d]	274.1[d]

[a] Including 'Short-term bills and bonds', 'Short-term borrowed funds', and 'Trade credits'.
[b] Including 'Short-term bills and bonds', 'Short-term borrowed funds'.
[c] Included in 'Other accounts payable'.
[d] Including 'Long-term bonds'.

Source: See Table 11.9; SCB, Finansräkenskaper, Fin K.11, 94:01.
Note: *n.e.c. = not elsewhere classified.

liabilities increased somewhat between 1977 and 1989 in Swedish companies, whereas in Denmark the ratio between short-term and total liabilities remained almost constant from 1977. Among long-term liabilities, bonds have been on average of minor importance, with a peak in 1989 when they represented 15 per cent of Finnish long-term liabilities, 28 per cent of Norwegian and 23 per cent of Swedish.

The financing of small and large Nordic manufacturing companies – a comparison

Unfortunately no data is available which would allow us to study the differences between companies of various sizes when it comes to their reliance on bonds during the process of transition. Consequently let us next try to discover whether there are any general differences in the debt financing of small Nordic manufacturing companies compared with that of their larger colleagues. As can be seen in Table 11.13, reliance on short-term debt was most common in small Danish companies and least common in large Finnish companies. During the 1980s the Nordic countries drew close to one another as regards the proportion of short-term debt; the Finnish companies were an

Table 11.13 Short-term debt in Nordic manufacturing companies, 1979–90 (as a percentage of total liabilities, ISIC 2–3)

Number of employees	Denmark[a]		Finland		Norway		Sweden	
	20–49	200–	20–49	100–	50–99	200–	20–49	200–
1979	n/a	n/a	54.2	37.1	50.4	33.5	40.6	31.8
1980	n/a	n/a	54.9	38.7	49.9	37.5	39.9	32.4
1981	n/a	n/a	52.4	37.4	48.9	42.6	40.8	33.2
1982	n/a	n/a	51.2	36.9	51.4	41.2	40.3	33.7
1983	n/a	n/a	50.9	36.8	48.1	39.6	40.9	32.3
1984	48.3	42.0	50.9	36.5	48.6	40.6	41.2	31.6
1985	47.7	41.0	44.0	33.8	49.9	43.3	40.1	32.7
1986	45.8	38.6	43.8	29.1	51.2	42.1	38.5	34.1
1987	45.3	38.3	40.3	29.4	48.6	41.7	42.3	34.4
1988	44.7	38.7	37.1	27.9	45.3	38.2	43.0	34.2
1989	45.9	39.7	37.8	29.5	43.9	39.7	43.3	38.8
1990	47.0	37.8	39.3	29.7	42.6	39.3	39.1	38.6

[a] Account statistics for all non-financial companies in 1984/85, and for industrial joint-stock companies from 1986–90.

Sources: Calculations are based on data from Central Statistical Bureau of Denmark, *Industrial Accounts Statistics*, various issues; Copenhagen Stock Exchange, *Annual Report*, various issues; Central Statistical Bureau of Finland, Database – Enterprises (unpublished data); Central Statistical Bureau of Norway, Database (unpublished data 1979–86) and *Statistics of Account*, various issues (1987–90); Central Statistical Bureau of Sweden, *Enterprises*, various issues (1979–87) and Database (unpublished data 1988–90).

exception here. At the beginning of the 1990s this proportion was almost the same as between the large Nordic manufacturing companies (again excluding the Finnish), whereas it still differed somewhat in the case of the small and medium-sized companies.

The gap between the short-term-debt share of total liability in small as against large Danish manufacturing companies in 1990 was about 10 per-centage points. A similar gap was registered for Finland, which in that case expressed a drop from the 15 per cent level. An even bigger gap was registered in Norway at the end of the 1970s and the beginning of the 1980s, but it then fell steadily to a few per cent in 1990. This was the case in Sweden too.

In the 1980s and at the beginning of the 1990s large Danish and Swedish companies relied to a small and diminishing extent on long-term debt, as can be seen in Table 11.14. The proportion of long-term debt at the beginning of the 1990s was highest in large Finnish companies and smallest in large Danish companies. In the small companies the proportion of long-term debt was also highest in Finnish companies. In Danish and Swedish small companies, the long-term-debt share of total liability was considerably higher than in the large companies in these two countries, but was still lower than the percentage in large Finnish and Norwegian companies. In Finland

Table 11.14 Long-term debt in Nordic manufacturing companies, 1979–90 (as a percentage of total liabilities, ISIC 2–3)

Number of employees	Denmark[a]		Finland		Norway		Sweden	
	20–49	200–	20–49	100–	50–99	200–	20–49	200–
1979	n/a	n/a	30.2	40.6	34.9	46.7	31.5	35.1
1980	n/a	n/a	31.3	39.9	36.4	41.5	28.9	34.7
1981	n/a	n/a	35.3	41.5	37.2	36.8	31.0	34.1
1982	n/a	n/a	35.9	43.1	32.4	38.9	30.4	32.4
1983	n/a	n/a	34.3	42.2	33.1	37.7	28.9	30.2
1984	16.9	15.5	34.2	41.3	29.7	34.6	26.6	25.6
1985	17.5	16.5	35.9	37.1	29.1	30.9	27.4	23.9
1986	19.5	16.2	35.6	40.1	28.0	31.6	26.5	22.2
1987	20.3	16.9	35.7	38.2	26.1	28.8	25.7	22.2
1988	22.0	15.9	39.3	35.8	28.3	30.3	25.2	22.2
1989	21.0	14.5	33.7	34.9	30.4	28.4	25.6	20.5
1990	22.3	15.7	34.6	36.3	31.9	28.6	24.3	21.2

[a] Account statistics for all non-financial companies in 1984/85, and for industrial joint-stock companies from 1986–90.

Sources: Calculations are based on data from Central Statistical Bureau of Denmark, *Industrial Accounts Statistics*, various issues; Copenhagen Stock Exchange, *Annual Report*, various issues; Central Statistical Bureau of Finland, Database – Enterprises (unpublished data); Central Statistical Bureau of Norway, Database (unpublished data 1979–86) and *Statistics of Accounts*, various issues (1987–90); Central Statistical Bureau of Sweden, *Enterprises*, various issues (1979–87) and Database (unpublished data 1988–90).

and Norway the long-term-debt share of total liability in small companies was almost always lower than in large companies. In one or two years only did the opposite apply. In Sweden a similar situation obtained as from 1984.

In an overall Nordic perspective the proportion of short-term debt (for working capital requirements) was higher than the proportion of long-term debt, except in large Finnish companies. The biggest difference between the shares of short-term and long-term debt appeared at the beginning of the 1990s in small and large Danish companies (23.6 and 24.7 percentage points respectively), while the smallest difference appeared in small and large Finnish companies (4.7 and –6.6 percentage points respectively).

Debt securitization in non-financial companies

Finally, debt securitization in the Nordic markets is illustrated in Tables 11.15 and 11.16. Generally speaking, securitization on the debt side in

Table 11.15 Securitization in the Nordic markets: the non-financial sector perspective, 1979–90 (securities as a percentage of interest-bearing debt in non-financial companies)

	Denmark[a]	Finland[a,b]	Norway[c]	Sweden
1979	n/a	4.1	11.0 (3.5–16.6)	10.6
1980	n/a	3.4	9.1 (6.2–16.2)	9.4
1981	n/a	3.1	10.2 (9.7–16.0)	8.8
1982	n/a	3.4	10.9 (7.4–20.0)	8.8
1983	7.6	3.6	11.1 (6.8–20.7)	8.8
1984	6.5	4.6	10.9 (5.7–18.2)	9.6
1985	6.6	6.1	12.3 (5.2–17.0)	10.8
1986	6.5	7.1	13.1 (4.5–18.6)	11.8
1987	5.8	8.7	15.4 (1.8–19.6)	11.4
1988	5.9	8.2	16.2 (1.4–19.6)	9.9
1989	5.3	7.3 (3.9–10.4)	16.5[d] (1.3–25.1)	8.2
1990	n/a	7.7 (1.9–9.2)	16.1[d] (0.7–21.6)	6.6

[a] Other domestic sectors. Other domestic sectors consist of public enterprises, private enterprises, non-profit institutions and households.
[b] The degree of securitization of small and medium-sized companies (number of employees between 20 and 49) and large companies (number of employees 100 and more) is given in parentheses.
[c] The degree of securitization of small and medium-sized companies (number of employees between 50 and 99) and large companies (number of employees 200 and more) is given in parentheses.
[d] Estimated value.

Sources: Based on data from Central Statistical Bureau of Denmark, Industri og energi, various issues; Central Statistical Bureau of Finland, Financial Statement Statistics of Industry, Database; Central Statistical Bureau of Finland, Financial Market Statistics, various issues; Central Statistical Bureau of Norway, Bank- og Kredittstatistikk, various issues, and Statistics of Accounts, Database; Central Statistical Bureau of Sweden, Financial Accounts, various issues.

companies gradually increased during the 1980s. The Swedish situation, with a peak in 1986 followed by a gradual decline, is an exception. The degree of securitization in the Nordic markets at the beginning of the 1990s, however, was far below that of the US market (about 60 per cent). The Nordic markets, with their fairly high debt ratios, can thus be seen as heavily bank-orientated. In Norway, as can be seen from the figures in parentheses, the securities share of total interest-bearing debt increased gradually in large non-financial companies, while it declined in small ones.

A closer examination of securitization, and with the focus on bonds in a Nordic comparison, shows (see Table 11.16) that historically bonds have had their greatest importance in Norwegian non-financial companies, where they accounted for 11 per cent of all interest-bearing debt in 1979 and 14.1 per cent in 1990. In Finnish companies the importance of bonds as an interest-bearing debt peaked in 1987 and in Sweden in 1986. Finnish companies none the less experienced an increase from 4.1 per cent in 1979 to 5.6 per cent in 1990, while the importance of bonds in Swedish companies dropped from 10.6 per cent in 1979 to 5.2 per cent in 1990. Bonds have played an insignificant role on the liability side in Danish companies.

THE EMPIRICAL ROLE OF BONDS IN NON-FINANCIAL COMPANIES – THE ASSET SIDE

Generally speaking, financial assets as a share of total assets increased during the 1980s in the United States, Germany, Italy, the United Kingdom and, especially, in France. A possible explanation of this is that the increase reflects changes in the desired composition of companies' portfolios in a world of high real interest rates and the availability of a greater range of financial instruments. The main part of the increase in the holdings of financial assets involved assets with long maturity times. Development on the asset side, however, was often dominated by a few companies. In France, for instance, 2 per cent of companies accounted for about 75 per cent of all purchases of financial assets during the period 1983–86.[51]

Table 11.17 shows big differences both among the Nordic countries and over time, as regards the role of bonds on the asset side. In the second half of the 1980s bonds exhibit their greatest importance on the asset side in Danish companies, while their importance is least in Norwegian companies. The pattern remained more or less unchanged at the beginning of the 1990s, although a slight increase could be noted in the importance of bonds as an investment alternative for Norwegian companies. In the second half of the 1980s Danish companies had more than 10 per cent of their assets in bonds, whereas Norwegian companies had a mere 1–3 per cent. Investment in bonds by Finnish and Swedish companies was around 5–7 per cent. However, this type of investment by Swedish companies was declining after a peak in 1987, whereas Finnish companies were increasing their investment in bonds during the period.

Table 11.16 Bond securitization in Nordic non-financial companies (outstanding bonds as a percentage of interest-bearing debt)

	Denmark[a]	Finland[b]	Norway	Sweden
1979	n/a	4.1	11.0	10.6
1980	n/a	3.4	9.1	9.4
1981	n/a	3.1	10.2	8.8
1982	n/a	3.4	10.9	8.8
1983	1.7	3.6	11.1	8.8
1984	1.1	4.6	10.9	8.7
1985	2.4	5.8	11.6	8.7
1986	2.4	6.6	11.9	9.6
1987	1.5	6.4	13.2	9.3
1988	1.2	5.3	14.3	8.2
1989	0.1	5.5	14.7	6.5
1990	n/a	5.6	14.1	5.2

[a] Manufacturing enterprises with twenty or more employees.
[b] Other domestic sectors. Other domestic sectors consist of public enterprises, private enterprises, non-profit institutions and households.

Sources: Based on data from Central Statistical Bureau of Denmark, *Industri og energi*, various issues; Central Statistical Bureau of Finland, *Financial Market Statistics*, various issues; Central Statistical Bureau of Norway, *Bank- og Kredittstatistikk*, various issues, and *Database*; Central Statistical Bureau of Sweden, *Financial Accounts*, various issues; and own estimates.

Table 11.17 Bonds in Nordic companies on the asset side (bond assets as a percentage of total assets. Outstanding bonds as a percentage of total assets (liabilities) in parentheses)

	Denmark[a]	Finland[b]	Norway[c]	Sweden[c]
1979	n/a	2.1 (2.7)	0.1 (6.0)	0.3 (5.9)
1980	n/a	2.2 (2.3)	0.1 (4.9)	0.3 (5.2)
1981	n/a	2.4 (2.1)	0.2 (5.6)	0.8 (5.0)
1982	n/a	2.9 (2.5)	0.2 (6.3)	0.9 (5.1)
1983	10.6 (0.4)	3.5 (2.9)	0.3 (6.2)	2.5 (4.9)
1984	11.2 (0.3)	4.0 (3.4)	0.4 (6.2)	2.4 (5.0)
1985	11.6 (0.6)	5.1 (4.3)	1.0 (6.4)	2.8 (4.9)
1986	12.3 (0.6)	5.5 (5.1)	1.6 (6.6)	7.2 (5.4)
1987	11.7 (0.6)	6.1 (4.9)	2.1 (7.3)	7.6 (5.2)
1988	10.9 (0.3)	5.9 (4.1)	2.6 (7.7)	7.2 (4.4)
1989	10.6 (0.0)	5.9 (4.2)	3.0 (7.5)	5.4 (3.6)
1990	n/a	7.3 (4.3)	n/a (6.5[d])	5.3 (2.8)

[a] Manufacturing enterprises with twenty or more employees. 'Other securities' as a percentage of total liabilities.
[b] Other domestic sectors. Other domestic sectors consist of public enterprises, private enterprises, non-profit institutions and households.
[c] Non-financial companies.
[d] Estimated value.

Sources: Central Statistical Bureau of Denmark, *Industri og energi*, various issues; Central Statistical Bureau of Finland, *Financial Market Statistics*, various issues; Central Statistical Bureau of Norway, *Bank- og Kredittstatistikk*, various issues, and *Database*; Central Statistical Bureau of Sweden, *Financial Accounts*, various issues; and own estimates.

Finally, let us compare the role of bonds on the asset and the liability side. Since the mid-1980s bonds have become most important on the asset side as a device for cash and risk management in Danish, Finnish and Swedish non-financial companies. In Norwegian companies they have had their greatest importance on the liability side. A large proportion of these bonds are issued abroad, which suggests that the motive may have been any of those listed at the beginning of this chapter.

CONCLUDING REMARKS ON THE ROLE OF BONDS AND BOND MARKETS TO NON-FINANCIAL COMPANIES

For the period of transition we have found some structural change as regards corporate funding behaviour in general, and the role of bonds in particular. To achieve comparability across countries as well as among companies of different sizes within a particular country, problems connected with the data have forced us to deal with two sets of data: one with non-financial companies and the other with manufacturing companies.

The global convergence in debt ratios that has been under way since the early 1980s has been apparent in the Nordic context as well. The ratios in all the Nordic countries have declined, but to differing extents, with the result that the range of Nordic debt ratios has also shrunk from 17 percentage points in 1981 to 9 per cent in 1991/92. Higher profitability and lower taxes were the main explanations to decreased ratios suggested above. Nordic companies (except in Denmark) were none the less still relatively highly leveraged at the beginning of the 1990s by international standards; the debt ratios of Finnish, Norwegian and Swedish non-financial companies were all in the range of 62–65 per cent.

The high debt ratios in the 1970s and 1980s in Finland, Norway and Sweden have been explained in terms of the double taxation and interest deduction arrangements, which in that period favoured debt financing in these countries. Up to the mid-1980s these three countries also had governments interested in impeding the development of securities markets, i.e. creating incentives for bank loans. Intra-Nordic differences in debt ratios were also found to reflect differences in industrial structure, with the predominance of the traditionally low-leveraged food and drug companies in Denmark, and with traditionally high-leveraged basic industries with large fixed assets in Finland (paper, pulp and wood) and Norway (oil industries). Sweden, with a mixture of basic industries and traditionally low-leveraged R&D-intensive industries, had debt ratios considerably below those of Finnish and Norwegian companies in the first part of the 1980s.

The Nordic debt ratios were found to be consistently higher in small manufacturing companies than in large ones. Further, debt ratios were found to be substantially higher in Finnish and Norwegian manufacturing companies than the corresponding ratios for the population of non-financial companies as a whole. This reflects the high relative value of fixed assets in the manufacturing industries in these countries.

The debt structure of Nordic non-financial companies has changed since 1977, but when it comes to the role of long-term debt as a substantial part of the total debt, the pattern has held in Finland and Norway. In 1991 the long-term-debt share of total debt was 60 per cent in Finland and 47 per cent in Norway, while in Denmark it was 30 per cent and in Sweden 36 per cent. The propensity to rely on other forms of long-term borrowing rather than bond issues also differs substantially across countries, with other types of borrowed long-term funds amounting to seven times the stock of bonds in the Finnish companies, five times the stock in the Swedish and three times the stock in the Norwegian. Here too the differences owe a good deal to the attitude of the national authorities as expressed in various regulations and policy measures, for instance measures such as tax rates and deregulations which affect the competitiveness of the banking sector. All other borrowed long-term funds are not made available through the domestic banking sector, however; some are borrowed from international banks and some from affiliates.

The relative importance of bonds can also be expressed with the help of our measure of debt securitization in a corporate perspective. This measure, as expressed by the securities share of interest-bearing debt in non-financial companies, showed that the Norwegian companies had by far the highest degree of securitization of the four Nordic countries. The same applied to bond securitization. In 1990 this share amounted to 14 per cent as compared to about 5 per cent for non-financial companies in Finland and Sweden. Moreover, Norwegian companies were the only Nordic ones in which the degree of securitization had risen since 1986–87. In assessing the role of the domestic bond markets in Norwegian non-financial companies we should also remember that, in 1990, 77 per cent of the stock of bonds issued by Norwegian non-financial companies were issued abroad (see Chapter 10).

The role of bonds in corporate risk and cash management also differed between the Nordic countries. Danish companies had on average the highest share of their assets in bonds, while Norway had the smallest share. With bonds occupying an insignificant position on the liability side, Danish companies benefited from the bond markets almost entirely on the asset side of the balance sheet. A somewhat similar situation applied in Finnish and Swedish companies from the mid-1980s on, when the bond share on the asset side exceeded that on the liability side, suggesting that the main role of bond markets to companies in these countries and in Denmark was to provide cash and risk management devices. The importance of the bond markets to Norwegian companies was on the liability side throughout the period, meeting a variety of needs ranging from fund raising to signalling.

NOTES

1   For some recent surveys on the question of capital structure, see Taggart (1985), Masulis (1988), Miller (1988), Allen (1990), and comments on Miller (1988) by Bhattacharya (1988), Modigliani (1988), Ross (1988), Stiglitz (1988) and Harris and Ravi (1991). Taggart (1985), Masulis (1988) and Harris and Ravi (1991) provide general surveys, while Allen (1990) focuses on security design.

2   Harris and Ravi (1991) identify four types of determinants of capital structure, which can be regarded as a regrouping of the categories used here. Their categories are based on the following objectives:

   - to ameliorate conflicts of interest among various groups with claims on the company's resources, including managers (the agency approach);
   - to convey private information to capital markets or to mitigate adverse selection effects (the asymmetric information approach);
   - to influence the nature of products or competition in the product/input market;
   - to affect the outcome of corporate control contests.

3   See, for example, Hansen (1986) and Rutterford (1985).

4   The issue represented 14.6 per cent of the pre-issue market value.

5   The issue represented 4.6 per cent of the pre-issue market value.

6   See, for example, Masulis (1988).

7   See, for instance, Warner (1977), Weiss (1990) and Wruck (1990).

8   See, for instance, Cutler and Summers (1988).

9   As discussed in Gilson (1990).

10   See, for instance, Hart and Moore (1990).

11   See, among others, Titman (1984) and Cornell and Shapiro (1987).

12   See Maksimovic (1988).

13   These ideas are developed in, for instance, Poitevin (1989), and Bolton and Scharfstein (1990).

14   See Brander and Lewis (1986).

15   See Glazer (1989).

16   See Sarig (1988).

17   See, for example, Jensen (1986, 1989), and Shleifer and Vishny (1989).

18   See also, Galai and Masulis (1976), and Smith and Warner (1979).

19   See Grossman and Hart (1982).

20   See Green and Talmor (1986).

21   Agency problems can be reduced by the use of managerial incentive schemes. See, for instance, Barnea et al. (1985), Brander and Poitevin (1989), Dybvig and Zender (1989). Counterwise arguments are presented by Narayanan (1987) and Haugen and Senbet (1987).

22   As discussed in Smith and Warner (1979).

23   Studies of the way a company's capital structure transmits to outside investors the information of insiders, began with the signalling of the proportion of debt (Ross 1977), and with the exploitation of managerial risk-aversion (Leland and Pyle 1977). A new research direction in which capital structure is assumed to be designed to mitigate such inefficiencies in the company's investment decisions as are caused by the information asymmetries, was triggered by Myers and Majluf (1984) and Myers (1984).

24   Discussed in Stiglitz and Weiss (1981).

25   See, for instance, Greenwald et al. (1984), Myers and Majluf (1984) and Narayanan (1988).

26   See, for instance, Bester (1985, 1987), and Besanko and Thakor (1987).

27 See Jaffe and Stiglitz (1990).
28 See Myers (1984).
29 See Brennan and Kraus (1987).
30 See, for instance, Gertner *et al.* (1988).
31 See, for instance, Heinkel (1982), Brennan and Kraus (1987) and Constantinides and Grundy (1989).
32 As discussed, for instance, in Smith (1986) and Masulis (1988).
33 See, for instance, Toy *et al.* (1974), Carleton and Silbermann (1977), Nakamura and Nakamura (1982), Friend and Hasbrouck (1988), Barton *et al.* (1989), Baskin (1989), and Chang and Rhee (1990).
34 See, for example, Bowen *et al.* (1982), Bradley *et al.* (1984), Long and Malitz (1985), Kester (1986), and Jensen (1989).
35 See, for example, Bradley *et al.* (1984), Castanias (1983), Long and Malitz (1985), Kester (1986), March (1982), Titman and Wessels (1988), and Chaplinski and Niehaus (1990).
36 The results of international studies of debt ratios and leverage should, as a general rule, be interpreted with caution. In measuring debt ratios there are differences as regards accounting standard as well as the inclusion or exclusion of accounts payable, accounts receivable, cash and other short-term debt. Moreover, in some cases debt-to-equity ratios are based on a ratio of the book value of equity, in others as the book value of the debt-to-market value of equity and, finally, in a few studies as the market value of the debt-to-market value of equity.
37 Borio (1990) notes this pattern in France and Italy among the G-7 countries.
38 Board of Governors of the Federal Reserve System (1992).
39 In Germany banks directly own almost 10 per cent of the stock of shares and, as a result of shares held in their custody, they influence another 40 per cent. In Japan banks hold directly about one-fifth of total shareholding, while corporations have about one-third (Borio 1990).
40 See Bowen *et al.* (1982), Bradley *et al.* (1984), Long and Malitz (1985) and Kester (1986).
41 For Canada, see Economic Council of Canada (1987); for Germany, Deutsche Bundesbank (1984); for Japan, Elston (1981); for United States, Titman and Wessels (1988); and for the United Kingdom, Benzie (1988).
42 The importance of debt is probably generally somewhat overestimated, since the table is based on balance sheet data with equity and debt at book rather than market value.
43 For instance, the offering of soft loans by the Danish government.
44 See, for instance, Taggart (1986) and Mayer (1990).
45 Research in the area of small business finance falls into the following six main categories: (1) small company access to financial markets; (2) the initial public offerings market; (3) the venture capital market; (4) small business failures; (5) ownership effect and company performance, and (6) others.
46 Aspects of small business finance are addressed by Jensen and Meckling (1976), which look particularly at agency costs; by Bates (1990), which concentrates on financial capital structure; and Day *et al.* (1985), which is concerned with taxes and financial policy.
47 In Tables 11.8–11.11, it has to be noted that limits on company size differ between the Nordic countries due to differences in data-gathering procedures.
48 With a question-mark regarding the Danish development; the only exception is the activity of small Norwegian non-financial companies, for which the average was slightly higher in the period 1988–90.
49 If the table were revised to include subsidies from the government, then during the 1980s subsidies should appear as a source of funds that was equally important

to Swedish non-financial companies as new equity issues.
50   About 91 per cent of all Swedish companies.
51   BIS (1992).

REFERENCES

Allen, F., 1990, 'The Changing Nature of Debt and Equity: A Financial Perspective',
    in Kopcke, R. and E. S. Rosengren (eds), *Are the Distinctions Between Debt and
    Equity Disappearing?*, Federal Reserve Bank of Boston, Boston, Conference Series
    No. 33, pp. 12–38.
Barnea, A., R. Haugen and L. Senbet, 1985, *Agency Problems and Financial
    Contracting*, Prentice-Hall, Englewood Cliffs, NJ.
Barton, S., H. Hill and S. Sundaram, 1989, 'An Empirical Test of Stakeholder Theory
    Predictions of Capital Structure', *Financial Management* (Spring), pp. 36–44.
Baskin, J., 1989, 'An Empirical Investigation of the Pecking Order Hypothesis',
    Financial Management (Spring), pp. 26–35.
Bates, T., 1990, 'Entrepreneur Human Capital Inputs and Small Business Longevity',
    The Review of Economics and Statistics, Vol. LXXII, No. 4, pp. 551–9.
Benzie, R.S., 1988, 'The Financial Behaviour of Industrial and Commercial Com-
    panies, 1970–96', *The Bank of England Quarterly Bulletin*, London, February,
    pp. 27–82.
Besanko, D. and A. Thakor, 1987, 'Competitive Equilibrium in the Credit Market
    under Asymmetric Information', *Journal of Economic Theory* 42, pp. 167–82.
Bester, H., 1985, 'Screening vs. Rationing in Credit Markets with Imperfect
    Information', *American Economic Review* 75, pp. 850–5.
Bester, H., 1987, 'The Role of Collateral in Credit Markets with Imperfect
    Information', *European Economic Review* 31, pp. 887–99.
Bhattacharya, S., 1988, 'Corporate Finance and the Legacy of Miller and Mod',
    Journal of Economic Perspectives 2, pp. 135–48.
BIS, 1992, *Annual Report*, Basle.
Board of Governors of the Federal Reserve System, 1992, *Flow of Funds Accounts*,
    Washington, DC.
Bolton, P. and D. Scharfstein, 1990, 'A Theory of Predation Based on Agency
    Problems in Financial Contracting', *American Economic Review* 80, pp. 93–106.
Borio, C.E.V., 1990, 'Leverage and Financing of Non-Financial Companies: An
    International Perspective', *BIS Economic Papers*, No. 27, May, BIS, Basle.
Bowen, R.M., L.A. Daily and C.C. Huber, Jr., 1982, 'Evidence on the Existence and
    Determinants of the Inter-industry Differences in Leverage', *Financial Manage-
    ment*, 11, pp. 10–20.
Bradley, M, G. Jarrel and E.H. Kim, 1984, 'On the Existence of an Optimal Structure:
    Theory and Evidence', *Journal of Finance* 39, pp. 857–78.
Brander, J.A. and T. Lewis, 1986, 'Oligopoly and Financial Structures: The Liability
    Effect', *American Economic Review*, No. 76, pp. 956–70.
Brander, J.A. and M. Poitevin, 1989, 'Management Compensation and the Agency
    Costs of Debt Finance', *Working Paper*, University of British Columbia.
Brennan, M. and A. Kraus, 1987, 'Efficient Financing under Asymmetric Informa-
    tion', *Journal of Finance* 42, pp. 1225–43.
Carleton, W. and I. Silbermann, 1977, 'Joint Determination of Return and Capital
    Structure, An Econometric Analysis', *Journal of Finance* 32, pp. 811–21.
Castanias, R., 1983, 'Bankruptcy Risk and Optimal Capital Structure', *Journal of
    Finance* 38, pp. 1617–35.
Chang, R. and S. Rhee, 1990, 'The Impact of Personal Taxes on Corporate Dividend

Policy and Capital Structure Decisions', *Financial Management* (Summer), pp. 21–31.

Chaplinsky, S. and G. Niehaus, 1990, 'The Determinants of Inside Ownership and Leverage', *Working Paper*, University of Minnesota.

Constantinides, G. and B. Grundy, 1989, 'Optimal Investment with Stock Repurchase and Financing as Signals', *Review of Financial Studies* 2, pp. 445–65.

Cornell, W.B. and A. Shapiro, 1987, 'Corporate Stakeholders and Corporate Finance', *Financial Management* (Spring), pp. 33–41.

Cutler, D. and L. Summers, 1988, 'The Costs of Conflict Resolution and Financial Distress: Evidence from the Texaco–Pennzoil Litigation', *Rand Journal of Economics* 19, pp. 157–72.

Day, T.E., Stoll, H.R. and R.E. Whaley, 1985, *Taxes, Financial Policy and Small Business*, Lexington Books, Lexington, Mass.

Deutsche Bundesbank, 1984, 'Annual Accounts of Small and Medium-sized Enterprises', *Monthly Report of the Deutsche Bundesbank*, Frankfurt a.M., April, pp. 22–9.

Dybvig, P. and J. Zender, 1989, 'Capital Structure and Dividend Irrelevance with Asymmetric Information', *Working Paper*, Yale School of Organization and Management, New Haven.

Economic Council of Canada, 1987, *A Framework of Financial Regulation – A Research Report*, Montreal.

Elston, C.D., 1981, 'The Financing of Japanese Industry', *Bank of England Quarterly Bulletin* (London) 21, pp. 510–18.

Fama, E.F. and M.H. Miller, 1972, *The Theory of Finance*, Holt, Rinehart & Winston, New York.

Friend, I. and J. Hasbrouck, 1988, 'Determinants of Capital Structure', in Chen, A. (ed.), *Research in Finance 7*, JAI Press, Greenwich, Conn.

Galai, D. and R. Masulis, 1976, 'The Option Pricing Model and the Risk Factor of Stock', *Journal of Financial Economics* 3, pp. 53–81.

Gandemo, B., 1990, *Näringslivets behov av externt kapital*; in SOU 1989:25 Rapporter till Finansieringsutredningen, Department of Industry.

Gertner, R., R. Gibbons and D. Scharfstein, 1988, 'Simultaneous Signalling to the Capital and Product Markets', *Rand Journal of Economics* 19, pp. 173–90.

Gilson, S., 1990, 'Bankruptcy, Boards, Banks, and Blockholders: Evidence on Changes in Corporate Ownership and Control when Firms Default', *Journal of Financial Economics* 27, pp. 355–87.

Glazer, J., 1989, 'Live and Let Live: Collusion Among Oligopolists with Long-Term Debt', *Working Paper*, Boston University.

Green, R., 1984, 'Investment Incentives, Debt, and Warrants', *Journal of Financial Economics*, No. 13, pp. 115–36.

Green, R. and E. Talmor, 1986, 'Asset Substitution and the Agency Costs of Debt Financing', *Journal of Banking and Finance* 10, pp. 391-9.

Greenwald, B., J.E. Stiglitz and A. Weiss, 1984, 'Informational Imperfections in the Capital Market and Macroeconomic Fluctuations', *American Economic Review*, Vol. 74, No. 2, pp. 194–9.

Grossman, S. and O. Hart, 1982, 'Corporate Financial Structure and Incentives', in McCall, J.M. (ed.), *The Economics of Information and Uncertainty*, Chicago Press, Chicago.

Hansen, R., 1986, 'Evaluating the Costs of a New Equity Issue', *Midland Corporate Finance Journal* 4, pp. 42–55.

Harris, M. and A. Ravi 1991, 'The Theory of Capital Structure', *Journal of Finance*, Vol. 46, No. 1 (March), pp. 297–355.

Hart, O. and J. Moore, 1990, 'A Theory of Corporate Financial Structure Based on the Seniority of Claims', *Discussion Paper* TE/90/217, London School of Economics.

Haugen, R. and L. Senbet, 1987, 'On the Resolution of Agency Problems Financial Instruments: A Reply', *Journal of Finance* 42, pp. 1091–5.

Heinkel, R., 1982, 'A Theory of Capital Structure Relevance under Imperfect Information', *Journal of Finance* 37, pp. 1141–50.

Jaffe, D. and J. Stiglitz, 1990, 'Credit Rationing', in Friedman, B. and F. Hahn (eds), *Handbook of Monetary Economics II*, Elsevier, New York.

Jensen, M.C., 1986, 'Agency Costs of Free Cash Flow, Corporate Finance, and Takeovers', *American Economic Review* 76, pp. 323–9.

Jensen, M.C., 1989, 'Eclipse of the Public Corporation', *Harvard Business Review* (September–October), pp. 61–74.

Jensen, M.C. and W.H. Meckling, 1976, 'Theory of the Firm: Managerial Behaviour, Agency Costs and Ownership Structure', *Journal of Financial Economics* 3, pp. 305–60.

Kester, C.W., 1986, 'Capital and Ownership Structure: A Comparison of United States and Japanese Manufacturing Corporations', *Financial Management*, pp. 5–16.

Leland, H.E. and D.H. Pyle, 1977, 'Information Asymmetries, Financial Structure and Financial Intermediation', *Journal of Finance*, pp. 371–87.

Long, M. and I. Malitz, 1985, 'The Investment-financing Nexus: Some Empirical Evidence', *Midland Corporate Finance Journal* 3, pp. 53–9.

Maksimovic, V., 1988, 'Capital Structure in Repeated Oligopoly', *Rand Journal of Economics* 19, pp. 389–407.

March, P., 1982, 'The Choice Between Equity and Debt: An Empirical Study', *Journal of Finance* 37, pp. 121–44.

Masulis, R.W., 1988, *The Debt/Equity Choice*, Ballinger Publishing Company, New York.

Mayer, D., 1990, 'Financial Systems, Corporate Finance, and Economic Development', in Hubbard, R. (ed.), *Asymmetric Information, Corporate Finance, and Investment*, University of Chicago Press, Chicago.

Miller, M.H., 1988, 'The Modigliani–Miller Propositions after Thirty Years', *Journal of Economic Perspectives* 2, pp. 99–120.

Modigliani, F., 1988, 'MM-past, Present, and Future', *Journal of Economic Perspectives* 2, pp. 149–58.

Modigliani, F. and M. Miller, 1958, 'The Cost of Capital, Corporation Finance, and the Theory of Investment', *American Economic Review* 48, pp. 261–97.

Myers, S.C., 1984, 'The Capital Structure Puzzle', *Journal of Finance* 39, pp. 575–92.

Myers, S.C. and N. Majluf, 1984, 'Corporate Financing and Investment Decisions when Firms have Information that Investors do not have', *Journal of Financial Economics* 13, pp. 187–221.

Nakamura, A. and N. Nakamura, 1982, 'On the Firm's Production, Capital Structure and Demand for Debt', *Review Economics and Statistics* 64, pp. 384–93.

Narayanan, M.P., 1987, 'On the Resolution of Agency Problems by Complex Financial Instruments: A Comment', *Journal of Finance* 42, pp. 1083–90.

Narayanan, M.P., 1988, 'Debt versus Equity under Asymmetric Information', *Journal of Financial and Quantitative Analysis* 23, pp. 39–51.

Oxelheim, L. and N. Andrén, 1995, 'On the Use of International Capital Markets', Mimeo, Institute of Economic Research, Lund.

Poitevin, M., 1989, 'Financial Signalling and the "Deep-Pocket" Argument', *Rand Journal of Economics* 20, pp. 26–40.

Ross, S., 1977, 'The Determination of Financial Structure: The Incentive Signaling Approach', *Bell Journal of Economics* 8, pp. 23–40.

Ross, S., 1988, 'Comment on the Modigliani-Miller Propositions', *Journal of Economics* 2, pp. 127–34.

Rutterford, J., 1985, 'An International Perspective on the Capital Structure Puzzle', *Midland Corporate Finance Journal* 3, pp. 60–72.

Sarig, O., 1988, 'Bargaining with a Corporation and the Capital Structure of the Firm', *Working Paper*, Tel Aviv University.

Shleifer, A. and R. Vishny, 1989, 'Management Entrenchment, The Case of Manager-Specific Investment', *Journal of Financial Economics* 25, pp. 123–39.

Smith, C., 1986, 'Investment Banking and the Capital Acquisition Product', *Journal of Financial Economics* 15, pp. 3–15.

Smith, C. and J. Warner, 1979, 'On Financial Contracting: An Analysis of Bond Covenants', *Journal of Financial Economics* 7, pp. 117–61.

Stiglitz, J.E., 1988, 'Why Financial Structure Matters', *Journal of Economic Policy*, pp. 121–6.

Stiglitz, J.E. and A. Weiss, 1981, 'Credit Rationing and Markets with Imperfect Information', *American Economic Review* 71, 393–411.

Taggart, R.A, 1985, 'Secular Patterns in the Financing of U.S. Corporations', in Friedman, B. (ed.), *Corporate Capital Structures in the U.S.*, University of Chicago Press, Chicago.

Taggart, R.A, 1986, 'Have U.S. Corporations Grown Financially Weak?', in Friedman, B.M. (ed.), *Financing Corporate Capital Formation*, University of Chicago Press, Chicago, pp. 13–34.

Titman, S., 1984, 'The Effects of Capital Structure on a Firm's Liquidation Decision', *Journal of Financial Economics* 13, pp. 137–51.

Titman, S. and R. Wessels, 1988, 'The Determinants of Capital Structure Choice', *Journal of Finance*, New York, March, pp. 1–19.

Toy, N., A. Stonehill, L. Remmers, R. Wright and T. Beeckhuisen, 1974, 'A Comparative International Study of Growth, Profitability, and Risk as Determinants of Corporate Debt Ratios in the Manufacturing Sector', *Journal of Financial and Quantitative Analysis* 9, pp. 875–86.

Warner, J., 1977, 'Bankruptcy Costs: Some Evidence', *Journal of Finance* 32, pp. 337–47.

Weiss, L., 1990, 'Bankruptcy Resolution, Direct Costs and Violation of Priority of Claims', *Journal of Financial Economics* 27, 285–317.

Wruck, K., 1990, 'Financial Distress, Reorganization and Organizational Efficiency', *Journal of Financial Economics* 27, pp. 419–44.

Chapter 12

Efficiency of secondary bond markets

Efficiency in the context of capital markets has been defined in many ways. To many researchers it is a matter of how the market participants handle information. According to this view an efficient bond market is a market where, at any one time, prices take all the available information into account. It is assumed that market participants formulate their decisions on the basis of the available information about bond prices and their relevant determinants.[1] But this definition of *informational efficiency*, which in fact contains three important sub-groups associated with the kind of information being considered,[2] only refers to the market's ability to process information so as to be able to use it to the best advantage. Hence, if a market is efficient as regards information, it is not necessarily so in the economists' usual sense of the word, i.e. that it provides services at the lowest cost in terms of the resources employed.

In this chapter we will look at the functioning of secondary markets, and our conception of efficiency will largely coincide with the economists' traditional view. The efficiency of the Nordic markets in terms of information will be analysed later in the book.[3] We will start by discussing the problems relating to the measurement of static efficiency, after which we will analyse the values we actually get for these measures. We will then look at ways of measuring dynamic efficiency, and measures adopted in the Nordic markets will be presented. The chapter concludes with some comments on the evolution of the efficiency of Nordic bond markets.

INDICATORS OF WELL-FUNCTIONING SECONDARY MARKETS

In the introduction to this book some important indicators of a well-functioning secondary bond market were listed, and were classified as indicators of static or dynamic efficiency. They were the following:

- a high degree of transparency;
- a multiplicity of maturities and issuers;

- low spread;
- high and continuous liquidity;
- a high level of adaptability as regards innovations.

In addition to these factors, the absence of political intervention should also be mentioned. It goes without saying that a market which is heavily regulated on the demand and supply sides and as regards prices, is not a 'well-functioning market'. Thus we can say that the first prerequisite of a well-functioning market is that a 'market' does in fact exist, i.e. that demand and supply are free to be balanced by the price. This does not imply a completely deregulated market. On the contrary, a minimum set of regulations is required to guarantee this freedom and the financial structure of the market. At the global level an essential part of this minimum set of regulations for the bond market is provided by the Association of International Bond Dealers (AIBD), while Euroclear and Cedel[4] furnish the market with generally accepted settlement systems.

To what extent, then, do the Nordic secondary bond markets meet the basic 'market' requirement? In earlier chapters we have noted that a secondary market existed in Denmark as far back as the 1970s, that such a market gradually emerged in Sweden after 1983 and that this was followed by a similar development in Norway and Finland. However, according to a stricter definition of the well-functioning market, taking into account all types of controls over domestic or cross-border bond transactions, no such market existed before – at the earliest – 1988 in Denmark, 1989 in Sweden and the early 1990s in Norway and Finland. Since some restrictions in excess of the minimum set mentioned above still obtained in Finland and Norway in the mid-1990s, it can be argued that these markets were still not fully mature at that date.

INDICATORS OF STATIC EFFICIENCY IN THE SECONDARY BOND MARKETS

Another aspect of the financial infrastructure of crucial importance to the functioning of markets, is the way in which trading is organized and information disseminated. Together these factors constitute the *transparency* of a market. In this sense the Nordic secondary markets were not functioning particularly well until the end of the 1980s, when stricter listing systems and rules about the reporting of trading in bonds were introduced. In order to get hold of bearer bonds, governments made registration mandatory.

The dissemination of information gradually improved in all countries after the mid-1980s, as a result of better registration routines and the introduction of electronic trading systems. In addition a new information system, Nordic Value Feed, was introduced in the early 1990s to provide information about the prices and trading volumes registered on all four Nordic stock markets.

The trend towards the decentralization of trade from the stock markets to OTC markets – as a result of improved information technology – had to be accompanied by stricter reporting requirements so that transparency could be maintained. Consequently all the Nordic countries established special institutions for the registration of trading. But at the present time (the mid-1990s), information about trading in Nordic bonds outside the Nordic region still lacks a registration procedure. The registration and reporting requirements on the Nordic bond markets are summarized in Table 12.1.

Another aspect of transparency concerns the listing practices. In 1991 the number of bonds listed on the Nordic stock exchanges was 2,315 (almost 100 per cent of all issues) on the Copenhagen Stock Exchange, 628 (about 50 per cent) at the Helsinki Stock Exchange; 938 (about two-thirds) on the Oslo Stock Exchange and 1,262 (close to 100 percent) on the Stockholm Stock Exchange. On the major global markets, the highest number of listed bonds, 12,679, was noted on the German Stock Exchange; the figures for the New York, Tokyo and Osaka, and London Stock Exchanges were 2,727, 2,546, and 4,606 respectively.[5] In the mid-1990s the pattern of listing differs considerably from country to country, ranging from 100 per cent of all issues in some countries to only a fraction of the total in others. On the largest government bond market, namely the US market, all bonds are at present listed on the New York Stock Exchange, while on the second largest government bond market, namely the Japanese market, only 10-year and 20-year bond issues are listed. However, on both these markets only a small fraction of trade takes place on the exchange. The existence of specialized brokers engaged in marrying the bids and offers of members of the dealing community and an efficient screen price service, ensure price transparency.

The organization of bond trading gives a fair picture of listing practices. Thus, in the early 1990s, the share of the total outstanding stock of bonds that was traded on the stock exchange differed between the Nordic countries. The smallest share was found for the Helsinki Stock Exchange; by far the biggest share of trading took place on the OTC market. Trade in Helibor[6] bank bonds predominated. Five major banks acted as market makers, and the interbank market between these Helibor banks played the most active role in the secondary market. The largest share of exchange trade was found in the Danish market, with almost all trading taking place through the exchange. In the early 1990s listed government bonds and notes predominated, although the outstanding stocks of mortgage bonds were bigger. In Norway many issues were small, and were seldom traded on the secondary market. It was often a case of private sector issues in the range of NOK 100–200 million or issues by municipalities in the region of NOK 200–400 million. Only about 50 issues in Norway exceeded NOK 1 billion, and a few bonds were very frequently traded. Almost four-fifths of the turnover in Norway was registered for mortgage bonds. On the Stockholm Exchange about one-third of listed issues – corresponding to slightly less than half the nominal value of

Table 12.1 Registration and reporting requirements on the Nordic bond markets

	Denmark		Finland		Norway		Sweden	
	Date of introduction	Regulated by:	Date of introduction	Regulated by:	Date of introduction	Regulated by:	Date of introduction	Regulated by:
Registration of bond loans	4 October 1982	The Securities Centre Act of 16 January 1991	1942 1 January 1970 1 January 1994	Act on Bonds[a] Act on Bonds and Debentures and Other Collective Debt Securities Securities Market Act	No obligation to register prior to the introduction of VPS (Verdipapir central) in 1986	Securities Registry Act of 1985	1863	Stock Exchange Regulation
Listing of bond loans	10 November 1983	Order on conditions of the admission of the Securities to Official Listing on the Copenhagen Stock Exchange, No. 418 of 31 May 1991	1 August 1989	Securities Market Act. Stock exchange regulation regulates the trading of shares and debt instruments	January 1981	Issuing control	1863	Stock Exchange Regulation
Reporting of trade in bonds	4 September 1987	Act on Copenhagen Stock Exchange, Consolidated Act No. 26 of 15 January 1982	No regulations		May 1981	The Stock Exchange Act	1985	Voluntary
Withholding tax	No tax		January 1991	Withholding Tax Law	No tax		No tax	
Book-entry securities	January 1983	The Securities Centre Act of 16 January 1991	August 1991	Law on Book Entry Securities	1986	Securities Registry Act of 1985	September 1993	VPC; by agreement

a The first Act on Bonds came into force in 1942, but registration was not made compulsory until the 1970 Act.

the domestic outstanding stock of bonds – were traded actively. Here, as on the Danish market, trading in listed government bonds and notes predominated.

Thus, in the mid-1990s, trading practice differs across the Nordic region, but a common feature is none the less that the most traded bonds all involve some sort of market-maker arrangements which constantly guarantee two-way prices. Usually is it the Nordic central banks that assume this role. The share of total bond trading on the stock exchange has shown a tendency to fall, but the decline in transparency thus caused was more than compensated by improved information systems.

Another characteristic of a well-functioning market is the *multiplicity* of alternative maturities and issuers in the supply of bonds. In this respect the Danish market, with its broad spectrum of maturities and large number of issues, may be regarded as the best. None the less, the Danish variety falls short of the US treasury market with its heavy trading in eight slices – 2-, 3-, 4-, 5-, 7-, 10-, 20- and 30-year bonds. The negative side of the Danish market, relative to the other Nordic markets, is the comparatively small amount of bonds issued direct on the domestic market by the Danish non-financial corporate sector. If we only take the distribution of loans over the various potential groups of issuers as the key criterion, then the Finnish market can be regarded as the best.

A third sign of the efficiency of a secondary bond market is a low *spread*.[7] Differences in this respect reflect inefficiencies, and are an expression of the competitive pressure on the market. Spread varies with maturity, size of deal and type of issue. When markets are to be compared in terms of spread, either the spread of representative species of similar issues or some form of average spread can thus be used. A low representative spread indicates a cost-efficient and competitive market. In the early 1990s, in terms of the representative bid-offer, the Nordic countries fell into two groups: one group consisting of Denmark and Sweden with a low spread approaching the size of the spread on the domestic US bond market, and the other made up of Finland and Norway with an average spread in the range of 5–10 basis points higher, expressed as a percentage of the amount traded.

Another way of measuring the spread is to use the J.P. Morgan Government Bond Index (see Table 12.2), in which three different liquidity sectors for bonds are calculated daily. The largest of the three sectors is classified as *Traded*, which contains a smaller, more liquid classification called *Active*. The third and the most liquid sector lies within the Active sector and is labelled *Benchmark*. This nesting of the sectors means that the data is nested as well, since the bonds included in calculating the Benchmark spread are also included in the computation of the Active spread, and bonds used in calculating the Active spread are also included in computing the Traded sector. According to Table 12.2, the bid–ask spread is higher in Denmark and Sweden than in the major financial centres, i.e. the US, the UK

Table 12.2 J.P. Morgan Government Bond Index (indicative price bid/ask spreads by liquidity)

	December 1990			December 1991			December 1992			December 1993		
	Benchmark	Active	Traded	Benchmark	Active	Traded	Benchmark	Active	Traded	Benchmark	Active	Traded
Australia	0.079	0.096	0.095	0.095	0.091	0.092	0.098	0.094	0.091	0.141	0.136	0.130
Belgium	0.200	0.313	0.356	0.200	0.200	0.275	0.010	0.133	0.183	0.100	0.145	0.154
Canada	0.160	0.207	0.216	0.100	0.124	0.128	0.092	0.103	0.111	0.099	0.100	0.112
Denmark	0.100	0.107	0.122	0.100	0.100	0.105	0.100	0.100	0.106	0.100	0.100	0.100
France	0.105	0.105	0.113	0.072	0.074	0.071	0.117	0.094	0.090	0.098	0.100	0.098
Germany	0.100	0.100	0.110	0.122	0.102	0.109	0.070	0.090	0.092	0.060	0.062	0.065
Italy	0.045	0.066	0.077	0.050	0.050	0.075	0.100	0.148	0.260	0.025	0.081	0.149
Japan	0.030	0.126	0.170	0.030	0.103	0.125	0.030	0.077	0.122	0.065	0.062	0.130
The Netherlands	0.100	0.121	0.163	0.100	0.114	0.123	0.100	0.107	0.108	0.122	0.103	0.106
Spain	0.070	0.105	0.129	0.100	0.102	0.107	0.123	0.135	0.130	0.100	0.100	0.100
Sweden	0.078	0.106	0.106	0.102	0.107	0.107	0.102	0.120	0.120	0.102	0.137	0.137
The United Kindom	0.088	0.098	0.101	0.105	0.104	0.107	0.086	0.085	0.086	0.087	0.084	0.087
The United States	n/a	n/a	n/a	0.044	0.045	0.059	0.016	0.033	0.058	0.027	0.028	0.058

Source: Based on data from J.P. Morgan Securities.

and Japan,[8] but it is well in parity with many other OECD markets.[9]

The fourth and perhaps most significant indication that a secondary bond market is functioning well is a high level of *liquidity*, as measured by the ratio between turnover and stock of bonds.[10] The stability of liquidity also deserves further consideration since it provides information about the continuity of the market and how it might function under different economic conditions.[11] Unfortunately, series of such measures are rarely published even though they provide important signals about a market and its vulnerability. Among other things they signal the degree of risk inherent in the market, i.e. the risk of its breakdown in a situation of general financial distress.

The reason for the difficulty in finding liquidity measures is that they are associated with problems which make it hard to interpret them or to use them in comparisons across markets or over time. Three kinds of problem can be distinguished: one related to the *numerator*, one to the *denominator*, and a third connected with the *process* of putting these two together. In the search for consistency a seemingly endless stack of empirical problems piles up. What we are aiming for here is a way of expressing total market liquidity as the total turnover in all relevant market segments relative to the market value of all outstanding bonds (in these segments).

What, then, is meant by relevant market segments? Some bonds are not intended for extensive trade, which suggests that we could divide the outstanding stock of bonds into two parts – one *tradable* and one *non-tradable* – and then claim that the liquidity of the tradable part as representative of the liquidity of the market. The tradable part also acts as a price-setter for the other part of the market, which consists of small issues, predominantly from private issuers. However, as soon as we introduce the concept of the relevant market segment, as opposed to the total market, we introduce discretion and face the problem of choosing an appropriate way of splitting the market in a way that allows for comparisons over time as well as across countries. Bearing this in mind, we can continue our review of the statistical problems.

Let us start with problems connected with the denominator and the market valuation of a stock of bonds corresponding to the definition above. The first task is to define the set of bonds appropriate for consideration. This brings us to the problem of defining the total set of outstanding loans, since not all bonds are registered. Assume that we solve the problem of identifying all missing non-registered loans by defining our population as consisting of registered bonds only. We then face the question of whether we should limit the relevant set to include listed bonds only, since in some markets information is only published for this set. Further, in some countries the stock markets only provide information about top lists. A market's listing praxis, i.e. the listing requirements and the scope of the listing are important, and they add further problems to our search for consistency. Once we have decided which definition of stock to use, we face the problem of finding the market valuation of that stock. However, regardless of which definition we use, a good proxy for market valuation in the case of bonds is the nominal value of the outstanding stock of bonds.[12]

The next category of empirical problems is connected with the numerator and the way in which turnover has been reported. One big worry concerns double-counting. For the user of international sources of statistics this can be a problem when it comes to international comparisons. Another dilemma concerns the transactions that are included in the turnover figures. Many sources give turnover data that includes both spot and forward transactions, while others include spot transactions only.[13] Unfortunately this is not generally stressed sufficiently in the presentation of international turnover data. And even when it is, it is still difficult to transform the data in order to achieve comparability. As well as the problem of the actual content of information, there is also the problem of differences in reporting require-ments. Some countries impose reporting requirements on all financial institutions which deal in bonds, while others rely on voluntary reporting. The introduction of improved systems for the registration and reporting of trading activities could distort comparisons over time.

Finally, there is the problem of finding a correspondence between numerator and denominator, i.e. matching a turnover figure for the numer-ator with the stock of bonds used in the denominator. Let us now face all the problems involved in measuring liquidity, by comparing the liquidity of the Nordic bond markets.

Table 12.3 shows that turnover of bonds on the Nordic stock exchanges has increased substantially since the beginning of the 1970s. However, a large part of the increase reflects the development of listing and better routines for reporting bond trading. This applies to the Danish increase in 1988, the Norwegian increase in 1987 and the dramatic Swedish upturn in 1985. Since that year, for instance, the figures for the Stockholm Stock Exchange also include dealing in government and mortgage bonds which takes place outside the Stockholm Stock Exchange but is reported to the exchange by brokerage firms. This change in the registration arrangements means that comparisons between pre- and post-1985 are not very relevant, and it also naturally reduces the historical compatibility between the Nordic countries. Compar-isons between Swedish and Finnish figures in particular become skewed, since the reported turnover on the Finnish Stock Exchange is just a small fraction of the total turnover on the domestic Finnish bond market, as the table shows.

The greatest problems are found in Finland. On 1 August 1992 a primary dealer system was introduced to improve the liquidity and transparency of the secondary market.[14] The main reason for this was the budget deficit which had started to grow in 1991. However, the substantial increase in 1992 and 1993 was followed by a very low figure for 1994 (FIM 2.1 billion). But

Table 12.3 Annual reported bond turnover, 1971–94 (billions of local currency units, nominal values)

	Denmark (DKK)	Finland (FIM)		Norway (NOK)	Sweden[a] (SEK)
	Stock Exchange	Stock Exchange	OTC[b]	Stock Exchange	Stock Exchange
1971	n/a	0.02		1.7	0.2
1972	n/a	0.42		2.1	0.3
1973	n/a	0.03		1.9	0.4
1974	n/a	0.02		2.8	0.5
1975	n/a	0.02		4.5	0.8
1976	n/a	0.02		4.2	1.1
1977	n/a	0.06		6.0	1.7
1978	n/a	0.15		3.0	3.1
1979	n/a	0.25		3.0	5.0
1980	22.2	0.34		8.8	9.4
1981	24.3	1.1		7.5	6.7
1982	25.8	2.4		4.7	7.5
1983	60.0	2.4		5.8	10.3
1984	54.0	5.0		20.4	10.0[c]
1985	78.8	9.0		75.9	1,250.0[d]
1986	102.1	6.5		78.6	1,196.2
1987	102.3	4.6		129.8	1,364.5
1988	988.2[e]	5.7		99.1	1,007.5
1989	1,801.1	7.4	16.2	180.9[f]	813.7[g]
1990	1,968.3	4.6	11.5	296.8	1,034.9
1991	2,189.4	1.3	32.5	424.5	1,874.3
1992	4,984.1	15.4	76.8 (36.3)	501.5	2,958.0
1993	11,259.8	60.1	287.2 (256.1)	1,583.7	5,330.2
1994	6,577.0[h]	2.1	522.6 (500.6)	1,529.6	7,757.6

[a] Including premium bonds.
[b] Consists of reported transactions in all Finnish markka-denominated bonds (bank bonds, corporate bonds and government bonds). Figures in parenthesis show the registered turnover for government benchmark bonds.
[c] Up to 1984 predominantly premium bonds (SEK 160 million interest-bearing bonds).
[d] A new registration system was introduced in 1985/86.
[e] An electronic trading system was introduced in September 1987 with limited availability. By 1988 stockbroker companies could trade on the system from their own offices.
[f] An electronic trading system, decentralized to the brokers' offices, was introduced.
[g] An electronic trading system called SAX (Stockholm Automated Exchange) was introduced.
[h] A new registration system. Figure including repurchase agreements is DKK 16,207.1 billion.

Sources: Based on data from Copenhagen Stock Exchange, *Database*; Helsinki Stock Exchange, *Database*; Bank of Finland, *Financial Markets, Statistical Review*, various issues; Oslo Stock Exchange, *Database*; and Stockholm Stock Exchange, *Annual report*, various issues.

the drop is deceptive. It was, rather, that an attempt to bring bond trading into the stock exchange had failed. Since there were no regulations about reporting the trade in bonds, Finnish brokers simply stopped reporting their trade to the stock exchange. However, the Bank of Finland and the Primary Dealers (PDs) then agreed that the PDs should report their transactions in markka-denominated bonds (including government benchmark bonds). Table 12.3 shows that despite the fall on the stock exchange, the trade in bonds increased noticeably at the beginning of the 1990s, primarily as a result of the growing budget deficit.

Table 12.3 also reveals some interesting features regarding the stability of turnover. In Norway and Sweden turnover fell in 1988, while in Denmark in particular, and to some extent in Finland, it continued to rise in nominal values. When the Swedish turnover is examined more closely, for instance, it can be seen that the daily turnover in government securities fell dramatically between 1987 and mid-1990: between 1987 and 1989 it fell by as much as 40 per cent. The reason for the accelerated drop in 1989 was that a turnover tax on interest-bearing securities was introduced that year. The tax brought the forward market in standardized interest contracts more or less to a standstill. After the tax was abolished in 1990, the market recovered. A dramatic increase then occurred in 1991, when the turnover was more than twice as high as in 1989. Allowing for all the statistical problems, Table 12.4 does suggest that in relative terms the turnover on the Nordic bond markets also increased as a share of GDP.

As we have noted liquidity measures express the risk of the non-completion of a transaction at a reasonable price, due to problems connected with the market rather than to problems connected with the loan as such. Hence, to be able to compare markets, we need measures of liquidity that are comparable across countries. Such measures are also required for assessing whether Nordic secondary markets meet international standards. Table 12.5 gives liquidity measures for the Nordic countries and for four major national bond markets. None of the measurement problems mentioned above

Table 12.4 Annual bond turnover on the Nordic stock exchanges (percentage of GDP)

Country	1975	1980	1985	1990	1993
Denmark	n/a	6	13	246	1,284
Finland	0	0	3	1	13
Norway	3	3	15	45	216
Sweden	0	2	138	76	368

Sources: Based on data from Copenhagen Stock Exchange, *Database*, Helsinki Stock Exchange, *Database*, Oslo Stock Exchange, *Database*; Stockholm Stock Exchange, *Annual Report*, various issues; Nordic Statistical Secretariat, *Yearbook of Nordic Statistics*, various issues; OECD, *National Accounts*, Vol. 1, 1994.

have disappeared, which means that the figures must be interpreted with caution. Thus we must remember that substantial jumps in the series can often be explained by changes in the procedures for registration, listing or reporting, while downturns can be explained by the emergence of OTC markets with no equivalent obligation as regards reporting. A conclusion

Table 12.5 Liquidity of national bond markets[a] (annual turnover as a percentage of outstanding stock at par value)

Country	1975	1980	1985	1990
Denmark[b]	n/a	5	8	153
Finland[c]	0	2	15	33
Norway[d]	36	21	60	107
Sweden[e]	0	3	188	104
Germany[f]	n/a	n/a	21	62
Japan[g]	n/a	60	561	417
United Kingdom[h]	192	214	218	769
United States[i]	286	438	1,087	1,202

[a] Turnover in derivatives not included.
[b] Annual turnover on the Copenhagen Stock Exchange as a percentage of outstanding stock of listed bonds. Traded on the exchange are government, mortgage, special institution, convertible, index-linked and foreign bonds.
[c] Annual turnover on the Helsinki Stock Exchange and over the counter as a percentage of outstanding stock of listed bonds.
[d] Annual turnover registered on the Oslo Stock Exchange as a percentage of outstanding stock of listed bonds. Traded on the exchange are government, government-guaranteed, government premium, municipality/county guaranteed, bank, insurance, mortgage bank, industrial and foreign bonds.
[e] Annual turnover on the Stockholm Stock Exchange as a percentage of outstanding stock of listed bonds. Traded on the exchange are government, government premium, mortgage, municipality, bank, industry, utility, ship, convertible and foreign bonds.
[f] Annual turnover on the German Stock Exchanges as a percentage of outstanding stock of listed bonds.
[g] Annual turnover in public and corporate bonds as a percentage of outstanding stock of bonds in Japan, where bonds held by government agencies, Bank of Japan, Postal Annuity, Postal Life Insurance and Trust Fund Bureau are excluded.
[h] Annual turnover of gilt-edged securities on stock exchanges as a percentage of outstanding stock of gilts. Note that the figures include gilts with maturities of less than one year.
[i] Annual turnover of US Treasury notes and bonds as a percentage of outstanding stock of US treasury notes and bonds.

Sources: Based on data from Copenhagen Stock Exchange, *Database*, and *Annual Report*; Central Statistical Bureau of Denmark, *Statistical Yearbook*, various issues; Helsinki Stock Exchange, *Database*; Central Statistical Bureau of Finland, *Financial Market Statistics*, various issues; Oslo Stock Exchange, *Database* and *Annual Report*; Central Statistical Bureau of Norway, *Credit Market Statistics* and *Bank- og Kredittstatistikk*, various issues; Stockholm Stock Exchange, *Annual Report*, various issues; Central Statistical Bureau of Sweden, *Database*; BIS (1992b); German Stock Exchange, *Database*; Central Statistical Office of UK, *Financial Statistics*, various issues; US Government, *Economic Report of the President*, 1992; Federal Reserve, *Federal Reserve Bulletin*, various issues; NYSE (1991); FIBV (1991); and own estimates.

based on our difficulty in finding good measures of liquidity, is that in the early 1990s most if not all markets can be said to possess a less than perfect transparency.

Table 12.5 indicates that historically the Nordic markets have had a level of liquidity significantly lower than that of the major international markets. In 1990 stocks on the Nordic markets were sold about once a year, while US stock was sold twelve times and UK stock eight. Of the Nordic countries Denmark had the most liquid market. The liquidity measures for Finland presented in the table are based on the sum of the turnover on the exchange and on the OTC market. In 1990 turnover on the stock exchange amounted to FIM 4.6 billion, while on the OTC market it was 11.5. However, since there was no reporting requirement, the OTC turnover may have been underestimated. In a similar vein, to demonstrate the vulnerability of the liquidity measures to differences in coverage, we can take an example from the Swedish market. If only trading in bonds covered by the daily list (i.e. the list of the most traded bonds) is included, then the liquidity measure for 1990 would have been a little over twice the stock.

Much of the same problems arise in connection with our international figures. If we study the liquidity of the New York Stock Exchange alone, for instance, we would get a very low liquidity measure, which in turn would imply that only a small fraction of the stock of US treasury notes and bonds is traded a year. The same observation can be made regarding the Japanese market, where about 95 per cent of the turnover is accounted for by large-lot OTC trading between banks and securities houses. When it comes to inconsistencies over time, not all jumps – despite warnings above – indicate the problems we have noted. For instance, the jump in the US measure from 1980 to 1985 was caused by efforts on the part of the US treasury to stimulate the market in 1984, among other things by the abolition of withholding tax. Similarly the dramatic increase in the liquidity of the Japanese market between 1980 and 1985 has its explanation: from 1984 the banks were permitted to act as dealers in the OTC market.

Gallant (1988) provides estimates of the liquidity of the non-Nordic markets for 1986. He estimates the liquidity of the German, Japanese, UK and US domestic bond markets at 7, 5, 9 and 12 times the stock of bonds respectively. When Gallant's figures are compared with those in Table 12.5, a large discrepancy appears between the two measures for the German market. However, we would have found a similar value if we had measured the liquidity of Bundesrepublikanleihe only. Further, following the liberal-izations of 1984-86, the German market was hit by a 10 per cent withholding tax during 1988 and 1989. As regards the deviation between Gallant's figure and ours for the UK market, a plausible explanation could be found in the Big Bang of 1986, which quadrupled turnover in the UK.

INDICATORS OF DYNAMIC EFFICIENCY IN THE SECONDARY BOND MARKETS

A dynamic market is assumed here to be a market which keeps in the forefront as regards financial innovations. According to the strictest definition such a market should respond to all imaginable demands by developing instruments for all types of risk and return, sliced in every possible way. Thus the relative degree of a market's dynamism is expressed by the time it takes for the market to meet these demands. However, to list all imaginable demands is not practicable, so we will adopt a modified measure here, based on the ability of a particular market to catch up with a benchmark market. Since this catch-up time differs for different kinds of innovation in a national market, the degree of dynamism may be expressed as an average of the lag times in that particular market. If one market has introduced innovations in all instruments, it will score zero in the 'lag' measure and will constitute the most efficient market in terms of dynamism. However, if another market is able to adopt the innovations at the very moment they are launched, it will be as efficient as the innovating market according the same measure. The concept of dynamic efficiency is thus closely related to informational efficiency.

A measure of the dynamic efficiency of a particular market can be expressed in two ways: as a measure of the process of adaptability *per se* or in terms of efficiency at a given point in time. The benchmark set of innovations can consist of all innovations known at the time of the comparison, or all imaginable innovations. As a measure of the historical degree of adaptability of a market we will use the average time a particular market needs to catch up with the market which first offered the instrument. A drawback of this approach, however, is that such an average says nothing about *when* the adoption of a particular innovation came about. The measure is of more historical than practical interest.

The other measure of dynamism considered here expresses the degree to which a particular market at a given point in time is still lagging behind an ideal (perfectly efficient) market in which all the relevant instruments have already been introduced. In the following exposition we will refer to the two types of measure as *measures of adaptability* and *measures of dynamic efficiency.*

In applying the different measures to the bond market we will consider three kinds of innovation: innovations connected with the issue of bonds, i.e. debt instruments such as floating rate bonds and zero coupon bonds; debt-equity hybrid instruments such as convertible bonds and bonds with warrants; and, finally, derivatives based on bonds such as futures and options.

The first appearance of different bond innovations on the global market

To be able to measure the adaptability and dynamic efficiency we have to identify the historical dates at which various bond instruments were first offered globally. This sounds like a fairly simple task, until one consults the literature in the field. Unfortunately, there appears to be no good description of the history of financial innovations. Thus, the task of finding a good benchmark set of the dates at which different innovations first appeared on a market, turns into the huge and cumbersome job of combining many separate sources which often provide conflicting figures. Although it is sometimes easy to see how the seemingly inconsistent timetables have arisen, I have often had to contact the original innovators to verify my conclusions.

Apart from direct errors or inconsistencies, the literature often gives different dates for the same instrument – dates reflecting different definitions. Without quoting specific instances one researcher may claim that an instrument appeared on the world market for the first time on a particular date, by which is meant the date when the instrument appeared on the OTC market, while another researcher may refer to the date on which the instrument was first offered on the stock exchange – in both cases without making the distinction explicit. Or some researchers may use the date when an instrument first appeared on the Euromarket, while others take the date it first appeared on a national market. Since the measurement of dynamic efficiency or adaptability depends on an appropriate measure of the dates when different instruments were introduced, it could be useful to look at these dates as applying to some major types of bond and bond-related innovations. Here follows a frame of reference regarding the dates when relevant innovations were marketed for the first time on a stock exchange or in over-the-counter trading.

Special debt instruments

Floating rate notes (FRN) are issued in many varieties. Floating rate notes are debt instruments with a coupon that changes periodically according to some predetermined interest rate benchmark, like LIBOR, STIBOR, etc. Floating rate notes in Eurodollars were introduced on the Euromarkets in May 1970 with an issue by Ente Nazionale per L'Energia Electtrica (ENEL), an Italian utility company (Walmsley 1991). A perpetual floater was first introduced by the National Westminster Bank in 1984, followed by Belgium with issues of USD 300 million, by Sweden with USD 750 million, and by Denmark with issues of USD 600 million. The first issue of a variable-spread FRN was made by the Nordic Investment Bank in December 1984. In February 1985 the minimax FRN was introduced with an issue by Denmark (Walmsley 1991). The growth of the FRN market between 1983 and 1986 can be largely attributed to the investment of Japanese funds in the Euromarkets.

Variable rate notes (VRN) have a coupon which is allowed to vary according to some predetermined formula. The VRN differs from the FRN in that conventional FRNs carry coupons fixed at a predetermined spread over an index rate. VRNs, in contrast, carry coupons whose spread above and below such an interest rate is refixed for each coupon period. The first VRN was issued on 21 July 1988 by Lloyd's Bank to revive the flagging interest in the FRN market. Two structures exist for VRN – the *Warburg structure* and the *Merill Lynch rate setting mechanism*. The Warburg structure uses an auction process at the start of each period to set the spread over the index rate, and the Merill Lynch rate setting mechanism implies an agreement, with clearly defined procedures in the event of failure to reach an agreement (Sarwal 1989). The first VRN was handled through Merill Lynch. In 1991 the Swedish mortgage institution Spintab became the first issuer of a Euroyen variable rate note.

Zero coupon bonds are single-payment long-term securities which do not call for periodic interest payments. These bonds are sold at a discount from par, and the investor's entire return is realized at maturity. In June 1966 the first Eurobond zero coupon was issued by the BP Tanker Company Limited. The first public offering of a domestic (USA) corporate zero coupon bond was made by the J.C. Penney Company Inc. in May 1981. In February 1990 the Bankers' Trust issued a zero coupon Eurobond on behalf of one of its customers, with an attached warrant on a basket of five stock indexes.

Junk bonds are corporate bonds carrying a high interest rate. They are issued in the domestic capital market by companies with low or no credit ratings, i.e. below Baa by Moodys and below BBB by S&P. This instrument was introduced in 1909 by John Moody. It accounted for 17 per cent of all funds raised through public US corporate debt issues between 1909 and 1943.[15] The market began to revive in 1977 when the banking firm Drexell Burnham Lambert started to underwrite new junk bonds.

The first *Eurobond* issue was issued by the Autostrada, the concessionaire and operator of toll motorways in Italy, in July 1963. There is some argument as to which was in fact the first Eurobond issue. Phillips, for example, issued US dollar bonds in the Netherlands in 1949 and 1951. In 1961 the Portuguese entity SACOR issued the equivalent of USD 5 million in seventeen-year bonds denominated in European Units of Account.[16] In 1963 the first Euro-Deutchmark bond issue and the first (and so far the only) Euro-Swiss franc bond issue also appeared. Norway made history in May 1964 by launching the first government bond in the form of a USD 25 million twenty-year bond. Norway was also first among the Nordic countries with an international issue in their own currency in 1979. Issues in other Nordic currencies had appeared by the mid-1980s. In March 1985 the first Danish Eurokroner bond was issued, while the first Swedish Eurokronor bond was issued in 1988 by the World Bank.[17]

The Fixed-rate Eurodollar bond market was reopened on 24 March 1980 with the announcement of a USD 500 million issue by Sweden. In June 1986 the Bull/Bear Bonds market was pioneered by Swedish Export Credit, with an issue for 20 billion yen. Denmark issued a five-year Bull/Bear bond loan in French francs in October 1986 (Walmsley 1991).

Index-linked bonds are bonds linked to inflation, stock prices, gold prices or something similar. During the 1980s the use of debt instruments linked to economic variables increased significantly. The first issue of a commodity-linked bond was for SACOR in 1961. The first silver-indexed issue – USD 25 million – was made by the Sunshine Mining Co. in April 1980. The first gold-index-linked bond was issued in February 1981 by Refinement. Earlier, the Mexican government had issued a bond linked to the oil price.[18]

Debt-equity hybrid instruments

Convertible bonds are corporate bonds which give the investor the right, but not the obligation, to convert the bond into another security, usually shares, at a price fixed on issue. Convertible securities can be traced back to the eighteenth century.[19] The first Euro convertible debenture was introduced at the end of 1963 by an international syndicate consisting of Canon Cameras, Takeda Chemical and Teijin.

An *equity warrant bond* entitles the warrant owner to buy the common stock of the issuer at a prespecified price. Normally the holder has the right to make the purchase at any time before or on a specified expiry date. In June 1964 the Istituto per la Ricostruzione Industriale (IRI) made the first Eurobond issue with warrants attached for shares in its subsidiary Società Finanziaria Siderurgica (FINSIDER). Warrants have been traded on the New York Stock Exchange (NYSE) since 13 April 1970 (NYSE 1991). A debt warrant permits the warrant owner to buy additional bonds from the issuer at the same price and yield as the host bond. A currency warrant entitles the warrant owner to exchange one currency for another at a fixed exchange rate. The first currency exchange warrants were issued by General Electric Credit in June 1987.

The *participating bond* is an instrument whereby the investor receives a return linked to the profitability of the issuing company. In Norway these bonds have been used by the savings banks to raise quasi-capital by issuing Primary Capital Certificates (PCC), as for example the issue by 'Spare-banken Moere' in February 1989 of NOK 100 million worth of PCCs, with a yield linked to the bank's profitability (Walmsley 1991).

Derivatives

Derivatives may be used for speculative as well as risk-covering purposes. The instruments are of two types. One is the standardized financial instrument traded on exchanges. The second is the individually created hedging product produced by intermediaries such as investment and commercial banks, i.e. OTC products. Prior to 1973, when the Chicago Board Options Exchange opened, all options were OTC instruments. OTC products are the main instrument used in hedging by corporations and others. In the case of derivatives I have looked for the first occasion on which a particular solution was used, regardless of whether it applied to bonds or money market instruments. The 'innovation' is embodied in the technical solution.

The first *interest rate future* was introduced in October 1975, but the first really successful interest rate futures contract was the 91-day Treasury Bill contract introduced by the International Monetary Market (IMM), which is a part of the Chicago Mercantile Exchange (CME), in January 1976.[20] Futures contracts are standardized contracts as regards size and delivery dates. In April 1989 the Marche à Terme d'Instruments Financiers (MATIF) and the London International Financial Future Exchange (LIFFE) introduced futures contracts on three-month Euro-Deutchmark interest rates (IMF 1991).

Interest rate options can be written on cash instruments or futures. The first exchange-traded interest rate option was introduced in 1980 on the European Options Exchange in Amsterdam (Sarwal 1989). It was based on Dutch guilder bonds. The OTC market in interest rate options has grown less vigorously than the markets for interest rate swaps and forward rate agreements.

An *interest rate swap* (IRS) involves the exchange of liabilities based on two different interest rates. The three main types of swap are *coupon swaps* (fixed rate to floating rate in the same currency), *basis swaps* (one floating rate index to another floating rate index), and *cross-currency interest rate swaps* (fixed rate in one currency to floating rate in another). The first interest rate swap was undertaken in 1981 between Citibank and Continental Illinois (Das, 1989). Liquidity in the IRS market, particularly in the short-term segment, is said to be very high. Banks use short-term IRSs principally to manage interest rate risk in their lending and funding portfolios. In 1985 the International Swap Dealers' Association and the British Bankers' Association produced a set of standardized dealing terms and documentation for interest rate swaps.

There are four innovations which borrowers and investors can use to protect themselves against adverse foreign exchange rate movements. These are:

- *currency forwards*;
- *currency futures contracts*;
- *currency option contracts*;
- *currency swaps*.

A *forward contract* is a private agreement between two parties. Forward contracts are not standardized, and the customer has to wait for the delivery date to realize the profit or loss on the position. The forward exchange market, including both outright forward and swap activities, is still very large and its liquidity is said to have remained deep. In the 1990s forwards have been superseded by instruments providing more efficient hedging and position-taking potential.

In May 1972 CME introduced *currency futures*, essentially as an alternative to the forward foreign exchange contract. A currency futures contract is a financial futures contract to buy or sell a standard amount of a specific currency. Listed currency futures and currency options are increasingly used to manage direct foreign exchange exposures. Futures contracts have succeeded because they are standardized.

Foreign currency options include two types: options on the foreign currency, and future options. The first currency options were introduced in Amsterdam in 1978. Options on foreign currencies in the USA have been traded on the Philadelphia Exchange since 1982. The OTC market for foreign currency options is the fastest growing segment of the foreign exchange market.

A currency swap is the exchange of a liability in one currency for a liability in another currency. The first year when a currency swap was undertaken – between Bos Kalis Westminister (a Dutch company) and ICI Finance (a British company) – was 1976.[21] However, the date most frequently cited as the real opening of the swap market is August 1981, when the classical currency swap between IBM and the World Bank took place.[22] A special variant known as the *parallel loan* was used during the 1960s and early 1970s. The longer-term currency swap market is said to be expanding, but up to the mid-1990s has been growing more slowly than other segments of the swap market. Currency and interest rate swaps were developed in the 1980s from the earlier practice of parallel back-to-back loans used to circumvent exchange-control regulations.

Forward rate agreements (FRA) are contracts which guarantee a client the borrowing or lending interest rate at a future time. FRAs were first introduced in the UK in late 1983 (Sarwal 1989). FRAs have become a very popular instrument for managing interest rate risk associated with foreign currency funding. The FRA market is generally believed to be the second largest segment, and in recent years one of the fastest-growing segments, of the OTC interest rate product market. FRAs are in essence an OTC interest rate futures contract.

Compared with listed futures, FRAs overcome the problems of contract specificity, margin calls, fixed forward dates, and the need to set up accounts and clearing facilities at exchanges (BIS 1992a). They also exist in standardized form.

The above description gives us a more precise set of benchmark dates to use in analysing adaptability and dynamic efficiency. Table 12.6 provides a summary of the dates. The different dates reflect the point

Table 12.6 Benchmark dates for innovations in the global market

Instrument	Year of first issue	Borrower (market)	Euro/country
Special debt instruments			
Floating rate notes (and bonds)	1970	ENEL	Euro
Variable Rate Notes	1988	Lloyd's Bank	UK
Zero coupon bonds	1981 (1966)	J.C. Penney (BP Tanker Company Lim.)	USA (Euro)
Junk bonds	1977 (1909)	Drexell Burnham Lambert (J. Moody)	USA
Eurobonds	1963	Autostrada	Euro
Index-linked bonds	1961	SACOR	Pre-Euro
Debt/equity hybrid instruments			
Convertible bonds	Eighteenth century		
Bonds with warrants	1964	IRI	Euro
Equity warrant bonds	1970	AT&T	NYSE
Derivatives			
Interest rate futures	1975	Chicago Commodity Exchanges	USA
Interest rate options	1980	European Options Exchange in Amsterdam	Netherlands
Interest rate swaps	1981	Citibanks and Continental Illinois	USA
Currency futures contracts	1972	Chicago Mercantile Exchange	USA
Currency options contracts	1978	Amsterdam	Netherlands
Currency swaps	1976	Bos Kalis Westminister v. ICI Finance	Netherlands/UK
FRAs	1983	UK	UK

in time when a particular bond or bond-related instrument was first offered publicly.

Introduction of different bonds and derivatives on the Nordic markets

The problems involved in finding the date when a particular innovation was first offered on the global bond markets are just as severe when it comes to Nordic markets. Generally speaking, moreover, the implementation of the various instruments has occurred fairly recently, which also means that it belongs to the era of the liberalization of the financial markets and the relaxation in registration and reporting requirements. However, to provide as comprehensive a picture as possible of the Nordic history of financial innovations, Table 12.7 lists more than one date for one and the same event; the first public offer of a particular financial instrument. The benchmark dates used in the calculations of adaptability and dynamic efficiency are the dates when the different innovations were made available for the first time on the different Nordic national markets.

At the end of 1992 all the Nordic countries in this study had options and futures markets. However, only a few of them dealt with instruments based on bonds. In Table 12.7, options and futures which were first offered outside the stock markets are registered in parentheses, indicating that it was a question of over-the-counter offers. In our measures of adaptability and dynamic efficiency we will use the earlier date of the two given for one and the same instrument.

The column 'Permitted from' in Table 12.7 gives the dates when a particular instrument became explicitly free to be marketed on the domestic stock exchange or a similar exchange. For a fairly short period these deregulations resulted in a 'grey zone', showing that new emerging market-places were not yet equated with traditional stock markets, and that they were thus allowed to offer innovations forbidden to the stock market. However, these market-places are regarded here as equivalent to the stock market.

Measures of the adaptability and dynamic efficiency of the Nordic bond markets

We have now sought to identify the dates when different bond innovations first appeared on the global markets and when these innovations were first marketed in the Nordic countries. By combining these two sets of information we can calculate measures of the adaptability and dynamic efficiency of the Nordic bond markets over time. Tables 12.8 and 12.9 demonstrate the basis of our calculations.

The next step in constructing a measure of the adaptability of the Nordic markets is to decide how to combine the observations in Table 12.8 into a single measure for each market, such that the measure describes the dynamic

Table 12.7 Dates of introduction of different bonds and bond-based derivatives on the Nordic exchanges (dates in parentheses show the date of introduction on the over-the-counter market, if it occurs prior to stock exchange introduction[a])

Instrument	Denmark		Finland		Norway		Sweden	
	Permitted from	First offered on the domestic market	Permitted from	First offered on the domestic market	Permitted from	First offered on the domestic market	Permitted from	First offered on the domestic market
Floating rate notes	1984	1984	1986	1988 (1986)		1991	1988[b]	1986
Variable rate notes		n.y.o.		n.y.o.		n.y.o.		1988
Zero coupon bonds		n.y.o.	1985	1991 (1986–87)	not allowed	n.y.o.[c]	1991	1991
Junk bonds		n.y.o.	not allowed	n.y.o.		n.y.o.		n.y.o.
Index-linked bonds	1982	1982	not allowed	n.y.o.[d]		1992	1991	1992 (1991)
Convertible bonds	1974	1974	1978	1982	1980	1980		1968
Bonds with warrants	1978	1990 (1985)	1978	1987 (1986)	1980	1984		1982 (1981)
Interest rate futures and forwards	1988	1988 (1985)	1988	n.y.o.[e] (1987)	1993	1993 (1985)		1988 (1984)
Interest rate options	1988	1988 (1986)		n.y.o. (1986)	1993	n.y.o. (1985)		1986
Interest rate swaps		n.y.o. (1988)		n.y.o. (1990)		n.y.o. (1983)		1988 (1986)
FRAs		n.y.o. (1988)		n.y.o. (1987)		n.y.o. (1987)		1988 (1987)

[a] Stock exchange or similar market-place.
[b] Intermediary institutes allowed to issue FRN loans.
[c] At the end of 1992, still regulated by the issuing controls (Emisjonsforskriften).
[d] At the end of 1992, still regulated by the 1985 Law on Indexation.
[e] Offered in January 1994.
Note: n.y.o. = not yet offered as of the end of 1992.

Table 12.8 The size of Nordic lags in adopting major international bond innovations (lags in years[a])

Instrument	Date of first issue/offer	Denmark	Finland	Norway	Sweden
Floating rate bonds	1970	14	16	21	16
Variable rate notes	1988	n.y.o.	n.y.o.	n.y.o.	0
Zero coupon bonds	1981	10	5	n.y.o.	10
Junk bonds	1977	n.y.o.	n.y.o.	n.y.o.	n.y.o.
Index-linked bonds	1961	21	n.y.o.	31	30
Convertible bonds	1946[b]	28	36	34	22
Bonds with warrants	1964	19	22	20	18
Interest rate options	1980	5	7	5	4
Interest rate futures	1975	11	11	10	11
Interest rate swaps	1981	7	9	2	5
FRAs	1983	5	4	4	4

[a] Calculated as the difference between the date when the bond-based instruments was first offered domestically (on the stock exchange or OTC), minus the date the instrument was first publicly offered.
[b] Post-war records.

Note: n.y.o. = not yet offered.

power of that particular market as well as lending itself to international comparisons. A possible measure could be an arithmetic mean based on the figures in the table, but this would entail giving the same weight to adaptability at the beginning of the 1990s as to adaptability during the 1970s. One solution would be to use exponentially decreasing weights, on the grounds that recent observations should have higher weights since they are more representative of the current degree of the adaptability of a particular market. Another rather similar alternative would be to shorten the period on which the calculation is based, i.e. the measure should be based on five- to ten-year periods only.

Tables like Table 12.8 thus serve to highlight the development of adaptability over time, while to meet decision-orientated demands it is necessary to develop a single statistical measure. An average measure calculated for a recent period meets these demands. We also have to solve the problem of handling instruments traded on the global market but not yet offered in one or more of the Nordic countries. Examples are junk bonds, not yet offered in any of the Nordic countries, or variable rate notes, still not offered in some of them. My way of solving this problem (see Table 12.10) is to assume that all innovations will be offered 'tomorrow'. The averages measured in this way may thus exaggerate the degree of adaptability.

Let us turn next to measuring the dynamic efficiency of the individual Nordic national bond markets at the beginning of the 1990s. In calculating this measure, a regulation prohibiting the use of a particular instrument is

Table 12.9 The lag in the dissemination of innovations to the Nordic national bond markets in 1992 (lags in years)

Instrument	Date of first issue	Denmark	Finland	Norway	Sweden
Floating rate bonds	1970	0	0	0	0
Variable rate notes	1988	4	4	4	0
Zero coupon bonds	1966	0	0	26*	0
Junk bonds	1977	15	15	15	15
Index-linked bonds	1961	0	31*	0	0
Convertible bonds	1946[a]	0	0	0	0
Bonds with warrants	1964	0	0	0	0
Interest rate futures	1975	0	0	0	0
Interest rate options	1980	0	0	0	0
Interest rate swaps	1981	0	0	0	0
FRAs	1983	0	0	0	0

[a] Post-war records.

Note: For example, the figure '15' for junk bonds indicates that junk bonds were not being offered on the Nordic national bond markets, despite the fact that they had appeared on the global market as far back as 1909. However, here we have used 1977 – the year when Drexell Burnham started to underwrite new junk bonds and the market revived – as the benchmark date. A '0' means that the instrument is offered on the domestic market. The * indicates that an instrument was not yet allowed in 1992, as in the case of zero coupon bonds in Norway and index-linked bonds in Finland.

treated as a dynamic inefficiency. Thus the measure should not be interpreted exclusively as an expression of the incompetence exclusively of financial engineers. The measures are presented in Table 12.9. An asterisk indicates that the instrument was still not allowed on the market at the end of 1992. The higher the measure, the lower the dynamic efficiency. Forty-six is the highest potential individual value, indicating that convertible bonds were not yet available in 1992. The lowest value is 0, indicating that a financial innovation was offered on that particular domestic market.

As can be seen in Table 12.10, over the 1960–1980 period as a whole, the Danish market was the most adaptive. The average lag before the Danish market introduced foreign innovations was about eleven years, as compared to six years for foreign innovations that appeared in the 1980s. The Danish bond market exhibited the highest degree of adaptability for the period 1960–70, while the Swedish market assumed that position during the 1980s.

The results presented in Table 12.10 are intuitively correct and convincing.[23] The Swedish bond market exhibits the highest degree of adaptability in the 1980s. The Danish and Finnish bond markets come next, while the Norwegian markets exhibit much less adaptability.

Table 12.10 shows that the Swedish market is also characterized by the highest dynamic efficiency. Perhaps this is not surprising, since in compar-

Table 12.10 Measures of adaptability and dynamic efficiency on the Nordic bond
markets, 1992

Adaptability	Denmark	Finland	Norway	Sweden
1960–1980	11.1	12.4	13.8	11.3
1960–1970	16.0	19.0	19.4	18.0
1980s	6.2	5.8	8.2	4.6
Dynamic efficiency	19 (2)	50 (3)	45 (3)	15 (1)

Note: The *adaptability* figure should be interpreted as the average number of years it takes
for a particular market to adopt an innovation, as measured from the date it first appeared on
the global market. The figures are calculated on the difference between the year when it first
appeared on the individual Nordic market, i.e. the lowest figure for each instrument in Table
12.7, and the year mentioned as benchmark date in Table 12.6. If an instrument had not been
introduced by 1992 – like zero coupon bonds in Norway – then 1992 has been used in the
calculation, which means that the adaptability of the Norwegian bond market has been
exaggerated. The figure for *dynamic efficiency* should be interpreted in the case of Denmark,
for instance, as if the market still lacks two instruments for which the sum of the lags is 19
years.

ison to the other Nordic countries Sweden has more large companies which
are able to issue bonds and which constantly follow the developments in the
international capital market. Further, the innovative Swedish company,
the Stockholm Option Market (OM), opened in 1985 and launched the
market in derivatives in Sweden. The company has since kept its position
among the leading participants in the global market. In terms of dynamic
efficiency the Nordic markets fall into two groups: one highly efficient group
consisting of Denmark and Sweden, and one that is less efficient consisting
of Finland and Norway. The reasons why the Finnish and Norwegian
markets are lagging behind are partly to do with regulations.

CONCLUDING REMARKS ON THE EFFICIENCY OF THE
SECONDARY MARKETS

Two types of efficiency on secondary markets have been analysed in this
chapter. The results as regards both static and dynamic efficiency point in the
same direction: the Danish and Swedish markets are only slightly less
efficient than the major national markets, while the Finnish and Norwegian
markets are distinctly less efficient than those of the other two. The
functioning of the Nordic secondary markets has also improved as regards
liquidity, although the liquidity of the Norwegian and Swedish markets
showed some shakiness towards the end of the 1980s. The difficulty in
finding good measures of liquidity reveals that the transparency of all four
markets is far from perfect. This problem, however, is a global one.

One explanation why the Swedish market pulled ahead of the other
Nordic markets in adopting financial innovations from abroad can be found

in the relative predominance of large and presumably financially well-informed companies in Sweden, which may have triggered the powerful innovative process in that country. However, the high level of efficiency in the Danish market shows that efficiency can have other explanations. Rather, in the Danish case, high efficiency reflects the liberal attitude adopted by the regulatory authorities. Thus the findings noted in this chapter may be seen largely as reflecting differences between the Nordic countries when it comes to their regulative systems. Consequently, we can assume that the differences manifest themselves in inefficiencies and in political risk premiums in the gap between domestic and foreign interest rates. The remaining chapters will address this issue.

NOTES

1   While supply is a function of the net finance requirements of the borrower, demand for bonds has many determinants, for instance: (1) changes in factors associated with the borrower such as credit status and quality, (2) proximity of the bond to repayment and maturity date, (3) changes in investors' expectations about the rate of inflation, (4) changes in investors' expectations about interest rate movements, (5) changes in investors' expectations about exchange rate movements, and (6) changes in the institutional setting. The uncertainty about these determinants constitutes risks of various kinds: credit risk, inflation risk, interest rate risk, exchange rate risk and political risk (as a general expression of the uncertainty about the rules of the market).

2   The three sub-groups are: (1) *weak* efficiency, implying that prices reflect all past information, (2) *semi-strong* efficiency in which prices fully reflect all publicly available information and (3) *strong* efficiency whereby prices reflect all information, publicly available and other.

3   In Chapter 14 we will round off our discussion of efficiency by introducing the remaining type of efficiency, namely that which is related to the lack of international financial integration and the existence of inefficiency wedges between rate on domestic as compared to foreign bonds. To a large extent this kind of efficiency focuses on how national bond rates respond to global news.

4   Euroclear was launched in 1968 by Morgan Guaranty, while its major competitor – Cedel – was founded in 1970. Both act as clearing houses for fixed income securities and equities.

5   Based on FIBV statistics (1991).

6   Helsinki interbank offered rate.

7   Spread refers here to the difference between the bid and offer price in the quotation of a bond. Another kind of spread or margin that is relevant is the difference between the offered prices of two different bonds, in particular the difference between the government rate as some kind of benchmark rate without credit risk and rates on other kinds of bonds. In that case spread will include credit risk and differences in liquidity premiums as well.

8   The spreads are calculated on a market capitalization basis as the sum of the weighted spread of the component bonds in each sector, with the following weights:

$$\frac{\text{bondprice} + \text{accrued}}{100 \times \text{par outstanding}} \Bigg/ \sum \frac{\text{all bond price} + \text{accrued}}{100 \times \text{par outstanding}}$$

9   Figures for Finland and Norway are not available.
10   Liquidity is an expression of the ability to deal in reasonable amounts at the current market prices. In general, the more recent the individual issue, the more liquid it is. After a while bonds tend to settle into the hands of institutional investors who plan to hold onto them until maturity.
11   Another way of measuring liquidity would be to measure the sensitivity of price to changes in volume.
12   Unlike in the case of the share, this proxy may be good so long as the use of zero-coupon bonds is not too excessive.
13   And forward transactions are sometimes big. At the beginning of the 1990s the forward trade in treasury bonds on the Swedish bond market, for instance, was only slightly smaller than the spot trade.
14   See Rantalainen (1993) for a further discussion about the primary dealer system, and Koskinen and Pylkkönen (1992) for a description of the Finnish bond market.
15   See, for example, Honeygold (1989).
16   See, for example, Gallant (1988).
17   See Danmarks Nationalbank, *Annual Report*, various issues; and The Swedish Central Bank, *Kredit- och valutaöversikt*, various issues.
18   See Walmsley (1985).
19   According to *The New Palgrave Dictionary of Money and Finance* (1992).
20   See, for example, Sarwal (1989).
21   See, for example, Cooper (1987).
22   See, for example, Fisher (1988) and Scott-Quinn (1990).
23   The reason why they appear intuitively correct is the role played in Sweden by the innovative company, the Stockholm Options Market (OM).

REFERENCES

Bank of Finland, 1991, *Financial Markets in Finland*, Helsinki.
BIS, 1992a, *Recent Developments in International Interbank Relations*, Basle.
BIS, 1992b, *The Liberalization of Japan's Financial Markets – Some Major Themes*, Basle.
Cooper, I., 1987, *New Financial Instruments*, The Chartered Institute of Bankers, London.
Das, S., 1989, *Swap Financing*, IFR Publishing Ltd, London.
FIBV, 1991, *Activities and Statistics, Annual Report*, Fédération Internationale des Bourses de Valeurs, Paris.
Fisher, III, F.G., 1988, *Eurobonds*, Euromoney Publications PLC, London.
Gallant, P., 1988, *The Eurobond Market*, Woodhead-Faulkner, Cambridge, England.
Honeygold, D., 1989, *International Financial Markets*, Woodhead-Faulkner, Cambridge, England.
IMF, 1991, *International Capital Markets, Developments and Prospects*, Washington, DC.
Koskinen, Y. and P. Pylkkönen, 1992, 'The Bond Market in Finland', *Bank of Finland Bulletin*, No. 6–7, pp. 2–6.
NYSE, 1991, *Fact book*, New York Stock Exchange.
Rantalainen, K., 1993, 'The Primary Dealer System in Finland', *Bank of Finland Bulletin*, No. 2, pp. 8–11.

Sarwal, A.K., 1989, *KPMG International Handbook of Financial Instruments and Transactions*, Butterworths, London.

Scott-Quinn, B., 1990, *Investment Banking: Theory and Practice*, Euromoney Books, London.

The New Palgrave Dictionary of Money and Finance, 1992, Macmillan, London.

Walmsley, J., 1985, *Dictionary of International Finance*, Macmillan, New York.

Walmsley, J., 1991, *Global Investing*, Macmillan, New York.

Chapter 13

Historical patterns in national bond rates

From Chapters 10–11 we have concluded that the role of the bond market in terms of direct corporate fund-raising is a minor one. But since the government bond rate is often used as a risk-free reference rate in corporate investment decisions, the way the bond markets operate is still a matter of great importance to companies. Inefficiencies that push up a country's bond rate will mean a lower level of domestic investment. It can also be assumed that increased volatility of bond rates will reduce the level of investment, since investors feel compelled to demand a compensatory increase in risk premiums. When the pricing of domestic – as opposed to international – bonds is subject to inefficiencies, the international competitiveness of the domestic industries will be affected because of the impact of capital costs on long-term sustainable profits.

The aim of this chapter is to describe and analyse the development of national interest rates, and to pave the way for an analysis of the gap between domestic and foreign bond rates in Chapter 14. First I will introduce the interest rate series that will be used in both chapters. Since we are interested in generalizing the results from the bond market so as to embrace the entire credit market, we need to study the relation between the various sectors of the national markets. Thus, I shall analyse the relation between five different rates. This will be followed by an analysis of the patterns in nominal rates, and a discussion of the level of financial integration between sectors in the same national market. I shall then address the development of real bond rates, both the actual and the expected. In conclusion I will look at the interest rate patterns on the national Nordic markets in the period of transition, and the similarities between them.

DESCRIPTION OF INTEREST RATE SERIES USED IN THE ANALYSIS

We have already discussed the difficulties that face any attempt to create comparability between international interest rates, as regards both the risks involved and the consistency over time. The idea that perfect comparability of interest rates can be achieved between countries and over time is an illusion. Temporary deviations from the general principle to which I subscribe have occurred even here, and these may reduce the comparability, but not to an extent that makes comparisons meaningless. It has naturally been most difficult to find good rates for the late 1970s and early 1980s when markets in the true sense of the word did not exist.

As a rule the rates used in Chapters 13 and 14 are the secondary market yields registered monthly at the end of a period.[1] For the international analysis of bond rates in Chapter 14 proxies for the global rate have been constructed. These rates were calculated as a weighted average of bond rates in certain major countries, usually the rates in the fifteen largest OECD countries. Representative trade weights were used for each Nordic country separately which meant that the international aggregates differ slightly between these countries. In creating the time series of Nordic bond rates and international aggregates my main data sources have been *World Financial Statistics* (Morgan Guaranty), *International Financial Statistics* (IMF), and *Main Economic Indicators* (OECD).

Two bond rates will be analysed, with government bond rates constituting one group and corporate bond rates the other. The *government bonds* included in the study generally have a maturity of five years and are issued by the central government. The aggregate in this case consists of rates for the US, the UK, Austria, Belgium, Denmark, Finland, France, Germany, Italy, the Netherlands, Norway, Sweden, Switzerland and Japan. The data source was *International Financial Statistics* (IMF) for all the countries except Finland, where the rates were provided by the Bank of Finland in the form of the tax-free rates on government bonds.

The rates on *corporate bonds* included in the study are the rates for bonds with a maturity of five years. Countries included in the aggregate are the US, the UK, Germany, the Netherlands, Sweden, Switzerland and Japan. The source for data on these rates was *World Financial Markets* (Morgan Guaranty). For Denmark corporate bond rates are available as quarterly data only, since extremely few issues have been undertaken (*International Financial Statistics*, IMF). The equivalent to the corporate bond rate for Finland is the rate on mass debentures (*Database*, Bank of Finland). For Norway the data source for the period up to 1982 was *World Financial Markets* (Morgan Guaranty); as from January 1983 the corporate bond yields were provided by the *International Financial Statistics* (IMF).[2] The Swedish bond rates for 1976 to July 1988 have been taken from *World Financial Markets* (Morgan Guaranty), and for August 1988 to November 1991 from *The Economist*.

Since the focus of this book is on the bond market, one part of the present chapter will examine the extent to which this market is integrated into the domestic credit market as a whole, i.e. the degree of domestic financial integration. Thus the relation between bond rates and rates in all other major segments of the domestic market will be analysed. The analysis is based not only on the correlation between government and corporate bond rates, but on rates from the three other main sectors as well, which means that data on the development of discount rates, treasury bill rates and prime rates is also needed.

From the data-collecting point of view, the official *discount rate* (DISC) is the least controversial rate. Even so, there have been measurement problems for some countries. This applies to Norway, for instance, where there has been no official discount rate for a long time. Discount rates have generally been retrieved from OECD's *Main Economic Indicators*, but this was not possible in the case of Norway. From 1984 on, the daily loan rate paid by banks on their borrowing in the Bank of Norway has been used as a proxy for the Norwegian discount rate (*Database*, Bank of Norway).

Treasury bill rates (TBRs) are measured as three-month rates. In the case of Denmark, the three-month money market rates for September 1976 to August 1988 (*Database*, Danmarks Nationalbank) and the three-month interbank rates for September 1988 to October 1991 (*Main Economic Indicators*, OECD) were used as the best proxies for the three-month treasury bill rate. As a Finnish treasury bill rate equivalent, the three-month forward FIM interest rate for January 1974 to December 1986 (*Database*, Bank of Finland) and the three-month Helibor[3] for January 1987 to December 1991 (*Database*, Bank of Finland) were used. Money market data for Norway prior to 1978 is difficult to find since the market was more or less non-existent. I have therefore used day-to-day domestic interbank rates as a proxy (*World Financial Markets*, Morgan Guaranty). As from January 1984 the three-month Nibor[4] (*Database*, Bank of Norway) has provided an equivalent for the Norwegian three-month treasury bill rate. Finally, for Sweden the rate for three-month treasury bills for January 1974 to September 1982 (*World Financial Markets*, Morgan Guaranty) has been registered, and from October 1982 the interest rate on treasury discount notes with ninety days outstanding maturity (*Database*, Swedish National Debt Office) has been used.

One more short-term rate has been registered, namely the three-month *lending rate to first-class borrowers (prime rate)* or its equivalent. The *World Financial Markets* (Morgan Guaranty) was used for the Danish, Finnish and Swedish rates. As a proxy for the Norwegian prime rate the three-month special-term deposit rates (*World Financial Markets*, Morgan Guaranty) were used for the period January 1974 to December 1979, and from the first quarter of 1980 the short-term (less than one year) rates provided by Norwegian commercial and savings banks in NOK to the public (*Database*, Bank of Norway).

THE DEVELOPMENT OF NOMINAL NATIONAL BOND RATES

As we have already noted, interest rate formation in the Nordic countries has changed fundamentally since the middle of the 1970s. The changeover from administratively determined interest rates to rates increasingly determined by the market can be expected to be reflected in new interest rate patterns. Let us now turn to an analysis of these patterns.

Peaks over the last twenty years

A break in the trend in Nordic nominal interest rates occurred in the mid-1950s, and was followed by gradually rising rates. A reversal appeared in Denmark and Norway at the beginning of the 1980s, whereas in Finland and Sweden no similar reversal occurred until the beginning of the 1990s. Danish rates peaked in 1982 at levels of about 22 per cent.[5] The same year the Norwegian rate also peaked, but at a level almost 10 per cent lower than this. It remained close to its peak level, however, for the rest of the decade. Rising Nordic bond rates at the beginning of the 1980s were largely a reflection of the general upward trend that followed the change in US monetary policy in October 1979.[6] As regards bond rate averages by the period, Table 13.1 shows trendwise differences between Danish and Norwegian rates on the one hand and Finnish and Swedish rates on the other. As in my earlier expositions the choice of subperiods in the tables reflects institutional changes. The choice of the same time-span for the subperiods in all the Nordic countries in order to facilitate comparisons, represents a compromise.

The table also provides an opportunity to compare the rates on government and corporate bonds in different periods. In a well-functioning market, the gap between corporate and government bond rates reflects the premium charged by the lenders/investors for the borrower's business risk. It may also to some extent reflect differences in liquidity between the two kinds of instrument, and differences related to the taxes imposed on them. No obvious inconsistencies in terms of a negative average margin between corporate and government bond rates can be found in Table 13.1.[7] Based on the average margin for the whole period, Swedish corporate borrowers have benefited from the lowest margin (0.3 of a percentage point), while Finnish corporate borrowers have on average had to bear the highest margin (3.2 percentage points). One major reason for the very large margin in Finland is that government bond rates were exempt from tax whereas corporate rates were not. In the most recent subperiod Finnish and Swedish margins are both at the top in a Nordic comparison. The economic turbulence at the beginning of the 1990s provides a plausible explanation for the higher business risk premium that Finnish and Swedish corporate borrowers had to pay at the time. The gap between corporate and government bond rates rose by 0.9

Table 13.1 Mean and standard deviation in national Nordic nominal interest rates, 1974 to June 1991 (end of period observations, quarterly data, annual rate as a percentage)

Interest rates	Denmark[a]		Finland		Norway		Sweden	
	Mean	Standard deviation	Mean	Standard deviation	Mean	Standard deviation	Mean	Standard deviation
1974–June 1991 (70 observations)								
Government bonds/notes	13.8	3.2	9.6	1.0	10.6	2.3	11.2	1.7
Corporate bonds	14.9	2.9	12.8	1.7	11.1	2.6	11.5	1.9
1974–1977 (16 observations)								
Government bonds/notes	13.5	1.0	9.8	0.7	7.3	0.4	8.9	0.8
Corporate bonds	14.9	1.5	15.1	1.6	7.6	0.4	9.0	0.9
1978–June 1989 (46 observations)								
Government bonds/notes	14.4	3.5	9.5	1.1	11.7	1.7	11.7	1.2
Corporate bonds	15.0	3.2	12.0	1.0	12.4	2.1	12.0	1.2
September 1989–June 1991 (8 observations)								
Government bonds/notes	10.4	0.6	9.3	0.9	10.6	0.4	12.6	1.3
Corporate bonds	10.9	0.3	12.7	0.8	10.9	0.4	13.7	1.3

[a] Rates on corporate bonds are registered as average rates.

percentage points in Finland and 0.8 in Sweden compared with the preceding period. Danish and Norwegian borrowers, on the other hand, faced no such increase between the third quarter of 1989 and the second quarter of 1991, when instead their business risk premiums were below the average for the study period as a whole.

Variability unchanged

The variability of interest rates can be measured in several ways. The most frequently used measure is the standard deviation, as demonstrated in Table 13.1. Generally speaking the standard deviations tended to increase between 1974–77 and 1978 to June 1989, to be followed by a decline in volatility between September 1989 and June 1991. The only exceptions from this pattern of volatility appear in the development of the two Swedish bond rates, whose variability continued to increase.

For the period as a whole Danish and Norwegian bond rates exhibit the highest standard deviation, while for the subperiod September 1989 to June 1991 the highest volatility is registered for the Swedish rates, followed by the Finnish. Corporate bond rates tended to be the most volatile, taking the period as a whole. Denmark is an exception here, but this can be explained by the fact that Danish corporate bond rates are measured as averages rather than end-of-period observations as in the other cases. For the most recent subperiod (September 1989 to June 1991), the volatility of the bond rates in a particular country is almost the same size regardless of the type of bond. The differences in interest-rate volatility across countries reflect changes in institutional and political arrangements. Denmark and Norway experienced the 'aftermath' of their internal liberalization (including a tax reform and a financial crisis) during the subperiod ending in June 1989, while the corresponding aftermath occurred in Finland and Sweden during the most recent subperiod.

The link between nominal interest rates in different sectors

Although this is not shown here, the Nordic discount rates were noticeably more variable in the period 1978 to June 1989 period than between 1974 and 1977. This reflected the growing use of the discount rate as a control instrument around the end of the 1970s. The interest rate environment in the Nordic region at the time meant that the development of the discount rate affected most other national interest rates. Tables 13.2–13.5 show that the relationship varied in strength between different types of interest as well as over time. In all the Nordic countries short-term interest rate movements exhibit the clearest covariation with discount rate movements. The discount rate had the strongest effect on the prime rate: over the period as a whole, 50–75 per cent of the variability in prime rates in Denmark, Finland and

Table 13.2 Covariation between Danish interest rate movements, 1974 to June 1991 (Pearson's coefficients of correlation, monthly data)

	Rate on treasury bills/discount notes	Prime rate	Rate on government bonds/notes	Discount rate
1974–June 1991 (209 observations[a])				
Rate on treasury bills/discount notes	1.00			
Prime rate	0.28*	1.00		
Rate on government bonds/notes	0.05	0.09	1.00	
Discount rate	0.34*	0.77*	0.15*	1.00
1978–June 1989 (138 observations)				
Rate on treasury bills/discount notes	1.00			
Prime rate	0.33*	1.00		
Rate on government bonds/notes	0.07	0.09	1.00	
Discount rate	0.41*	0.75*	0.21*	1.00
July 1989–June 1991 (24 observations)				
Rate on treasury bills/discount notes	1.00			
Prime rate	0.74*	1.00		
Rate on government bonds/notes	0.60*	0.26	1.00	
Discount rate	0.33	0.36*	−0.14	1.00

[a] Correlation coefficients involving treasury bills are based on 177 observations.

Note: Since Danish corporate bond rates are registered only as quarterly averages they are excluded from the table. * means significant positive correlation at the 5 per cent level.

Sweden can be traced to changes in discount rates.

As we have already noted, the role of the discount rate in monetary policy became weaker again during the 1980s in all the Nordic countries. In Sweden, for instance, its function was reduced when a penalty rate on the banks' borrowing from the central bank was introduced. Although the correlation between changes in discount rates and other interest rates has declined in the most recent subperiod, the correlation between changes in discount rates and prime rates was still significant in the early 1990s in all the Nordic countries.

Table 13.3 Covariation between Finnish interest rate movements, 1974 to June
1991 (Pearson's coefficients of correlation, monthly data)

	Rate on treasury bills/discount notes	Prime rate	Rate on government bonds/notes	Rate on corporate bonds	Discount rate
1974–June 1991 (209 observations)					
Rate on treasury bills/discount notes	1.00				
Prime rate	0.06	1.00			
Rate on government bonds/notes	−0.02	0.18*	1.00		
Rate on corporate bonds	0.05	0.01	−0.02	1.00	
Discount rate	0.02	0.87*	0.21*	−0.02	1.00
1978–June 1989 (138 observations)					
Rate on treasury bills/discount notes	1.00				
Prime rate	0.11	1.00			
Rate on government bonds/notes	−0.05	0.17*	1.00		
Rate on corporate bonds	0.13	0.00	0.14*	1.00	
Discount rate	0.07	0.88*	0.22*	−0.01	1.00
July 1989–June 1991 (24 observations)					
Rate on treasury bills/discount notes	1.00				
Prime rate	0.51*	1.00			
Rate on government bonds/notes	0.06	0.24*	1.00		
Rate on corporate bonds	0.35*	0.14	−0.03	1.00	
Discount rate	0.11	0.81*	0.26*	−0.05	1.00

Note: * means significant positive correlation at the 5 per cent level.

Table 13.4 Covariation between Norwegian interest rate movements, 1974 to June 1991 (Pearson's coefficients of correlation, monthly data)

	Rate on treasury bills/discount notes	Prime rate	Rate on government bonds/notes	Rate on corporate bonds	Discount rate
1974–June 1991					
Rate on treasury bills/discount notes (150 observations)	1.00				
Prime rate (153 observations)	0.14	1.00			
Rate on government bonds/notes (209 observations)	0.03	0.09	1.00		
Rate on corporate bonds (93 observations)	0.17	0.09	0.09	1.00	
Discount rate (209 observations)	0.10	0.09	0.23*	0.04	1.00
1978–June 1989					
Rate on treasury bills/discount notes (126 observations)	1.00				
Prime rate (106 observations)	0.14	1.00			
Rate on government bonds/notes (138 observations)	0.00	0.07	1.00		
Rate on corporate bonds (69 observations)	0.20*	0.09	0.14	1.00	
Discount rate (138 observations)	0.09	0.16	0.02	0.11	1.00
July 1989–June 1991 (24 observations)					
Rate on treasury bills/discount notes	1.00				
Prime rate[a]	0.63*	1.00			
Rate on government bonds/notes	0.48*	0.34	1.00		
Rate on corporate bonds	0.37*	0.28	0.37*	1.00	
Discount rate	0.15	0.70*	0.03	0.31	1.00

[a]Quarterly data.

Note: * means significant positive correlation at the 5 per cent level.

Table 13.5 Covariation between Swedish interest rate movements, 1974 to June 1991 (Pearson's coefficients of correlation, monthly data)

	Rate on treasury bills/discount notes	Prime rate	Rate on government bonds/notes	Rate on corporate bonds	Discount rate
1974–June 1991 (209 observations)					
Rate on treasury bills/discount notes	1.00				
Prime rate	0.51*	1.00			
Rate on government bonds/notes	0.29*	0.10	1.00		
Rate on corporate bonds	0.40*	0.28*	0.69*	1.00	
Discount rate	0.55*	0.69*	0.15*	0.36*	1.00
1978–June 1989 (138 observations)					
Rate on treasury bills/discount notes	1.00				
Prime rate	0.51*	1.00			
Rate on government bonds/notes	0.21*	−0.02	1.00		
Rate on corporate bonds	0.39*	0.26*	0.60*	1.00	
Discount rate	0.60*	0.69*	0.11	0.39*	1.00
July 1989–June 1991 (24 observations)					
Rate on treasury bills/discount notes	1.00				
Prime rate	0.41*	1.00			
Rate on government bonds/notes	0.62*	0.35*	1.00		
Rate on corporate bonds	0.65*	0.31	0.84*	1.00	
Discount rate	0.18	0.42*	0.17	0.29	1.00

Note: * means significant positive correlation at the 5 per cent level.

Stronger links between different segments in the national Nordic financial markets

Tables 13.2–13.5 show that during the period under investigation there was a growing correlation between changes in different types of nominal interest rates. The correlation between short-term and long-term rates increased, at least as regards the relation between bond rates and the rates on treasury bills. Also, the association between short-term rates grew stronger, with a slightly different picture in Sweden where the relationship was strong over the whole period.

Further, if we compare the period July 1989 to June 1991 with the period 1978 to June 1989, we find that the correlation between the two kinds of domestic bonds increased; the Finnish rates were the only exception. This greater correlation was due to the deregulations. In the past, the investment requirements imposed by the central banks on the commercial banks and insurance companies meant that the rates on government bonds lived a life of their own (see Chapter 7).

The correlation pattern thus suggests a growing association between movements in bond rates and movements in other types of interest rate, a correlation which indicates an increasing integration between the bond market and other segments of the national credit markets in the individual Nordic countries. This interpretation does not seem too bold, since the existence of a potential time-varying risk premium, for instance, will mean that the correlation is far from perfect even under perfect internal integration of the markets.

Mixed empirical support for the Fisher Effect

According to the Fisher Effect, changes in expected inflation should be reflected in the nominal interest rate in a one-to-one relationship. In other words, in an empirical analysis we would expect to find a strong correlation between the nominal interest rate and expected inflation. We can see from Tables 13.6–13.9, which display different naïve ways of estimating expected inflation, that for the period as a whole this correlation is significant for a few combinations of interest rates and forms of expected inflation, i.e. for the Danish rates and to some extent for the Finnish. But we can see improvements when we look at the results for Norway and Sweden in the latest subperiod. In Denmark the correlation pattern shows the reverse tendency.

The tables show that the pattern of expectations differs between the countries and over time, as well as within individual countries. For the period as a whole Denmark shows the highest correlation between interest rates and inflation when the inflation estimate is based on producer prices. Using an inflation estimate based on the last four quarters in the preceding period seems adequate. The correlation vanishes in the subperiod 1986 to June 1991. In the case of Finland, an inflation estimate based on consumer prices gives the highest correlation with the nominal interest rate. Inflation during the last four quarters also provides the highest correlation here. In the subperiod the correlation pattern remains more or less unchanged.

Norwegian nominal interest rates exhibit no correlation with inflation in the period as a whole. In the subperiod, however, a significant pattern appears. Consumer prices show the highest correlation, but producer prices are also significantly correlated with the Norwegian nominal interest rates in

Table 13.6 Correlation between nominal interest rate and 'expected' inflation in Denmark (quarterly data)

Interest rates	Consumer price change (number of lagged quarters)					Producer price change (number of lagged quarters)				
	-4	-3	-2	-1	A	-4	-3	-2	-1	A
1974–June 1991										
Government bonds/notes[a]	0.65*	0.62*	0.57*	0.44*	0.44*	0.68*	0.67*	0.65*	0.59*	0.56*
Corporate bonds[a]	0.71*	0.71*	0.64*	0.53*	0.46*	0.62*	0.62*	0.62*	0.55*	0.63*
1986–June1991										
Government bonds/notes[b]	0.19	0.20	0.10	0.01	-0.20	-0.05	0.10	0.16	0.19	0.18
Corporate bonds[b]	0.19	0.12	-0.04	-0.07	-0.22	0.07	0.18	0.20	0.22	0.31

[a] The number of observations is 69.
[b] The number of observations is 22.

Note: The nominal interest rate is correlated with expected inflation equal to actual inflation (A = the case of perfect information), and to quarterly inflation based on the observed rate for the last preceding quarter, the two last quarters, etc. The * coefficient of correlation is significantly positive at the 5 per cent level.

Table 13.7 Correlation between nominal interest rate and 'expected' inflation in Finland (quarterly data)

Interest rates	Consumer price change (number of lagged quarters)					Producer price change (number of lagged quarters)				
	-4	-3	-2	-1	A	-4	-3	-2	-1	A
1974–June 1991										
Government bonds/notes[a]	-0.49	-0.47	-0.46	-0.40	-0.48	-0.28	-0.30	-0.32	-0.30	-0.40
Corporate bonds[a]	0.73*	0.68*	0.63*	0.50*	0.44*	-0.04	-0.05	-0.02	-0.01	-0.05
1986–June1991										
Government bonds/notes[b]	0.40*	0.22	0.04	0.05	-0.06	-0.18	-0.23	-0.28	-0.33	-0.46
Corporate bonds[b]	0.43*	0.22	0.01	-0.01	0.01	-0.15	-0.19	-0.25	-0.30	-0.48

[a]The number of observations is 70.
[b]The number of observations is 20.

Note: See Table 13.6.

Table 13.8 Correlation between nominal interest rate and 'expected' inflation in Norway (quarterly data)

Interest rates	Consumer price change (number of lagged quarters)					Producer price change (number of lagged quarters)				
	-4	-3	-2	-1	A	-4	-3	-2	-1	A
1974–June 1991										
Government bonds/notes[a]	-0.09	-0.09	-0.11	-0.08	-0.08	0.53*	-0.46	-0.37	-0.28	-0.26
Corporate bonds[a]	-0.04	-0.05	-0.10	-0.07	-0.07	-0.49	-0.42	-0.35	-0.26	-0.25
1986–June1991										
Government bonds/notes[b]	0.91*	0.80*	0.71*	0.48*	0.44*	0.69*	0.66*	0.52*	0.43*	0.35
Corporate bonds[b]	0.92*	0.80*	0.66*	0.38*	0.38*	0.65*	0.58*	0.40*	0.32*	0.27

[a]The number of observations is 70.
[b]The number of observations is 21.

Note: See Table 13.6.

Table 13.9 Correlation between nominal interest rate and 'expected' inflation in Sweden (quarterly data)

Interest rates	Consumer price change (number of lagged quarters)					Producer price change (number of lagged quarters)				
	-4	-3	-2	-1	A	-4	-3	-2	-1	A
1974–June 1991										
Government bonds/notes[a]	0.04	0.01	-0.04	0.02	0.01	-0.23	-0.21	-0.17	-0.03	-0.01
Corporate bonds[a]	-0.11	-0.12	-0.15	-0.07	-0.08	-0.39	-0.36	-0.30	-0.18	-0.18
1986–June1991										
Government bonds/notes[b]	0.72*	0.67*	0.56*	0.49*	0.37*	0.32	0.31	0.36	0.35	0.05
Corporate bonds[b]	0.71*	0.66*	0.57*	0.48*	0.37*	0.14	0.16	0.22	0.23	-0.05

[a] The number of observations is 70.
[b] The number of observations is 22.

Note: See Table 13.6.

this period. The highest correlation appears when the calculations are based on an inflation estimate equal to the actual inflation in the preceding year. In Norway, unlike the other Nordic countries, we also find strong correlations in the subperiod between interest rates and actual inflation. Swedish interest rates, like the Norwegian, are not correlated with inflation for the period as a whole. However, the correlation increases in the subperiod and reaches significant levels when the inflation estimate is based on consumer prices.

The results, in terms of empirical support for the Fisher Effect, are mixed. For the period as a whole we have found some support for Danish and Finnish rates. However, this vanished in the subperiod. But for the Norwegian and Swedish rates the support grew stronger and appeared to be significant in the latest period. As regards the lag structure, we found that the 'perfect foresight' estimate of future inflation generally shows a lower correlation with the nominal interest rate than naïve estimates based on recent history. Among the possible estimates from the preceding year, we found the highest correlation between the annual inflation rate and the nominal interest rate. The fact that the correlations increase monotonically calls for an explanation. One reason is probably connected with seasonal fluctuations.

REAL NATIONAL BOND RATES

Real bond rates in the Nordic countries rose substantially during the first half of the 1980s.[8] For the first time in fifty years the Nordic rates reached levels not far from those of the late 1920s and early 1930s. At the beginning of the 1990s they were all approaching the two-digit level. The trend is exemplified in Figure 13.1 for the case of Sweden, where it can be seen that after twenty years when real interest rates were between 0 and 4 per cent, the mid-1970s represented a period of negative real interest rates due to the inflation explosion at the time of the first oil crisis. From the middle of the 1970s there was then a rising trend in Nordic real interest rates, which was not reversed until the beginning of the 1990s.

Violent fluctuations in the real bond rate

Tables 13.10-13.13 show that both actual and expected[9] real bond rates have fluctuated a good deal. Expected real bond rates have generally fluctuated less than actual rates. This is consistent with the observation that when inflation is abnormally high or low, people expect it to return to the 'normal' level. During the subperiod September 1989 to June 1991 the variation diminished in all cases. A comparison of Table 13.1 with Tables 13.10–13.13 also shows that the variation in expected and actual real rates is considerably greater than the variation in corresponding nominal rates.[10] Thus, we find that the assumption in the Fisher Effect of a more or less constant 'expected'

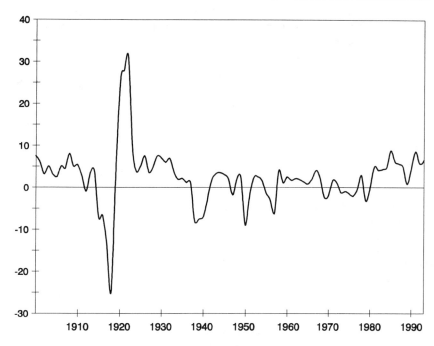

Figure 13.1 Real interest rate trend, 1900–93, Sweden (annual average value)

Source: For the period 1900–78 the figure is based on Ståhl (1980). The updating refers to the real interest rate on government bonds/government notes.
Note: The interest rate is based on four somewhat different series of quotations of discount rate and the rate of government bonds, but it can be regarded as a good approximation of the interest rate trend during the present study.

real rate of interest is not empirically confirmed.[11]

Is the inverted Fisher Effect a more adequate description?

Another way of analysing the Fisher Effect is to look at the correlation between expected inflation and the expected real bond rate. Given a *constant* real interest rate according to the Fisher Effect, we should expect a zero correlation. Fisher argued that changes in real rates are to be seen as a secular phenomenon. Table 13.14 suggests, however, that there is a strong negative relationship between the expected real interest rate and inflation in the perfect foresight case. This inverted 1:1 relationship between changes in the real interest rate and inflation expectations has been reported by Carmichael and Stebbing (1983) and many other researchers, and has been dubbed the 'inverted Fisher Effect'. Some researchers emphasize an explanatory value in the time horizon and claim, like Virén (1987), that an extended inverted Fisher Effect provides the best description of changes in the nominal

Table 13.10 Mean and standard deviation in Danish real bond rates, 1974 to June 1991 (end of period observations, quarterly data, annual rate as a percentage)

Interest rates	Actual real interest rate		Expected real interest rate	
	Mean	Standard deviation	Mean	Standard deviation
1974–June 1991 (70 observations)				
Government bonds/notes	6.6	4.7	6.4	4.6
Corporate bonds[a]	7.3	4.5	7.1	4.2
1974–1977 (16 observations)				
Government bonds/notes	3.1	5.8	2.7	6.0
Corporate bonds	4.5	6.1	4.1	5.7
1978–June 1989 (46 observations)				
Government bonds/notes	7.5	3.9	7.5	3.6
Corporate bonds	8.1	3.6	8.1	3.2
September 1989–June 1991 (8 observations)				
Government bonds/notes	7.9	2.7	7.6	2.6
Corporate bonds	8.9	3.0	7.0	0.3

[a] Rates on corporate bonds are registered as average rates.
Note: The consumer price index is used in calculating the real interest rate.

Table 13.11 Mean and standard deviation in Finnish real bond rates, 1974 to June 1991 (end of period observations, quarterly data, annual rate as a percentage)

Interest rates	Actual real interest rate		Expected real interest rate	
	Mean	Standard deviation	Mean	Standard deviation
1974–June 1991 (70 observations)				
Government bonds/notes	3.1	6.2	2.8	6.2
Corporate bonds	4.6	4.8	4.4	4.8
1974–1977 (16 observations)				
Government bonds/notes	−3.5	6.4	−4.2	6.1
Corporate bonds	1.8	5.7	1.1	5.5
1978–June 1989 (46 observations)				
Government bonds/notes	4.4	4.3	4.4	4.4
Corporate bonds	4.9	4.3	4.8	4.2
September 1989–June 1991 (8 observations)				
Government bonds/notes	8.4	3.1	8.0	2.7
Corporate bonds	8.5	3.0	8.1	2.9

Note: See Table 13.10.

Table 13.12 Mean and standard deviation in Norwegian real bond rates, 1974 to June 1991 (end of period observations, quarterly data, annual rate as a percentage)

Interest rates	Actual real interest rate		Expected real interest rate	
	Mean	Standard deviation	Mean	Standard deviation
1974–June 1991 (70 observations)				
Government bonds/notes	3.0	5.6	2.8	5.7
Corporate bonds	3.6	5.8	3.4	5.8
1974–1977 (16 observations)				
Government bonds/notes	–2.0	4.7	–2.1	5.1
Corporate bonds	–1.7	4.7	–1.7	5.1
1978–June 1989 (46 observations)				
Government bonds/notes	4.0	5.2	3.8	5.2
Corporate bonds	4.7	5.4	4.5	5.3
September 1989–June 1991 (8 observations)				
Government bonds/notes	7.0	2.7	7.0	2.8
Corporate bonds	7.3	2.9	7.4	2.9

Note: See Table 13.10.

Table 13.13 Mean and standard deviation in Swedish real bond rates, 1974 to June 1991 (end of period observations, quarterly data, annual rate as a percentage)

Interest rates	Actual real interest rate		Expected real interest rate	
	Mean	Standard deviation	Mean	Standard deviation
1974–June 1991 (70 observations)				
Government bonds/notes	2.9	5.5	2.7	5.6
Corporate bonds	3.2	5.7	3.0	5.8
1974–1977 (16 observations)				
Government bonds/notes	–1.0	4.6	–1.4	5.4
Corporate bonds	–1.0	4.6	–1.4	5.4
1978–June 1989 (46 observations)				
Government bonds/notes	4.2	4.3	4.0	4.3
Corporate bonds	4.5	4.6	4.3	4.6
September 1989–June 1991 (8 observations)				
Government bonds/notes	3.1	9.4	3.0	9.1
Corporate bonds	4.2	9.4	4.0	9.1

Note: See Table 13.10.

Table 13.14 Correlation between real bond rates and inflation in the Nordic
countries (quarterly data)

Real interest rate	Consumer price change	Producer price change
Denmark 1974–June 1991		
Government bonds/notes (70 observations)	−0.79	−0.84
Corporate bonds (64 observations)	−0.82	−0.87
Denmark 1986–June 1991 (6 observations)		
Government bonds/notes	−0.95	−0.98
Corporate bonds	−0.96	−0.99
Finland 1974–June 1991 (70 observations)		
Government bonds/notes	−0.98	−0.99
Corporate bonds	−0.95	−0.98
Finland 1986–June 1991 (22 observations)		
Government bonds/notes	−0.96	−0.99
Corporate bonds	−0.95	−0.99
Norway 1974–June 1991 (70 observations)		
Government bonds/notes	−0.91	−0.94
Corporate bonds	−0.89	−0.93
Norway 1986–June 1991 (21 observations)		
Government bonds/notes	−0.96	−0.97
Corporate bonds	−0.90	−0.93
Sweden 1974–June 1991 (70 observations)		
Government bonds/notes	−0.95	−0.95
Corporate bonds	−0.94	−0.95
Sweden 1986–June 1991 (22 observations)		
Government bonds/notes	−0.98	−0.96
Corporate bonds	−0.98	−0.96

Note: All coefficients are significant at the 5 per cent level.

interest rate in the short run, while the classical Fisher Effect gives the best description in the longer term.

Is the interest rate determined abroad?

It is only to be expected that in periods when the nominal interest rate was administratively determined, the rate should exhibit deviations from the Fisher Effect. But it is interesting to note that during the 1980s, when interest rates were increasingly market-determined, the deviations were not reduced.

We could of course extend the analysis to allow for taxes and other factors, but instead I shall conclude this analysis of the Fisher Effect here. The conclusion is that the relationship fails to describe interest rate formation in a satisfactory manner, which means that many new explanatory variables can come into the picture. Some of these indicate that the Nordic national interest rates are determined outside the individual countries concerned.

CONCLUDING REMARKS ON BOND RATES

The observations made in this chapter support the view that the Fisher Effect does not hold, and that changes in expected inflation affect the expected real interest rate rather than the nominal interest rate. Moreover, whenever naïve inflation estimates are used, they should be based on observations of inflation over the whole preceding year, rather than just the last quarter.

As regards patterns in individual national bond rates, we found that the Danish rates exhibit the highest volatility when measured for the period as a whole, while the more regulated markets in the Nordic region have experienced considerably lower volatility. In the most recent subperiod the Danish – and, even more, the Norwegian – bond rates fluctuated considerably less than the Finnish or Swedish rates. Thus the first two of these markets have become the least risky in a Nordic comparison.

We have no convincing indications in the Nordic region that the presence of capital controls has implied rates less volatile than in periods without such controls. Not even internal control measures reduced volatility in any consistent way. Rather, we have found many indications that periods of heavy regulation have meant higher interest rate volatility when compared with periods with less rigorous external and/or internal regulations.

The correlations between different sectors of the national financial markets have changed over time as well as across the Nordic region during the period of the investigation. In the deregulated period many interest rates were tied to the discount rate. Consequently, we find a strong correlation whenever discount rates are involved. In the more recent subperiod this correlation became weaker in most countries in the wake of the deregulations. However, in all four countries a significant correlation still existed in the early 1990s between prime rates and discount rates. As regards domestic financial integration, the correlation pattern observed between bond rates and other types of nominal interest rate provides an indication of increasing integration between the bond market and other segments of the national credit markets in the individual Nordic countries.

For the period of the investigation as a whole we have found real bond rates to be at a long-term sustainable level of about 3 per cent in Finland, Norway and Sweden, whereas it has been considerably higher in Denmark. However, when we restrict ourselves to observations of the transition phase for the individual countries, we find similar experiences in all four countries. The way the transition was handled in Denmark – the liberal way – can be assumed to have caused a higher real interest rate of some percentage points, and consequently substantial social costs as well. In the mid-1990s the Danish transition seems to be completed, as indicated by a low business risk, and, as we will see in the next chapter, a 'low' interest rate gap between the domestic and foreign interest rates.

The other Nordic countries show average real rates at about 3 per cent for the entire period of the investigation. However, there are many indications that the costs of the transitions are still to be paid. In contrast to Denmark, the other countries all benefited from negative real rates in the mid-1970s, but once the transition got started the real rates increased. In the last subperiod in the study they all had high rates, except Sweden. However, in the Swedish case high nominal rates and high volatility in real rates indicated instability. In the aftermath, Finland and Sweden experienced high real rates. We can thus conclude that Norway will manage to come through the transition at a fairly low cost, while in Finland and Sweden the cost may ultimately be high.

NOTES

1   Of the several common ways of calculating interest rates on long-term loans - yield at maturity, current yield and yield on a discount basis - I have tried to stick to the first one.
2   From 1983, Norwegian rates are average yields.
3   Helsinki interbank offered rate.
4   Norwegian interbank offered rate.
5   Graphs illustrating the development of Nordic bond rates are shown in the next chapter.
6   It included a change in focus from interest rates to the money supply.
7   If a negative margin had appeared, there could have been three main reasons:

   • a lack of comparability between government and corporate rates, e.g. in terms of maturity;
   • taxes may have affected interest rates differently;
   • it may be an indication of inefficiency.

8   The real interest (r^R) is calculated here as

$$1 + r^R = (1 + r)/(1 + \hat{P}).$$

If, for example, the nominal interest rate is 8 per cent and inflation is 8 per cent, the real interest rate will be 0 per cent. Given a nominal interest rate of 8 per cent and inflation at 4 per cent, the real interest rate will be 3.84 per cent.

For small values of r, r^R and $\hat{P}$ the simpler formula should have been a good approximation:

$$r^R \approx r - \hat{P}.$$

In case the interest rates are measured as interest intensities, i.e. we assume continual returns, the alternative would have been the relationship

$$e^{r^R} = e^{r-\hat{P}} = e^r/e^{\hat{P}}$$

where e is the base for the natural logarithms.

9   When estimating the expected real interest rate I follow our observations from the previous section and use the inflation rate in the immediately preceding year as an expression of the market's inflation expectations. Several authors (e.g. Hooper 1984, Sachs 1985, and Coe and Golub 1986) have successfully used naïve proxies like this – and generally with more success than when sophisticated econometric forecasts were used (e.g. Schaefer and Loopesko 1983).

10   If the covariance between nominal interest rates and expected inflation is zero or negative, the result would be trivial, as can be seen from this formula:

$$var(r^R) = var(r - \hat{P}^*) = var(r) + var(\hat{P}^*) - 2\ cov\ (r, \hat{P}^*) \tag{13.1}$$

According to the Fisher Effect, however, we should expect cov($r, \hat{P}^*$) > 0.

11   A survey of interest rate theory would show that there is great uncertainty in the interpretation of empirical tests of the Fisher Effect (see Oxelheim 1990). We should be particularly careful when interpreting results based on the long-term real interest rates, since the likelihood that the market's way of estimating future inflation deviates from the procedure of using the latest registered inflation rate increases with the maturity.

REFERENCES

Carmichael, J. and P.W. Stebbing, 1983, 'Fisher's Paradox and the Theory of Interest', *American Economic Review*, September, pp. 619–30.

Coe, D.T. and S.S. Golub, 1986, 'Exchange Rates and Real Long-Term Interest Rate Differentials: Evidence for Eighteen OECD Countries', OECD Department of Economics and Statistics, *Working Paper*, No. 28, February.

Fama, E.F., 1970, 'Efficient Capital Markets', *Journal of Finance*, Vol. 25, No. 2 (May), pp. 383–416.

Hooper, P., 1984, 'International Repercussions of the US Budget Deficit', *Federal Reserve Board International Finance Discussion Paper*, No. 246, September.

Leamer, E. and R. Stern, 1972, *Problems in the Theory and Empirical Estimation of International Capital Movements*, NBER, New York.

Oxelheim, L., 1990, *International Financial Integration*, Springer Verlag, Heidelberg.

Sachs, J.D., 1985, 'The Dollar and the Policy Mix: 1985', *Brookings Papers on Economic Activity*, No. 1, Brookings Institution, Washington, DC.

Schaefer, J.R. and B.E. Loopesko, 1983, 'Floating Exchange Rates after Ten Years', *Brookings Papers on Economic Activity*, No. 1, pp. 1–87.

Ståhl, I., 1980, 'Realräntans utveckling i Sverige 1900–1978', in Dahlmén E. and G. Eliasson, (eds), *Industriell utveckling i Sverige*, IUI, Stockholm.

Virén, M., 1987, 'Inflation, Hedging and the Fisher Hypothesis', *Journal of Macroeconomics*, Vol. 9, No. 1, pp. 45–57.

Chapter 14

Bond rate fluctuations in a global perspective

We have now reached the stage where we are ready to study the link between bond rates on individual national markets, and the link between these rates and the 'global' bond rate. The latter rate is envisaged as a rate exerting an influence on all national markets albeit varying in strength according to the degree of international financial integration. The US bond rate and a weighted average of bond rates in the OECD countries can be seen as competing proxies for the global bond rate.[1]

The previous chapters have provided convincing signs of deviations from purchasing power parity and strong grounds for assuming the existence of exchange rate risk as well as political risks. In Chapters 8 and 9 we found indications that during the period under investigation there was neither goods market integration nor monetary or political integration. In the period in question there was thus no perfect *total* international integration of Nordic financial markets in general, or of the bond markets in particular. However, the different elements in this imperfection remain to be explored. An important question to be addressed in the present chapter thus concerns the size of the risk premiums but also the size of the inefficiencies, and consequently the degree of *direct* integration of the Nordic national bond markets.

In Chapter 2 the distinction between *de jure* and *de facto* integration was emphasized. As a by-product of our analysis of the inefficiencies, we should also discover when these inefficiencies seem to have disappeared. In line with the argument put forward in Chapter 5, the date when this occurred is also the date when the market became integrated *de facto*.

In this chapter we will try to get some idea of the extent to which Nordic companies have suffered a competitive disadvantage as a result of interest rates that are higher than those of their foreign competitors. As we have seen, this disadvantage hits companies which are locked into the domestic capital market by a variety of barriers. In other words it applies predominantly to small and medium-sized companies. Shifts in the gap between foreign and Nordic rates may then explain variations in the relative performance of different industries at different times.

The chapter opens with a discussion of the development of the total integration of Nordic bond markets, and an analysis of the covariation between Nordic and foreign real bond rates. The rest of the chapter is devoted to an analysis of the gap between domestic and foreign nominal bond rates. First I describe the gaps and follow this with an analysis of the covariation between nominal bond rates, thus emphasizing the degree of direct bond market integration. I then discuss the potential dates of the *de facto* integration of Nordic bond markets and conclude with a summary of the results.

THE DEGREE OF TOTAL INTEGRATION OF NATIONAL BOND MARKETS

In perfect totally integrated markets, where international purchasing power parity and the International Fisher Effect prevail, all expected real interest rates would be the same. A test of real interest rate parity is thus also a test of this kind of financial integration. In the real world, under a fixed exchange rate regime such as existed for long periods in the Nordic countries, big temporary deviations from purchasing power parity can arise which are taken into account when the market forms its expectations. If these imbalances are not corrected during the period reflected in the interest rate, there will be substantial movements in the actual real interest rate. In such an environment the actual real rate – as a proxy for the expected rate – is not thus a good indicator of total financial integration. None the less, a good many studies are based on an analysis of actual rates.

Test of real interest rate parity

Studies of total financial integration based on real interest rate parity all report that a gap exists between expected real interest rates, and that these rates are far from perfectly correlated between countries.[2] Thus, they indicate a fairly low degree of (total) financial integration.

Frankel and MacArthur (1988), for instance, report the counterintuitive result that even during the 1980s capital mobility remained low between the major industrialized countries. They used a set of forward rate data for twenty-four countries to decompose the real interest differential into two parts: the covered interest differential or political premium, and the real forward discount or currency risk premium. The latter was further decomposed into the exchange risk premium and expected real depreciation.[3] Frankel and MacArthur found some explanatory value in the political premium, but in general the currency premium appeared to be a more important determinant of the real interest differential. Of the two currency factors, the authors found expected real depreciation to be as large and as variable as the exchange risk premium. They concluded that it was imperfect integration of goods markets rather than of financial markets, which was responsible for the fact that real interest rates were not equalized. Thus, they found the low level of total financial integration to be caused by a low level of indirect financial integration.

Gaps between real interest rates in different currencies

Large gaps between real interest rates[4] in different currencies were a characteristic feature of the second half of the 1970s and the first half of the 1980s. Since the collapse of the Bretton Woods agreement substantial differences have occurred between the real rates for DEM and USD in the case of short-term rates, for instance on three-month treasuries. This applied to both actual and expected real interest rates. During the later 1970s the actual real rate in the USA was as much as 5 percentage points lower than the corresponding German rate. The reverse applied during the early 1980s. Many researchers have used these differentials in an attempt to explain exchange rate movements over the last decade. For long periods there has also been a convincing empirical connection between observed exchange movements and expected changes in the real interest rate differential.

A comparison of the real rate on corporate bonds issued in the G-10 countries over different periods reveals that German corporate bonds generated the highest real rate throughout the 1970s.[5] The biggest country differentials appear in the years immediately after the collapse of the Bretton Woods system and the first oil crisis. During that period investors may have been affected by some confusion in assessing the choice of policies in different countries. The UK was pursuing an expansive monetary policy, while West Germany and Switzerland, for example, preferred a more contractive approach. In such a situation the market was probably unable to form sufficiently realistic expectations about the subsequent inflation explosion. The period immediately following the choice of a new target for US monetary policy in October 1979 witnessed an increase in the real rates on US corporate bonds to the same levels as the German rates. In the first half of the 1990s expected real bond rates in the three major OECD countries – the US, Germany and Japan – converged at around 4.5 per cent and the gaps between them were more or less negligible in this period.[6]

The average gaps between Nordic national and foreign real *ex post* bond rates have decreased during the 1980s. As from the mid-1980s all the Nordic rates exceeded the US rate. An outlier appears in 1989, namely the Swedish real *ex post* rate which was particularly low due to a peak in inflation in 1990. In the early 1990s all the Nordic bond rates were substantially higher than the US and OECD rates. The gap grew and during the early 1990s individual Nordic government bond rates could exceed the US rate by as much as 6 percentage points, as was shown in Figure 3.4, whereas the gaps between the Nordic rates and the OECD rate were somewhat smaller.

Covariation between Nordic national and foreign real interest rates

Equal expected real bond rates is our indication of *total* bond market integration. It has already been noted that Nordic expected real bond rates have varied substantially over time. But the question to be answered in this section is the extent to which they have covaried with expected foreign real bond rates.

Let us thus turn to a study of the correlation between changes in real bond rates, looking at the results country by country.[7] For the period 1974 to June 1991, Table 14.1 shows that changes in Danish bond rates were significantly correlated with changes in OECD rates. From 1979–1985 the correlation was high, whereas between 1986 and June 1991 it became insignificant. In the later period the US rate took over the role as the rate exerting the strongest influence on Danish rates. The correlation pattern of changes in actual rates conveys the same message as the pattern of changes in expected rates.

As can be seen in Table 14.2 the Finnish pattern is a contrast to the Danish. A strong indication of a major influence on Finnish rates from changes in the OECD rate is found. Up to the end of the 1970s the US rates made a strong impact on the Finnish rates. However, after that date this influence declined. In the period from 1986 to June 1991 it was still significant, although considerably less than the influence from changes in OECD rates. In the period from 1986 to June 1991 expected changes in the OECD rate on government bonds and on corporate bonds accounted for almost 70 per cent of the variability in expected changes in the corresponding Finnish rates.[8] There was also a tendency towards greater correlation between expected changes.

The Norwegian correlation pattern resembles the Danish, as the role of the US rate was enhanced in the period from 1986 to June 1991, after having played a minor role in the early 1980s. In the later period, as shown in Table 14.3, there were only small differences in correlation patterns for expected as against actual changes, and for government as against corporate bonds.

As in the case of Denmark and Norway the impact of changes in US rates on changes in Swedish domestic rates also increased, as did the correlation between expected changes as compared to the correlation between actual changes. The correlation pattern for the period between 1986 and June 1991 was very homogeneous and the range of the eight coefficients shown in Table 14.4 was small.

For the Nordic countries as a group it can be said that, for the whole period from 1974 to June 1991, the covariation with the level of the OECD bond rate was clearly the strongest. However, evidence of greater influence from changes in US rates is found for the 1986 to June 1991 period. The difference between actual and expected quantities is small. As a rule there was increasing correlation between expected changes.

Table 14.1 Correlation between Danish real bond rate movements and corresponding movements in the OECD bond rate and the US bond rate, 1974 to June 1991 (quarterly data)

Real rates	1974–June 1991		1979–1985		1986–June 1991	
	Actual	Expected	Actual	Expected	Actual	Expected
OECD government bonds	0.36*	0.29*	0.54*	0.49*	0.22	0.16
US government bonds	0.06	–0.09	0.25	–0.01	0.48*	0.38*
OECD corporate bonds	0.34*	0.31*	0.49*	0.47*	0.20	0.29
US corporate bonds	0.03	–0.08	0.19	–0.01	0.44*	0.46*

Note: * marks the significance in two-tailed tests at the 5 per cent level. The actual real bond rate is estimated as the rate at the beginning of the quarter minus actual inflation during the quarter. Expected real bond rate is estimated as the rate at the beginning of the quarter minus expected inflation in the shape of the inflation during the preceding year. Weighting has been based on trade weights.

Table 14.2 Correlation between Finnish real bond rate movements and corresponding movements in the OECD bond rates and the US bond rate, 1974 to June 1991 (quarterly data)

Real rates	1974–June 1991		1979–1985		1986–June 1991	
	Actual	Expected	Actual	Expected	Actual	Expected
OECD government bonds	0.27*	0.29*	0.63*	0.61*	0.79*	0.83*
US government bonds	0.29*	0.23*	0.36*	0.28	0.49*	0.50*
OECD corporate bonds	0.25*	0.31*	0.60*	0.63*	0.77*	0.83*
US corporate bonds	0.27*	0.22*	0.37*	0.23	0.50*	0.48*

Note: See note to Table 14.1.

Table 14.3 Correlation between Norwegian real bond rate movements and corresponding movements in the OECD bond rate and the US bond rate, 1974 to June 1991 (quarterly data)

Real rates	1974–June 1991		1979–1985		1986–June 1991	
	Actual	Expected	Actual	Expected	Actual	Expected
OECD government bonds	0.34*	0.37*	0.53*	0.55*	0.38*	0.39*
US government bonds	0.23*	0.19*	0.08	-0.01	0.60*	0.58*
OECD corporate bonds	0.34*	0.37*	0.54*	0.55*	0.38*	0.39*
US corporate bonds	0.25*	0.18	0.13	-0.02	0.58*	0.59*

Note: See note to Table 14.1.

Table 14.4 Correlation between Swedish real bond rate movements and corresponding movements in the OECD bond rate and the US bond rate, 1974 to June 1991 (quarterly data)

Real rates	1974–June 1991		1979–1985		1986–June 1991	
	Actual	*Expected*	*Actual*	*Expected*	*Actual*	*Expected*
OECD government bonds	0.46*	0.40*	0.42*	0.35	0.58*	0.52*
US government bonds	0.33*	0.22	0.11	−0.16	0.58*	0.53*
OECD corporate bonds	0.49*	0.36*	0.48*	0.30	0.58*	0.52*
US corporate bonds	0.34*	0.21	0.17	−0.20	0.57*	0.54*

Note: See note to Table 14.1.

The total integration of different Nordic national financial markets is far from perfect

Our study of the correlation between changes in real bond rates reveals that the covariations have fluctuated over time, suggesting that the total integration of the Nordic national bond market has also shifted. These observations accord well with the fluctuations that have been noted in the gaps between expected real bond rates in the Nordic countries and abroad. However, the overwhelming impression from the study of the cross-correlation between changes in real bond rates is that the correlation did increase between the 1979–85 period and the period from 1986 to June 1991, and that there was thus *a clear indication of a further approach towards perfect total financial integration.* This may be because monetary integration and/or the integration between goods markets has improved. Thus, direct financial integration may not necessarily have increased. Since the total financial integration is not perfect, we will continue our analysis to find out how far the imperfection is generated by direct disintegration as manifest in a gap between the risk-adjusted expected returns from different markets, measured in a common currency.

GAPS BETWEEN NOMINAL NATIONAL AND FOREIGN BOND RATES

In this section we will examine the size of the gaps between nominal domestic and foreign bond rates, and correlation patterns. Let us start by reviewing what is actually contained in the interest gap, and then proceed to an empirical analysis of the development of the gap between national bond rates and our two proxies for the global rate.

Analysis of deviations from the International Fisher Effect

In exploring the gap between nominal bond rates and trying to infer something about the level of direct financial integration, I adopt a rate-of-return perspective and subscribe to the law of one price for interest rates. As was discussed in Chapter 5 this can be studied in terms of the empirical validity of two of its expressions: the International Fisher Effect and the interest rate parity theorem.[9] The International Fisher Effect[10] expresses this law by taking the market's expectations regarding future exchange rate movements into consideration. However, to the extent that the matching of interest rates leaves some risks unmatched, the investor is regarded as being risk-neutral. It is thus assumed that different distributions of probability, as regards exchange movements, do not generate any demand for a risk premium. The same applies to a premium for any increase in uncertainty associated with political changes, such as adjustments in taxes. If the assumption of risk-neutrality holds, and the gap between two interest rates corresponds to the exchange expectations at every point in time, then the direct financial integration of the market is perfect.

Consequently, if an empirical test of this integration is to be satisfactorily underpinned, we must have information about the market's exchange expectations. If we do not have such information, we will have to make do (as is commonly done) with the actual (*ex post*) exchange rate movements and subscribe to the perfect foresight assumption. But the fact that we have no access to market expectations about exchange rate changes causes some problems, since an analysis based on observed exchange rate movements instead of these expectations in fact includes an analysis of the two hypotheses on the right-hand side of equation 14.1.

$$S_{t+n} - IFE_t(n) = [S_{t+n} - S^*_{t+n}] + [S^*_{t+n} - IFE_t(n)] \qquad (14.1)$$

The deviation between the actual future spot rate (S_{t+n}) and the forecast from the International Fisher Effect [$IFE_t(n)$] can thus be subdivided into a deviation between the actual future rate and market expectation (S^*_{t+n}) and a deviation between market expectation and the forecast [$IFE_t(n)$].

The subdivision according to formula 14.1 shows that conclusions about integration based on *ex post* analysis can be difficult to interpret. For example, the market expectation may be correct, even though the actual exchange rate does not assume the relevant value. This situation can arise, within the limits of efficiency, if the transaction costs are so great that the financial transaction is not economically defensible. The source of the interest gap – whether it depends on the market expectation deviating from the International Fisher Effect or on the presence of transaction costs – will determine any conclusions about the inefficiency and disintegration of the markets. The difficulty lies in judging the relative weight of the two causes.

Yet another source of systematic deviation when it comes to empirical testing is to be found in the investors' risk-aversion and their demands for a risk premium to compensate for the exchange and political risks. Thus, any conclusions about the inefficiency of the market must also allow for an evaluation of these premiums.[11]

In an interview study reported in Oxelheim (1990) it was found that about half the business leaders interviewed placed great confidence in the International Fisher Effect, while the other half were equally convinced that the theory does not hold. This could mean that half the market also acts in accordance with its belief in the Effect, while the other half provides one explanation of the *ex post* deviations. On top of which, possible market inefficiencies also affect the outcome.

Government bond rates

We can see in Figures 14.1–14.8 that from 1982/83 the Nordic *government bond* rates (apart from the Finnish) have been more or less consistently higher that the US and OECD rates. The reason why Finnish rates are an exception, however, is that they are tax free. Since the OECD rates have proved to be the most influential during the period as a whole, we will emphasize the gap between them and the Nordic national rates.

The Danish rates have exceeded our OECD proxy for the global rate all the time since 1974. In the Nordic region as a whole the largest gaps are registered for Denmark, where they sometimes exceed 10 percentage points. However, the Danish gaps began to fall radically from the beginning of 1983, in a period when big issues of government bonds coincided with non-resident investors being allowed once again to invest in Danish krone-denominated government bonds. But a new big gap appeared in 1986–87, i.e. at the time of the Danish 'potato diet'. The gaps then became very small as from the time *de jure* external deregulation was completed.

Finnish gaps were among the smallest in the region, but they are difficult to interpret on account of differences between the Finnish and the global rate as regards tax. Nor can the Finnish rates be easily converted into a taxable

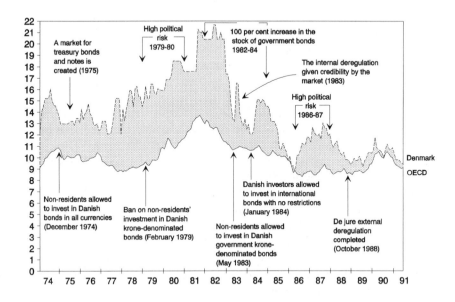

Figure 14.1 Government bond rates, Denmark as against OECD, 1974 to June 1991 (per cent per year, monthly data, end of period)

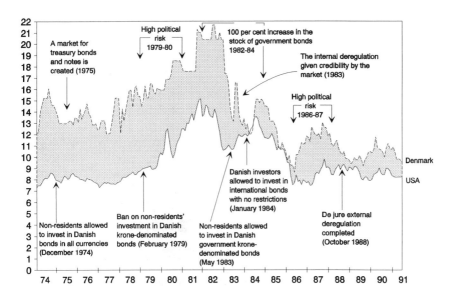

Figure 14.2 Government bond rates, Denmark as against USA, 1974 to June 1991 (per cent per year, monthly data, end of period)

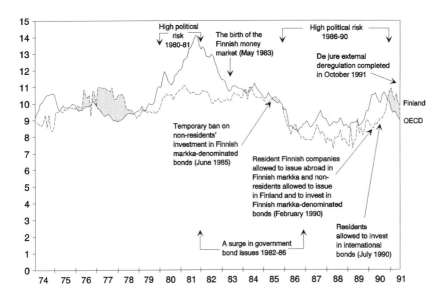

Figure 14.3 Government bond rates, Finland as against OECD, 1974 to June 1991 (per cent per year, monthly data, end of period)

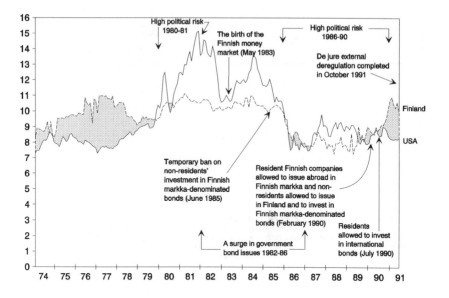

Figure 14.4 Government bond rates, Finland as against USA, 1974 to June 1991 (per cent per year, monthly data, end of period)

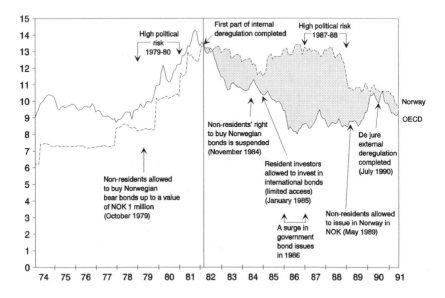

Figure 14.5 Government bond rates, Norway as against OECD, 1974 to June 1991 (per cent per year, monthly data, end of period)

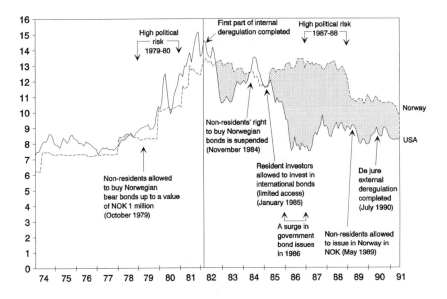

Figure 14.6 Government bond rates, Norway as against USA, 1974 to June 1991 (per cent per year, monthly data, end of period)

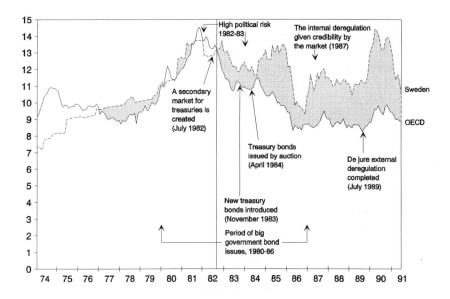

Figure 14.7 Government bond rates, Sweden as against OECD, 1974 to June 1991 (per cent per year, monthly data, end of period)

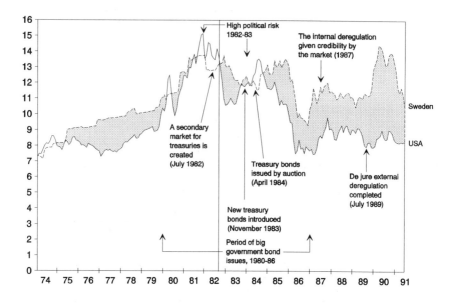

Figure 14.8 Government bond rates, Sweden as against USA, 1974 to June 1991 (per cent per year, monthly data, end of period)

equivalent, since for most of the period a marginal tax rate applied. Bearing all this in mind, it is found that except for a few years in the 1970s (1976–78), the Finnish bond rates were more or less consistently below the global rates; occasionally, at the beginning of the 1980s, as much as 4 percentage points below. The size of the gap diminished from 1982 onwards, but the Finnish rates did not pass the OECD rates until the mid-1990s, when non-resident investors were again allowed to invest in Finnish markka-denominated government bonds and resident Finnish investors were allowed to invest in international bonds. Moreover, after August 1989, the Finnish government stopped issuing tax-free government bonds.

The Norwegian rates were consistently below the global rates until the beginning of 1982. Thereafter they were above the global rate for the remainder of the period of investigation, with gaps sometimes exceeding 6 percentage points. The biggest gaps of the 1980s occurred in the period 1986–87, at the time of the dramatic drop in the price of crude oil and its aftermath, i.e. in a period of high political risks. As from the *de jure* completion of external deregulation, the gap became quite small.

The Swedish rates were well below the OECD rate in the mid-1970s. At the time of the introduction of the new exchange rate regime in August 1977, they began to overtake the OECD rate. However, big gaps did not appear until after the Swedish devaluation in the autumn of 1982. At the beginning of the 1990s the Swedish rates were sometimes 5 percentage points above the global rates.

Thus in the case of the government bond rate – the risk-free benchmark rate used by the corporate sector – we find that something happened in all the Nordic countries in the 1981–82 period. A downturn in the global bond rate occurred in 1981. The Danish rate followed but at a higher pace, which meant a diminishing gap. In Finland the gaps also decreased, but as a result of a more or less unchanged Finnish rate. The Norwegian and Swedish rates did not follow the downturn in the global rate in 1981–83, which meant that big gaps appeared. To summarize: since autumn 1982 the Danish, Norwegian and Swedish rates have been consistently above the global rate, whereas the Finnish (tax-free) rates did not overtake the global rate until the beginning of the 1990s.

Corporate bond rates

In the case of gaps between national and global corporate bond rates – which tell us something about the relative cost of capital for Nordic companies – Figures 14.9–14.16 reveal patterns similar to those applying to government bond rates. There is one exception, however: unlike Finnish government bond rates (which are tax-free), Finnish corporate bond rates (which are taxable) have exceeded the OECD rates – not only now and then but for almost the whole period of the investigation. In this sense they resemble the Danish rates, with gaps of about 9 percentage points in the 1970s. While the Danish and Finnish rates were far above the OECD rate, for some years (1974–77) the Norwegian and Swedish rates were below it, sometimes by as much as about 4 percentage points. In the period 1981–82 something happened which, as in the case of government bond rates, made all the Nordic rates overtake the OECD rates – the Danish and Finnish rates by up to 4 or 5 percentage points, and the Norwegian and Swedish rates by up to 6 or 7. Hence, after 1982, companies from all the Nordic countries suffered a cost-of-capital disadvantage with implications for their international competitiveness.

The completion of *de facto* external integration

The consistently higher Nordic bond rates after 1982 can hardly be regarded as an intended result of economic policy-making. Rather, it is as though the central-bank-generated wedges had disappeared and the rates had been allowed to reflect the market's *expectations* and its demands for *premiums* for carrying various types of risk. Although some general market inefficiency may remain, I interpret the patterns appearing in Figures 14.1–14.8 as indicating that the Danish bond market was *de facto* integrated as far back

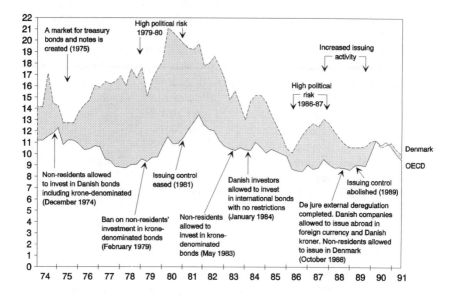

Figure 14.9 Corporate bond rates, Denmark as against OECD, 1974 to June 1991 (per cent per year, quarterly data, end of period)

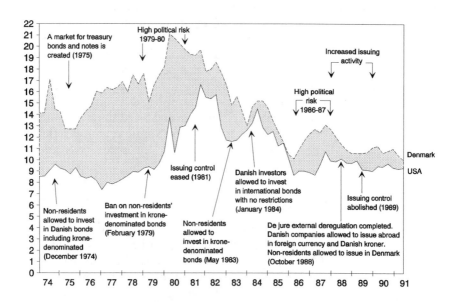

Figure 14.10 Corporate bond rates, Denmark as against USA, 1974 to June 1991 (per cent per year, quarterly data, end of period)

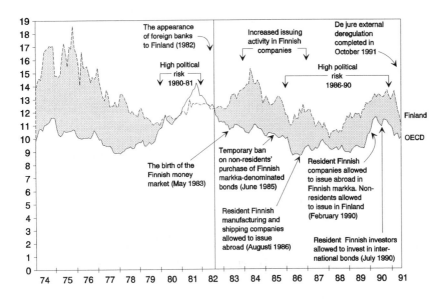

Figure 14.11 Corporate bond rates, Finland as against OECD, 1974 to June 1991 (per cent per year, monthly data, end of period)

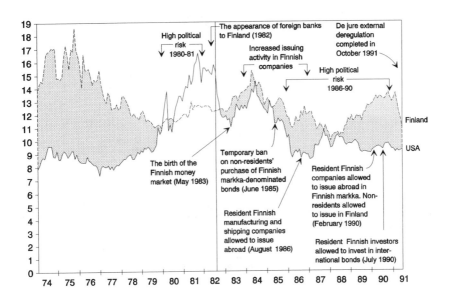

Figure 14.12 Corporate bond rates, Finland as against USA, 1974 to June 1991 (per cent per year, monthly data, end of period)

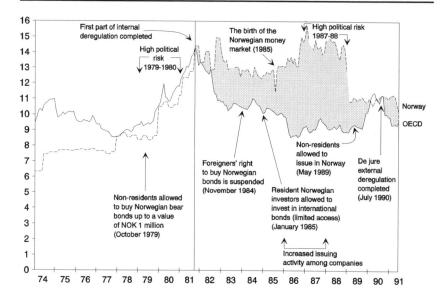

Figure 14.13 Corporate bond rates, Norway as against OECD, 1974 to June 1991 (per cent per year, monthly data, end of period)

Note: Quarterly data January 1974–December 1982. Missing data July–August 1983, March–April 1987, January 1988 and January 1989.

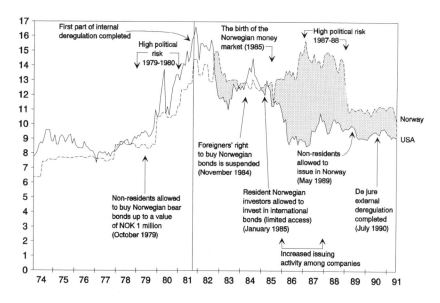

Figure 14.14 Corporate bond rates, Norway as against USA, 1974 to June 1991 (per cent per year, monthly data, end of period)

Note: See Table 14.13.

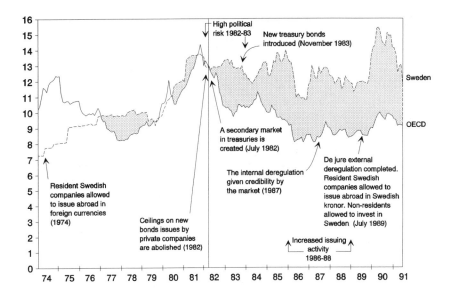

Figure 14.15 Corporate bond rates, Sweden as against OECD, 1974 to June 1991 (per cent per year, monthly data, end of period)

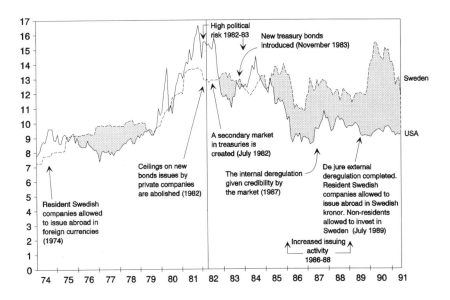

Figure 14.16 Corporate bond rates, Sweden as against USA, 1974 to June 1991 (per cent per year, monthly data, end of period)

as 1974, whereas the Norwegian and Swedish market became integrated in the period 1981–82. The temporary ban on non-residents' purchase of Norwegian NOK-denominated and Danish DKK-denominated government bonds seems to have had no effect on the *de facto* integration, as expressed in the interest rate gaps. We were not able to make any strong inferences from the Finnish government bond rate gap about *de facto* integration. The Finnish corporate bond rate gaps, however, indicate that *de facto* external integration occurred at about the same time as the Norwegian and Swedish markets became integrated.

The temporary gaps found in all the Nordic countries in 1983, just after the completion of the *de facto* external integration, are largely a reflection of risk premiums. The real exchange rate patterns discussed in Chapter 8 provide further support for this view, since they show that after the devaluations of the Nordic currencies in 1982, there do not seem to have been any substantial expected exchange rate changes to motivate Nordic interest rates above the OECD rate.

Spill-over effects of nominal bond rate fluctuations in a regional perspective

In Chapter 13 we found that the variability of the five major interest rates in each of the Nordic countries had changed over time. Short-term and long-term rates became more variable during the 1980s for most combinations of interest rate/country. The variability of different interest rates within countries was found to be extremely 'contagious'. How contagious, then, is this variability in a regional perspective? Can we find any patterns of significant intra-Nordic correlations?

Table 14.5 shows that for the whole of the period investigated some intra-Nordic coefficients of correlation are significantly positive. A strong correlation existed between Swedish and Finnish and between Swedish and Norwegian government and corporate bond rates.

Table 14.6 shows that the Danish rates were closely linked to Swedish bond rates in the subperiod from 1987 to June 1991.[12] Finnish bond rates also show strong positive correlation with Swedish rates, but the significance is weak in the case of government bond rates. In this subperiod the highest single coefficient is found between the movements in Danish and Swedish government bond rates.

Thus the links between Swedish bond rates on the one hand and Danish and Finnish on the other have grown stronger, whereas the opposite is true of the link between the Norwegian and Swedish rates. In the subperiod Norwegian rates show no correlation at all with other Nordic bond rates. On this count Norway has thus experienced diminishing intra-Nordic bond market integration, whereas Denmark has become increasingly more integrated.

Table 14.5 Covariation between movements in Nordic national bond rates, 1974 to June 1991 (Pearson coefficients of correlation, quarterly data)

Country	Interest rate	Denmark BOND	Denmark DCBY	Finland BOND	Finland DCBY	Norway BOND	Norway DCBY	Sweden BOND	Sweden DCBY
Denmark	BOND	1.0							
	DCBY		1.0						
Finland	BOND	0.25*	0.02	1.0					
	DCBY	0.08	0.14		1.0				
Norway	BOND	-0.15	0.08	0.07	0.11	1.0			
	DCBY	0.06	0.18	0.11	0.11		1.0		
Sweden	BOND	0.13	0.18	0.26*	0.23*	0.23*	0.20	1.0	
	DCBY	0.11	0.17	0.30*	0.28*	0.30*	0.30*		1.0

Note: BOND equals rate on government bond and DCBY equals rate on corporate bond. * means a coefficient of correlation that is significantly positive at a 5 per cent level. The number of observations is 70.

Table 14.6 Covariation between movements in Nordic national bond rates, 1987 to June 1991 (Pearson coefficients of correlation, quarterly data)

Country	Interest rate	Denmark		Finland		Norway		Sweden	
		BOND	DCBY	BOND	DCBY	BOND	DCBY	BOND	DCBY
Denmark	BOND	1.0							
	DCBY		1.0						
Finland	BOND	0.16	−0.06	1.0					
	DCBY	0.29	0.00		1.0				
Norway	BOND	0.06	0.02	−0.03	0.11	1.0			
	DCBY	−0.11	−0.06	−0.07	−0.09		1.0		
Sweden	BOND	0.65*	0.53*	0.35	0.39	0.28	−0.02	1.0	
	DCBY	0.63*	0.51*	0.43*	0.53*	0.38	−0.01		1.0

Note: BOND equals rate on government bond and DCBY equals rate on corporate bond. * means a coefficient of correlation that is significantly positive at a 5 per cent level. The number of observations is 18.

COVARIATION BETWEEN NATIONAL AND GLOBAL NOMINAL BOND RATES

As was discussed in Chapter 5, temporary segmentation may be expressed by the time it takes for changes in the global rate to be reflected in the national rate, this lag being one dimension of our measure of direct financial integration. A significant *positive* correlation between contemporary changes is seen as an indication of financial integration. How far then, and with what time lag, do the Nordic national nominal bond rates covary with the global rate? Table 14.7 shows the pattern of cross-correlations between changes in the global rate and in the rate in the USA on the one hand, and the Nordic rates on the other. The time lag is expressed in the number of months that pass before a particular Nordic national interest rate exhibits any significant responsiveness.

The size and pattern of lags together provide an ambivalent sign of greater covariation

In the case of Denmark, Table 14.7 shows significant and growing coefficients of correlation between the Danish and the US government bond rates. The same applies to the correlation between the Danish and the OECD rates, but at a lower level. However, the first of these correlations appeared with a higher number of lags than in the case of the relation between changes in the Danish and the OECD rates, which makes it hard to decide which rate had the strongest influence on the Danish rate.

In the case of the Finnish rates the greater impact of changes in the OECD rate rather than the US rate is obvious. In the case of government bond rates, the correlation increased and the time it took for changes in the global rate to influence Finnish rates grew significantly shorter. The correlation pattern for corporate bond rates is insignificant.

Changes in nominal Norwegian bond rates were influenced by changes in the corresponding US rates. From Table 14.7 we can see increasing coefficients of correlation, as well as an increasing number of lags. Taken together these two indications complicate the interpretation in terms of increasing integration in the Norwegian bond market.

In the Swedish case the OECD rate exerts the greater influence on both kinds of bond rate. However, the influence of the US rates has increased, and the number of lags has decreased.

The correlation between the national and the OECD rates has thus increased, and the time lag has diminished in the case of the Danish, Finnish and Swedish government bond rates. For these markets we have consequently found an indication of greater direct financial integration as from the mid-1980s. As regards the corporate bond market we received a similar indication for the Swedish market. In the case of the other markets we can

Table 14.7 Maximal correlation between lagged bond rate movements, Nordic rates as compared to global rates, 1974 to June 1991 (monthly observations; lag in number of months)

Interest rate	Period	Maximal correlation	
		OECD rate	US rate
Denmark[a]			
Government bonds	Jan 1974–June 1991	0.17* (4)	0.17* (5)
	Jan 1978–June 1991	0.16 (4)	0.19* (5)
	Jan 1986–June 1991	0.29* (1)	0.40* (30)
Finland			
Government bonds	Jan 1974–June 1991	0.17 (33)	0.17* (32)
	Jan 1978–June 1991	0.19* (32)	0.22* (32)
	Jan 1986–June 1991	0.29* (2)	0.23* (2)
Corporate bonds	Jan 1974–June 1991	0.12 (1)	0.16 (33)
	Jan 1978–June 1991	0.15 (28)	0.18 (33)
	Jan 1986–June 1991	0.22 (29)	0.26 (29)
Norway			
Government bonds	Jan 1974–June 1991	0.17 (16)	0.15 (16)
	Jan 1978–June 1991	0.18 (16)	0.17 (16)
	Jan 1986–June 1991	0.28 (12)	0.29* (36)
Corporate bonds	Jan 1974–June 1991	0.17 (36)	0.32* (13)
	Jan 1978–June 1991	0.17 (36)	0.33* (13)
	Jan 1986–June 1991	0.26 (29)	0.31* (13)
Sweden			
Government bonds	Jan 1974–June 1991	0.26* (2)	0.23* (2)
	Jan 1978–June 1991	0.27* (1)	0.24* (13)
	Jan 1986–June 1991	0.46* (1)	0.33* (1)
Corporate bonds	Jan 1974–June 1991	0.23* (2)	0.15 (2)
	Jan 1978–June 1991	0.25* (2)	0.16 (2)
	Jan 1986–June 1991	0.44* (2)	0.29* (2)

[a] Rates on corporate bonds are excluded due to lack of monthly data.

Note: The lag in number of months on which the reported coefficient of correlation is calculated, is given in brackets. For example, (9) signifies the correlation between the change in foreign bond rates and the change in the corresponding domestic rate nine months later. * means absolute deviations from zero with a probability less than 1 per cent under the null hypothesis of no positive correlation.

see no conclusive indications of their integration into the OECD bond market. For both the Norwegian markets, for instance, we find a significant correlation between the Norwegian bond rates and the US bond rates, albeit accompanied by a high and growing number of time lags. Thus the signals are not always unequivocal as regards a possible increase in the influence of global bond rate movements.

It has to be emphasized, however, that the lack of indications of stronger integration should be interpreted with caution, since this lack may simply be reflecting changes in foreign exchange policy between the subperiods concerned. When there are formally fixed or semi-fixed exchange rates, or when there is little variation in the rates, it may be enough to examine the covariation between nominal uncovered interest rates. But when floating exchange rates obtain, or if there are parity changes, such an approach can be expected to prove inadequate.

Nevertheless, many researchers use the size of the cross-correlation between domestic and foreign nominal interest rates as an expression of the level of direct financial integration. Although large parity changes were infrequent in the Nordic exchange rate arrangements in the period 1986 to June 1991,[13] it appears in our present case that if we disregard foreign exchange rate effects, it will be difficult to interpret the results.

When a simple regression analysis with changes in the national Nordic interest rates was performed as a function of earlier changes in foreign rates, indications of misspecifications were found. Important explanatory variables that are missing are the effects of exchange rates.[14] A simple device would thus be to allow for these effects in the shape of the forward premium and to study the correlation between the individual Nordic national rates and the corresponding foreign rate, covered on the forward market for foreign exchange. By adopting such a procedure we would have been able to eliminate the problem of exchange rate expectations and exchange rate risk. However, the problem of political risk would have remained, since in the absence of a Euroversion of the different Nordic currencies for the whole period of the study, the comparison would have to be made between national interest rates. Unfortunately, the Nordic forward markets are 'thin' as regards long-term contracts with the great majority of transactions referring to three-month or shorter contracts, and no such analysis can therefore be performed here.

Does the historical survey of nominal bond rates thus far give us any indication that *direct* integration between the Nordic and foreign bond markets has increased? Indeed it does. We have found indications that national policy-makers are less able to pursue policies with a view to keeping the long-term bond rates at a low level. Thus we found that by 1982 the ability of national authorities to insert wedges between their own national bond rate and the global rate had disappeared in all the Nordic countries. From 1983 on, we have seen that the bond rates in all these countries have substantially exceeded the global rate. The disappearance of central-bank-induced inefficiencies, and probably also a substantial part of the market inefficiencies,[15] led us to assume the presence of premiums – sometimes even large ones – for political and exchange rate risk.

POLITICAL RISK PREMIUMS IN THE BOND RATE GAPS

We have seen quite substantial gaps between national bond rates on the one hand and the OECD and US bond rates on the other. A pertinent question here concerns the relative size of the different elements in the gap. In view of the findings in Chapters 6–9 we have good grounds to believe that all the elements have existed, albeit varying in strength over time.

It would have been best to perform the analysis of the different elements of the gap within a multivariate model framework on the lines suggested in Chapter 5. However, since we are interested in the development over time and in comparing subperiods, but at the same time are restricted to using quarterly data, our opportunities for studying short subperiods are rather limited. When the model is applied to longer periods, however, the political risk premium in Denmark in the period from mid-1986 to the end of 1987 has been identified as representing about 1.5 percentage points of the gap between the Danish government bond rate and the corresponding OECD rate.[16] Similarly, in January 1989, when the Swedish government announced the abolition of the remaining capital controls, the gap between the Swedish government bond rate and the OECD rate contained a political risk premium of about 2 percentage points.[17]

Here we will try instead to identify and eliminate in a gradual process the different elements in the bond rate gap. In doing so we will focus on the government bond rate because of its role as the risk-free benchmark rate. The alternative, namely of using the corporate bond rate, would probably have caused difficulties in the interpretation of the results, since the potential prevalence of some unmatched business risks makes it possible that a premium for these risks could be embodied in the bond rates. Considering the different character of the industrial core in the four Nordic countries, i.e. a difference between the core companies which are also the ones that might benefit from issuing on the bond market, such a risk premium is not unlikely.[18] In the case of Finland, however, we have no choice but to study the gap between corporate bond rates, since the tax exemption of Finnish government bond rates makes these rates inappropriate for the analysis.

In order to capture the potential size of the risk premiums we have to eliminate from the gaps the exchange rate expectations that prevailed at the time when the interest rate gap was created. It goes without saying that the task of eliminating the exchange rate expectations is an extremely difficult one. There are two main ways of approaching it. One is the perfect foresight alternative, i.e. we assume that the market actors 'knew' exactly what was going to happen as regards the change in the exchange rate. The other way is to assume that the market actors believe in purchasing power parity, i.e. their exchange rate expectation equals their expectation about the development of relative inflation.[19] Here we are trapped again, unless we add some further assumptions: that the actors have perfect foresight as regards the development of relative inflation, or that they use an adaptive way of forming their expectations about this development. Hence the two alternatives actually mean that we are comparing either *ex post* real bond rates or *ex ante* real bond rates. In the second case we have found indications that the actors form this kind of expectation on a basis of relative inflation from the preceding year. Another purchasing power parity approach is to assume that the actors believe in the mean-reverting feature of the PPP process and that they always include the current deviation from parity as a complement to the forecasted exchange rate change as estimated from relative inflation.

In the analysis, we have used the alternative procedures as proxies for the expected change in exchange rates and have looked for consensus results. The elimination of these expected exchange rate changes as estimated by the proxies has left us with a residual gap containing inefficiency, exchange and political risk premiums. In Chapter 5 we distinguished between two types of inefficiency: general market inefficiency and the central-bank-induced inefficiency. Since in this chapter we have found indications that the second of these disappeared as far back as 1974 for Danish rates and in the period 1981–82 for the national bond rates of the other three countries in the region, only some market inefficiency probably remains, of which the main systematic component is the transaction cost. Depending on the view we subscribe to, the transaction costs can be described (in its narrowest form) as the bid–ask spread or (in its widest) as an estimate including the information cost as well. The literature suggests a maximum for this cost not exceeding 0.5 percentage points.[20] Globalization reduces this cost because of the accompanying increase in competition. If we then assume that market inefficiency in excess of the transaction cost is random, the calculation of an average will cancel out this inefficiency, leaving us with a gap containing the exchange and political risk premiums plus a transaction cost of 0.5 percentage points at most.

Table 14.8 shows the size of the different averages in various periods after the completion of *de facto* external integration. The periods have been identified by our political risk proxies as high-risk periods. Here, unlike the presentation in Chapter 9, we have calculated the political risk by multiplying our proxy for the government's propensity to intervene by our proxy for its need to do so. In the table we find four estimates for each country and risk period. The two cases in which the market's exchange rate expectations are based on an assumption about perfect foresight – actual exchange rate or relative inflation for next year – show risk premiums of about the same size.

The table shows that the sum of the exchange and political risk premiums have been substantial during the periods identified as high-risk periods. In 1987, the year after the tax reform and the potato diet, the gap between the Danish and OECD bond rates, for instance, contains risk premiums of about 2 percentage points, after the elimination of a potential transaction cost of about 0.5 percentage points. The size of the risk premiums is fairly consistent

Table 14.8 Average gaps in periods of high political risk (quarterly data)

		Denmark	Finland	Norway	Sweden
Period of high political risk		1986:2–1987:3	1988:4–1990:2	1986:4–1988:2	1990:1–1990:4
Average bond rate gap in the high risk period		2.9	2.4	4.3	4.0
Representative average from the same institutional period (see Table 15.2)		2.4	2.2	3.4	3.3
Average bond rate gap cleared from expected exchange rate changes	Bondgap – actual exchange rate change $(t+1)$	2.8	2.5	4.1	3.7
	Bondgap – relative inflation from previous year $(t-1)$	3.7	1.1	−3.8	1.5
	Bondgap – relative inflation for next year $(t+1)$	3.1	3.4	5.9	3.4
	Bondgap – [relative inflation for next year $(t+1)$ plus correction for accumulated deviation from PPP at time]	−7.1	5.5	5.6	1.0
Exchange rate risk in the high political risk period above		fairly low	low	low	low

Note: Inflation is based on changes in producer price index.

with the econometric estimate, reported earlier in this study, of a political risk premium for that period of about 1.5 percentage points. If we combine our estimate of the risk premium with the interest rate sensitivity of the Danish economy presented in Chapter 3, we find that the risk premium corresponds to a 1.6 to 2 percentage points lower growth in the Danish GDP than would otherwise have obtained over the remaining years of the 1980s.

In Norway we similarly find a high political risk between mid-1986 and mid-1987, the turbulent period in the wake of the dramatic fall in the price of crude oil, which led to a temporary turnaround in the Norwegian current account. The risk premiums amount to about 3.5 percentage points after the elimination of transaction costs. However, in both Denmark and Norway the completion of the *de jure* deregulation began to pay off almost immediately in terms of lower risk premiums.

In Finland and Sweden, after the completion of *de facto* external deregulation, periods of high political risk did not appear until the end of the 1980s and the beginning of the 1990s. At that time the risk premiums reached the same levels as those in Denmark and Norway a couple of years earlier. In Sweden, and to some extent Finland, the risk premiums continued to increase noticeably in the first part of the 1990s, and in the mid-1990s they reached the Danish and Norwegian top levels of 1986–87.

Our next step is to split the risk premiums into their political and exchange rate parts. Unfortunately the different exchange risk proxies we discussed in Chapter 8 would have to be further elaborated to fit this task. For instance, we would have to consider the location – in domestic or foreign hands – of the bulk of the stock of bonds. To enable a comparison I have reduced the exchange risk to its inflation components. Hence, Figure 14.17 shows the development of relative inflation, whereby a high value indicates a potentially high exchange risk premium for investing in that particular market. We can see that the exchange risk measured in this way has been very low in Norway since the *de facto* external deregulation was completed. The gap between the variances in inflation at home and in the OECD countries has been around 1 per cent only. With the exception of Finland in 1986, exchange risk also seems to have been low in the whole Nordic region. We can thus conclude that the main part of the sum of risk premiums consists of the *political risk* premium. Thus, in the mid-1990s the Finnish and Swedish policy-makers have some way to go before gaining the same credibility as their colleagues in the neighbouring countries.

CONCLUDING REMARKS ABOUT BOND RATE GAPS

This chapter opened with an investigation of the total international integration of the Nordic bond markets. Although earlier in the book we had found many indications that this type of integration was far from perfect, its development none the less seemed to call for further exploration. The gaps

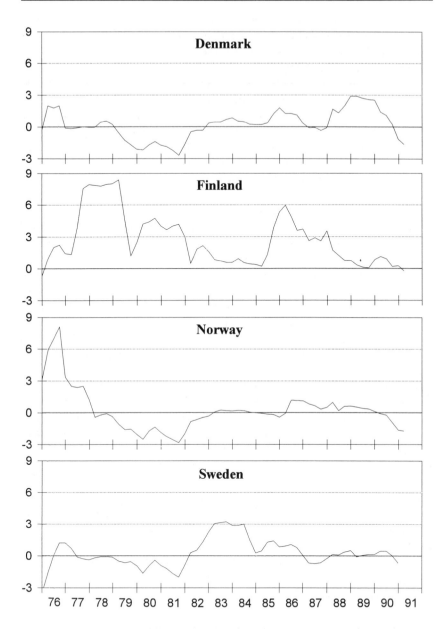

Figure 14.17 Relative variance in inflation as a measure of currency risk in the Nordic region (quarterly data, end of period observations)

Note: Calculated as the difference between the variance in domestic inflation and the OECD inflation. The variances are based on annual inflation measured on monthly observations over the preceding twenty-four months.

between the Nordic and the global real bond rates diminished in the second half of the 1980s and the correlation between them increased from the mid-1980s onwards, which was taken as an indication of growing total financial integration. The indication was weak, however, since the gaps increased again at the beginning of the 1990s. The question then to be addressed was whether the increase in total integration was caused by greater direct or indirect financial integration. Hence, our next step was to analyse the gaps between the Nordic and the global nominal bond rates, to be able to make a statement about the degree of direct financial integration. The decision to take this step also sprang from an interest in revealing the existence of inefficiencies, as a complement to the findings discussed in Chapter 12.

The analysis of *direct* financial integration started with an examination of the gaps between the Nordic rates on the one hand and the US and OECD rates on the other. This examination also provided some insight into intra-Nordic financial market integration. From our observations of correlation patterns we found that from the mid-1980s onwards, the Danish, Finnish and Swedish bond markets were closely linked to each other, whereas the Norwegian markets showed no links at all with the other Nordic markets. However, we should not let the results tempt us to adopt too far-reaching an interpretation – especially about the intra-Nordic links of the Norwegian market – since so long as we ignore exchange rate expectations, the results can be regarded as providing a weak indication only of intra-Nordic integration.

The development of the Nordic rates relative to that of our proxies for the global rate, provides quite a clear pattern. Given that governments prefer low bond rates to high, and that they also look at the nominal rate as a policy variable, it was found that Nordic governments had been able to isolate the national bond markets over long periods during the last two decades. The only market that showed interest rates consistently above the global rate throughout the period was the Danish market. Here, we got a solid indication that the Danish bond market has been integrated into the global market since 1974, the beginning of the period studied. Our observations embraced the government and the corporate bond markets. However, as we discovered in Chapter 10, the second of these was rather insignificant.

In the case of the Finnish bond market we received mixed signals. Regarding the government bond sector it was difficult to draw any conclusions at all, since the Finnish government bond rates were tax-free and the global rate was not. The indication, if any, was that this market was not *de facto* integrated until just before the completion of the *de jure* external integration in 1991. In the corporate bond sector, however, things looked quite different. Since – except for a few years at the beginning of the 1980s – Finnish corporate bond rates have been consistently above the OECD rates, we concluded that this sector was *de facto* integrated throughout the period of the investigation – or, if we allow for the above exception, at least since the autumn of 1982.

On the Norwegian bond market we found convincing indications that *de facto* integration occurred in the period 1981–82. As regards the gap between Norwegian and OECD rates the indication was the same for both sectors of the bond market. The gradual process of *de facto* external integration, as expressed in the Norwegian bond rates drawing closer to the global rates, started around 1979.

De facto integration of the Swedish bond market was completed in the autumn of 1982. The signals before that are difficult to interpret, since periods of negative gaps have been succeeded by periods of positive gaps. The alternative date for *de facto* integration is the beginning of 1977. However, the period 1980–82 exhibits some brief periods when the global rate exceeded the Swedish bond rate. In view of this I suggested the autumn of 1982 as the most convincing date for the *de facto* external integration.

For the region as a whole, on a basis of our assumptions about policy-makers' preferences, we may conclude that the Danish market has been *de facto* integrated throughout the period of the investigation, and the Finnish, Norwegian and Swedish markets at least since 1982.

Our analysis of the interest gaps provided further insight into the relative importance of the different elements in the gaps, including the size of inefficiencies. We found the risk premiums to be substantial in periods identified as characterized by high political risk. After gradually eliminating the different elements in the interest gap we found the risk premium to be a substantial part of this gap. At the time of the Danish 'potato-diet', it amounted to about 2 percentage points, of which about 1.5 percentage points constituted the political risk premium. At the time of the dramatic decrease in the price of crude oil, the risk premium constituted about 3.5 percentage points of the gap between the Norwegian interest rate and the OECD rate. Since we found no indication of exchange risk we concluded that the premium was almost entirely a compensation for political risk. In the case of Finland and Sweden we found high risk premiums at the end of the 1980s and the beginning of the 1990s.

The debate about the declining international competitiveness of the Nordic countries, particularly noticeable in Finland and Sweden, may not simply be a matter of fluctuating currencies affecting the goods and services markets, as the debate will have it, but also to a great extent a matter of an unfavourable development in the relative cost of capital. We have found indications that an important element in this development is the presence of a premium charged by the investor for investing in assets under the jurisdiction of authorities with a high propensity to intervene, i.e. to change the market rules. In the transition phase this premium can be seen as a characteristic feature of the gap between the global bond rate and the rate on bonds in political economies such as the Nordic, which are all ranked among the top five as regards total tax burden.

NOTES

1   Henceforth I shall refer to the weighted average of the OECD countries' interest rates as the OECD rate. The weights in the respective national currency baskets have been used.

2   See, for example, Mishkin (1984a, 1984b), Cumby and Obstfeld (1984), Mark (1985), Cumby and Mishkin (1986), Gaab et al. (1986), Frankel and MacArthur (1988) and Oxelheim (1990).

3   Meese and Rogoff (1986) use co-integration analysis. They explore the relationship between real interest rate differentials and real exchange rates by testing to see whether the two series can be represented as a co-integrated process (see Granger 1983). The evidence they find suggests that there is no common influence inducing non-stationarity in real interest rate differentials and real exchange rates.

4   The calculation of the real interest rate refers back to the conclusions reached in Chapter 13, and is thus based on a simple approximation of the market's inflation expectations with the inflation the preceding year. Other measures such as official inflation forecasts, interview data about the market's inflation expectations, time-series analysis, etc, all have their drawbacks and ultimately only seem to confirm the result provided by the simple approximation.

5   See Oxelheim (1990).

6   See OECD (1994).

7   We should be cautious about interpreting the statistical measure. Long-term rates may be more affected by developments in the business cycle and changes in business conditions than short-term rates. A relatively large part of the covariation between long-term rates may thus be illusory, and may come from some common underlying factor.

8   Provided by squaring the coefficient in Table 14.2.

9   It has become usual to regard the absence of deviations from interest rate parity as a sign of *perfect capital mobility*. Similarly, the absence of deviations from the International Fisher Effect is regarded as a sign of *perfect substitutability*.

10   The International Fisher Effect dates back to the turn of the century, but what we could call the standard theory of the pricing of *international* financial securities did not really begin to evolve until the late 1960s and early 1970s. See, for example, Grubel (1968), Grubel and Fadner (1971), Levy and Sarnat (1970), Solnik (1973), Adler and Dumas (1975), and Grauer et al. (1976).

11   Aliber (1974) suggests that the systematic difference between the interest differential and the observed exchange rate change must be analysed in terms of two risks, an exchange risk and a political risk. Aliber concentrates on the information content in different rates of interest, and assumes that national interest rates, unlike Eurorates, contain premiums for political risks. Thus, by using the forward rate, Aliber felt able to distinguish the premium for exchange risk from the premium for political risk. He found the premium for both risks to be about the same size, and took the presence of risk premiums to mean that we can expect the interest differential to give a biased estimate of future exchange rate movements. Aliber demonstrates that the International Fisher Effect needs to be extended by the inclusion of terms for the premiums for exchange and political risks.

12   The subperiod includes no major parity changes as regards exchange rates to be defended within a fixed exchange rate arrangement.

13   The devaluation of the Norwegian krone in 1986 was the only Nordic parity change in the period 1986 to June 1991 (see also Chapter 8).

14   For example, for a regression analysis with changes in the Swedish interest rate

on treasury bills as a function of earlier changes in trade-weighted rate on international treasury bills, the Durbin–Watson values were as low as 0.4–0.5. In a regression analysis in which changes in the Swedish interest rate is the dependent variable and changes in covered foreign rates the independent variable, the Durbin–Watson values came close to the expected value 2.

15   Many reports show that inefficiencies in terms of risk-free profit opportunities have more or less vanished in the computerized financial landscape of the 1980s and after.

16   See Oxelheim (1995).

17   See Oxelheim (1990).

18   Such differences are discussed in Oxelheim and Gärtner (1994).

19   On the basis of an interview study Oxelheim (1990) reports a strong belief in the purchasing power parity relationship among Swedish top managers.

20   See, for example, Oxelheim (1990) for an analysis of the transaction costs in the Swedish case as compared to some international observations.

REFERENCES

Adler, M. and B. Dumas, 1975, 'Optimal International Acquisitions', *Journal of Finance*, Vol. 30, March, pp. 1–20.

Aliber, R., 1974, 'Attributes of National Monies and the Interdependence of National Monetary Policies', in Aliber, R. (ed.), *National Monetary Policies and the International Financial System*, University of Chicago, Studies in Business and Society, Series 3, Chicago and London, pp. 111–26.

Cumby, R.E. and M. Obstfeld, 1984, 'International Interest Rate and Price Level Linkages under Flexible Exchange Rates: A Review of Recent Evidence', in Bilson, J.F.O. and R.C. Marston (eds), *Exchange Rate Theory and Practice*, University of Chicago Press, NBER, Chicago, pp. 121–52.

Cumby, R.E. and F. Mishkin, 1986, 'The International Linkage of Real Interest Rates: The European–U.S. Connection', *Journal of International Money and Finance* 5, pp. 5–29.

Frankel, J.A. and A. MacArthur, 1988, 'Political vs Currency Premia in International Real Interest Differentials', *European Economic Review*, Vol. 32, pp. 1083–121.

Gaab, W., M.J. Granziol and M. Horner, 1986, 'On Some International Parity Conditions: An Empirical Investigation', *European Economic Review*, No. 30, pp. 683–713.

Granger, C.W.J., 1983, 'Co-integrated Variables and Error-correcting Models', Unpublished Discussion Paper, No. 83–139, University of California, San Diego.

Grauer, F.L.A., R.H. Litzenberger and R.E. Stehle, 1976, 'Sharing Rules and Equilibrium in an International Capital Market under Uncertainty', *Journal of Financial Economics*, Vol. 3, pp. 233–56.

Grubel, H.G., 1968, 'Internationally Diversified Portfolios: Welfare Gains and Capital Flows', *American Economic Review*, Vol. 58, No. 5 (December), pp. 1299–1317.

Grubel, H.G. and K. Fadner, 1971, 'The Interdependence of International Equity Markets', *Journal of Finance*, Vol. 26, No. 1 (March), pp. 89–94.

Levy, H. and M. Sarnat, 1970, 'International Diversification of Investment Portfolios', *American Economic Review*, Vol. 60, September, pp. 668–75.

Mark, N.C., 1985, 'Some Evidence on the International Inequality of Real Interest Rates', *Journal of International Money and Finance* 4, pp. 189–208.

Mascaro, A. and A. Meltzer, 1983, 'Long- and Short-Term Interest Rates in a Risky World', *Journal of Monetary Economics*, Vol. 12. No. 4, pp. 485–518.

Meese, R.A. and K. Rogoff, 1986, 'Was It Real? The Exchange Rate–Interest Differential Relation 1973–84,' *Journal of Economic Dynamics and Control* 10, pp. 297–8.

Mishkin, F.S., 1984a, 'The Real Interest Rate: A Multicountry Empirical Study', *Canadian Journal of Economics* 17, No. 2, pp. 283–311.

Mishkin, F.S., 1984b, 'Are Real Interest Rates Equal across Countries? An Empirical Investigation of International Parity Conditions', *Journal of Finance* 39, pp. 1345–58.

OECD, 1994, *Economic Outlook*, No. 56, December, Paris.

Oxelheim, L., 1990, *International Financial Integration*, Springer Verlag, Heidelberg.

Oxelheim, L., 1995, 'On the Measurement of Political Risk', Mimeo, Lund University, Lund.

Oxelheim, L. and R. Gärtner, 1994, 'Small Country Manufacturing Industries in Transition – The Case of the Nordic Region', *Management International Review*, Vol. 34, No. 4, pp. 331–56.

Solnik, B., 1973, *European Capital Markets, Towards a General Theory of International Investment*, Lexington Books, Lexington, Mass.

Chapter 15

National financial markets in transition
Summary of a regional experience of the globalization process

This book has been devoted to an analysis of the globalization of national financial markets in general and of bond markets in particular. In a review of the dimensions that could potentially be considered in an evaluation of the path followed in the transition of particular national markets, we found these to be so many that the analysis obviously had to be narrowed down to include only a few of the most important. Among these it was considered that the way politicians act was most crucial to the outcome of the process. A close examination of their role in the process of regulation/deregulation therefore seemed justified. For this purpose the devices employed in regulation and deregulation were divided into two categories: internal and external regulative or deregulative devices. Within each category we then made a further division based on the distinction between the point when various control devices were *de facto* deregulated (i.e. when they were no longer effective), and the point when they were deregulated *de jure* (i.e. the control measures were officially abolished).

In the general discussion at the beginning of the book the problems involved in measuring the actual degree of globalization or financial integration were elaborated. I distinguished four measures, of which two were dismissed as being based on unreliable measures of capital flows – flows which I claimed were becoming increasingly more difficult to measure the higher the degree of financial integration. The two measures that remained, and which I used here, are based on the correlation between savings and investments and on an analysis of interest rate gaps. On the basis of these gaps I distinguished three kinds of integration: total, indirect and direct financial integration.

The aim of the book has been to see how the process of transition was reflected in the way savings were channelled into investments that promoted economic growth. Since at an early stage of the book we found good reason to assume a positive relationship between investment and growth, the study concentrated thenceforth on the savings-to-investment relationship only. We looked first at certain aspects of the globalization of financial markets in general, but focused later exclusively on bond markets.

The hypothesis about the optimal sequence of deregulation

The role of the regulating authorities was discussed in terms of the order in which different regulative and deregulative measures are undertaken. We formulated a hypothesis about the 'optimal' sequence, seeing it as a process starting out with a tax reform that eliminated all distortive tax incentives, proceeding to the completion of the *de jure* internal deregulation, and terminating in the completion of the *de jure* external deregulation. The hard fact is that internal distortions have to be corrected under the protection of a still-functioning external barrier. But we also hypothesized that when *de facto* integration precedes *de jure* integration, heavy social costs may arise, so that according to our argument the time between *de facto* and *de jure* integration should be as short as possible in the 'optimal' deregulative process.

Signs of deviation from the optimal route towards integration

A review of some prominent examples of globalization in the recent past provided us with two main models for the dismantling of capital controls: the gradual approach and the single-stroke approach. We also noted periods of reregulation in the long-term perspective as well as in the recent past. As regards the effects of deregulation, it was found that in many countries the abolition of capital controls was followed by an appreciation in the currency of the country concerned, a high national real interest rate and large gaps between domestic and foreign nominal interest rates. We also found indications that the countries which proceeded most rapidly with their deregulative process in the 1980s were also the ones with the highest inflation and current account deficits at the beginning of the 1990s. Finally, we noted that at the end of the 1980s, after a decade of deregulation, the world had to face the emergence of a severe financial crisis, a crisis which it is feared in the mid-1990s may become systemic. We have thus found much to suggest that the way the transition proceeds and how policy-makers interfere, may greatly affect the ultimate outcome.

Bond market efficiency is crucial to corporate investments

After reviewing the most important elements in the process of transition and experiences of globalization in general, I proceeded to an empirical analysis of the process, concentrating on a particular part of the overall financial system – namely, the bond market. The choice of this market was motivated by the role played by bonds in corporate investment decisions (the government bond rate being the risk-free benchmark rate and the corporate bond rate being a cost-of-capital proxy), rather than by the recognizedly insignificant role played by bonds in the funding of companies. Nevertheless, in the empirical analysis I paid particular attention to the way both these roles developed in the process of transition. More specifically I looked at the importance of national primary bond markets in the funding of domestic non-financial companies, and at the development of the efficiency of national secondary bond markets.

REGIONAL ASPECTS OF THE TRANSITION PHASE

For the empirical illustration of the process of transition I chose a regional approach. The homogeneity of the Nordic region in relevant aspects such as disclosure norms and accounting, as well as their cultural and social similarity, meant that this region was an excellent example. The four countries – Denmark, Finland, Norway and Sweden – also proved to be very alike in important economic dimensions: they are all small, open, political economies which have opted for similar monetary regimes.

In our review of the main features to take into account in the evaluation of the deregulative process, we found that the initial state of the economy was important. A major regional feature in this context was that for roughly thirty or forty years all the Nordic countries had been relying on rigorous capital controls. Another regional feature was that all these countries were members of the top five group of countries with the highest relative tax burden. On numerous occasions during the process of transformation the importance of this feature was very evident, and it will presumably be subject to traumatic changes in the future, once the completion of the external deregulation is fully comprehended by the policy-makers and market actors concerned. The perfect mobility of capital that characterizes perfect financial integration will act as a catalyst in the harmonization of taxes. A third aspect of the initial state that proved important in explaining differences in the globalization of the individual financial markets in the Nordic region was the industrial structure, as expressed in the size distribution of companies and the degree of internationalization and knowledge-intensity in their industry.

If we look at some general indications of the ultimate success of the process of globalization of Nordic financial markets, we can see differences between the individual countries. Although it is too early in the mid-1990s to draw conclusions about the success of different approaches, we have noted big differences between Denmark and Norway on the one hand and Finland and Sweden on the other, as regards certain factors potentially attributable to the process of globalization. Thus, the second two countries have high interest rates, a gradually depreciating currency, and high foreign indebtedness in relation to OECD standards. Further, an unsatisfactorily low level of real investment also suggests that the process of transition may have diverged from the 'optimal' model.

With the 'last' deregulative measure in Finland in October 1991, the globalization of the Nordic region was more or less completed. We have thus had an opportunity to follow the entire process of the deregulation of a whole region. To be able to assess the real permanent implications of the way the globalization was undertaken, however, we would have needed another five to ten years to study the aftermath.

Only weak signs of the deregulative process being contagious in the region

At an early stage in the book we found reason to believe that deregulation is contagious, and that in a region as close-knit as the Nordic we could therefore expect globalization to occur more or less simultaneously in all the member countries. It seemed likely, too, that the transparency prevailing in the region would work in the same direction. Nor did such a scenario appear far-fetched, since regional negotiations had been going on for a long time about the creation of a Nordic financial market. And certainly there had been cooperation in many relevant aspects over the last twenty years before globalization actually took off. And even after this there was some regional cooperation, or at least coordination, but it was fairly rare. At a very comprehensive level the regional globalization process might also appear to have been contagious: the fact that the completion of *de jure* external deregulation occurred within three years throughout the region supports such a view. However, at the detailed week-to-week or month-to-month level the evidence is scarce. In our analysis we found no clear country advantage or drawback in being part of a region during the phase of transition. While Denmark had been a member of the EU for many years, membership for Finland and Sweden became the solution to their search for a 'refuge' in the new globalized financial environment.

SAVINGS PATTERNS AND THE EXISTENCE OF POLITICAL RISKS

Before trying to draw some more detailed conclusions about the process of transformation, we should look at various aspects of savings which appear interesting and which may explain the lack of economic success referred to in the previous section. In the Nordic region we have noted some patterns which deviate from those in the major OECD countries: (1) a very low level of private savings, (2) a strong correlation between government and private savings, and (3) great volatility in private savings. Comparisons of the absolute level of savings soon run up against difficulties. How important, for instance, are social security schemes or women's rates of participation in the labour force? The first of the above patterns is thus difficult to interpret, but the second two lend themselves more readily to comparisons. They can be taken as indicating that no crowding-out by governments in Denmark, Finland or Sweden has occurred and, thus, that no direct effects on interest rates and investments can be expected from the governments' savings patterns. But the governments, with their frequent changes in the rules affecting savings, have forced private-sector saving to meet their requirements. This will be taken as reflecting their general propensity to change the market rules, which will consequently contribute to the political risk; and even more so in an integrated market. The effect of this signal from the policy-makers can be expected to express itself in higher interest rates, due to the higher premiums charged by investors for bearing this risk. And, more importantly, in the long term it will thus reduce the level of investment in these countries compared to the levels that would otherwise have obtained.

Finally, in private savings we found a very pronounced reaction to the deregulation, and later also to the emergence of a national financial crisis. This pattern seemed to reflect accurately the point at which the private sector decided that the *de facto* internal deregulation of the market was really credible. Further, we assumed that the point at which private sector saving started to increase again, reflected the time when that sector first perceived the financial crises that occurred in each one of the Nordic countries. We could see from this pattern that the downturn in Finnish and Swedish private sector savings occurred after the crises had hit Denmark. The private sector in the first two countries obviously learned nothing from what was happening in their Nordic neighbours or indeed in most other OECD countries.

WHAT TRIGGERED THE GLOBALIZATION, AND WHEN?

What, then, were the driving forces behind the globalization of the Nordic national financial markets? Although many factors may have interacted, the internationalization of business and banks and the increase in public sector borrowing emerged as the two main forces. However, the corporate sector's financial activities also contributed, for instance their efforts in the 1970s to create various 'grey markets' in order to bypass existing regulations.

The year of the first oil crisis, 1973, appears to have been the time when the whole process began. However, it is not quite so easy to establish an exact starting-point, if we also examine the credibility of the policy-makers' commitment to deregulation, particularly as the Nordic countries represent different traditions when it comes to their governments' views on the importance of a functioning market. Danish politicians were early proponents of a deregulated market, while for a long time the other Nordic governments tried to maintain the status quo and to reap the benefits of a heavily regulated market in the shape of the cheap financing of budget deficits and housing. Although nominally they all got started in the early 1970s, the credibility of the Finnish, Norwegian and Swedish efforts was probably rather shaky because of the signals sent out by the policy-makers in these countries: their extensive use of issuing controls, investment obligations, liquidity requirements and interest-rate regulations all served to eliminate the incentives for the emergence of well-functioning secondary markets. Throughout the 1980s, however, the financial markets in the four countries were converging, mainly because their policy-makers were seeking consciously to improve the functioning of secondary markets so as to be able to influence interest rates by way of open market operations.

In global terms the 1980s presented politicians with new and possibly fewer policy options. Small open economies with fixed exchange rate regimes found it difficult to lower their interest rates in order to encourage domestic investment, because the efficiency of the capital controls had become eroded and capital flows tended to equalize risk-adjusted domestic and international rates. For the period of transition as a whole we have found that the international or 'global' rate which exerted the greatest influence on the Nordic national interest rates was a weighted OECD rate. This represented a switch in influence patterns, since up to at least the mid-1970s the US interest rate was regarded as the unchallenged 'leader' which dictated interest levels in the rest of the world. However, we found some indications that the US influence on national rates was growing again from the mid-1980s onwards. As a rule, in the early 1980s, Nordic policy-makers also began to realize that it had become almost impossible to control overall credit availability, in particular for specific purposes such as private consumption. Thus to some extent, with a possible exclusion of Danish policy-makers, they were being forced into the globalization process in order to avoid large welfare losses.

INTERNAL DEREGULATION AND TAX REFORMS

The elimination of distortive tax incentives was seen as a vital task which policy-makers had to tackle at an early stage in the process of globalization. In all the Nordic countries tax rules favoured debt financing for much of the period of transition, and they were one of the reasons for capital remaining locked up in some companies instead of being transferred to other possibly more efficient parts of the corporate sector. More specifically this may have meant that capital was locked into mature industries rather than being channelled into growth industries. Tax reforms that completely eliminate all distortive incentives are difficult to find. Thus, my choice of *the* major tax reform in that respect in each country in the region has been to some extent subjective. In terms of the globalization, the most important tax reforms in Denmark and Norway seem to have been those undertaken in 1986, while the major tax reforms in Finland appeared in 1989 and in Sweden in 1991.

The credibility of internal deregulation as reflected in savings patterns

The date of the completion of the *de facto* internal integration can be derived from the shift in savings patterns mentioned above. In these terms we thus found that completion occurred in Denmark in 1983, in Finland in 1988, in Norway in 1985 and in Sweden in 1987. These dates were then compared with the dates of the *de jure* deregulation. In such a comparison we found that the bulk of regulative devices had been dismantled before the date of the *de facto* completion. The fact that the private sector reaction came much later than the implementation of this part of the *de jure* deregulation may mean that this deregulation was not yet regarded as completely credible, (1) because of the way politicians had acted, (2) because too many devices still remained, or (3) because the external *de jure* deregulation had not yet started – all of which meant that the private sector was still waiting for the authorities to send a convincing signal of their intention to cease their efforts to steer the availability of credits. One of the main internal regulations which was lifted much later was issuing control. This was not lifted until 1989 in Denmark, 1991 in Sweden, 1993 in Finland and 1995 in Norway. Some rules still remained even after these dates, but they were aimed primarily at ensuring a sound and safe financial infrastructure.

The creation of 'markets' was important to the process of globalization

While the *de jure* external deregulation began in most of the Nordic countries as far back as the mid-1970s, as a result of the current account imbalances which followed the first oil crisis, the necessary *de jure* internal deregulation of financial markets which signalled that the government had accepted the creation of 'markets', did not start in Norway, Sweden or Finland until much later. Denmark had moved earlier and was well equipped as regards markets, with a functioning interbank market by 1970, a market for negotiated deposits by 1973 and a market for treasury notes and bonds by 1975. But the growing internationalization of business and banking in the other three countries was creating the conditions for such markets there too, and the creation of 'grey markets' mentioned above constituted one step in this direction.

In general, the integration of the bond markets in the Nordic countries started with the creation of money markets. However, if in the case of Denmark we choose 1975, the year the market for treasury bonds and notes was created, as the year when a functioning market was first established there, we can say that here the creation of a bond market coincided with the creation of a money market.

Functioning secondary markets did not appear in Finland until the beginning of the 1990s. But embryos of markets outside the 'grey' sector can be found ever since the appearance in 1982 of foreign banks in the country. The deregulation of their activities promoted competition between banks, thus also encouraging the development of a money market in Finland. May 1983 is sometimes regarded as the date of birth of the Finnish money market. That was the month when banks were given permission to transfer part of the funding costs of their free market funds into their lending rates, and the call-money market was changed so that there would be a single common interest rate for all banks. However, apart from this interbank market, there was no proper functioning market until 1991. The explanation of the late appearance of 'markets' in Finland lies in the relatively low public borrowing need in the 1980s compared with the other Nordic countries and in certain peculiarities in the tax system. A new tax law in 1989 sought to mitigate those problems. The new law stated that the tax exemption of bonds and deposits was to depend on their rate of interest rather than on the type of account. Then, at the beginning of 1991, an amendment to the tax law came into force, according to which a flat final tax is based on interest earnings at source. At the same time deductions for payments were reduced. All these reforms were aimed at neutrality in the tax treatment of different instruments.

In Norway and Sweden money markets were also created before bond markets. The move towards a financial market in Norway – apart from the interbank market which had existed since 1971 – began in the mid-1970s when in the middle of the international recession Norwegian fiscal policy became expansive, and future oil revenues were exploited in advance. Government spending and lending rose. In the period 1980–82 the temporary dismantling of some internal regulations was effected, but was reversed in 1983 when direct controls were applied on practically all markets. By the beginning of 1984 a new wave of deregulation began, since when the Norwegian authorities have favoured deregulation. A functioning Norwegian money market was born in 1985, in the shape of a market for certificates of deposit issued by banks and other financial institutions. The same year the Norwegian government also started to use the interest rate on treasury bills as a signal for the short-term money market rate, and the rate on government bonds as a signal for long-term interest rates.

In Sweden all the markets were created in the early 1980s. At that time Swedish companies evinced little investment activity and their cash reserves were high, in particular as a result of two huge devaluations and the locking-in effect of capital controls and tax rules. At the same time the government deficits were growing substantially and there were strong incentives for companies to direct excess funds towards the government. As the efficiency of the current regulations declined, the central bank became interested in creating a market so as to be able to influence the interest rate level and the liquidity of the banks through open market operations. In March 1980 the banks began to issue certificates of deposit, following the abolition of the tax on such issues, and this date is often regarded as the start of the Swedish money market. In 1982 a treasury bill market emerged, and in 1983 a government bond market and a market for commercial paper.

EXTERNAL DEREGULATION AS A GRADUAL PROCESS

Many signs during the 1980s suggested that external regulation was losing its efficacy in all four countries. A gradual *de jure* deregulation was also in progress. None the less the deregulation processes in the four countries developed differently, both in their speed and in their content. In Denmark the deregulation process began to generate big visible changes as early as in the second half of the 1970s, while in Finland no really big changes appeared until the end of the 1980s. In a regional perspective the completion of the dismantling of capital controls started in Denmark in October 1988, and terminated with the abolition of the last regulations in Finnish capital controls in October 1991.

The process of liberalization and integration has sometimes been blamed for causing difficulties for the policy-making authorities. The process of change itself is difficult to administer and may result in unforeseen problems and sudden adjustments. To bring financial developments back under control, temporary reversals of recent liberalization measures have also occurred in all the Nordic countries since the late 1970s. For instance, Denmark (1979) and Norway (1984) were both forced to suspend the right for non-residents to buy domestic krone-denominated bonds. In most cases the reintroduction of restrictions was specifically declared to be temporary, since the underlying difficulties were regarded as being short-lived, caused by transitory complications in the very rapid introduction of a new financial regime.

Total financial integration is still less than perfect

Our measures of financial integration indicated that total financial integration had increased but was still far from perfect. The reason for this less-than-perfect total financial integration was to be found in indirect disintegration – the segmentation of the goods and services market, monetary segmentation and the lack of political coordination – rather than in direct disintegration of financial markets.

De facto *external integration occurred much earlier than* de jure *integration*

While we could date the completion of the *de jure* external integration of all the Nordic markets to the period 1988–91, *de facto* integration had occurred much earlier. Taking the development of the gap between national and OECD rates as our measure we found that Denmark was *de facto* integrated as early as 1974, while Norway and Sweden followed in 1982. In Finland the signals were rather mixed, with some indicating *de facto* integration at around the same period as Norway and Sweden, and others suggesting a date at the beginning of the 1990s.

The main reasons for undertaking *de facto* deregulation were different in the different countries. The Danish decision to let non-residents invest in Danish krone bonds, for instance, hastened the early *de facto* integration of the Danish market. However, a similar decision in the Finnish and Norwegian cases was not sufficient to cause *de facto* integration there. One plausible explanation of this could be that the possibility for companies to borrow abroad was still restricted; another could be the temporary ban on the right of non-residents to invest in bonds denominated in the currencies of the two countries. But such a ban was also imposed in Denmark without having any noticeable impact on the interest rate gap. The decision by the Swedish authorities in 1974 to encourage domestic companies to borrow abroad, to help the government to finance the current account deficit in the wake of the first oil crisis, was the start of the erosion of the Swedish capital controls; an erosion that was not complete until almost a decade later. Thus, the opening up for cross-border transactions is a necessary but not sufficient criteria for *de facto* external deregulation to occur.

The creation of a secondary market for bonds should also be considered in a discussion about the timing of *de facto* external integration. The early *de facto* external deregulation of the Danish bond market came about at the time of the simultaneous emergence of a bond market and the granting of permission to non-residents to buy Danish bonds in all currencies. In the other three Nordic countries, *de facto* external integration of the national markets followed the completion of the first part of the internal deregulation. This development thus pinpoints the two crucial requirements that have to be met before a market becomes integrated: the existence of an embryonic national market in the true sense of the word, and opportunities for investors to choose between domestic or foreign investment alternatives, either directly or indirectly by way of financial engineering.

Intra-regional integration has also increased

How closely are the Nordic bond markets related to each other? We have noted above that as far as deregulative measures are concerned there seem to have been very few indications of contagious action, but this does not exclude the possibility of a close relationship between interest rates on the different Nordic markets. We also found that growing international financial integration was accompanied by a closer correlation between the bond rates in the Nordic area, with the exception of the Norwegian rates.

DEVIATIONS FROM THE 'OPTIMAL' INTEGRATION SEQUENCE

Table 15.1 displays the differences in the process of globalization of the Nordic bond markets. Individually the countries all opted for a *gradual* process, but even so the order of events differed significantly. The Danish model involved external *de facto* deregulation in the mid-1970s, paired with the appearance of a financial market in the true sense of the word. A long period of transition then followed, up to the necessary tax reform in 1986. The internal deregulation can be said to have won credibility by 1983: non-residents were once again permitted to invest in Danish krone-denominated bonds, and a change in savings patterns signalled a belief in the new regime. Until the deregulation had reached this stage the political risk premiums had remained high, as the gap between the Danish and OECD rates indicate. A new period of high political risk appeared in the period 1986–87, i.e. at the time of the tax reform and the 'potato-diet' cure. Although some internal regulations remained in the early 1990s, the globalization can be regarded as nicely terminated by the time the last capital controls were dismantled in October 1988. Thus we see some deviations from the optimal order: the tax reform should have come much earlier, preferably as early as the mid-1970s,

Table 15.1 The sequence of events in the deregulation process

		Hypothetical 'optimal' order	Denmark	Finland	Norway	Sweden
Tax reform effective as from		1	1986 (1991)	1989 (1993)	1986 (1992)	1991 (1983)
De facto internal deregulation	Embryo of a market appears for the first time	2	1975	1983	1985	1980
	Gained credibility	3	1983	1988	1985	1987
De jure internal deregulation completed		4	1989	1993	1995	1991
De facto external deregulation gained credibility		5	1974	1982 (1990)	1982	1982
De jure external deregulation completed		6	October 1988	October 1991	July 1990	July 1989

and if it had done so, then *de jure* external deregulation should have been effected in 1983.

In the Norwegian and Swedish cases we could say that all the deregulative devices should have been introduced before the external deregulation had become inefficient, i.e. they should have been effected before 1982. If we have identified the Finnish *de facto* external deregulation correctly as occurring in 1982 (the alternative year would be 1990), then we can say that the Finnish *de jure* deregulation should have been completed earlier than that year. Thus, the fact that policy-makers in these three countries continued to rely on regulatory internal devices without having the protection of functioning external controls probably gave rise to high additional social costs.

In Norway this social cost was reduced by the implementation of a tax reform as early as 1986, i.e. the year after the internal deregulation had gained credibility, whereas at the other extreme the tax reform in Sweden was not introduced until the *de jure* external deregulation was complete. In Norway a high political risk appeared in the period 1986–87. The premium that was charged by the market for the changes in the market rules following the fall in the price of crude oil and the related current account imbalance, may not have been fully compensated by a desired economic outcome, since policy autonomy had disappeared with the *de facto* external integration. A narrow gap between the Norwegian and OECD rates appeared after the Norwegian parliament presented measures for completing the dismantling of any remaining capital controls at the beginning of 1990. That some internal regulations such as issuing control still remained, had obviously not affected the credibility of the globalization process, which has to be regarded as complete by July 1990.

The sequence of events in the Finnish and Swedish deregulations shows many signs of having been handled in a less-than-optimal way. The Swedish and Finnish governments, and to some extent the Norwegian, were probably forced into *de jure* deregulation by the decision of the EU to dismantle all capital controls in the EU area. In this light the process can be regarded as being contagious. The most flagrant example of inoptimality was the late introduction of the tax reform, which should have been accomplished before the internal deregulation had gained credibility (in 1987 in Sweden and in 1988 in Finland). Another circumstance that may have generated welfare losses was the late date for *de jure* external deregulation and *de jure* internal deregulation relative to the *de facto* erosion of the efficacy of the capital controls.

As is shown in Table 15.2, the gaps between the national Finnish and Swedish bond rates on the one hand and the OECD rates on the other were high in the first half of the 1990s, which may indicate that the market was still confused about the signals from the governments and the central banks of these countries and was thus charging a high political risk premium. Since we can expect the gaps to be lower on average in a floating exchange rate

Table 15.2 Average gaps between the national and the global bond rates in different institutional periods, 1974–94:4 (quarterly data, percentage points)

Periods	Denmark	Finland	Norway	Sweden
Prior to the external *de facto* deregulation	(→1974) –	(1974–1981) 2.9	(1974–1981) –1.8	(1974–1981) –0.3
Post external *de facto* deregulation but prior to the appearance of 'markets'	(1974–1975:2) 3.9	(1983–1983–2) 2.0	(1983–1985:2) 1.7	
Post external *de facto* integration and the appearance of markets but prior to the point in time when internal deregulation gained credibility	(1975:3–1983:2) 5.5	(1983:3–1988:2) 2.4		(1983–1987:1) 1.9
Period between *de facto* internal and external deregulation but prior to *de jure* external deregulation	(1983:3–1988:3) 2.4	(1988:3–1991:2) 2.2	(1985:3–1990:2) 3.4	(1987:3–1988:2) 2.4
Post *de jure* external deregulation — with fixed exchange rate	(1988:4–1993:3) 0.6	(1991:3–1992:3) 4.3	(1990:3–1992:3) 0.1	(1988:3–1991:2) 2.7
Post *de jure* external deregulation — with floating exchange rate	(1993:4–1994:4)[a] 0.4	(1992:3–1994:4) 2.6	(1992:4–1994:4) –1.4	(1992:4–1994:4) 2.0
In the mid-1990s (January 1995)	0.6	0.9	–0.1	3.0

Note: [a] Period with broad fluctuation band

environment than in a fixed rate environment, this may even indicate an increasing political risk in the two countries. The high premiums in Finland and Sweden go a long way to explain the deteriorating economic positions of the two countries during the first half in that period, such as low rates of new industrial investment and a declining competitiveness of investments already made. The consequences are also hitting small and medium-sized companies harder than larger companies. The inoptimal sequence of events in the deregulation may thus also go some way to explaining the poor prospects for the Finnish and Swedish economies at the present time.

Any estimation of the social cost of pursuing inadequate policies under the assumption of segmented markets is difficult, since in one case – Denmark – 'completion' of the *de jure* deregulation simply meant the final dismantling of some minor details, while in the other countries it embraced the hard core of their former regulations. Thus the main social cost could be expected to appear in all four countries from 1982–83 onwards. For example, when the Swedish authorities imposed a tax on securities at a time when capital controls still obtained but *de facto* integration had become established, a social cost was bound to arise. The size of the cost will have to be estimated in terms of the cost of restoring a Swedish money market that was more or less wiped out overnight following the introduction of the tax.

The cost of transition is high in political economies

The pattern of frequent periods of high political risk that we have identified is probably typical of the transition process in political economies, i.e. economies characterized by a tax burden that is high relative to GDP. In our analysis of the gap between Nordic national bond rates and the OECD rate we found that the premium for political risk during long periods of the process constituted a large part of the interest rate gap. An important lesson here is thus that the costs generated by the incremental increase in domestic interest rates, in the shape of this risk premium, should be incorporated whenever government's interventions are evaluated in a cost–benefit analysis.

At certain periods during the process of transition the political risk premium has been considerable. In Denmark, at the time of the 'potato-diet', it represented about 1.5 percentage points of the gap between the Danish and the OECD bond rates and can be claimed to account for 1.2 to 1.5 percentage points lower growth in the Danish GDP over the last years of the 1980s than would otherwise have obtained. In Sweden, in January 1989 just prior to the announcement by the Swedish government that capital controls would be abolished during the coming year, the risk premiums represented about 2 percentage points of the gap between the Swedish and the OECD bond rates.

In the mid-1990s political risk premiums in Sweden, and to some extent Finland, are high following numerous emergency packages presented by politicians in both countries who in this way have signalled their strong propensity to intervene. A high foreign indebtedness also indicates a need for intervention. By the same type of estimate, the premiums in Denmark and Norway are found to be low.

The 'cost' of policy-making in the aftermath of the globalization can be estimated for Sweden, for example, in terms of the impact of the political risk premium on economic growth. Since we have found that the various kinds of inefficiencies have been more or less eliminated, now representing at most a transaction cost of 0.5 per cent, it would seem that the gaps between domestic and foreign interest rates are made up of risk premiums and exchange expectations only. Whatever approach we then subscribe to as regards the exchange rate expectations in the mid-1990s – when the Swedish krona is 'undervalued' in PPP terms – these risk premiums appear as the main element in the gaps. In addition, our proxy for exchange risk – relative variance in inflation rates – indicates that the premium for exchange risk is low or insignificant. It can thus be argued that the political risk premium, reflecting the way the transition has been handled, accounts for Swedish interest rates being about 2.5 percentage points higher than would otherwise have obtained. Based on the interest rate sensitivity of the Swedish GDP (as estimated by the National Institute of Economic Research, Stockholm, in December 1994), a risk premium of the size that is found in January 1995 will, if it persists the whole year, cause a 1.5 percentage point lower GDP growth than would otherwise be obtained over 1996–97. The factors contributing to the political risk include the reinstatement in 1995 of double taxation, which has meant a great step backwards, in terms of globalization, by reintroducing both sectorial and international tax wedges.

The cost of the financial crisis is a 'learning' cost

The crisis in the Nordic financial systems at the beginning of the 1990s can be explained more as a question of inadequate financial competence and the inadequacy and low transparency of various policy measures, than as something directly generated by the deregulations. The authorities should somehow have 'helped' the market to learn how to deal with the new market conditions. When people feel they lack the necessary knowledge they often tend to watch what others are doing, trying not to deviate too much from the norm in deciding what factors to consider and what weight to give them. Such copy-cat behaviour seems to provide a plausible explanation for the kind of overall market behaviour which often appears to reflect more implicit consensus about the future than the prevailing uncertainties seem to warrant.

With hindsight the crowd can be shown to have been either right or wrong. When it has been wrong, there may be the makings of a financial crisis, as we have seen in the real estate business and the banking industry. The likelihood of this kind of spurious consensus may be greater in small countries such as the Nordic. Small countries in general opt for policy autonomy. The conclusion to be drawn from these two observations is that the politicians in the Nordic countries may long have been aggravating the national financial crises by pursuing policies aimed at isolating the domestic financial market; one element of the cost of these policies appeared ultimately at the time of national financial crisis in the shape of a learning cost.

Efforts to curb financial engineering are not usually successful

History has shown that the authorities have to be cautious when attempting to intervene in an innovative process. This applies particularly to small open economies like those in the Nordic region. Nevertheless, the authorities in the Nordic countries have shown a high propensity to intervene and to distort the market structure of their national financial markets. This has meant that many financial activities have been located abroad, with obvious implications for domestic companies and probably also for industrial growth. A hopeful sign, suggesting that innovations cannot always be stifled, is the emergence of the innovative Swedish company Stockholm Option Market (OM). This company has proved to be highly innovative in an international comparison, and is unique as an example of a privately owned market-place. Moreover, it is among the global top ten in terms of turnover.

GLOBALIZATION AND STRUCTURAL CHANGES TO NATIONAL CREDIT MARKETS

The links between the different sectors of the individual Nordic financial markets grew stronger during the 1980s, indicating less reliance on the part of policy-makers on sectorial wedges, and greater internal financial integration. Without pushing these bond market findings too far, we can assume that they may to some extent apply to the national market as a whole. In some periods sectorial wedges have spurred the development of one sector at the expense of another, but in the 1980s the deregulation did not lead to any major changes in the structure of the Nordic national credit markets. If any changes could be called structural, they would be the appearance of a Finnish money market, which reduced the market share of bank loans from its high level of 91 per cent in 1980 to 77 per cent in 1990, and the reduced market shares of the Swedish bond market in that period.

Institutional changes of a temporary kind have occurred

There have been structural changes as regards the range of special corporate financial services. A great many new financial institutions aimed at answering the new and growing need of the corporate sector for financial alternatives were established during the process of transition. Some of these, however, such as the leasing companies and most finance companies, emerged as a result of the regulatory distortions and more or less disappeared again once the distortions were eliminated by the deregulation. Others, such as factoring companies, are still in the market. The turbulence during the transition phase also led to the emergence of stronger supervisory institutions.

GLOBALIZATION AND CORPORATE INDEBTEDNESS

Debt ratios have changed rather drastically during the transition period, which suggests a Nordic convergence of a kind that was also typical on a global scale. The decline in indebtedness was most pronounced in Finland and Norway. The falling Nordic debt ratios may reflect not only the globalization, but also a possible decline in the importance of credit markets in general and bond markets in particular. In so far as this last holds good, it is to a large extent a result of the shift in many industries away from material resources and towards the immaterial, especially in the high-technology companies whose rapid growth has run parallel with the process of globalization. Knowledge-intensive operations such as marketing, R&D and various kinds of services have become more important. In the absence of collaterals these 'soft investments' have to be financed to a greater extent by equity capital, either internally generated through operating profits or created by the input of new risk capital. Thus in terms of corporate funding, the liberalization and vitalization of the equity markets may be more important than that of the credit markets.

Some changes, as in the degree of securitization for instance, also occurred, but were later reversed. Up to 1987 Swedish non-financial companies, for example, experienced an increase in the proportion of securities on the debt side. After this, the importance of securities declined in favour of bank loans predominantly denominated in foreign currencies. In 1988 and 1989 bank lending to companies increased at an annual rate of about 50 per cent. However, Swedish non-financial companies did not cease issuing securities during this period; in fact they increased their issues of Euro-commercial papers as well, so that such programmes corresponded to about half the banks' lending during these years. Total lending by Swedish banks to companies more than doubled between 1987 and 1990, which outweighed the earlier increase in the market shares of the securities markets.

Lending by Finnish banks exhibited a similar surge in 1987, albeit at a much lower rate. As in Sweden, lending in foreign currencies showed the highest percentage increase. In Norway, bank lending was high in the mid-1980s, but went into reverse at the end of the decade. In 1989 the banks' lending to companies fell by about 30 per cent, which still left Norwegian companies in the lead as regards the securities share of total interest-rate-bearing debt. In Denmark the banks' lending to non-financial companies remained at roughly the same level. Denmark tends to differ from the other Nordic countries since the structure of its credit market matches the US structure (i.e. a market-based financial system), while the structure in the other countries resembles that of bank-orientated financial systems such as the German.

A negative effect of the rapid progress of liberalization may be expected in that short-term considerations come to dominate over long-term. However, we found no clear indication that the liability side of non-financial companies actually changed in this way during the process of transition. In Sweden the proportion of short-term to long-term debt increased, whereas in Finland the opposite was true and in Denmark and Norway the proportion remained unchanged. Nor did we find any indications that the process brought any shift towards a debt securitization pattern more resembling that of non-financial companies in the United States.

TO WHAT EXTENT DID THE TRANSITION AFFECT THE BOND MARKET STRUCTURE?

In the early 1990s some major structural differences still obtain between the Danish and the other Nordic markets. One such difference concerns the role of domestic bonds in the total domestic credit stock. The total outstanding stock of domestic bonds represents almost half the domestic credit stock in Denmark, while it constitutes only 13–23 per cent of the total in the other Nordic countries.

Another difference emerges if we look at the share of the domestic Danish credit stock represented by issues made by Danish companies and compare this with the corresponding share in the other Nordic countries. Direct bond issues by Danish corporations are few, reflecting a tradition whereby it has been possible to borrow through Danish mortgage institutions. These institutions have dominated the Danish bond market and have issued between 50–75 per cent of the total stock of Danish bonds. In addition to traditional loans from the financial institutions, the Euro-commercial paper programme has been the main source of funds for Danish companies.

Trends emerging from the transformation of primary bond markets

The far-reaching transformation of the Nordic national bond markets in the 1980s is reflected in a number of trends, e.g. in the structure of total markets, in issuing behaviour, in investment behaviour, and in other features as well. In the early 1990s, the trends on all or most of the Nordic national markets with regard to *general market development* are:

- a growing total stock of bonds as a percentage of national GDP;

- diminishing or unchanged importance of domestic bond issues in the total domestic credit stock;
- a growing amount (in real terms) of international bond issues from the mid-1980s onwards;
- a falling share of Nordic issues in the total stock of international issues.

With regard to the *issuing behaviour* of different groups of borrowers the trends that deserve attention are the following:

- a diminishing share of government issues of the total outstanding stock of bonds (except in Denmark);
- an increasing share of issues of financial institutions of the total outstanding stock of bonds (except in Denmark);
- a growing bank bond share of the total outstanding stock of bonds;
- less reliance on bonds in the financing of non-financial companies as from 1985–87 (except in Norway).

The relative importance of issues by mortgage institutions has increased in Norway and Sweden, but although the importance of the Swedish institutions matches that of the Danish in amounts issued, the credit policies of Danish institutions may mean that indirectly they are more helpful to domestic non-financial companies than their counterparts in the other Nordic countries. We have found that bonds in general play a very minor role on the liability side of Nordic non-financial companies. The importance of bond loans as a share of the liability side of non-financial companies is highest in Norwegian companies, and almost insignificant in Danish companies. The international bond market has been most important to Norwegian companies and least important to Danish companies, going by the size of their international issues relative to their domestic issues. By turning to the international market, non-financial companies may have escaped all the inefficiencies and risk premiums attached to the domestic market. Hence, they may have gained some of the advantages of diversification, but they also had to assume an exchange risk (except when the international issues were denominated in their home currency).

With regard to *investment behaviour*, the discernible trends are:

- a diminishing share of bond assets in the bank portfolios;
- a growing share of bond assets in the portfolios of non-financial companies;
- a growing share in the hands of foreigners.

Trends emerging from the transformation of secondary bond markets

The efficiency of the Nordic bond markets was the second of the special issues to be addressed in this book. We have found a number of indicators for static efficiency which show that the Danish and Swedish markets are approaching the efficiency of the benchmark market, the US treasury market. The Finnish and Norwegian markets have shown an improvement in efficiency but are still lagging somewhat behind the other Nordic markets in terms of transparency, spreads and liquidity. The same grouping also applies with regards to the dynamic efficiency of Nordic national markets. In the early 1990s the Swedish secondary market emerges as having the highest dynamic efficiency, closely followed by the Danish market; the Finnish and Norwegian markets, on the other hand, still lack certain important financial innovations. This should not be interpreted as an expression of the incompetence of Finnish and Norwegian financial engineers, however, but rather of a continuing political interest in controlling the development of the financial market.

The major trends in the Nordic secondary markets may be summarized as follows:

- an increasing degree of transparency;
- diminishing spread;
- increasing liquidity, although this is still unstable and is inferior to other major markets;
- growing dynamic efficiency.

In addition to its role as an efficient provider of price information to companies, a functioning secondary market also plays a part in corporate cash and risk management. Here we have found that Danish companies benefit the most, as can be seen in the share of their assets invested in bonds, while Norwegian companies have made the least use of such investments. Throughout the 1980s and at the beginning of the 1990s the share of bonds on the asset side exceeded that on the liability side of Danish companies. The same applied to Finnish and Swedish companies from the mid-1980s onwards.

Direct vs indirect issues in corporate funding

The development of the Nordic national bond markets reflects two types of political set-up which have produced two kinds of model for corporate funding: the Danish model based on *indirect* financing via loans from mortgage institutions which have raised capital by issuing bonds, and the Finnish, Norwegian and Swedish model whereby the non-financial companies turn *directly* to the bond market with their own issues. Although from the beginning of the 1990s the two models have become blurred, they can serve as useful paradigms. Since it costs a lot, especially when it comes to international issues, to gain enough recognition to get an issue successfully placed with investors, scale effects could be invoked as an argument in favour of the Danish model.

At the level of the small and medium-sized companies, mortgage institutions in particular contribute in many ways. Their mere existence puts pressure on the loan rates of bank credits: they offer a possibility that would otherwise be closed to these types of company, and in particular they offer an opportunity to entrepreneurs to start companies by taking loans with property as their collateral. The high level of activity among mortgage institutions in Denmark in the 1980s, as compared to the other Nordic countries, may perhaps help to explain the relatively high incidence of small companies in Denmark. The mortgage institutions can be conceived as differing from the banks in that they specialize particularly on the assessment of collateral. Their business is transparent, which allows for favourable issuing terms. As a rule it is only large companies with excellent credit rating which may find it advantageous to turn directly to the market. Since the company itself may then face higher transaction costs and credit risk premiums, a financial case for going to the bond market exists only when these additional items add up to more than the 'value-added' contribution charged by a mortgage institution.

In retrospect the Danish model does appear to have been successful in many ways. The Danish government's attitude to the 'market' has helped to curtail the number of changes in the market rules, and thus also to keep the political risk premium – encapsulated in the domestic risk-free interest rate – low in comparison with the general Nordic standard in the new globalized environment. This attitude has also meant that the Danish mortgage institutions have had a long time in which to develop their skill in operating in a deregulated environment, which should in the end provide them with access to relatively low funding costs. We can thus assume that in the mid-1990s the Danish model is offering capital to Danish corporate borrowers (in particular to small and medium-sized companies) at a risk-adjusted cost that is lower than in the other Nordic countries.

GLOBALIZATION AND THE FUNDING OF SMALL AND MEDIUM-SIZED COMPANIES

Although we have found the Nordic financial markets to be integrated in terms of capital flow, the correlation between savings and investment shows that Denmark and Finland may still be segmented. In these two countries domestic savings during the 1980s and the beginning of the 1990s were still of considerable importance to domestic investments. This contrasts some-what with what we might have expected, at least in the case of Denmark as being the most liberal of the Nordic countries over the last twenty years or so in terms of cross-border financial transactions. However, a closer look reveals that our findings are not inconsistent. Although Denmark is integrated as regards the freedom to undertake cross-border financial transactions, the bulk of the country's small and medium-sized companies are unable for reasons of cost to exploit this opportunity, and have to rely on domestic savings instead. Since we found that investments are about 60–80 per cent financed by retained earnings, there are policy implications here: if the aim is to stimulate investment faster and to avoid inefficiency costs in the channelling of savings into investments, governments should make it possible for companies to retain more of their profits.

The role of governments in corporate funding

The government must not solve the corporate funding problem by supplying capital at under the international rate adjusted for project and credit risk. First, such a move would not be well received in a world characterized by high economic integration. Subsidies of this kind could trigger trade and investment wars. Second, it would mean the launching of projects with poor competitive edge in international terms – negative net-values, if an appropriate discount rate is used. Hence, the subsidized rate will contribute to the destruction of capital. What policy-makers have to tackle is the deviation of national project risk-adjusted rates from the corresponding international rates. In order to enhance the competitiveness of domestic companies, governments should emphasize the elimination of such deviations. This may be effected either by adequate policy-making (perhaps simply geared to ensuring the basic financial infrastructure and increased transparency) aimed at eliminating inefficiencies and macroeconomic risks, or by subsidizing companies for risk premiums that may be regarded as induced by the government's own policy.

Some special problems still face small companies

The liberalization of the financial markets has also led to the appearance of new and more sophisticated financial instruments. The efficient utilization of these financial opportunities calls for corporate investment in new equipment and qualified personnel. This is more readily accepted in large companies, because they know they can benefit from financial economies of scale. Large companies may therefore improve their financial position, while smaller ones with scarce resources and less opportunities for exploiting the potential economies of scale may have problems in adjusting to the rapid developments of the financial market. Moreover, many of the biggest Nordic companies have established their own in-house banks and investment companies, which are pursuing large-scale operations in the financial markets.

SOME LESSONS TO BE LEARNT FROM THE PROCESS OF TRANSITION

There are some general lessons to be learnt from our regional example of the globalization of national financial markets. Let us look at them in the chronological order in which they appear to policy-makers in the process of globalization. First, 'distorting' tax incentives have to be eliminated. Second, the preparedness of the market to face a deregulation should be assessed. As a part of this an assessment of the vulnerability of domestic industries to external deregulation has to be undertaken. Third, some market actors will need to be educated in order to be able to handle the new situation. The quality of the information available for risk assessment and the pricing of risk should be improved. Fourth, internal deregulation has to be speeded up before external deregulation is launched. Fifth, markets in the true sense of the word must be created. Sixth, the policy-makers must signal their interest in the sustainability of these markets if the process of globalization is to gain credibility. Seventh, in deciding about the timing of the external deregulation, politicians must constantly monitor the cost of intervention. They should therefore consider the sum of the premiums charged by the market for exchange rate risk and political risk. Finally, when it comes to the abolition of capital controls, they should not be tempted to introduce subsidies but instead should be rather restrictive on this front. To avoid the waste or destruction of capital, politicians should at most subsidize companies to an amount equal to the risk premiums they themselves have created.

Further, a subsidy which might be regarded as less 'unfair' in the eyes of international competition could consist of subsidies to new rating institutes, or to the rating itself to release small and medium-sized companies from their heavy reliance on the domestic banking industry.

SOME PERCEIVED THREATS

The rapidly growing stock of domestic bonds in the hands of foreigners has caused some uneasiness about a possible rush of returning papers, in face of an impending depreciation of the domestic currency. There is general concern among market participants that this will trigger a wave of re-regulation once a government has had such an experience. The Danish market, for instance, went through a period of such uncertainty at the end of 1985 and at the beginning of 1986, when the direction of capital movements went into reverse: krone bonds were returned and private residents invested heavily in foreign shares. However, a rise in interest rate differentials in March 1986 stopped the outflow of capital at that time, and no new regulations were introduced. In the mid-1990s a big share of the outstanding stocks of Nordic bonds is in the hands of non-residents, and this constitutes a potential threat.

Changes in the financial markets and in the monetary policy options have limited the policy choices available to an extent as yet unknown. In many ways the limitations may even be welcome as an incentive to policy-makers not to create big imbalances or to diverge in any other way from the paths compatible with well-functioning financial markets. Fiscal policy and income policy have had to assume a bigger role in regulating overall activity and price developments. And as regards encouraging structural development, taxation policy has acquired a central role, taking over certain parts of the traditional monetary policy. However, should serious imbalances develop, the reduced autonomy of monetary policy may prove to be a very inconvenient restriction on policy choices. Discretionary rules and selective policies previously posed a temptation to politicians. If policy-makers are still tempted to use such instruments, the result is likely to be high social costs following from the increasing effect of political risk premiums on interest rates.

The high unemployment rates of the mid-1990s seem to have triggered a race between countries to attract direct investments from abroad in order to create more jobs. In a globalized world, however, the freedom for policy-makers to accomplish anything within the limits of their short political mandates and using devices compatible with fair competition, is much restricted. The temptation to use the economic equivalent of a dose of anabolic steroids just to make the investment opportunities look attractive very quickly, may be too strong – something that would ultimately lead to the outbreak of an investment war. History shows that disputes, wars and financial distress are followed by periods of extensive regulation. There is thus a non-negligible likelihood that a period of global efforts to control capital flows may ensue. The regulation–liberalization pendulum will continue to swing from one side to the other of what should be regarded as the minimum set of regulations required to guarantee the market infrastructure, to maintain a sound market and to ensure 'fair' competition. Although some elements in the liberalization may be seen as irreversible, others may still lend themselves to re-regulation, thus engendering a great leap downwards in global welfare.

Author index

Subject index

NB. Figures in bold type indicate a table or figure on the page.